SAINT CHRYSOSTOM

HOMILIES ON THE GOSPEL OF SAINT MATTHEW

PART 1

NICENE AND POST-NICENE
CHURCH FATHERS: SERIES 1

VOLUME 17

CATHOLIC EDITION

TRANSLATED BY
PHILIP SCHAFF

THE CHURCH FATHERS

AETERNA PRESS

PUBLISHED BY AETERNA PRESS.
COVER DESIGN BY AETERNA PRESS.

NICENE AND POST-NICENE CHURCH FATHERS SERIES 1: 25 VOLUMES

COMPLETE SET: 3 SERIES, 63 VOLUMES

CATHOLIC EDITION. CONTAINS CHURCH FATHERS AUTHOR TEXTS ONLY, WITHOUT PROTESTANT INTRODUCTIONS, ELUCIDATIONS, PREFACES OR FOOTNOTES.

THE CHURCH FATHERS COMPLETE COLLECTION: COMPOSED OF 3 SERIES, 63 VOLUMES, 65 AUTHORS, 500 TEXTS COMPOSED OF 1,000 BOOKS, 18,000 CHAPTERS, 16 MILLION WORDS.

SCHAFF, PHILIP (1819–1893) (EDITOR) PRINT BASIS: NEW YORK: CHRISTIAN LITERATURE PUBLISHING CO., 1886.

A SELECT LIBRARY OF THE NICENE AND POST-NICENE FATHERS OF THE CHRISTIAN CHURCH.

EDITED BY PHILIP SCHAFF, D.D., LL.D., PROFESSOR IN THE UNION THEOLOGICAL SEMINARY, NEW YORK, IN CONNECTION WITH A NUMBER OF PATRISTIC SCHOLARS OF EUROPE AND AMERICA.

T&T CLARK EDINBURGH WM. B. EERDMANS PUBLISHING COMPANY GRAND RAPIDS, MICHIGAN.

ISBN-13: 978-1-78516-276-3

AVAILABLE AS AN E-BOOK:
WWW.AETERNAPRESS.COM

CONTENTS

A Commentary On The Gospel Of St. Matthew: Part 1

THE HOMILIES OF ST. JOHN CHRYSOSTOM, ARCHBISHOP OF CONSTANTINOPLE.

TRANSLATED BY

REV. SIR GEORGE PREVOST, BARONET, M.A.,

OF ORIEL COLLEGE, OXFORD.

REVISED, WITH NOTES, BY

REV. M. B. RIDDLE, D.D.,

PROFESSOR OF NEW TESTAMENT EXEGESIS IN THE WESTERN THEOLOGICAL SEMINARY AT ALLEGHENY, PA.

The Homilies Of St. John Chrysostom, Archbishop Of Constantinople, On The Gospel Of St. Matthew

HOMILY I

It were indeed meet for us not at all to require the aid of the written Word, but to exhibit a life so pure, that the grace of the Spirit should be instead of books to our souls, and that as these are inscribed with ink, even so should our hearts be with the Spirit. But, since we have utterly put away from us this grace, come, let us at any rate embrace the second best course.

For that the former was better, God hath made manifest, both by His words, and by His doings. Since unto Noah, and unto Abraham, and unto his offspring, and unto Job, and unto Moses too, He discoursed not by writings, but Himself by Himself, finding their mind pure. But after the whole people of the Hebrews had fallen into the very pit of wickedness, then and thereafter was a written word, and tables, and the admonition which is given by these.

And this one may perceive was the case, not of the saints in the Old Testament only, but also of those in the New. For neither to the apostles did God give anything in writing, but instead of written words He promised that He would give them the grace of the Spirit: for "He," saith our Lord, "shall bring all things to your remembrance." And that thou mayest learn that this was far better, hear what He saith by the Prophet: "I will make a new covenant with you, putting my laws into their mind, and in their heart I will write them," and, "they shall be all taught of God." And Paul too, pointing out the same superiority, said, that they had received a law "not in tables of stone, but in fleshy tables of the heart."

But since in process of time they made shipwreck, some with regard to doctrines, others as to life and manners, there was again need that they should be put in remembrance by the written word.

2. Reflect then how great an evil it is for us, who ought to live so purely as not even to need written words, but to yield up our hearts, as books, to the Spirit; now that we have lost that honor, and are come to have need of these, to fail again in duly employing even this second remedy. For if it be a blame to stand in need of written words, and not to have brought down on ourselves the grace of the Spirit; consider how heavy the charge of not choosing to profit even after this assistance, but rather treating what is written with neglect, as if it were cast forth without purpose, and at random, and so bringing down upon ourselves our punishment with increase.

But that no such effect may ensue, let us give strict heed unto the things that are written; and let us learn how the Old Law was given on the one hand, how on the other the New Covenant.

3. How then was that law given in time past, and when, and where? After the destruction of the Egyptians, in the wilderness, on Mount Sinai, when smoke and fire were rising up out of the mountain, a trumpet sounding, thunders and lightnings, and Moses entering into the very depth of the cloud. But in the new covenant not so,—neither in a wilderness, nor in a mountain, nor with smoke and darkness and cloud and tempest; but at the beginning of the day, in a house, while all were sitting together, with great quietness, all took place. For to those, being more unreasonable, and hard to guide, there was need of outward pomp, as of a wilderness, a mountain, a smoke, a sound of trumpet, and the other like things: but they who were of a higher character, and submissive, and who had risen above mere corporeal imaginations, Yea, for it was removal of punishment, and remission of sins, and "righteousness, and sanctification, and redemption," and adoption, and an inheritance of Heaven, and a relationship unto the Son of God, which he came declaring unto all; to enemies, to the perverse, to them that were sitting in darkness. What then could ever be equal to these good tidings? God on earth, man in Heaven; and all became mingled together, angels joined the choirs of men, men had fellowship with the angels, and with the other powers above: and one might see the long war brought to an end, and reconciliation made between God and our nature, the devil brought to shame, demons in flight, death destroyed, Paradise opened, the curse blotted out, sin put out of the way, error driven off, truth returning, the word of godliness everywhere sown, and flourishing in its growth, the polity of those above planted on the earth, those powers in secure intercourse with us, and on earth angels continually haunting, and hope abundant touching things to come.

Therefore he hath called the history good tidings, forasmuch as all other things surely are words only without substance; as, for instance, plenty of wealth, greatness of power, kingdoms, and glories, and honors, and whatever other things among men are accounted to be good: but those which are published by the fishermen would be legitimately and properly called good tidings: not only as being sure and immoveable blessings, and beyond our deserts, but also as being given to us with all facility.

For not by laboring and sweating, not by fatigue and suffering, but merely as being beloved of God, we received what we have received.

5. And why can it have been, that when there were so many disciples, two write only from among the apostles, and two from among their followers? (For

one that was a disciple of Paul, and another of Peter, together with Matthew and John, wrote the Gospels.) It was because they did nothing for vainglory, but all things for use.

"What then? Was not one evangelist sufficient to tell all?" One indeed was sufficient; but if there be four that write, not at the same times, nor in the same places, neither after having met together, and conversed one with another, and then they speak all things as it were out of one mouth, this becomes a very great demonstration of the truth.

6. "But the contrary," it may be said, "hath come to pass, for in many places they are convicted of discordance." Nay, this very thing is a very great evidence of their truth. For if they had agreed in all things exactly even to time, and place, and to the very words, none of our enemies would have believed but that they had met together, and had written what they wrote by some human compact; because such entire agreement as this cometh not of simplicity. But now even that discordance which seems to exist in little matters delivers them from all suspicion, and speaks clearly in behalf of the character of the writers.

But if there be anything touching times or places, which they have related differently, this nothing injures the truth of what they have said. And these things too, so far as God shall enable us, we will endeavor, as we proceed, to point out; requiring you, together with what we have mentioned, to observe, that in the chief heads, those which constitute our life and furnish out our doctrine, nowhere is any of them found to have disagreed, no not ever so little.

But what are these points? Such as follow: That God became man, that He wrought miracles, that He was crucified, that He was buried, that He rose again, that He ascended, that He will judge, that He hath given commandments tending to salvation, that He hath brought in a law not contrary to the Old Testament, that He is a Son, that He is only-begotten, that He is a true Son, that He is of the same substance with the Father, and as many things as are like these; for touching these we shall find that there is in them a full agreement.

And if amongst the miracles they have not all of them mentioned all, but one these, the other those, let not this trouble thee. For if on the one hand one had spoken of all, the number of the rest would have been superfluous; and if again all had written fresh things, and different one from another, the proof of their agreement would not have been manifest. For this cause they have both treated of many in common, and each of them hath also received and declared something of his own; that, on the one hand, he might not seem superfluous, and cast on the heap to no purpose; on the other, he might make our test of the truth of their affirmations perfect.

7. Now Luke tells us also the cause wherefore he proceeds to write: "that thou mayest hold," saith he, "the certainty of the words wherein thou hast been instructed;" that is, that being continually reminded thou mayest hold to the certainty, and abide in certainty.

But as to John, he hath himself kept silence touching the cause; yet, (as a tradition saith, which hath come down to us from the first, even from the Fathers,) neither did he come to write without purpose; but forasmuch as it had been the care of the three to dwell upon the account of the dispensation, and the doctrines of the Godhead were near being left in silence, he, moved by Christ, then and not till then set himself to compose his Gospel. And this is manifest both from the history itself, and from the opening of his Gospel. For he doth not begin like the rest from beneath, but from above, from the same point, at which he was aiming, and it was with a view to this that he composed the whole book. And not in the beginning only, but throughout all the Gospel, he is more lofty than the rest.

Of Matthew again it is said, that when those who from amongst the Jews had believed came to him, and besought him to leave to them in writing those same things, which he had spoken to them by word, he also composed his Gospel in the language of the Hebrews. And Mark too, in Egypt, is said to have done this self-same thing at the entreaty of the disciples.

For this cause then Matthew, as writing to Hebrews, sought to shew nothing more, than that He was from Abraham, and David; but Luke, as discoursing to all in general, traces up the account higher, going on even to Adam. And the one begins with His generation, because nothing was so soothing to the Jew as to be told that Christ was the offspring of Abraham and David: the other doth not so, but mentions many other things, and then proceeds to the genealogy.

8. But the harmony between them we will establish, both by the whole world, which hath received their statements, and by the very enemies of the truth. For many sects have had birth, since their time, holding opinions opposed to their words; whereof some have received all that they have said, while some have cut off from the rest certain portions of their statements, and so retain them for themselves. But if there were any hostility in their statements, neither would the sects, who maintain the contrary part, have received all, but only so much as seemed to harmonize with themselves; nor would those, which have parted off a portion, be utterly refuted by that portion; so that the very fragments cannot be hid, but declare aloud their connexion with the whole body. And like as if thou shouldest take any part from the side of an animal, even in that part thou wouldest find all the things out of which the

whole is composed;—nerves and veins, bones, arteries, and blood, and a sample, as one might say, of the whole lump;—so likewise with regard to the Scriptures; in each portion of what is there stated, one may see the connexion with the whole clearly appearing. Whereas, if they were in discord, neither could this have been pointed out, and the doctrine itself had long since been brought to nought: "for every kingdom," saith He, "divided against itself shall not stand." But now even in this shines forth the might of the Spirit, namely, in that it prevailed on these men, engaged as they were in those things which are more necessary and very urgent, to take no hurt at all from these little matters.

Now, where each one was abiding, when he wrote, it is not right for us to affirm very positively.

But that they are not opposed to each other, this we will endeavor to prove, throughout the whole work. And thou, in accusing them of disagreement, art doing just the same as if thou wert to insist upon their using the same words and forms of speech.

9. And I do not yet say, that those likewise who glory greatly in rhetoric and philosophy, having many of them written many books touching the same matters, have not merely expressed themselves differently, but have even spoken in opposition to one another (for it is one thing to speak differently and another to speak at variance); none of these things do I say. Far be it from me to frame our defense from the frenzy of those men, neither am I willing out of falsehood to make recommendations for the truth.

But this I would be glad to inquire: how were the differing accounts believed? how did they prevail? how was it that, while saying opposite things, they were admired, were believed, were celebrated everywhere in the world?

And yet the witnesses of what they said were many, and many too were the adversaries and enemies thereof. For they did not write these things in one corner and bury them, but everywhere, by sea and by land, they unfolded them in the ears of all, and these things were read in the presence of enemies, even as they are now, and none of the things which they said offended any one. And very naturally, for it was a divine power that pervaded all, and made it to prosper with all men.

10. For if it had not been so, how could the publican, and the fisherman, and the unlearned, have attained to such philosophy? For things, which they that are without have never been able to imagine, no not in a dream, are by these men with great certainty both published and made convincing, and not in their lives only, but even after death: neither to two men, nor twenty men, nor an hundred, nor a thousand, nor ten thousand, but to cities, nations, and

people, both to land and sea, in the land both of Greeks and barbarians, both inhabited and desert; and all concerning things far beyond our nature. For leaving the earth, all their discourse is concerning the things in heaven, while they bring in unto us another principle of life, another manner of living: both wealth and poverty, freedom and slavery, life and death, our world and our polity, all changed.

Not like Plato, who composed that ridiculous Republic, or Zeno, or if there be any one else that hath written a polity, or hath framed laws. For indeed, touching all these, it hath been made manifest by themselves, that an evil spirit, and some cruel demon at war with our race, a foe to modesty, and an enemy to good order, oversetting all things, hath made his voice be heard in their soul. When, for example, they make their women common to all, and stripping virgins naked in the Palaestra, bring them into the gaze of men; and when they establish secret marriages, mingling all things together and confounding them, and overturning the limits of nature, what else is there to say? For that these their sayings are all inventions of devils, and contrary to nature, even nature herself would testify, not tolerating what we have mentioned; and this, though they write not amidst persecutions, nor dangers, nor fightings, but in all security and freedom, and deck it out with many ornaments from many sources. But these doctrines of the fishermen, chased as they were, scourged and in jeopardy, both learned and unlearned, both bond and free, both kings and private soldiers, both barbarians and Greeks, have received with all good will.

11. And thou canst not say, that it was because these things were trifling and low, that they were easily to be received by all men: nay, for these doctrines are far higher than those. For as to virginity, they never imagined even the name thereof so much as in a dream, nor yet of voluntary poverty, nor of fasting, nor of any other of those things that are high.

But they that are of our part not only exterminate lust, they chastise not only the act, but even an unchaste look, and insulting language, and disorderly laughter, and dress, and gait, and clamor, and they carry on their exactness even to the smallest things, and have filled the whole earth with the plant of virginity. And touching God too, and the things in heaven, they persuade men to be wise with such knowledge as no one of those hath at any time been able so much as to conceive in his mind. For how could they, who made for gods images of beasts, and of monsters that crawl on the earth, and of other things still more vile?

Yet these high doctrines were both accepted and believed, and they flourish every day and increase; but the others have passed away, and perished, having disappeared more easily than spiders' webs.

And very naturally, for they were demons that published these things; wherefore besides their uncleanness, their obscurity is great, and the labor they require greater. For what could be more ridiculous than that "republic," in which, besides what I have mentioned, the philosopher, when he hath spent lines without number, that he may be able to shew what justice is, hath over and above this prolixity filled his discourse with much indistinctness? This, even if it did contain anything profitable, must needs be very useless for the life of man. For if the husbandman and the smith, the builder and the pilot, and every one who subsists by the labor of his hands, is to leave his trade, and his honest toils, and is to spend such and such a number of years in order to learn what justice is; before he has learnt he will often times be absolutely destroyed by hunger, and perish because of this justice, not having learnt anything else useful to be known, and having ended his life by a cruel death.

12. But our lessons are not such; rather Christ hath taught us what is just, and what is seemly, and what is expedient, and all virtue in general, comprising it in few and plain words: at one time saying that, "on two commandments hang the Law and the Prophets;" that is to say, on the love of God and on the love of our neighbor: at another time, "Whatsoever ye would that men should do to you, do ye also to them; for this is the Law and the Prophets."

And these things even to a laborer, and to a servant, and to a widow woman, and to a very child, and to him that appeareth to be exceedingly slow of understanding, are all plain to comprehend and easy to learn. For the lessons of the truth are like this; and the actual result bears witness thereto. All at least have learned what things they are to do, and not learned only, but been emulous also of them; and not in the cities alone nor in the midst of the market places, but also in the summits of the mountains.

Yea, for there wilt thou see true wisdom abounding, and choirs of angels shining forth in a human body, and the commonwealth of Heaven manifested here on earth. For a commonwealth did these fishermen too write for us, not with commands that it should be embraced from childhood, like those others, nor making it a law that the virtuous man must be so many years old, but addressing their discourse generally to every age. For those lessons are children's toys, but these are the truth of things.

And as a place for this their commonwealth they have assigned Heaven, and God they have brought in as the framer thereof, and as lawgiver of the statutes there set; as indeed was their duty. And the rewards in their commonwealth are not leaves of bay nor olive, nor an allowance of meat in the public hall, nor statues of brass, these cold and ordinary things, but a life which hath no end, and to become children of God, to join the angels' choir, and to stand by the royal throne, and to be always with Christ. And the popular guides of this commonwealth are publicans, and fishermen, and tent-makers, not such as have lived for a short time, but such as are now living for ever. Therefore even after their death they may possibly do the greatest good to the governed.

This republic is at war not with men, but with devils, and those incorporeal powers. Wherefore also their captain is no one of men, nor of angels, but God Himself. And the armor too of these warriors suits the nature of the warfare, for it is not formed of hides and steel, but of truth and of righteousness, and faith, and all true love of wisdom.

13. Since then the aforesaid republic is both the subject on which this book was written, and it is now proposed for us to speak thereof, let us give careful heed to Matthew, discoursing plainly concerning this: for what he saith is not his own, but all Christ's, who hath made the laws of this city. Let us give heed, I say, that we may be capable of enrolment therein, and of shining forth among those that have already become citizens thereof, and are awaiting those incorruptible crowns. To many, however, this discourse seems to be easy, while the prophetic writings are difficult. But this again is the view of men who know not the depth of the thoughts laid up therein. Wherefore I entreat you to follow us with much diligence, so as to enter into the very ocean of the things written, with Christ for our guide at this our entering in.

But in order that the word may be the more easy to learn, we pray and entreat you, as we have done also with respect to the other Scriptures, to take up beforehand that portion of the Scripture which we may be going to explain, that your reading may prepare the way for your understanding (as also was the case with the eunuch), and so may greatly facilitate our task.

14. And this because the questions are many and frequent. See, for instance, at once in the beginning of his Gospel, how many difficulties might be raised one after the other. As first, wherefore the genealogy of Joseph is traced, who was not father of Christ. Secondly, whence may it be made manifest that He derives His origin from David, while the forefathers of Mary, who bare Him, are not known, for the Virgin's genealogy is not traced? Thirdly, on what account Joseph's genealogy is traced, when he had nothing to do with the birth; while with regard to the Virgin, who was the very mother, it is not shown of what fathers, or grandfathers, or ancestors, she is sprung.

And along with these things, this is also worth inquiry, wherefore it can be, that, when tracing the genealogy through the men, he hath mentioned women also; and why since he determined upon doing this, he yet did not mention them all, but passing over the more eminent, such as Sarah, Rebecca, and as many as are like them, he hath brought forward only them that are famed for some bad thing; as, for instance, if any was a harlot, or an adulteress, or a mother by an unlawful marriage, if any was a stranger or barbarian. For he hath made mention of the wife of Uriah, and of Thamar, and of Rahab, and of Ruth, of whom one was of a strange race, another an harlot, another was defiled by her near kinsman, and with him not in the form of marriage, but by a stolen intercourse, when she had put on herself the mask of an harlot; and touching the wife of Uriah no one is ignorant, by reason of the notoriety of the crime. And yet the evangelist hath passed by all the rest, and inserted in the genealogy these alone. Whereas, if women were to be mentioned, all ought to be so; if not all but some, then those famed in the way of virtue, not for evil deeds.

See you how much care is required of us straightway in the first beginning? and yet the beginning seems to be plainer than the rest; to many perhaps even superfluous, as being a mere numbering of names.

After this, another point again is worth inquiry; wherefore he hath omitted three kings. For if, because they were exceeding ungodly, he therefore passed by their names in silence, neither should he have mentioned the others, that were like them.

And this again is another question; why, after having spoken of fourteen generations, he hath not in the third division maintained the number.

And wherefore Luke hath made mention of other names, and not only not all of them the same, but also many more of them, while Matthew hath both fewer and different, though he too hath ended with Joseph, with whom Luke likewise concluded.

Ye see how much wakeful attention is needed on our part, not only for explanation, but even that we may learn what things we have to explain. For neither is this a little matter, to be able to find out the difficulties; there being also this other hard point, how Elizabeth, who was of the Levitical tribe, was kinswoman to Mary.

15. But that we may not overload your memory, by stringing many things together, here let us stay our discourse for a time. For it is enough for you in order that ye be thoroughly roused, that you learn the questions only. But if ye long for their solution also, this again depends on yourselves, before we speak. For if I see you thoroughly awakened, and longing to learn, I will endeavor to add the solution also; but if gaping and not attending, I will conceal both the difficulties, and their solution, in obedience to a divine law. For, saith He,

"Give not the holy things to the dogs, neither cast ye your pearls before swine, lest they trample them under their feet."

But who is he that tramples them under foot? He that doth not account these things precious, and venerable. And who, it may be asked, is so wretched as not to esteem these things venerable, and more precious than all? He who doth not bestow on them so much leisure as on the harlot women in the theatres of Satan. For there the multitude pass the whole day, and give up not a few of their domestic concerns for the sake of this unseasonable employment, and they retain with exactness whatever they have heard, and this though it be to the injury of their souls, that they keep it. But here, where God is speaking, they will not bear to tarry even a little time.

Therefore, let me warn you, we have nothing in common with Heaven, but our citizenship goes no further than words. And yet because of this, God hath threatened even hell, not in order to cast us therein, but that He might persuade us to flee this grievous tyranny. But we do the opposite, and run each day the way that leads thither, and while God is commanding us not only to hear, but also to do what He saith, we do not submit so much as to hearken.

When then, I pray thee, are we to do what is commanded, and to put our hand to the works, if we do not endure so much as to hear the words that relate to them, but are impatient and restless about the time we stay here, although it be exceedingly short?

16. And besides, when we are talking of indifferent matters, if we see those that are in company do not attend, we call what they do an insult; but do we consider that we are provoking God, if, while He is discoursing of such things as these, we despise what is said, and look another way?

Why, he that is grown old, and hath travelled over much country, reports to us with all exactness the number of stadia, and the situations of cities, their plans, and their harbors and markets; but we ourselves know not even how far we are from the city that is in Heaven. For surely we should have endeavored to shorten the space, had we known the distance. That city being not only as far from us as Heaven is from the earth, but even much farther, if we be negligent; like as, on the other hand, if we do our best, even in one instant we shall come to the gates thereof. For not by local space, but by moral disposition, are these distances defined.

But thou knowest exactly the affairs of the world, as well new as old, and such too as are quite ancient; thou canst number the princes under whom thou hast served in time past, and the ruler of the games, and them that gained the prize, and the leaders of armies, matters that are of no concern to thee; but who hath become ruler in this city, the first or the second or the third, and for how long, each of them; and what each hath accomplished, and brought to pass, thou hast not imagined even as in a dream. And the laws that are set in this city thou wilt not endure to hear, nor attend to them, even when others tell thee of them. How then, I pray thee, dost thou expect to obtain the blessings that are promised, when thou dost not even attend to what is said?

17. But though never before, now, at any rate, let us do this. Yea, for we are on the point of entering into a city (if God permit) of gold, and more precious than any gold.

Let us then mark her foundations, her gates consisting of sapphires and pearls; for indeed we have in Matthew an excellent guide. For through his gate we shall now enter in, and much diligence is required on our part. For should He see any one not attentive, He casts him out of the city.

Yes, for the city is most kingly and glorious; not as the cities with us, divided into a market-place, and the royal courts; for there all is the court of the King. Let us open therefore the gates of our mind, let us open our ears, and with great trembling, when on the point of setting foot on the threshold, let us worship the King that is therein. For indeed the first approach hath power straightway to confound the beholder.

For the present we find the gates closed; but when we see them thrown open (for this is the solution of the difficulties), then we shall perceive the greatness of the splendor within. For there also, leading thee with the eyes of the Spirit, is one who offers to show thee all, even this Publican; where the King sitteth, and who of His host stand by Him; where are the angels, where the archangels; and what place is set apart for the new citizens in this city, and what kind of way it is that leads thither, and what manner of portion they have received, who first were citizens therein, and those next after them, and such as followed these. And how many are the orders of these tribes, how many those of the senate, how many the distinctions of dignity.

Let us not therefore with noise or tumult enter in, but with a mystical silence.

For if in a theatre, when a great silence hath been made, then the letters of the king are read, much more in this city must all be composed, and stand with soul and ear erect. For it is not the letters of any earthly master, but of the Lord of angels, which are on the point of being read.

If we would order ourselves on this wise, the grace itself of the Spirit will lead us in great perfection, and we shall arrive at the very royal throne, and attain to all the good things, by the grace and love towards man of our Lord Jesus Christ, to whom be glory and might, together with the Father and the Holy Ghost, now and always, even for ever and ever. Amen.

HOMILY II

MATT. I. 1

"The book of the generation of Jesus Christ, the Son of David, the Son of Abraham."

Do ye indeed remember the charge, which we lately made you, entreating you to hearken unto all the things that are said with all silence, and mystical quietness? For we are to-day to set foot within the holy vestibule, wherefore I have also put you in mind of the charge.

Since, if the Jews, when they were to approach "a mountain that burned, and fire, and blackness, and darkness, and tempest;"—or rather when they were not so much as to approach, but both to see and to hear these things from afar;—were commanded for three days before to abstain from their wives, and to wash their garments, and were in trembling and fear, both themselves and Moses with them; much more we, when we are to hearken to such words, and are not to stand far from a smoking mountain, but to enter into Heaven itself, ought to show forth a greater self-denial; not washing our garments, but wiping clean the robe of our soul, and ridding ourselves of all mixture with worldly things. For it is not blackness that ye shall see, nor smoke, nor tempest, but the King Himself sitting on the throne of that unspeakable glory, and angels, and archangels standing by Him, and the tribes of the saints, with those interminable myriads.

For such is the city of God, having "the Church of the first-born, the spirits of the just, the general assembly of the angels, the blood of sprinkling," whereby all are knit into one, and Heaven hath received the things of earth, and earth the things of Heaven, and that peace hath come which was of old longed for both by angels and by saints.

Herein standeth the trophy of the cross, glorious, and conspicuous, the spoils won by Christ, the first-fruits of our nature, the booty of our King; all these, I say, we shall out of the Gospels know perfectly. If thou follow in becoming quietness, we shall be able to lead thee about everywhere, and to show where death is set forth crucified, and where sin is hanged up, and where are the many and wondrous offerings from this war, from this battle.

Thou shalt see likewise the tyrant here bound, and the multitude of the captives following, and the citadel from which that unholy demon overran all things in time past. Thou wilt see the hiding places, and the dens of the robber, broken up now, and laid open, for even there also was our King present.

But be not thou weary, beloved, for if any one were describing a visible war, and trophies, and victories, wouldest thou feel no satiety at all; nay, thou wouldest not prefer either drink or meat to this history. But if that kind of narrative be welcome, much more this. For consider what a thing it is to hear, how on the one side God from Heaven, arising "out of the royal thrones, leaped down " unto the earth, and even unto hell itself, and stood in the battle array; and how the devil on the other hand set himself in array against Him; or rather not against God unveiled, but God hidden in man's nature.

And what is marvellous, thou wilt see death destroyed by death, and curse extinguished by curse, and the dominion of the devil put down by those very things whereby he did prevail. Let us therefore rouse ourselves thoroughly, and let us not sleep, for lo, I see the gates opening to us; but let us enter in with all seemly order, and with trembling, setting foot straightway within the vestibule itself.

2. But what is this vestibule? "The book of the generation of Jesus Christ, Son of David, Son of Abraham."

"What sayest thou? Didst thou not promise to discourse of the Only-begotten Son of God, and dost thou make mention of David, a man born after a thousand generations, and say that he is both father and ancestor?" Stay, seek not to learn all at once, but gently and by little and little. Why, it is in the vestibule that thou art standing, by the very porch; why then dost thou hasten towards the inner shrine? As yet thou hast not well marked all without. For neither for a while do I declare unto thee that other generation: or rather not even this which cometh after, for it is unutterable, and unspeakable. And before me the Prophet Esaias hath told thee this; where when proclaiming His passion, and His great care for the world, and admiring who He was, and what He became, and whither He descended, he cried out loud and clear, saying thus, "Who shall declare His generation?"

It is not then of that we are now to speak, but of this beneath, this which took place on earth, which was amongst ten thousand witnesses. And concerning this again we will relate in such wise as it may be possible for us, having received the grace of the Spirit. For not even this may any one set forth altogether plainly, forasmuch as this too is most awful. Think not, therefore, it is of small things thou art hearing, when thou hearest of this birth, but rouse up thy mind, and straightway tremble, being told that God hath come upon earth. For so marvellous was this, and beyond expectation, that because of these things the very angels formed a choir, and in behalf of the world offered up their praise for them, and the prophets from the first were amazed at this, that "He was seen upon earth, and conversed with men ." Yea, for it is far beyond all thought to hear that God the Unspeakable, the Unutterable, the Incomprehensible, and He that is equal to the Father, hath passed through a virgin's womb, and hath vouchsafed to be born of a woman, and to have Abraham and David for forefathers. But why do I say Abraham and David? For what is even more amazing, there are those women, whom we have lately mentioned.

3. Hearing these things, arise, and surmise nothing low: but even because of this very thing most of all shouldest thou marvel, that being Son of the Unoriginate God, and His true Son, He suffered Himself to be called also Son of David, that He might make thee Son of God. He suffered a slave to be father to Him, that He might make the Lord Father to thee a slave.

Seest thou at once from the beginning of what nature are the Gospels? If thou doubt concerning the things that pertain to thee, from what belongs to Him believe these also. For it is far more difficult, judging by human reason, for God to become man, than for a man to be declared a Son of God. When therefore thou art told that the Son of God is Son of David and of Abraham, doubt not any more that thou too, the son of Adam, shall be son of God. For not at random, nor in vain did He abase Himself so greatly, only He was minded to exalt us. Thus He was born after the flesh, that thou mightest be born after the Spirit; He was born of a woman, that thou mightest cease to be the son of a woman.

Wherefore the birth was twofold, both made like unto us, and also surpassing ours. For to be born of a woman indeed was our lot, but "to be born not of blood, nor of the will of flesh, nor of man," but of the Holy Ghost, was to proclaim beforehand the birth surpassing us, the birth to come, which He was about freely to give us of the Spirit. And everything else too was like this. Thus His baptism also was of the same kind, for it partook of the old, and it partook also of the new. To be baptized by the prophet marked the old, but the coming down of the Spirit shadowed out the new. And like as though any one were to place himself in the space between any two persons that were standing apart, and stretching forth both his hands were to lay hold on either side, and tie them together; even so hath He done, joining the old covenant with the new, God's nature with man's, the things that are His with ours.

Seest thou the flashing brightness of the city, with how great a splendor it hath dazzled thee from the very beginning? how it hath straightway shown the King in thine own form; as though in a camp? For neither there doth the king always appear bearing his proper dignity, but laying aside the purple and the diadem, he often disguises himself in the garb of a common soldier. But there it is, lest by being known he should draw the enemy upon himself; but here on the contrary, lest, if He were known, He should cause the enemy to fly from the conflict with Him, and lest He should confound all His own people: for His purpose was to save, not to dismay.

4. For this reason he hath also straightway called Him by this title, naming Him Jesus. For this name, Jesus, is not Greek, but in the Hebrew language it is thus called Jesus; which is, when interpreted into the Greek tongue, "A Saviour." And He is called a Saviour, from His saving His people.

Seest thou how he hath given wings to the hearer, at once speaking things familiar, and at the same time by these indicating to us things beyond all hope? I mean that both these names were well known to the Jews. For, because the things that were to happen were beyond expectation, the types even of the names went before, in order that from the very first all the unsettling power of novelty might be taken away. Thus he is called Jesus, who after Moses brought the people into the land of promise. Hast thou seen the type? Behold the truth. That led into the land of promise, this into heaven, and to the good things in the heavens; that, after Moses was dead, this after the law had ceased; that as a leader, this as a King.

However, lest having heard the word Jesus, thou shouldest by reason of the identity of the name be perplexed, he hath added, "Jesus Christ, Son of David." But that other was not of David, but of another tribe.

5. But wherefore doth he call it a "book of the generation of Jesus Christ," while yet this book hath not the birth only, but the whole dispensation? Because this is the sum of the whole dispensation, and is made an origin and root of all our blessings. As then Moses calleth it the book of heaven and earth, although he hath not discoursed of heaven and earth only, but also of all things that are in the midst thereof; so also this man hath named his book from that which is the sum of all the great things done. For that which teems with astonishment, and is beyond hope and all expectation, is that God should become man. But this having come to pass, all afterwards follows in reasonable consequence.

6. But wherefore did he not say, "the Son of Abraham," and then "the Son of David?" It is not, as some suppose, that he means to proceed upward from the lower point, since then he would have done the same as Luke, but now he doth the contrary. Why then hath he made mention of David? The man was in the mouths of all, both from his distinction, and from the time, for he had not been so very long since dead, like Abraham. And though God made promises to both, yet the one, as old, was passed over in silence, while the other, as fresh and recent, was repeated of all. Themselves, for instance, say, "Doth not Christ come of the seed of David, and out of Bethlehem, the town where David was?" And no man called Him Son of Abraham, but all Son of David;

and that because this last was more in the recollection of all, both on account of the time, as I have already said, and because of his royalty. On this principle again all the kings whom they had in honor after his time were named from him, both by the people themselves and by God. For both Ezekiel and other prophets besides speak of David as coming and rising again; not meaning him that was dead, but them who were emulating his virtue. And to Hezekiah He saith, "I will defend this city, for mine own sake and for my servant David's sake." And to Solomon too He said, that for David's sake He rent not the kingdom during his lifetime. For great was the glory of the man, both with God and with men.

On account of this he makes the beginning at once from him who was more known, and then runs up to his father; accounting it superfluous, as far as regards the Jews, to carry the genealogy higher up. For these were principally the persons held in admiration; the one as a prophet and a king, the other as a patriarch and a prophet.

7. "But whence is it manifest that He is of David?" one may say. For if He was not sprung of a man, but from a woman only, and the Virgin hath not her genealogy traced, how shall we know that He was of David's race? Thus, there are two things inquired; both why His mother's genealogy is not recited, and wherefore it can be that Joseph is mentioned by them, who hath no part in the birth: since the latter seems to be superfluous, and the former a defect.

Of which then is it necessary to speak first? How the Virgin is of David. How then shall we know that she is of David? Hearken unto God, telling Gabriel to go unto "a virgin betrothed to a man (whose name was Joseph), of the house and lineage of David." What now wouldest thou have plainer than this, when thou hast heard that the Virgin was of the house and lineage of David?

Hence it is evident that Joseph also was of the same. Yes, for there was a law, which bade that it should not be lawful to take a wife from any other stock, but from the same tribe. And the patriarch Jacob also foretold that He should arise out of the tribe of Judah, saying on this wise: "there shall not fail a ruler out of Judah, nor a governor out of his loins, until He come for whom it is appointed, and He is the expectation of the Gentiles."

"Well; this prophecy doth indeed make it clear that He was of the tribe of Judah, but not also that He was of the family of David. Was there then in the tribe of Judah one family only, even that of David, or were there not also many others? And might it not happen for one to be of the tribe of Judah, but not also of the family of David?"

Nay, lest thou shouldest say this, the evangelist hath removed this suspicion of thine, by saying, that He was "of the house and lineage of David."

And if thou wish to learn this from another reason besides, neither shall we be at a loss for another proof. For not only was it not allowed to take a wife out of another tribe, but not even from another lineage, that is, from another kindred. So that if either we connect with the Virgin the words, "of the house and lineage of David," what hath been said stands good; or if with Joseph, by that fact this also is proved. For if Joseph was of the house and lineage of David, he would not have taken his wife from another than that whence he himself was sprung.

"What then," one may say, "if he transgressed the law?" Why, for this cause he hath by anticipation testified that Joseph was righteous, on purpose that thou mightest not say this, but having been told his virtue, mightest be sure also that he would not have transgressed the law. For he who was so benevolent, and free from passion, as not to wish, even when urged by suspicion, to attempt inflicting punishment on the Virgin, how should he have transgressed the law for lust? he that showed wisdom and self-restraint beyond the law (for to put her away, and that privily, was to act with self-restraint beyond the law), how should he have done anything contrary to the law; and this when there was no cause to urge him?

8. Now that the Virgin was of the race of David is indeed from these things evident; but wherefore he gave not her genealogy, but Joseph's, requires explanation. For what cause was it then? It was not the law among the Jews that the genealogy of women should be traced. In order then that he might keep the custom, and not seem to be making alterations from the beginning, and yet might make the Virgin known to us, for this cause he hath passed over her ancestors in silence, and traced the genealogy of Joseph. For if he had done this with respect to the Virgin, he would have seemed to be introducing novelties; and if he had passed over Joseph in silence, we should not have known the Virgin's forefathers. In order therefore that we might learn, touching Mary, who she was, and of what origin, and that the laws might remain undisturbed, he hath traced the genealogy of her espoused husband, and shown him to be of the house of David. For when this hath been clearly proved, that other fact is demonstrated with it, namely, that the Virgin likewise is sprung from thence, by reason that this righteous man, even as I have already said, would not have endured to take a wife from another race.

There is also another reason, which one might mention, of a more mystical nature, because of which the Virgin's forefathers were passed over in silence;

but this it were not seasonable now to declare, because so much has been already said.

9. Wherefore let us stay at this point our discourse concerning the questions, and in the meanwhile let us retain with accuracy what hath been revealed to us; as, for instance, why he mentioned David first; wherefore he called the book, "a book of the generation;" on what account he said, "of Jesus Christ;" how the birth is common and not common; whence it was that Mary was shown to be from David; and wherefore Joseph's genealogy is traced, while her ancestors are passed over in silence.

For if ye retain these things, ye will the more encourage us with respect to what is to come; but if ye reject and cast them from your mind, we shall be the more backward as to the rest. Just as no husbandman would care to pay attention to a soil which had destroyed the former seed.

Wherefore I entreat you to revolve these things. For from taking thought concerning such matters, there springs in the soul some great good, tending unto salvation. For by these meditations we shall be able to please God Himself; and our mouths will be pure from insults, and filthy talking, and reviling, while they are exercising themselves in spiritual sayings; and we shall be formidable to the devils, while arming our tongue with such words; and we shall draw unto ourselves God's grace the more, and it will render our eye more piercing. For indeed both eyes and mouth and hearing He set in us to this intent, that all our members may serve Him, that we may speak His words, and do His deeds, that we may sing unto Him continual hymns, that we may offer up sacrifices of thanksgiving, and by these may thoroughly purify our consciences.

For as a body will be more in health when enjoying the benefits of a pure air, even so will a soul be more endued with practical wisdom when nourished in such exercises as these. Seest thou not even the eyes of the body, that when they abide in smoke they are always weeping; but when they are in clear air, and in a meadow, and in fountains and gardens, they become more quick-sighted and more healthy? Like this is the soul's eye also, for should it feed in the meadow of spiritual oracles, it will be clear and piercing, and quick of sight; but should it depart into the smoke of the things of this life, it will weep without end, and wail both now and hereafter. For indeed the things of this life are like smoke. On this account also one hath said, "My days have failed like smoke." He indeed was referring to their shortness of duration, and to their unsubstantial nature, but I would say that we should take what is said, not in this sense alone, but also as to their turbid character.

For nothing doth so hurt and dim the eye of the soul as the crowd of worldly anxieties and the swarm of desires. For these are the wood that feedeth this smoke. And as fire, when it lays hold of any damp and saturated fuel, kindles much smoke; so likewise this desire, so vehement and burning, when it lays hold of a soul that is (so to speak) damp and dissolute, produces also in its way abundance of smoke. For this cause there is need of the dew of the Spirit, and of that air, that it may extinguish the fire, and scatter the smoke, and give wings to our thoughts. For it cannot, it cannot be that one weighed down with so great evils should soar up to heaven; it is well if being without impediment we can cleave our way thither; or rather it is not possible even so, unless we obtain the wing of the Spirit.

Now if there be need both of an unencum bered mind, and of spiritual grace, that we may mount up to that height; what if there be none of these things, but we draw to ourselves whatever is opposite to them, even a satanical weight? how shall we be able to soar upwards, when dragged down by so great a load? For indeed, should any one attempt to weigh our words as it were in just balances; in ten thousand talents of worldly talk he will scarcely find an hundred pence of spiritual words, or rather, I should say, not even ten farthings. Is it not then a disgrace, and an extreme mockery, that if we have a servant, we make use of him for the most part in things necessary, but being possessed of a tongue, we do not deal with our member so well even as with a slave, but on the contrary make use of it for things unprofitable, and mere makeweights? And would it were only for makeweights: but now it is for what are contrary and hurtful and in no respect advantageous to us. For if the things that we spoke were profitable to us, they would assuredly be also pleasing to God. But as it is, whatever the devil may suggest, we speak it all, now laughing, and now speaking wittily; now cursing and insulting, and now swearing, lying, and taking false oaths; now murmuring, and now making vain babblings, and talking trifles more than old wives; uttering all things that are of no concern to us.

For, tell me, who of you that stand here, if he were required, could repeat one Psalm, or any other portion of the divine Scriptures? There is not one.

And it is not this only that is the grievous thing, but that while ye are become so backward with respect to things spiritual, yet in regard of what belongs to Satan ye are more vehement than fire. Thus should any one be minded to ask of you songs of devils and impure effeminate melodies, he will find many that know these perfectly, and repeat them with much pleasure.

10. But what is the answer to these charges? "I am not," you will say, "one of the monks, but I have both a wife and children, and the care of a house-

hold." Why, this is what hath ruined all, your supposing that the reading of the divine Scriptures appertains to those only, when ye need it much more than they. For they that dwell in the world, and each day receive wounds, these have most need of medicines. So that it is far worse than not reading, to account the thing even "superfluous:" for these are the words of diabolical invention. Hear ye not Paul saying, "that all these things are written for our admonition"?

And thou, if thou hadst to take up a Gospel, wouldest not choose to do so with hands unwashed; but the things that are laid up within it, dost thou not think to be highly necessary? It is because of this, that all things are turned upside down.

For if thou wouldest learn how great is the profit of the Scriptures, examine thyself, what thou becomest by hearing Psalms, and what by listening to a song of Satan; and how thou art disposed when staying in a Church, and how when sitting in a theatre; and thou wilt see that great is the difference between this soul and that, although both be one. Therefore Paul said, "Evil communications corrupt good manners." For this cause we have need continually of those songs, which serve as charms from the Spirit. Yes, for this it is whereby we excel the irrational creatures, since with respect to all other things, we are even exceedingly inferior to them.

This is a soul's food, this its ornament, this its security; even as not to hear is famine and wasting; for "I will give them," saith He, "not a famine of bread, nor a thirst of water, but a famine of hearing the word of the Lord."

What then can be more wretched? when the very evil, which God threatens in the way of punishment, this thou art drawing upon thine head of thine own accord, bringing into thy soul a sort of grievous famine, and making it the feeblest thing in the world? For it is its nature both to be wasted and to be saved by words. Yea, this leads it on to anger; and the same kind of thing again makes it meek: a filthy expression is wont to kindle it to lust, and it is trained to temperance by speech full of gravity.

But if a word merely have such great power, tell me, how is it thou dost despise the Scriptures? And if an admonition can do such great things, far more when the admonitions are with the Spirit. Yes, for a word from the divine Scriptures, made to sound in the ear, doth more than fire soften the hardened soul, and renders it fit for all good things.

11. In this way too did Paul, when he had found the Corinthians puffed up and inflamed, compose them, and make them more considerate. For they were priding themselves on those very things, touching which they ought to have been ashamed, and to have hid their face. But after they had received the letter,

hear the change in them, of which the Teacher himself hath borne witness for them, saying on this wise: for "this very thing, that ye sorrowed after a godly sort, what carefulness it wrought in you, yea, what clearing of yourselves, yea, what indignation, yea, what zeal, yea, what revenge." In this way do we bring to order servants and children, wives, and friends, and make our enemies friends.

In this way the great men too, they that were dear to God, became better. David, for instance, after his sin, when he had had the benefit of certain words, then it was that he came unto that most excellent repentance; and the apostles also by this mean became what they did become, and drew after them the whole world.

"And what is the profit," one may say, "when any one hears, but doeth not what is said?" No little will the profit be even from hearing. For he will go on to condemn himself, and to groan inwardly, and will come in time also to do the things that are spoken of. But he that doth not even know that he hath sinned, when will he cease from his negligence? when will he condemn himself?

Let us not therefore despise the hearing of the divine Scriptures. For this is of Satan's devising; not suffering us to see the treasure, lest we should gain the riches. Therefore he saith that the hearing the divine laws is nothing, lest he should see us from the hearing acquiring the practice also.

Knowing then this his evil art, let us fortify ourselves against him on all sides, that being fenced with this armor, we may both abide unconquered ourselves, and smite him on the head: and thus, having crowned ourselves with the glorious wreaths of victory, we may attain unto the good things to come, by the grace and love towards man of our Lord Jesus Christ, to whom be glory and might for ever and ever. Amen.

HOMILY III

MATT. I. 1

"The book of the generation of Jesus Christ, the Son of David, the Son of Abraham."

Behold a third discourse, and we have not yet made an end of the prefatory matter. It was not then for nought that I said, It is the nature of these thoughts to have a great depth.

Come, then, let us speak to-day what remains. What is it then that is now required? Why Joseph's genealogy is traced, who had no part in the birth. And one cause we have mentioned already; but it is necessary to mention likewise the other, that which is more mystical and secret than the first. What then is this? He would not that it should be manifest to the Jews, at the time of the birth, that Christ was born of a virgin.

Nay, be not troubled at the strangeness of the saying. For it is no statement of mine, but of our fathers, wonderful and illustrious men. For if He disguised many things from the first, calling Himself Son of Man, and hath not everywhere clearly unfolded to us even His equality with the Father; why dost thou wonder at His having for a time disguised this also, taking order as He was for a certain great and marvellous purpose? and would have condemned her for adultery. For if in regard to the other matters, for which they had frequent precedents likewise in the old dispensation, they were quite shameless in their obstinacy (for so, because He had cast out devils, they called Him possessed; and because He healed on the Sabbath day, they supposed Him to be an adversary of God; and yet oftentimes even before this had the Sabbath been broken), what would they not have said, if this had been told them? Especially as they had all time before this on their side, in that it never had produced any such thing. For if after so many miracles they still called Him son of Joseph, how before the miracles would they have believed that He was born of a virgin?

It is then for this reason that both Joseph has his genealogy traced, and the Virgin betrothed to him. For if even he, who was both a just and wondrous man, required many things, in order that he should receive that which had come to pass; an angel, and the vision in dreams, and the testimony from the prophets; how could the Jews, being both dull and depraved, and of so unfriendly spirit towards Him, have admitted this idea into their minds? For the strangeness and novelty thereof would be sure greatly to disturb them, and the fact that they had never so much as heard of such a thing having happened in the times of their forefathers. For as the man who was once persuaded that He is Son of God, would after that have no cause to doubt concerning this too; so he who was accounting Him to be a deceiver and an adversary of God, how could he but have been yet more offended by this, and have been led on unto the opposite notion? For this cause neither do the apostles at the first directly say this, but while of His resurrection they discourse much and often (forasmuch as of this there were examples in the times before, although not such as this); that He was born of a virgin they do not say always: nay, not even His mother herself ventured to utter this. See, for instance, what saith the Virgin even to Himself: "Behold, Thy father and I have sought Thee." For if this suspicion had been entertained, neither would He any longer have been accounted to be a Son of David, and this opinion not being held, many other evils besides would have arisen. For this cause neither do the angels say these things to all, but to Mary only, and Joseph; but when showing to the shepherds the glad tidings of that which was come to pass, they no longer added this.

2. But why is it, that having mentioned Abraham, and having said that "he begat Isaac, and Isaac, Jacob;" and not having made any mention of his brother; when he is come to Jacob, he remembers both "Judah, and his brethren"? Now there are some that say, it was because of the perverseness of Esau, and of the rest that came before. But I should not say this; for if it were so, how is it that he a little after mentions such women? It being out of contraries, in this place, that His glory is manifested; not by having great forefathers, but low and of little account. For to the lofty One it is a great glory to be able to abase Himself exceedingly. Wherefore then did He not mention them? Because Saracens, and Ishmaelites, and Arabians, and as many as are sprung from those ancestors, have nothing in common with the race of the Israelites. For this cause then he passes over those in silence, and hastens on to His forefathers, and those of the Jewish people. Wherefore he saith, "And Jacob begat Judas and his brethren." For at this point the race of the Jews begins to have its peculiar mark.

3. "And Judas begat Phares and Zara of Thamar." "What doest thou, O man, putting us in remembrance of a history that contains an unlawful intercourse?" But why is this said? Since, if we were recounting the race of a mere man, one might naturally have been silent touching these things; but if of God Incarnate, so far from being silent, one ought to make a glory of them, showing forth His tender care, and His power. Yea, it was for this cause He came, not to escape our disgraces, but to bear them away. Therefore as He is the more admired, in that He not only died, but was even crucified (though the thing be opprobrious, yet the more opprobrious the more doth it show Him full of love to man), so likewise may we speak touching His birth; it is not only because He took flesh upon Him, and became man, that we justly stand amazed at Him, but because He vouchsafed to have also such kinsfolk, being in no respect ashamed of our evils. And this He was proclaiming from the very beginnings of His birth, that He is ashamed of none of those things that belong to us; while He teaches us also hereby, never to hide our face at our forefathers' wickedness, but to seek after one thing alone, even virtue. For such a man, though he have an alien for his ancestor, though he have a mother who is a prostitute, or what you will, can take no hurt thereby. For if the whoremonger himself, being changed, is nothing disgraced by his former life, much

more will the wickedness of his ancestry have no power to bring to shame him that is sprung of an harlot or an adulteress, if he be virtuous.

But he did these things not only to instruct us, but also to bring down the haughtiness of the Jews. For since they, negligent about virtue in their own souls, were parading the name of Abraham, thinking they had for a plea their forefathers' virtue; he shows from the very beginning that it is not in these things men ought to glory, but in their own good deeds.

Besides this, he is establishing another point also, to show that all are under sin, even their forefathers themselves. At least their patriarch and namesake is shown to have committed no small sin, for Thamar stands against him, to accuse his whoredom. And David too had Solomon by the wife whom he corrupted. But if by the great ones the law was not fulfilled, much more by the less. And if it was not fulfilled, all have sinned, and Christ's coming is become necessary.

For this cause he made mention also of the twelve patriarchs, by this again bringing down their pride at the noble birth of their fathers. Because many of these also were born of women that were slaves; but nevertheless the difference of the parents did not make a difference in the children. For all were equally both patriarchs and heads of tribes. For this is the precedence of the Church, this the prerogative of the nobility that is among us, taking its type from the beginning. So that whether thou be bond or free, thou hast from thence nothing more nor less; but the question is all about one thing only, namely, the mind, and the disposition of the soul.

4. But besides what we have said, there is another cause also, wherefore he hath mentioned even this history; for to be sure, Zara's name was not cast at random on that of Phares. (For indeed it was irrelevant, and superfluous, when he had mentioned Phares, from whom he was to trace Christ's genealogy, to mention Zara also.) Wherefore then did he mention him? When Thamar was on the point of giving birth to them, the pangs having come upon her, Zara put forth his hand first. Then the midwife, when she saw this, in order that the first should be known, bound his hand with scarlet; but the child, when he was bound, drew in his hand, and when he had drawn it in, Phares came forth first, and then Zara. The midwife when she saw this said, "Why was the hedge broken up for thee?"

Seest thou the dark expression of mysteries? For it was not without purpose that these things were recorded for us: since neither was it worth our study to learn, what it might be that the midwife said; nor worth a narrative to know, that he who came out second, put forth his hand first. What then is the mysterious lesson? First, from the name of the child we learn what is inquired, for

Phares is "a division," and "a breach." And moreover from the thing itself, which took place; for it was not in the order of nature that, having thrust out his hand, he should draw it in again when bound; these thing neither belonged to a movement directed by reason, nor did they take place in the way of natural consequence. For after the hand had found its way out, that another child should come forth before was perhaps not unnatural; but that he should draw it back, and give a passage for another, was no longer after the manner of children at the birth, but the grace of God was present with the children, ordering these things, and sketching out for us by them a sort of image of the things that were to come.

What then? Some of those who have examined these things accurately say, that these children are a type of the two nations. And so in order that thou mightest learn that the polity of the latter people shone forth previously to the origin of the former, the child that hath the hand stretched forth doth not show itself entire, but draws even it in again; and after his brother had glided forth whole, then he too appears entire. And this took place also with regard to the two nations. I mean, that after the polity of the Church had been manifested in the times of Abraham, and then had been withdrawn in the midst of its course, the Jewish people came, and the legal polity, and then the new people appeared entire with their own laws. Wherefore also the midwife saith, "Why was the hedge broken up for thee?" because the law coming in had broken in upon the freedom of the polity. For indeed the Scripture is ever wont to call the law a hedge; as the prophet saith: "Thou hast broken down her hedge, so that all they which pass by the way do pluck off her grapes:" and, "I have set a hedge about it:" and Paul, "Having broken down the middle wall of the hedge." But others say, that the saying, "Why was the hedge broken up for thee?" was spoken touching the new people: for this at its coming put down the law.

5. Seest thou that it was not for few nor small causes that he brought to our remembrance the whole history concerning Judah? For this end he hath mentioned Ruth also and Rahab, the one an alien, the other an harlot, that thou mayest learn that He came to do away with all our ills. For He hath come as a Physician, not as a Judge. Therefore in like manner as those of old took harlots for wives, even so God too espoused unto Himself the nature which had played the harlot: and this also prophets from the beginning declare to have taken place with respect to the Synagogue. But that spouse was ungrateful towards Him who had been an husband to her, whereas, the Church, when once delivered from the evils received from our fathers, continued to embrace the Bridegroom.

See, for instance, what befell Ruth, how like it is to the things which belong to us. For she was both of a strange race, and reduced to the utmost poverty, yet Boaz when he saw her neither despised her poverty nor abhorred her mean birth, as Christ having received the Church, being both an alien and in much poverty, took her to be partaker of the great blessings. But even as Ruth, if she had not before left her father, and renounced household and race, country and kindred, would not have attained unto this alliance; so the Church too, having forsaken the customs which men had received from their fathers, then, and not before, became lovely to the Bridegroom. Of this therefore the prophet discourses unto her, and saith, "Forget thy people, and thy father's house, so shall the king have pleasure in thy beauty." This Ruth did too, and because of this she became a mother of kings, even as the Church did likewise. For of her David himself sprung. So then to shame them by all these things, and to prevail on them not to be high-minded, he hath both composed the genealogy, and brought forward these women. Yes, for this last, through those who intervened, was parent to the great king, and of these David is not ashamed. For it cannot, nay, it cannot be that a man should be good or bad, obscure or glorious, either by the virtue or by the vice of his forefathers; but if one must say somewhat even paradoxical, he shines forth the more, who not being of worthy ancestors, has yet become excellent.

6. Let no one therefore be high-minded on account of these matters, but let him consider the forefathers of the Lord, and put away all his haughtiness, and let good actions be his pride; or rather, not even these. For thus it was that the Pharisee came to be inferior to the Publican. Thus, if thou wouldest show the good work to be great, have no high thought, and thou hast proved it so much the greater. Make account that thou hast done nothing, and then thou hast done all. For if, being sinners, when we account ourselves to be what we are, we become righteous, as indeed the Publican did; how much more, when being righteous we account ourselves to be sinners. Since if out of sinners men are made righteous by a lowly mind (although this were not to be lowly-minded but to be right-minded); if then to be right-minded avails so much in the case of sinners, consider what will not lowliness of mind do with respect to righteous men.

Do not then mar thy labors, nor cast away from thee the fruits of thy toils, neither run thou in vain, making frustrate all thy labor after the many courses thou hast run. Nay, for thy Lord knows thy good works better than thou dost. Though thou give but a cup of cold water, not even this doth He overlook; though thou contribute but a farthing, though thou shouldest utter a sigh only, He receives it all with great favor and is mindful thereof, and assigns for it great rewards.

But wherefore dost thou search out thine own doings, and bring them out before us continually? Knowest thou not, that if thou praise thyself, God will no more praise thee? even as if thou bewail thyself, He will not cease proclaiming thee before all. For it is not at all His will that thy labors should be disparaged. Why do I say, disparaged? Nay, He is doing and contriving all things, so that even for little He may crown thee; and He goes about seeking excuses, whereby thou mayest be delivered from hell. For this cause, though thou shouldest work but the eleventh hour of the day, He gives thy wages entire; and though thou afford no ground of salvation, He saith, "I do it for mine own sake, that my name be not profaned:" though thou shouldest sigh only, though thou shouldest only weep, all these things He quickly catches hold of, for an occasion of saving thee.

Let us not therefore lift up ourselves, but let us declare ourselves unprofitable, that we may become profitable. For if thou call thyself approved, thou art become unprofitable, though thou wert approved; but if useless, thou art become profitable, even though thou wert reprobate.

7. Wherefore it is necessary to forget our good actions. "Yet how is it possible," one may say, "not to know these things with which we are well acquainted?" How sayest thou? Offending thy Lord perpetually, thou livest delicately, and laughest, and dost not so much as know that thou hast sinned, but hast consigned all to oblivion; and of thy good actions canst thou not put away the memory? And yet fear is a stronger kind of thing. But we do the very contrary; on the one hand, whilst each day we are offending, we do not so much as put it before our mind; on the other, if we give a little money to a poor person, this we are ever revolving. This kind of conduct comes of utter madness, and it is a very great loss to him who so makes his reckoning. For the secure storehouse of good works is to forget our good works. And as with regard to raiment and gold, when we expose them in a market-place, we attract many ill-meaning persons; but if we put them by at home and hide them, we shall deposit them all in security: even so with respect to our good deeds; if we are continually keeping them in memory, we provoke the Lord, we arm the enemy, we invite him to steal them away; but if no one know of them, besides Him who alone ought to know, they will lie in safety.

Be not therefore for ever parading them, lest some one should take them away. As was the case with the Pharisee, for bearing them about upon his lips; whence also the devil caught them away. And yet it was with thanksgiving he made mention of them, and referred the whole to God. But not even did this suffice Him. For it is not thanksgiving to revile others, to be vainglorious before many, to exalt one's self against them that have offended. Rather, if thou art giving thanks to God, be content with Him only, and publish it not unto men, neither condemn thy neighbor; for this is not thanksgiving. Wouldest thou learn words of thanksgiving? hearken unto the Three Children, saying, "We have sinned, we have transgressed. Thou art righteous, O Lord, in all that thou hast done unto us, because thou hast brought all things upon us by a true judgment." For to confess one's own sins, this is to give thanks with confession unto God: a kind of thing which implies one to be guilty of numberless offenses, yet not to have the due penalty exacted. This man most of all is the giver of thanks.

8. Let us beware therefore of saying anything about ourselves, for this renders us both odious with men and abominable to God. For this reason, the greater the good works we do, the less let us say of ourselves; this being the way to reap the greatest glory both with men and with God. Or rather, not only glory from God, but a reward, yea, a great recompense. Demand not therefore a reward that thou mayest receive a reward. Confess thyself to be saved by grace, that He may profess Himself a debtor to thee; and not for thy good works only, but also for such rightness of mind. For when we do good works, we have Him debtor for our good works only; but when we do not so much as think we have done any good work, then also for this disposition itself; and more for this, than for the other things: so that this is equivalent to our good works. For should this be absent, neither will they appear great. For in the same way, we too, when we have servants, do then most approve them when, after having performed all their service with good will, they do not think they have done anything great. Wherefore, if thou wouldest make thy good deeds great, do not think them to be great, and then they will be great.

It was in this way that the centurion also said, "I am not fit that thou shouldest enter under my roof;" because of this, he became worthy, and was "marvelled at" above all Jews. On this wise again Paul saith, "I am not meet to be called an apostle;" because of this he became even first of all. So likewise John: "I am not meet to loose the latchet of His shoe;" because of this he was the "friend of the Bridegroom," and the hand which he affirmed to be unworthy to touch His shoes, this did Christ draw unto His own head. So Peter too said, "Depart from me, for I am a sinful man;" because of this he became a foundation of the Church.

For nothing is so acceptable to God as to number one's self with the last. This is a first principle of all practical wisdom. For he that is humbled, and bruised in heart, will not be vainglorious, will not be wrathful, will not envy his neighbor, will not harbor any other passion. For neither when a hand is bruised, though we strive ten thousand times, shall we be able to lift it up on high. If therefore we were thus to bruise our heart likewise, though it were stirred by ten thousand swelling passions, it could not be lifted up, no, not ever so little. For if a man, by mourning for things pertaining to this life, drives out all the diseases of his soul, much more will he, who mourns for sins, enjoy the blessing of self-restraint.

9. "But who," one may say, "will be able thus to bruise his own heart?" Listen to David, who became illustrious chiefly because of this, and see the contrition of his soul. How after ten thousand good works, and when he was on the point of being deprived of country, and home, and life itself, at the very season of his calamity, seeing a vile and outcast common soldier trample on the turn of his fortunes and revile him; so far from reviling him again, he utterly forbad one of his captains, who was desirous to have slain him, saying, "Let him alone, for the Lord hath bidden him." And again, when the priests desired to carry about the ark of God with him, he did not permit it; but what doth he say? "Let me set it down in the temple, and if God deliver me from the dangers that are before me, I shall see the beauty thereof; but if He say to me, I have no delight in thee, behold, here am I, let Him do to me as seemeth good unto Him." And that which was done with regard to Saul, again and again, even oftentimes, what excellence of self-restraint doth it not show? Yea, for he even surpassed the old law, and came near to the apostolic injunctions. For this cause he bore with contentedness all that came from the Lord's hands; not contending against what befell him, but aiming at one object alone, namely, in everything to obey, and follow the laws set by Him. And when after so many noble deeds on his part, he saw the tyrant, the parricide, the murderer of his own brother, that injurious, that frenzied one, possessing in his stead his own kingdom, not even so was he offended. But "if this please God," saith he, "that I should be chased, and wander, and flee, and that he should be in honor, I acquiesce, and accept it, and do thank God for His many afflictions." Not like many of the shameless and impudent ones, who when they have not done, no not the least part of his good works, yet if they see any in prosperity, and themselves enduring a little discouragement, ruin their own souls by ten thousand blasphemies. But David was not such an one; rather he showed forth all modesty. Wherefore also God said, "I have found David, the son of Jesse, a man after mine own heart."

Such a spirit as this let us too acquire, and whatever we may suffer we shall bear it easily, and before the Kingdom, we shall reap here the gain accruing from lowliness of mind. Thus "learn," saith He, "of me, for I am meek and lowly in heart, and ye shall find rest unto your souls." Therefore in order that we may enjoy rest both here and hereafter, let us with great diligence implant in our souls the mother of all things that are good, I mean humility. For thus we shall be enabled both to pass over the sea of this life without waves, and to end our voyage in that calm harbor; by the grace and love towards man of our Lord Jesus Christ, to whom be glory and might for ever and ever. Amen.

HOMILY IV

MATT. I. 17

"So all the generations from Abraham to David are fourteen generations, and from David until the carrying away into Babylon are fourteen generations, and from the carrying away into Babylon unto Christ are fourteen generations."

He hath divided all the generations into three portions, to indicate that not even when their form of government was changed did they become better, but alike under an aristocracy, and under a king, and under an oligarchy, they were in the same evil ways, and whether popular leaders, or priests, or kings controlled them, it was no advantage to them in the way of virtue.

But wherefore hath he in the middle portion passed over three kings, and in the last, having set down twelve generations, affirmed them to be fourteen? The former question I leave for you to examine; for neither is it needful for me to explain all things to you, lest ye should grow indolent: but the second we will explain. To me then he seems in this place to be putting in the place of a generation, both the time of the captivity, and Christ Himself, by every means connecting Him with us. And full well doth he put us in mind of that captivity, making it manifest that not even when they went down thither, did they become more sober-minded; in order that from everything His coming may be shown to be necessary.

"Why then," one may say, "doth not Mark do this, nor trace Christ's genealogy, but utter everything briefly?" It seems to me that Matthew was before the rest in entering on the subject (wherefore he both sets down the genealogy with exactness, and stops at those things which require it): but that Mark came after him, which is why he took a short course, as putting his hand to what had been already spoken and made manifest.

How is it then that Luke not only traces the genealogy, but doth it through a greater number? As was natural, Matthew having led the way, he seeks to teach us somewhat in addition to former statements. And each too in like manner imitated his master; the one Paul, who flows fuller than any river; the other Peter, who studies brevity.

2. And what may be the reason that Matthew said not at the beginning, in the same way as the prophet, "the vision which I saw," and "the word which came unto me"? Because he was writing unto men well disposed, and exceedingly attentive to him. For both the miracles that were done cried aloud, and they who received the word were exceeding faithful. But in the case of the prophets, there were neither so many miracles to proclaim them; and besides, the tribe of the false prophets, no small one, was riotously breaking in upon them: to whom the people of the Jews gave even more heed. This kind of opening therefore was necessary in their case.

And if ever miracles were done, they were done for the aliens' sake, to increase the number of the proselytes; and for manifestation of God's power, if haply their enemies having taken them captives, fancied they prevailed, because their own gods were mighty: like as in Egypt, out of which no small "mixed multitude" went up; and, after that, in Babylon, what befell touching the furnace and the dreams. And miracles were wrought also, when they were by themselves in the wilderness; as also in our case: for among us too, when we had just come out of error, many wonderful works were shown forth; but afterwards they stayed, when in all countries true religion had taken root.

And what took place at a later period were few and at intervals; for example, when the sun stood still in its course, and started back in the opposite direction. And this one may see to have occurred in our case also. For so even in our generation, in the instance of him who surpassed all in ungodliness, I mean Julian, many strange things happened. Thus when the Jews were attempting to raise up again the temple at Jerusalem, fire burst out from the foundations, and utterly hindered them all; and when both his treasurer, and his uncle and namesake, made the sacred vessels the subject of their open insolence, the one was "eaten with worms, and gave up the ghost," the other "burst asunder in the midst." Moreover, the fountains failing, when sacrifices were made there, and the entrance of the famine into the cities together with the emperor himself, was a very great sign. For it is usual with God to do such things; when evils are multiplied, and He sees His own people afflicted, and their adversaries greatly intoxicated with their dominion over them, then to display His own power; which he did also in Persia with respect to the Jews.

3. Wherefore, that he was not acting without an object, or by chance, when he distributed Christ's forefathers into three portions, is plain from what hath been said. And mark, too, whence he begins, and where he ends. From Abraham to David; from David to the captivity of Babylon; from this unto Christ Himself. For both at the beginning he put the two in close succession, David and Abraham, and also in summing up he mentions both in the same way.

And this, because, as I have already said, it was to them that the promises were made.

But why can it be, that as he mentioned the captivity of Babylon, he did not mention also the descent into Egypt? Because they had ceased to be any longer afraid of the Egyptians, but the Babylonians they dreaded still. And the one thing was ancient, but the other fresh, and had taken place of late. And to the one they were carried down for no sins, but to the other, transgressions were the cause of their being removed.

And also with regard to the very names, if any one were to attempt to translate their etymologies, even thence would he derive great matter of divine speculation, and such as is of great importance with regard to the New Testament: as, for instance, from Abraham's name, from Jacob's, from Solomon's, from Zorobabel's. For it was not without purpose that these names were given them. But lest we should seem to be wearisome by running out a great length, let us pass these things by, and proceed to what is urgent.

4. Having then mentioned all His forefathers, and ending with Joseph, he did not stop at this, but added, "Joseph the husband of Mary;" intimating that it was for her sake he traced his genealogy also. Then, lest when thou hast heard of the "husband of Mary," thou shouldest suppose that Christ was born after the common law of nature, mark, how he sets it right by that which follows. "Thou hast heard," saith he, "of an husband, thou hast heard of a mother, thou hast heard a name assigned to the child, therefore hear the manner too of the birth." "The birth of Jesus Christ was on this wise." "Of what kind of birth art thou telling me, I pray thee, since thou hast already mentioned His ancestors?" "I still wish to tell thee the manner also of His birth." Seest thou, how he wakens up the hearer? For as though he were about to speak of something unusual, he promises to tell also the manner thereof.

And observe a most admirable order in the things he hath mentioned. For he did not proceed directly to the birth, but puts us in mind first, how many generations he was from Abraham, how many from David, and from the captivity of Babylon; and thus he sets the careful hearer upon considering the times, to show that this is the Christ who was preached by the prophets. For when thou hast numbered the generations, and hast learnt by the time that this is He, thou wilt readily receive likewise the miracle which took place in His birth. Thus, being about to tell of a certain great thing, His birth of a virgin, he first shadows over the statement, until he hath numbered the generations, by speaking of "an husband of Mary;" or rather he doth even put in short space the narration of the birth itself, and then proceeds to number also the years, reminding the hearer, that this is He, of whom the patriarch Jacob had said, He should then at length come, when the Jewish rulers had come to an end; of whom the prophet Daniel had proclaimed beforehand, that He should come after those many weeks. And if any one, counting the years spoken of to Daniel by the angel in a number of weeks, would trace down the time from the building of the city to His birth, by reckoning he will perceive the one to agree with the other.

5. How then was He born, I pray thee? "When as His mother Mary was espoused:" He saith not "virgin," but merely "mother;" so that his account is easy to be received. And so having beforehand prepared the hearer to look for some ordinary piece of information, and by this laying hold of him, after all he amazes him by adding the marvellous fact, saying, "Before they came together, she was found with child of the Holy Ghost." He saith not, "before she was brought to the bridegroom's house;" for indeed she was therein. It being the way of the ancients for the most part to keep their espoused wives in their house: in those parts, at least, where one may see the same practised even now. Thus also Lot's sons-in-law were in his house with him. Mary then herself likewise was in the house with Joseph.

And wherefore did she not conceive before her espousal? It was, as I said at first, that what had been done might be concealed awhile, and that the Virgin might escape every evil suspicion. For when he, who had most right of all to feel jealousy, so far from making her a show, or degrading her, is found even receiving and cherishing her after her conception; it was quite clear that, unless he had fully persuaded himself that what was done was of the operation of the Holy Spirit, he would not have kept her with him, and ministered to her in all other things. And most properly hath he said, that "she was found' with child," the sort of expression that is wont to be used with respect to things strange, and such as happen beyond all expectation, and are unlooked for.

Proceed therefore no further, neither require anything more than what hath been said; neither say thou, "But how was it that the Spirit wrought this of a virgin?" For if, when nature is at work, it is impossible to explain the manner of the formation; how, when the Spirit is working miracles, shall we be able to express these? And lest thou shouldest weary the evangelist, or disturb him by continually asking these things, he hath said who it was that wrought the miracle, and so withdrawn himself. "For I know," saith he, "nothing more, but that what was done was the work of the Holy Ghost."

6. Shame on them who busy themselves touching the generation on high. For if this birth, which hath witnesses without number, and had been proclaimed so long a time before, and was manifested and handled with hands, can by no man be explained; of what excess of madness do they come short

who make themselves busy and curious touching that unutterable generation? For neither Gabriel nor Matthew was able to say anything more, but only that it was of the Spirit; but how, of the Spirit, or in what manner, neither of them hath explained; for neither was it possible.

Nor think that thou hast learnt all, by hearing "of the Spirit;" nay, for we are ignorant of many things, even when we have learnt this; as, for instance, how the Infinite is in a womb, how He that contains all things is carried, as unborn, by a woman; how the Virgin bears, and continues a virgin. How, I pray thee, did the Spirit frame that Temple? how did He take not all the flesh from the womb, but a part thereof, and increased it, and fashioned it? For that He did come forth of the Virgin's flesh, He hath declared by speaking of "that which was conceived in her;" and Paul, by saying, "made of a woman;" whereby he stops the mouths of them that say, Christ came among us as through some conduit. For, if this were so, what need of the womb? If this were so, He hath nothing in common with us, but that flesh is of some other kind, and not of the mass which belongs to us. How then was He of the root of Jesse? How was He a rod? how Son of man? how was Mary His mother? how was He of David's seed? how did he "take the form of a servant?" how "was the Word made flesh?" and how saith Paul to the Romans, "Of whom as concerning the flesh Christ came, who is God over all?" Therefore that He was of us, and of our substance, and of the Virgin's womb, is manifest from these things, and from others beside; but how, is not also manifest. Do not either thou then inquire; but receive what is revealed, and be not curious about what is kept secret.

7. "And Joseph her husband, being," saith he "a just man, and not willing to make her a public example, was minded to put her away privily."

Having said that it was of the Holy Ghost, and without cohabitation, he establishes his statement in another way again. Lest any one should say, "Whence doth this appear? Who hath heard, who hath seen any such thing ever come to pass?"—or lest you should suspect the disciple as inventing these things to favor his Master;—he introduces Joseph as contributing, by what he underwent, to the proof of the things mentioned; and by his narrative all but says, "If thou doubt me, and if thou suspect my testimony, believe her husband." For "Joseph," saith he, "her husband, being a just man." By "a just man" in this place he means him that is virtuous in all things. For both freedom from covetousness is justice, and universal virtue is also justice; and it is mostly in this latter sense that the Scripture uses the name of justice; as when it saith, "a man that was just and true;" and again, "they were both just." Being then "just," that is good and considerate, "he was minded to put her away privily." For this intent he tells what took place before Joseph's being fully informed, that thou mightest not mistrust what was done after he knew. However, such a one was not liable to be made a public example only, but that she should also be punished was the command of the law. Whereas Joseph remitted not only that greater punishment, but the less likewise, namely, the disgrace. For so far from punishing, he was not minded even to make an example of her. Seest thou a man under self-restraint, and freed from the most tyrannical of passions. For ye know how great a thing jealousy is: and therefore He said, to whom these things are clearly known, "For full of jealousy is the rage of a husband;" "he will not spare in the day of vengeance:" and "jealousy is cruel as the grave." And we too know of many that have chosen to give up their lives rather than fall under the suspicion of jealousy. But in this case it was not so little as suspicion, the burden of the womb entirely convicting her. But nevertheless he was so free from passion as to be unwilling to grieve the Virgin even in the least matters. Thus, whereas to keep her in his house seemed like a transgression of the law, but to expose and bring her to trial would constrain him to deliver her to die; he doth none of these things, but conducts himself now by a higher rule than the law. For grace being come, there must needs henceforth be many tokens of that exalted citizenship. For as the sun, though as yet he show not his beams, doth from afar by his light illumine more than half the world; so likewise Christ, when about to rise from that womb, even before He came forth, shone over all the world. Wherefore, even before her travail, prophets danced for joy, and women foretold what was to come, and John, when he had not yet come forth from the belly, leaped from the very womb. Hence also this man exhibited great self-command, in that he neither accused nor upbraided, but only set about putting her away.

8. The matter then being in this state, and all at their wits' end, the angel comes to solve all their difficulties. But it is worth inquiring, why the angel did not speak sooner, before the husband had such thoughts: but, "when he thought on it," not until then, he came; for it is said, "While he thought on these things, the angel" comes. And yet to her he declares the good tidings even before she conceived. And this again contains another difficulty; for even though the angel had not spoken, wherefore was the Virgin silent, who had been informed by the angel; and why, when she saw her betrothed husband in trouble, did she not put an end to his perplexity?

Wherefore then did not the angel speak before Joseph became troubled. For we must needs explain the former difficulty first. For what reason then did he not speak? Lest Joseph should be unbelieving, and the same happen to him as to Zacharias. For when the thing was visible, belief was thenceforth easy; but when it had not yet a beginning, it was not equally easy to receive his saying. For this reason the angel spake not at the first, and through the same cause the Virgin too held her peace. For she did not think to obtain credit with her betrothed husband, in declaring to him a thing unheard of, but rather that she should provoke him the more, as though she were cloking a sin that had been committed. Since if she herself, who was to receive so great a favor, is affected somewhat after the manner of man, and saith, "How shall this be, seeing I know not a man?" much more would he have doubted; and especially when hearing it from the woman who was under suspicion. Wherefore the Virgin saith nothing to him, but the angel, the time demanding it, presents himself to him.

9. Why then, it may be asked, did he not so in the Virgin's case also, and declare the good tidings to her after the conception? Lest she should be in agitation and great trouble. For it were likely that she, not knowing the certainty, might have even devised something amiss touching herself, and have gone on to strangle or to stab herself, not enduring the disgrace. For wondrous indeed was that Virgin, and Luke points out her excellency, saying, that when she heard the salutation, she did not straightway pour herself out, neither did she accept the saying, but "was troubled," seeking "what manner of salutation this might be." Now she who was of such perfect delicacy would even have been distracted with dismay at the thought of her shame, not expecting, by whatever she might say, to convince any one who should hear of it, but that what had happened was adultery. Therefore to prevent these things, the angel came before the conception. Besides that, it was meet that womb should be free from trouble which the Maker of all things entered; and the soul rid of all perturbation, which was thought worthy to become the minister of such mysteries. For these reasons He speaks to the Virgin before the conception, but to Joseph at the time of travail.

And this many of the simpler sort, not understanding, have said there is a discordance; because Luke saith it was Mary to whom he declared the good tidings, but Matthew, that it was Joseph; not knowing that both took place. And this sort of thing it is necessary to bear in mind throughout the whole history; for in this way we shall solve many seeming discordances.

10. The angel then comes, when Joseph is troubled. For in addition to the causes mentioned, with a view also to the manifestation of his self-command, he defers his coming. But when the thing was on the point of taking place, then at last he presents himself. "While he thought on these things, an angel appeareth to Joseph in a dream."

Seest thou the mildness of the husband? So far from punishing, he did not even declare it to any one, no not even to her whom he suspected, but was thinking it over with himself, as aiming to conceal the cause even from the Virgin herself. For neither is it said that he was minded to "cast her out," but to "put her away," so very mild and gentle was the man. "But while he is thinking on these things, the angel appeareth in a dream."

And why not openly, as to the shepherds, and to Zacharias, and to the Virgin? The man was exceedingly full of faith, and needed not this vision. Whereas the Virgin, as having declared to her very exceeding good tidings, greater than to Zacharias, and this before the event, needed also a marvellous vision; and the shepherds, as being by disposition rather dull and clownish. But this man, after the conception, and wide the interval between the two men; wherefore neither was there need of rebuke.

But by saying, "fear not," he signifies him to have been afraid, lest he should give offense to God, as retaining an adulteress; since, if it had not been for this, he would not have even thought of casting her out. In all ways then he points out that the angel came from God, bringing forward and setting before him all, both what he thought to do, and what he felt in his mind.

Now having mentioned her name, he stayed not at this, but added also, "thy wife;" whereas he would not have called her so, if she had been corrupted. And here he calls her that is espoused "a wife;" as indeed the Scripture is wont to call betrothed husbands sons-in-law even before marriage.

But what means, "to take unto thee?" To retain her in his house, for in intention she had been now put away by him. "Her, being put away, do thou retain," saith he, "as committed unto thee by God, not by her parents. And He commits her not for marriage; but to dwell with thee; and by my voice doth He commit her." Much as Christ Himself afterwards committed her to His disciple, so even now unto Joseph.

12. Then having obscurely signified the matter in hand, he mentioned not the evil suspicion; but, in a manner more reverent and seemly, by telling the cause of travail he removed this also; implying that the very thing which had made him afraid, and for which he would have cast her out,—this very thing, I say, was a just cause why he should take her and retain her in his house. Thus more than entirely doing away with his distress. "For she is not only free," saith he, "from unlawful intercourse, but even above all nature is her conception. Not only therefore put away thy fear, but even rejoice more exceedingly, for that which is conceived in her is of the Holy Ghost.'"

A strange thing it was which he spake of, surpassing man's reason, and above all the laws of nature. How then is he to believe, to whom such tidings are altogether new? "By the things that are past," saith he, "by the revelations." For with this intent he laid open all things that were in his mind, what he felt, what he feared, what he was resolved to do;—that by these he might assure himself of this point.

Or rather, not by things past only, but like wise by things to come, he wins him over. "And she shall bring forth," saith he, "a Son, and thou shalt call His name Jesus." "For do not thou, because He is of the Holy Ghost, imagine that thou art an alien to the ministry of this dispensation. Since although in the birth thou hast no part, but the Virgin abode untouched, nevertheless, what pertains to a father, not injuring the honor of virginity, that do I give thee, to set a Name on that which is born: for "thou shalt call Him." For though the offspring be not thine, yet shalt thou exhibit a father's care towards Him. Wherefore I do straightway, even from the giving of the name, connect thee with Him that is born."

Then lest on the other hand any one should from this suspect him to be the father, hear what follows, with what exact care he states it. "She shall bring forth," he saith, "a Son:" he doth not say, "bring forth to thee," but merely "she shall bring forth," putting it indefinitely: since not to him did she bring forth, but to the whole world.

13. For this cause too the angel came bringing His name from Heaven, hereby again intimating that this is a wondrous birth: it being God Himself who sends the name from above by the angel to Joseph. For neither was this without an object, but a treasure of ten thousand blessings. Wherefore the angel also interprets it, and suggests good hopes, in this way again leading him to belief. For to these things we are wont to be more inclined, and therefore are also fonder of believing them.

So having established his faith by all, by the past things, by the future, by the present, by the honor given to himself, he brings in the prophet also in good time, to give his suffrage in support of all these. But before introducing him, he proclaims beforehand the good things which were to befall the world through Him. And what are these? Sins removed and done away. "For He shall save His people from their sins."

Here again the thing is signified to be beyond all expectation. For not from visible wars, neither from barbarians, but what was far greater than these, from sins, he declares the glad tidings of deliverance; a work which had never been possible to any one before.

But wherefore, one may ask, did he say, "His people," and not add the Gentiles also? That he might not startle the hearer yet a while. For to him that listens with understanding he darkly signified the Gentiles too. For "His people" are not the Jews only, but also all that draw nigh and receive the knowledge that is from Him.

And mark how he hath by the way discovered to us also His dignity, by calling the Jewish nation "His people." For this is the word of one implying nought else, but that He who is born is God's child, and that the King of those on high is the subject of his discourse. As neither doth forgiving sins belong to any other power, but only to that single essence.

14. Forasmuch then as we have partaken of so great a gift, let us do everything not to dishonor such a benefit. For if even before this honor, what was done was worthy of punishment, much more now, after this unspeakable benefit. And this I say not now for no cause, but because I see many after their baptism living more carelessly than the uninitiated, and having nothing peculiar to distinguish them in their way of life. It is, you see, for this cause, that neither in the market nor in the Church is it possible to know quickly who is a believer and who an unbeliever; unless one be present at the time of the mysteries, and see the one sort put out, the others remaining within. Whereas they ought to be distinguished not by their place, but by their way of life. For as men's outward dignities are naturally to be discovered by the outward signs with which they are invested, so ours ought to be discernible by the soul. That is, the believer ought to be manifest not by the gift only, but also by the new life. The believer ought to be the light and salt of the world. But when thou dost not give light even to thyself, neither bind up thine own gangrene, what remains, whereby we are to know thee? Because thou hast entered the holy waters? Nay, this to thee becomes a store of punishment. For greatness of honor is, to them who do not choose to live worthy of the honor, an increase of vengeance. Yea, the believer ought to shine forth not only by what he hath received from God, but also by what he himself hath contributed; and should be discernible by everything, by his gait, by his look, by his garb, by his voice. And this I have said, not that display, but that the profit of beholders, may be the rule by which we frame ourselves.

15. But now, what things soever I might seek to recognize thee by, I find thee in all points distinguished by the contraries of the same. For whether by thy place I would fain discern thee, I see thee spending thy day in horse races, and theatres, and scenes of lawlessness, in the wicked assemblies in the market places, and in companies of depraved men; or by the fashion of thy countenance, I see thee continually laughing to excess, and dissolute as a grinning and abandoned harlot; or by thy clothes, I see thee in no better trim than the people on the stage; or by thy followers, thou art leading about parasites and flatterers; or by thy words, I hear thee say nothing wholesome, nothing neces-

sary, nothing of moment to our life; or by thy table, yet heavier from thence will the charge against thee appear.

By what then, tell me, am I to recognize the believer in thee, while all the things I have mentioned give the contrary sentence? And why do I say, the believer? since I can not clearly make out whether thou art a man. For when thou art like an ass, kicking, and like a bull, wantoning, and like a horse neighing after women; when thou dost play the glutton like the bear, and pamper thy flesh as the mule, and bear malice like the camel; also?

Further, if I were bidding thee make another man gentle, not even so ought I to seem as one enjoining impossible things; however, thou mightest then object that thou hast not the control of another's disposition, and that it doth not altogether rest with thee. But now it is thine own wild beast, and a thing which absolutely depends on thee. What plea then hast thou? or what fair excuse wilt thou be able to put forth, turning as thou art a lion into a man, and regardless that thou thyself art of a man becoming a lion; upon the beast bestowing what is above nature, but for thyself not even preserving what is natural? Yea, while the wild beasts are by thine earnest endeavors advanced into our noble estate, thou art by thyself cast down from the throne of the kingdom, and thrust out into their madness. Thus, imagine, if thou wilt, thy wrath to be a kind of wild beast, and as much zeal as others have displayed about lions, so much do thou in regard of thyself, and cause that way of taking things to become gentle and meek. Because this too hath grievous teeth and talons, and if thou tame it not, it will lay waste all things. For not even lion nor serpent hath such power to rend the vitals as wrath, with its iron talons continually doing so. Since it mars, we see, not the body only, but the very health likewise of the soul is corrupted by it, devouring, rending, tearing to pieces all its strength, and making it useless for everything. For if a man nourishing worms in his entrails, shall not be able so much as to breathe, his inward parts all wasting away; how shall we, having so large a serpent eating up all within us (it is wrath I mean), how, I say, shall we be able to produce anything noble?

17. How then are we to be freed from this pest? If we can drink a potion that is able to kill the worms within us and the serpents. "And of what nature," it will be asked, "may this potion be, that hath such power?" The precious Blood of Christ, if it be received with full assurance, (for this will have power to extinguish every disease); and together with this the divine Scriptures carefully heard, and almsgiving added to our hearing; for by means of all these things we shall be enabled to mortify the affections that mar our soul. And then only shall we live; for now surely we are in no better state than the dead: forasmuch as it cannot be, that while those passions live, we should live too,

but we must necessarily perish. And unless we first kill them here, they will be sure to kill us in the other life; or rather before that death they will exact of us, even here, the utmost penalty. Yes, for every such passion is both cruel and tyrannical and insatiable, and never ceases to devour us every day. For "their teeth are the teeth of a lion," or rather even far more fierce. For the lion, as soon as ever he is satisfied, is wont to leave the carcass that hath fallen in his way; but these passions neither are satisfied, nor do they leave the man whom they have seized, until they have set him nigh the devil. For so great is their power, that the very service which Paul showed forth to Christ, despising both hell and the kingdom for His sake, even this same do they require of them whom they have seized. For whether it be with the love of women, or of riches, or of glory, that any one is entangled, he laughs at hell thenceforth, and despises the kingdom, that he may work the will of these. Let us not then doubt Paul when he saith that he so loved Christ. For when some are found so doing service to their passions, how should that other afterwards seem incredible? Yea, and this is the reason why our longing for Christ is feebler, because all our strength is consumed on this love, and we rob, and defraud, and are slaves to vainglory; than which what can be more worthless?

For though thou shouldest become infinitely conspicuous, thou wilt be nothing better than the base: rather for this selfsame cause thou wilt even be baser. For when they who are willing to give thee glory, and make thee illustrious, do for this very cause ridicule thee, that thou desirest the glory which comes of them, how can such instances fail to turn the contrary way in regard of thee. For indeed this thing is among those which attract censure. So that even as in the case of one desiring to commit adultery or fornication, should any one praise or flatter him, by this very act he becomes an accuser rather than a commender of the person indulging such desires: so with regard to him who is desirous of glory; when we all praise, it is accusation rather than praise which we bestow on those who wish to be made glorious.

18. Why then bring upon thyself that, from which the very opposite is wont to befall thee. Yea, if thou wilt be glorified, despise glory; so shalt thou be more illustrious than any. Why feel as Nebuchadnezzar felt? For he too set up an image, thinking from wood and from a senseless figure to procure to himself an increase of fame, and the living would fain appear more glorious by the help of that which hath no life. Seest thou the excess of his madness; how, thinking to do honor, he rather offered insult, to himself? For when it appears that he is relying rather on the lifeless thing, than on himself and the soul that lives in him, and when for this cause he advances the stock unto such high precedence, how can he be other than ridiculous, endeavoring as he doth to

adorn himself, not by his way of living, but by planks of wood? Just as if a man should think proper to give himself airs, because of the pavement of his house, and his beautiful staircase rather than because he is a man. Him do many too amongst us imitate now. For as he for his image, so some men claim to be admired for their clothes, others for their house; or for their mules and chariots, and for the columns in their house. For inasmuch as they have lost their being as men, they go about gathering to themselves from other quarters such glory as is full of exceeding ridicule.

But as to the noble and great servants of God, not by these means, but by such as best became them, even by such did they shine forth. For captives as they were, and slaves, and youths, and strangers, and stripped of all resources of their own, they proved at that time far more awful than he who was invested with all these things. And while Nebuchadnezzar found neither so great an image, nor satraps, nor captains of the host, nor endless legions, nor abundance of gold, nor other pomp, enough to meet his desire, and to show him great; to these, on the other hand, stripped of all this, their high self-restraint alone was sufficient, and showed him that wore the diadem and the purple, as much inferior in glory to those who had no such thing, as the sun is more glorious than a pearl. For they were led forth in the midst of the whole world, being at once youths, and captives, and slaves, and straightway on their appearance the king darted fire from his eyes, and captains, and deputies, and governors, and the whole amphitheatre of the devil, stood around; and a voice of pipes from all sides, and of trumpets, and of all music, borne up to Heaven, was sounding in their ears, and the furnace burned up to a boundless height, and the flame reached the very clouds, and all was full of terror and dismay. But none of these things dismayed them, but they laughed it all to scorn, as they would children mocking them, and exhibited their courage and meekness, and uttering a voice clearer than those trumpets, they said, "Be it known unto thee, O king." For they did not wish to affront the king, no not so much as by a word, but to declare their religion only. For which cause, neither did they extend their speech to any great length, but set forth all briefly; "For there is," say they, "a God in Heaven, who is able to deliver us," "why showest thou me the multitude? why the furnace? why the sharpened swords? why the terrible guards? our Lord is higher and more mighty than all these."

Then when they considered that it was possible that God might be willing even to permit them to be burnt; lest, if this should come to pass, they might seem to be speaking falsehoods; they add this also and say, "If this happen not, be it known unto thee, O king, that we serve not thy gods." For had they said, "Sins are the cause of His not delivering us, should He fail to deliver," they would not have been believed. Wherefore in this place they are silent on that subject, though they speak of it in the furnace, again and again alleging their sins. But before the king they say no such thing; only, that though they were to be burnt, they would not give up their religion.

For it was not for rewards and recompenses that they did what they did, but out of love alone; and yet they were in captivity too, and in slavery, and had enjoyed no good thing. Yea, they had lost their country, and their freedom, and all their possessions. For tell me not of their honors in the king's courts, for holy and righteous as they were, they would have chosen ten thousand times rather to have been beggars at home, and to have been partakers of the blessings in the temple. "For I had rather," it is said, "be an outcast in the house of my God, than to dwell in the tents of sinners." And "one day in thy courts is better than thousands." They would have chosen then ten thousand times rather to be outcasts at home, than kings in Babylon. And this is manifest, from what they declare even in the furnace, grieving at their continuance in that country. For although themselves enjoyed great honors, yet seeing the calamities of the rest they were exceedingly vexed; and this kind of thing is most especially characteristic of saints, that no glory, nor honor, nor anything else should be more precious to them than their neighbor's welfare. See, for example, how even when they were in a furnace, they made their supplication for all the people. But we not even when at large bear our brethren in mind. And again, when they were inquiring about the dreams, they were looking "not to their own but the common good," for that they despised death they showed by many things afterwards. But everywhere they put themselves forward, as wishing to prevail with God by importunity. Next, as not accounting themselves either to be sufficient, they flee to the Fathers; but of themselves they said that they offer nothing more than "a contrite spirit."

19. These men then let us also imitate. Because now too there is set up a golden image, even the tyranny of Mammon. But let us not give heed to the timbrels, nor to the flutes, nor to the harps, nor to the rest of the pomp of riches; yea, though we must needs fall into a furnace of poverty, let us choose it, rather than worship that idol, and there will be "in the midst a moist whistling wind." Let us not then shudder at hearing of "a furnace of poverty." For so too at that time they that fell into the furnace were shewn the more glorious, but they that worshipped were destroyed. Only then all took place at once, but in this case some part will be accomplished here, some there, some both here and in the day that is to come. For they that have chosen poverty, in order that they might not worship mammon, will be more glorious both here

and then, but they that have been rich unjustly here, shall then pay the utmost penalty.

From this furnace Lazarus too went forth, not less glorious than those children; but the rich man who was in the place of them that worshipped the image, was condemned to hell. For indeed what we have now mentioned was a type of this. Wherefore as in this instance they who fell into the furnace suffered no hurt, but they who sat without were laid hold of with great fierceness, so likewise shall it be then. The saints walking through the river of fire shall suffer no pain, nay they will even appear joyous; but they that have worshipped the image, shall see the fire rest upon them fiercer than any wild beast, and draw them in. So that if any one disbelieves hell, when he sees this furnace, let him from the things present believe things to come, and fear not the furnace of poverty, but the furnace of sin. For this is flame and torment, but that, dew and refreshment; and by this stands the devil, by that, angels wafting aside the flame.

20. These things let them hear that are rich, that are kindling the furnace of poverty. For though they shall not hurt those others, "the dew" coming to their aid; yet themselves they will render an easy prey to the flame, which they have kindled with their own hands.

Then, an angel went down with those children; now, let us go down with them that are in the furnace of poverty, and by alms-deeds let us make a "dewy air," and waft the flame quite aside, that we may be partakers of their crowns also; that the flames of hell may likewise be scattered by the voice of Christ saying, "Ye saw me an hungered, and fed me." For that voice shall then be with us instead of a "moist wind whistling" through the midst of the flame. Let us then go down with alms-giving, unto the furnace of poverty; let us behold them that in self-restraint walk therein, and trample on the burning coals; let us behold the marvel, strange and beyond thought, a man singing praise in a furnace, a man giving thanks in fire, chained unto extreme poverty, yet offering much praise to Christ. Since they, who bear poverty with thankfulness, really become equal to those children. For no flame is so terrible as poverty, nor so apt to set us on fire. But those children were not set on fire; rather, on their giving thanks to the Lord, their bonds too were at once loosed. So likewise now, if when thou hast fallen into poverty, thou art thankful, both the bonds are loosened, and the flame extinguished; or though it be not extinguished (what is much more marvellous), it becomes a fountain instead of a flame: which then likewise came to pass, and in the midst of a furnace they enjoyed a pure dew. For the fire indeed it quenched not, but the burning of those cast in it altogether hindered. This one may see in their case also who live by the rules of wisdom, for they, even in poverty, feel more secure than the rich.

Let us not therefore sit down without the furnace, feeling no pity towards the poor; lest the same befall us as then befell those executioners. For if thou shouldest go down to them, and take thy stand with the children, the fire will no longer work thee any harm; but if thou shouldest sit above and neglect them in the flame of their poverty, the flame will burn thee up. Go down therefore into the fire, that thou mayest not be burnt up by the fire; sit not down without the fire, lest the flame catch hold of thee. For if it should find thee amongst the poor, it will depart from thee; but if alienated from them, it will run upon thee quickly, and catch thee. Do not therefore stand off from them that are cast in, but when the devil gives command to cast them that have not worshipped gold into the furnace of poverty, be not thou of them that cast others in, but of them that are cast in; that thou mayest be of the number of the saved, and not of the burned. For indeed it is a most effectual dew, to be held in no subjection by desire of wealth, to be associate with poor persons. These are wealthier than all, who have trampled under foot the desire of riches. Forasmuch as those children too, by despising the king at that time, became more glorious than the king. And thou therefore, if thou despise the things of the world, shalt become more honorable than all the world; like those holy men, "of whom the world was not worthy."

In order then to become worthy of the things in Heaven, I bid thee laugh to scorn things present. For in this way thou shalt both be more glorious here, and enjoy the good things to come, by the grace and love towards man of our Lord Jesus Christ; to whom be glory and might for ever and ever. Amen.

HOMILY V

MATT. I. 22, 23

"Now all this was done, that it might be fulfilled which was spoken of the Lord by the Prophet, saying, Behold, a Virgin shall be with child, and shall bring forth a Son, and they shall call His name Emmanuel."

I Hear many say, "While we are here, and enjoying the privilege of hearing, we are awed, but when we are gone out, we become altered men again, and the flame of zeal is quenched." What then may be done, that this may not come to pass? Let us observe whence it arises. Whence then doth so great a change in us arise? From the unbecoming employment of our time, and from the company of evil men. For we ought not as soon as we retire from the Communion, to plunge into business unsuited to the Communion, but as soon as ever we get home, to take our Bible into our hands, and call our wife and children to join us in putting together what we have heard, and then, not before, engage in the business of life.

For if after the bath you would not choose to hurry into the market place, lest by the business in the market you should destroy the refreshment thence derived; much more ought we to act on this principle after the Communion. But as it is, we do the contrary, and in this very way throw away all. For while the profitable effect of what hath been said to us is not yet well fixed, the great force of the things that press upon us from without sweeps all entirely away.

That this then may not be the case, when you retire from the Communion, you must account nothing more necessary than that you should put together the things that have been said to you. Yes, for it were the utmost folly for us, while we give up five and even six days to the business of this life, not to bestow on things spiritual so much as one day, or rather not so much as a small part of one day. See ye not our own children, that whatever lessons are given them, those they study throughout the whole day? This then let us do likewise, since otherwise we shall derive no profit from coming here, drawing water daily into a vessel with holes, and not bestowing on the retaining of what we have heard even so much earnestness as we plainly show with respect to gold and silver. For any one who has received a few pence both puts them into a bag and sets a seal thereon; but we, having given us oracles more precious than either gold or costly stones, and receiving the treasures of the Spirit, do not put them away in the storehouses of our soul, but thoughtlessly and at random suffer them to escape from our minds. Who then will pity us after all this, plotting against our own interests, and casting ourselves into so deep poverty? Therefore, that this may not be so, let us write it down an unalterable law for ourselves, for our wives, and for our children, to give up this one day of the week entire to hearing, and to the recollection of the things we have heard. For thus with greater aptness for learning shall we approach what is next to be said; and to us the labor will be less, and to you the profit greater, when, bearing in memory what hath been lately spoken, ye hearken accordingly to what comes afterwards. For no little doth this also contribute towards the understanding of what is said, when ye know accurately the connexion of the thoughts, which we are busy in weaving together for you. For since it is not possible to set down all in one day, you must by continued remembrance make the things laid before you on many days into a kind of chain, and so wrap it about your soul: that the body of the Scriptures may appear entire.

Therefore let us not either to-day go on to the subjects set before us, without first recalling what was lately said to our memory.

2. But what are the things set before us to-day? "Now all this was done, that it might be fulfilled which was spoken of the Lord by the prophet, saying." In a tone worthy of the wonder, with all his might he hath uttered his voice, saying, "Now all this was done." For when he saw the sea and the abyss of the love of God towards man, and that actually come to pass which never had been looked for, and nature's laws broken, and reconciliations made, Him who is above all come down to him that is lower than all, and "the middle walls of partition broken," and the impediments removed, and many more things than these done besides; in one word he hath put before us the miracle, saying, "Now all this was done that it might be fulfilled which was spoken of the Lord." For, "think not," saith he, "that these things are now determined upon; they were prefigured of old." Which same thing, Paul also everywhere labors to prove.

And the angel proceeds to refer Joseph to Isaiah; in order that even if he should, when awakened, forget his own words, as newly spoken, he might by being reminded of those of the prophet, with which he had been nourished up continually, retain likewise the substance of what he had said. And to the woman he mentioned none of these things, as being a damsel and unskilled in them, but to the husband, as being a righteous man and one who studied the prophets, from them he reasons. And before this he saith, "Mary, thy wife;" but now, when he hath brought the prophet before him, he then trusts him with the name of virginity; for Joseph would not have continued thus unshaken, when he heard from him of a virgin, unless he had first heard it also from Isaiah. For indeed it was nothing novel that he was to hear out of the prophets, but what was familiar to him, and had been for a long time the subject of his meditations. For this cause the angel, to make what he said easy to be received, brings in Isaiah. And neither here doth he stop, but connects the discourse with God. For he doth not call the saying Isaiah's, but that of the God of all things. For this cause he said not, "that it might be fulfilled which was spoken of Isaiah," but "which was spoken of the Lord." For the mouth indeed was Isaiah's, but the oracle was wafted from above.

3. What then saith this oracle? "Behold, a virgin shall be with child, and shall bring forth a son, and they shall call His name Emmanuel."

How was it then, one may say, that His name was not called Emmanuel, but Jesus Christ? Because he said not, "thou shalt call," but "they shall call," that is, the multitude, and the issue of events. For here he puts the event as a name: and this is customary in Scripture, to substitute the events that take place for names.

Therefore, to say, "they shall call" Him "Emmanuel," means nothing else than that they shall see God amongst men. For He hath indeed always been amongst men, but never so manifestly.

But if Jews are obstinate, we will ask the, when was the child called, "Make speed to the spoil, hasten the prey?" Why, they could not say. How is it then that the prophet said, "Call his name Maher-shalal-hash-baz?" Because, when he was born, there was a taking and dividing of spoils, therefore the event that took place in his time is put as his name. And the city, too, it is said, shall be called "the city of righteousness, the faithful city Sion." And yet we nowhere find that the city was called "righteousness," but it continued to be called Jerusalem. However, inasmuch as this came to pass in fact, when the city underwent a change for the better, on that account he saith it is so called. For when any event happens which marks out him who brings it to pass, or who is benefited by it, more clearly than his name, the Scripture speaks of the truth of the event as being a name to him.

4. But if, when their mouths are stopped on this point, they should seek another, namely, what is said touching Mary's virginity, and should object to us other translators, saying, that they used not the term "virgin," but "young woman;" in the first place we will say this, that the Seventy were justly entitled to confidence above all the others. For these made their translation after Christ's coming, continuing to be Jews, and may justly be suspected as having spoken rather in enmity, and as darkening the prophecies on purpose; but the Seventy, as having entered upon this work an hundred years or more before the coming of Christ, stand clear from all such suspicion, and on account of the date, and of their number, and of their agreement, would have a better right to be trusted.

But even if they bring in the testimony of those others, yet so the tokens of victory would be with us. Because the Scripture is wont to put the word "youth," for "virginity;" and this with respect not to women only, but also to men. For it is said, "young men and maidens, old men with younger ones." And again, speaking of the damsel who is attacked, it saith, "if the young woman cry out," meaning the virgin.

And what goes before also establishes this interpretation. For he doth not merely say, "Behold, the Virgin shall be with child," but having first said, "Behold, the Lord Himself shall give you a sign," then he subjoins, "Behold, the Virgin shall be with child." Whereas, if she that was to give birth was not a virgin, but this happened in the way of marriage, what sort of sign would the event be? For that which is a sign must of course be beyond the course of common events, it must be strange and extraordinary; else how could it be a sign?

5. "Then Joseph, being raised from sleep, did as the angel of the Lord had bidden him." Seest thou obedience, and a submissive mind? Seest thou a soul truly wakened, and in all things incorruptible? For neither when he suspected something painful or amiss could he endure to keep the Virgin with him; nor yet, after he was freed from this suspicion, could he bear to cast her out, but he rather keeps her with him, and ministers to the whole Dispensation.

"And took unto him Mary his wife." Seest thou how continually the evangelist uses this word, not willing that that mystery should be disclosed as yet, and annihilating that evil suspicion?

And when he had taken her, "he knew her not, till she had brought forth her first-born Son." He hath here used the word "till," not that thou shouldest suspect that afterwards he did know her, but to inform thee that before the birth the Virgin was wholly untouched by man. But why then, it may be said, hath he used the word, "till"? Because it is usual in Scripture often to do this, and to use this expression without reference to limited times. For so with respect to the ark likewise, it is said, "The raven returned not till the earth was dried up." And yet it did not return even after that time. And when discoursing also of God, the Scripture saith, "From age until age Thou art," not as fixing limits in this case. And again when it is preaching the Gospel beforehand, and saying, "In his days shall righteousness flourish, and abundance of peace, till the moon be taken away," it doth not set a limit to this fair part of creation. So then here likewise, it uses the word "till," to make certain what was before the birth, but as to what follows, it leaves thee to make the inference. Thus, what it was necessary for thee to learn of Him, this He Himself hath said; that the Virgin was untouched by man until the birth; but that which both was seen to be a consequence of the former statement, and was acknowledged, this in its turn he leaves for thee to perceive; namely, that not even after this, she having so become a mother, and having been counted worthy of a new sort of travail, and a child-bearing so strange, could that righteous man ever have endured to know her. For if he had known her, and had kept her in the place of a wife, how is it that our Lord commits her, as unprotected, and having no one, to His disciple, and commands him to take her to his own home?

How then, one may say, are James and the others called His brethren? In the same kind of way as Joseph himself was supposed to be husband of Mary. For many were the veils provided, that the birth, being such as it was, might be for a time screened. Wherefore even John so called them, saying, "For neither did His brethren believe in Him."

6. Nevertheless they, who did not believe at first, became afterwards admirable, and illustrious. At least when Paul and they that were of his company were come up to Jerusalem about decrees, they went in straightway unto James. For he was so admired as even to be the first to be entrusted with the bishop's office. And they say he gave himself up to such great austerity, that even his members became all of them as dead, and that from his continual praying, and his perpetual intercourse with the ground, his forehead became so callous as to be in no better state than a camel's knees, simply by reason of his striking it so against the earth. This man gives directions to Paul himself, when he was after this come up again to Jerusalem, saying, "Thou seest, brother, how many thousands there are of them that are come together." So great was his understanding and his zeal, or rather so great the power of Christ. For they that mock Him when living, after His death are so filled with awe, as even to die for Him with exceeding readiness. Such things most of all show the power of His resurrection. For this, you see, was the reason of the more glorious things being kept till afterwards, viz. that this proof might become indisputable. For seeing that even those who are admired amongst us in their life, when they are gone, are apt to be forgotten by us; how was it that they, who made light of this Man living, afterwards thought Him to be God, if He was but one of the many? How was it that they consented even to be slain for His sake, unless they received His resurrection on clear proof?

7. And these things we tell you, that ye may not hear only, but imitate also his manly severity, his plainness of speech, his righteousness in all things; that no one may despair of himself, though hitherto he have been careless, that he may set his hopes on nothing else, after God's mercy, but on his own virtue. For if these were nothing the better for such a kindred, though they were of the same house and lineage with Christ, until they gave proof of virtue; what favor can we possibly receive, when we plead righteous kinsmen and brethren, unless we be exceeding dutiful, and have lived in virtue? As the prophet too said, intimating the selfsame thing, "A brother redeemeth not, shall a man redeem?" No, not although it were Moses, Samuel, Jeremiah. Hear, for example, what God saith unto this last, "Pray not thou for this people, for I will not hear thee." And why marvellest thou if I hear not thee? "Though Moses himself and Samuel stood before me," I would not receive their supplication for these men." Yea, if it be Ezekiel who entreats, he will be told, "Though Noah stand forth, and Job, and Daniel, they shall deliver neither sons nor daughters." Though the patriarch Abraham be supplicating for them that are most

incurably diseased, and change not, God will leave him and go His way, that he may not receive his cry in their behalf. Though again it be Samuel who is doing this, He saith unto him, "Mourn not thou for Saul." Though for his own sister one entreat, when it is not fitting, he again shall have the same sort of answer as Moses, "If her father had but spit in her face."

Let us not then be looking open-mouthed towards others. For it is true, the prayers of the saints have the greatest power; on condition however of our repentance and amendment. Since even Moses, who had rescued his own brother and six hundred thousand men from the wrath that was then coming upon them from God, had no power to deliver his sister; and yet the sin was not equal; for whereas she had done despite but to Moses, in that other case it was plain impiety, what they ventured on. But this difficulty I leave for you; while that which is yet harder, I will try to explain.

For why should we speak of his sister? since he who stood forth the advocate of so great a people had not power to prevail for himself, but after his countless toils, and sufferings, and his assiduity for forty years, was prohibited from setting foot on that land, touching which there had been so many declarations and promises. What then was the cause? To grant this favor would not be profitable, but would, on the contrary, bring with it much harm, and would be sure to prove a stumbling-block to many of the Jews. For if when they were merely delivered from Egypt, they forsook God, and sought after Moses, and imputed all to him; had they seen him also lead them into the land of promise, to what extent of impiety might they not have been cast away? And for this reason also, let me add, neither was his tomb made known.

And Samuel again was not able to save Saul from the wrath from above, yet he oftentimes preserved the Israelites. And Jeremiah prevailed not for the Jews, but some one else he did haply cover from evil by his prophecy. And Daniel saved the barbarians from slaughter, but he did not deliver the Jews from their captivity.

And in the Gospels too we shall see both these events come to pass, not in the case of different persons, but of the same; and the same man now prevailing for himself and now given up. For he who owed the ten thousand talents, though he had delivered himself from the danger by entreaty, yet again he prevailed not, and another on the contrary, who had before thrown himself away, afterwards had power to help himself in the greatest degree. But who is this? He that devoured his Father's substance.

So that on the one hand, if we be careless, we shall not be able to obtain salvation, no not even by the help of others; if, on the other hand, we be watchful, we shall be able to do this by ourselves, and by ourselves rather than by others. Yes; for God is more willing to give His grace to us, than to others for us; that we by endeavoring ourselves to do away His wrath, may both enjoy confidence towards Him, and become better men. Thus He had pity on the Canaanitish woman, thus He saved the harlot, thus the thief, when there was none to be mediator nor advocate.

8. And this I say, not that we may omit supplicating the saints, but to hinder our being careless, and entrusting our concerns to others only, while we fall back and slumber ourselves. For so when He said, "make to yourselves friends," he did not stop at this only, but He added, "of the unrighteous mammon;" that so again the good work may be thine own; for it is nothing else but almsgiving which He hath here signified. And, what is marvellous, neither doth He make a strict account with us, if we withdraw ourselves from injustice. For what He saith is like this: "Hast thou gained ill? spend well. Hast thou gathered by unrighteousness? scatter abroad in righteousness." And yet, what manner of virtue is this, to give out of such gains? God, however, being full of love to man, condescends even to this and if we thus do, promises us many good things. But we are so past all feeling, as not to give even of our unjust gain, but while plundering without end, if we contribute the smallest part, we think we have fulfilled all. Hast thou not heard Paul saying, "He which soweth sparingly, shall reap also sparingly"? Wherefore then dost thou spare? What, is the act an outlay? is it an expense? Nay, it is gain and good merchandise. Where there is merchandise, there is also increase; where there is sowing, there is also reaping. But thou, if thou hadst to till a rich and deep soil, and capable of receiving much seed, wouldest both spend what thou hadst, and wouldest borrow of other men, accounting parsimony in such cases to be loss; but, when it is Heaven which thou art to cultivate, which is exposed to no variation of weather, and will surely repay thine outlay with abundant increase, thou art slow and backward, and considerest not that it is possible by sparing to lose, and by not sparing to gain.

9. Disperse therefore, that thou mayest not lose; keep not, that thou mayest keep; lay out, that thou mayest save; spend, that thou mayest gain. If thy treasures are to be hoarded, do not thou hoard them, for thou wilt surely cast them away; but entrust them to God, for thence no man makes spoil of them. Do not thou traffic, for thou knowest not at all how to gain; but lend unto Him who gives an interest greater than the principal. Lend, where is no envy, no accusation, nor evil design, nor fear. Lend unto Him who wants nothing, yet hath need for thy sake; who feeds all men, yet is an hungered, that thou mayest not suffer famine; who is poor, that thou mayest be rich. Lend there, where thy return cannot be death, but life instead of death. For this usury is

the harbinger of a kingdom, that, of hell; the one coming of covetousness, the other of self-denial; the one of cruelty, the other of humanity. What excuse then will be ours, when having the power to receive more, and that with security, and in due season, and in great freedom, without either reproaches, or fears, or dangers, we let go these gains, and follow after that other sort, base and vile as they are, insecure and perishable, and greatly aggravating the furnace for us? For nothing, nothing is baser than the usury of this world, nothing more cruel. Why, other persons' calamities are such a man's traffic; he makes himself gain of the distress of another, and demands wages for kindness, as though he were afraid to seem merciful, and under the cloak of kindness he digs the pitfall deeper, by the act of help galling a man's poverty, and in the act of stretching out the hand thrusting him down, and when receiving him as in harbor, involving him in shipwreck, as on a rock, or shoal, or reef.

"But what dost thou require?" saith one; "that I should give another for his use that money which I have got together, and which is to me useful, and demand no recompense?" Far from it: I say not this: yea, I earnestly desire that thou shouldest have a recompense; not however a mean nor small one, but far greater; for in return for gold, I would that thou shouldest receive Heaven for usury. Why then shut thyself up in poverty, crawling about the earth, and demanding little for great? Nay, this is the part of one who knows not how to be rich. For when God in return for a little money is promising thee the good things that are in Heaven, and thou sayest, "Give me not Heaven, but instead of Heaven the gold that perisheth," this is for one who wishes to continue in poverty. Even as he surely who desires wealth and abundance will choose things abiding rather than things perishing; the inexhaustible, rather than such as waste away; much rather than little, the incorruptible rather than the corruptible. For so the other sort too will follow. For as he who seeks earth before Heaven, will surely lose earth also, so he that prefers Heaven to earth, shall enjoy both in great excellency. And that this may be the case with us, let us despise all things here, and choose the good things to come. For thus shall we obtain both the one and the other, by the grace and love towards man of our Lord Jesus Christ; to whom be glory and might for ever and ever. Amen.

HOMILY VI

MATT. II. 1, 2

"When Jesus was born in Bethlehem of Judaea in the days of Herod the king, behold, there came wise men from the east to Jerusalem, saying, Where is He that is born King of the Jews? for we have seen His star in the east, and are come to worship Him."

We have need of much wakefulness, and many prayers, that we may arrive at the interpretation of the passage now before us, and that we may learn who these wise men were, and whence they came, and how; and at whose persuasion, and what was the star. Or rather, if ye will, let us first bring forward what the enemies of the truth say. Because the devil hath blown upon them with so violent a blast, as even from this passage try to arm them against the words of truth.

What then do they allege? "Behold," say they, "even when Christ was born a star appeared; which is a sign that astrology may be depended on." How then, if He had His birth according to that law, did He put down astrology, and take away fate, and stop the mouths of demons, and cast out error, and overthrow all such sorcery?

And what moreover do the wise men learn from the star of itself? That He was King of the Jews? And yet He was not king of this kingdom; even as He said also to Pilate, "My kingdom is not of this world." At any rate He made no display of this kind, for He had neither guards armed with spear or shield, nor horses, nor chariots of mules, nor any other such thing around Him; but He followed this life of meanness and poverty, carrying about with Him twelve men of mean estate.

And even if they knew Him to be a king, for what intent are they come? For surely this is not the business of astrology, to know from the stars who are born, but from the hour when men are born to predict what shall befall them: so it is said. But these were neither present with the mother in her pangs, nor did they know the time when He was born, neither did they, beginning at that moment, from the motion of the stars compute what was to happen: but conversely, having a long time before seen a star appear in their own country, they come to see Him that was born.

Which circumstance in itself would afford a still greater difficulty even than the former. For what reason induced them, or the hope of what benefits, to worship one who was king so far off? Why, had He been to reign over themselves, most assuredly not even so would the circumstance be capable of a reasonable account. To be sure, if He had been born in royal courts, and with His father, himself a king, present by Him, any one would naturally say, that they, from a wish to pay court to the father, had worshipped the child that was born, and in this way were laying up for themselves beforehand much ground of patronage. But now when they did not so much as expect Him to be their own king, but of a strange nation, far distant from their country, neither seeing

Him as yet grown to manhood; wherefore do they set forth on so long a journey, and offer gifts, and this when dangers were sure to beset their whole proceeding? For both Herod, when he heard it, was exceedingly troubled, and the whole people was confounded on being told of these things by them.

"But these men did not foresee this." Nay, this is not reasonable. For let them have been ever so foolish, of this they could not be ignorant, that when they came to a city under a king, and proclaimed such things as these, and set forth another king besides him who then reigned, they must needs be bringing down on themselves a thousand deaths.

2. And why did they at all worship one who was in swaddling clothes? For if He had been a grown man, one might say, that in expectation of the succor they should receive from Him, they cast themselves into a danger which they foresaw; a thing however to the utmost degree unreasonable, that the Persian, the barbarian, and one that had nothing in common with the nation of the Jews, should be willing to depart from his home, to give up country, and kindred, and friends, and that they should subject themselves to another kingdom.

But if this be foolish, what follows is much more foolish. Of what nature then is this? That after they had entered on so long a journey, and worshipped, and thrown all into confusion, they went away immediately. And what sign at all of royalty did they behold, when they saw a shed, and a manger, and a child in swaddling clothes, and a poor mother? And to whom moreover did they offer their gifts, and for what intent? Was it then usual and customary, thus to pay court to the kings that were born in every place? and did they always keep going about the whole world, worshipping them who they knew should become kings out of a low and mean estate, before they ascended the royal throne? Nay, this no one can say.

And for what purpose did they worship Him at all? If for the sake of things present, then what did they expect to receive from an infant, and a mother of mean condition? If for things future, then whence did they know that the child whom they had worshipped in swaddling clothes would remember what was then done? But if His mother was to remind Him, not even so were they worthy of honor, but of punishment, as bringing Him into danger which they must have foreseen. Thence at any rate it was that Herod was troubled, and sought, and pried, and took in hand to slay Him. And indeed everywhere, he who makes known the future king, supposing him in his earliest age in a private condition, doth nothing else than betray him to slaughter, and kindle against him endless warfare.

Seest thou how manifold the absurdities appear, if we examine these transactions according to the course of human things and ordinary custom? For not these topics only, but more than these might be mentioned, containing more matter for questions than what we have spoken of. But lest, stringing questions upon questions, we should bewilder you, come let us now enter upon the solution of the matters inquired of, making a beginning of our solution with the star itself.

3. For if ye can learn what the star was, and of what kind, and whether it were one of the common stars, or new and unlike the rest, and whether it was a star by nature or a star in appearance only, we shall easily know the other things also. Whence then will these points be manifest? From the very things that are written. Thus, that this star was not of the common sort, or rather not a star at all, as it seems at least to me, but some invisible power transformed into this appearance, is in the first place evident from its very course. For there is not, there is not any star that moves by this way, but whether it be the sun you mention, or the moon, or all the other stars, we see them going from east to west; but this was wafted from north to south; for so is Palestine situated with respect to Persia.

In the second place, one may see this from the time also. For it appears not in the night, but in mid-day, while the sun is shining; and this is not within the power of a star, nay not of the moon; for the moon that so much surpasses all, when the beams of the sun appear, straightway hides herself, and vanishes away. But this by the excess of its own splendor overcame even the beams of the sun, appearing brighter than they, and in so much light shining out more illustriously.

In the third place, from its appearing, and hiding itself again. For on their way as far as Palestine it appeared leading them, but after they set foot within Jerusalem, it hid itself: then again, when they had left Herod, having told him on what account they came, and were on the point of departing, it shows itself; all which is not like the motion of a star, but of some power highly endued with reason. For it had not even any course at all of its own, but when they were to move, it moved; when to stand, it stood, dispensing all as need required: in the same kind of way as the pillar of the cloud, now halting and now rousing up the camp of the Jews, when it was needful.

In the fourth place, one may perceive this clearly, from its mode of pointing Him out. For it did not, remaining on high, point out the place; it not being possible for them so to ascertain it, but it came down and performed this office. For ye know that a spot of so small dimensions, being only as much as a shed would occupy, or rather as much as the body of a little infant would take up, could not possibly be marked out by a star. For by reason of its immense height, it could not sufficiently distinguish so confined a spot, and discover it to them that were desiring to see it. And this any one may see by the moon, which being so far superior to the stars, seems to all that dwell in the world, and are scattered over so great an extent of earth,—seems, I say, near to them every one. How then, tell me, did the star point out a spot so confined, just the space of a manger and shed, unless it left that height and came down, and stood over the very head of the young child? And at this the evangelist was hinting when he said, "Lo, the star went before them, till it came and stood over where the young Child was."

4. Seest thou, by what store of proofs this star is shown not to be one of the many, nor to have shown itself according to the order of the outward creation? And for what intent did it appear? To reprove the Jews for their insensibility, and to cut off from them all occasion of excuse for their willful ignorance. For, since He who came was to put an end to the ancient polity, and to call the world to the worship of Himself, and to be worshipped in all land and sea, straightway, from the beginning, He opens the door to the Gentiles, willing through strangers to admonish His own people. Thus, because the prophets were continually heard speaking of His advent, and they gave no great heed, He made even barbarians come from a far country, to seek after the king that was among them. And they learn from a Persian tongue first of all, what they would not submit to learn from the prophets; that, if on the one hand they were disposed to be candid, they might have the strongest motive for obedience; if, on the other hand, they were contentious, they might henceforth be deprived of all excuse. For what could they have to say, who did not receive Christ after so many prophets, when they saw that wise men, at the sight of a single star, had received this same, and had worshipped Him who was made manifest. Much in the same way then as He acted in the case of the Ninevites, when He sent Jonas, and as in the case of the Samaritan and the Canaanitish women; so He did likewise in the instance of the magi. For this cause He also said, "The men of Nineveh shall rise up, and shall condemn:" and, "the Queen of the South shall rise up, and shall condemn this generation:" because these believed the lesser things, but the Jews not even the greater.

"And wherefore," one may say, "did He attract them by such a vision?" Why, how should He have done? Sent prophets? But the magi would not have submitted to prophets. Uttered a voice from above? Nay, they would not have attended. Sent an angel? But even him they would have hurried by. And so for this cause dismissing all those means, God calleth them by the things that are familiar, in exceeding condescension; and He shows a large and extraordinary star, so as to astonish them, both at the greatness and beauty of its appearance, and the manner of its course.

In imitation of this, Paul also reasons with the Greeks from an heathen altar, and brings forward testimonies from the poets. And not without circumcision doth he harangue the Jews. Sacrifices he makes the beginning of his instruction to them that are living under the law. For, since to every one what is familiar is dear, both God, and the men that are sent by Him, manage things on this principle with a view to the salvation of the world. Think it not therefore unworthy of Him to have called them by a star; since by the same rule thou wilt find fault with all the Jewish rites also, the sacrifices, and the purifications, and the new moons, and the ark, and the temple too itself. For even these derived their origin from Gentile grossness. Yet for all that, God, for the salvation of them that were in error, endured to be served by these things, whereby those without were used to serve devils; only He slightly altered them; that He might draw them off by degrees from their customs, and lead them towards the highest wisdom. Just so He did in the case of the wise men also, not disdaining to call them by sight of a star, that He might lift them higher ever after. Therefore after He hath brought them, leading them by the hand, and hath set them by the manger; it is no longer by a star, but by an angel that He now discourses unto them. Thus did they by little and little become better men.

This did He also with respect to them of Ascalon, and of Gaza. For those five cities too (when at the coming of the ark they had been smitten with a deadly plague, and found no deliverance from the ills under which they lay)—the men of them called their prophets, and gathered an assembly, and sought to discover an escape from this divine scourge. Then, when their prophets said that they should yoke to the ark heifers untamed, and having their first calves, and let them go their way, with no man to guide them, for so it would be evident whether the plague was from God or whether it was any accident which brought the disease;—("for if," it is said, "they break the yoke in pieces for want of practice, or turn where their calves are lowing, it is a chance that hath happened;' but if they go on right, and err not from the way, and neither the lowing of their young, nor their ignorance of the way, have any effect on them, it is quite plain that it is the hand of God that hath visited those cities:")—when, I say, on these words of their prophets the inhabitants of those cities obeyed and did as they were commanded, God also followed up the counsel of the prophets, showing condescension in that instance also, and counted it not unworthy of Himself to bring to effect the prediction of the prophets, and to make them seem trustworthy in what they had then said. For so the good achieved was greater, in that His very enemies themselves bore witness to the power of God; yea, their own teachers gave their voice concerning Him. And one may see many other such things brought about by God. For what took place with respect to the witch, is again like this sort of dispensation; which circumstance also you will now be able to explain from what hath been said.

With respect to the star, we have said these things, and yet more perhaps may be said by you; for, it is said, "Give occasion to a wise man, and he will be yet wiser:" but we must now come to the beginning of what hath been read.

5. And what is the beginning? "When Jesus was born in Bethlehem of Judaea, in the days of Herod the king, behold, there came wise men from the east to Jerusalem." While wise men followed under the auspices of a star, these believed not, with prophets even sounding in their ears. But wherefore doth he mention to us both the time and the place, saying, "in Bethlehem," and "in the days of Herod the king?" And for what reason doth he add his rank also? His rank, because there was also another Herod, he who slew John: but that was a tetrarch, this a king. And the place likewise, and the time, he puts down, to bring to our remembrance ancient prophecies; whereof one was uttered by Micah, saying, "And thou, Bethlehem, in the land of Judah, art by no means the least among the princes of Judah;" and the other by the patriarch Jacob, distinctly marking out to us the time, and setting forth the great sign of His coming. For, "A ruler," saith he, "shall not fail out of Judah, nor a leader out of his loins, until He come for whom it is appointed, and He is the expectation of the Gentiles."

And this again is worth inquiry, whence it was that they came to entertain such a thought, and who it was that stirred them up to this. For it doth not seem to me to be the work of the star only, but also of God, who moved their soul; which same kind of thing He did also in the case of Cyrus, disposing him to let the Jews go. He did not however so do this as to destroy their free will, since even when He called Paul from above by a voice, He manifested both His own grace and Paul's obedience.

And wherefore, one may ask, did He not reveal this to all the wise men of the East? Because all would not have believed, but these were better prepared than the rest; since also there were countless nations that perished, but it was to the Ninevites only that the prophet was sent; and there were two thieves on the cross, but one only was saved. See at least the virtue of these men, not only by their coming, but also by their boldness of speech. For so that they may not seem to be a sort of impostors, they tell who showed them the way, and the length of their journey; and being come, they had boldness of speech: "for we are come," that is their statement, "to worship Him:" and they were afraid neither of the people's anger, nor of the tyranny of the king. Whence to me at least they seem to have been at home also teachers of their countrymen. For they who here did not shrink from saying this, much more would they speak boldly in their own country, as having received both the oracle from the angel, and the testimony from the prophet.

6. But "when Herod," saith the Scripture, "had heard, he was troubled, and all Jerusa lem with him." Herod naturally, as being king, and afraid both for himself and for his children; but why Jerusalem? Surely the prophets had foretold Him a Saviour, and Benefactor, and a Deliverer from above. Wherefore then was Jerusalem troubled? From the same feeling which caused them before also to turn away from God when pouring His benefits on them, and to be mindful of the flesh-pots of Egypt, while in the enjoyment of great freedom.

But mark, I pray thee, the accuracy of the prophets. For this selfsame thing also had the prophet foretold from the first, saying, "They would be glad, if they had been burnt with fire; for unto us a Child is born, unto us a Son is given."

But nevertheless, although troubled, they seek not to see what hath happened, neither do they follow the wise men, nor make any particular inquiry; to such a degree were they at once both contentious and careless above all men. For when they had reason rather to pride themselves that the king was born amongst them, and had attracted to Him the land of the Persians, and they were on the point of having all subject to them, as though their affairs had advanced towards improvement, and from the very outset His empire had become so glorious; nevertheless, they do not even for this become better. And yet they were but just delivered from their captivity there; and it was natural for them to think (even if they knew none of those things that are high and mysterious, but formed their judgment from what is present only), "If they thus tremble before our king at His birth, much more when grown up will they fear and obey Him, and our estate will be more glorious than that of the barbarians."

7. But none of these things thoroughly awakens them, so great was their dullness, and with this their envy also: both which we must with exact care root out of our mind; and he must be more fervent than fire who is to stand in such an array. Wherefore also Christ said, "I am come to send fire on earth, and I would it were already kindled." in the same lot with it, even so godly tears are a germ of perpetual and unfading joy. In this way the very harlot became more honorable than virgins when seized by this fire. That is, being

thoroughly warmed by repentance, she was thenceforth carried out of herself by her longing desire toward Christ; loosing her hair, and drenching with her tears His holy feet, and wiping them with her own tresses, and exhausting the ointment. And all these were outward results, but those wrought in her mind were far more fervent than these; which things God Himself alone beheld. And therefore, every one, when he hears, rejoices with her and takes delight in her good works, and acquits her of every blame. But if we that are evil pass this judgment, consider what sentence she obtained from that God who is a lover of mankind; and how much, even before God's gifts, her repentance caused her to reap in the way of blessing.

For much as after a violent burst of rain, there is a clear open sky; so likewise when tears are pouring down, a calm arises, and serenity, and the darkness that ensues on our sins quite disappears. And like as by water and the spirit, so by tears and confession are we cleansed the second time; unless we be acting thus for display and vanity: for as to a woman whose tears were of that sort, I should call her justly condemnable, more than if she decked herself out with lines and coloring. For I seek those tears which are shed not for display, but in compunction; those which trickle down secretly and in closets, and in sight of no man, softly and noiselessly; those which arise from a certain depth of mind, those shed in anguish and in sorrow, those which are for God alone; such as were Hannah's, for "her lips moved," it is said, "but her voice was not heard;" however, her tears alone uttered a cry more clear than any trumpet. And because of this, God also opened her womb, and made the hard rock a fruitful field.

If thou also weep thus, thou art become a follower of thy Lord. Yea, for He also wept, both over Lazarus, and over the city; and touching Judas He was greatly troubled. And this indeed one may often see Him do, but nowhere laugh, nay, nor smile but a little; no one at least of the evangelists hath mentioned this. Therefore also with regard to Paul, that he wept, that he did so three years night and day, both he hath said of himself, and others say this of him; but that he laughed, neither hath he said himself anywhere, neither hath so much as one other of the saints, either concerning him, or any other like him; but this is said of Sarah only, when she is blamed, and of the son of Noe, when for a freeman he became a slave.

9. And these things I say, not to suppress all laughter, but to take away dissipation of mind. For wherefore, I pray thee, art thou luxurious and dissolute, while thou art still liable to such heavy charges, and are to stand at a fearful judgment-seat, and to give a strict account of all that hath been done here? Yes: for we are to give an account both of what we have sinned willingly, and what

against our will:—for "whosoever shall deny me," saith He, "before men, him will I also deny before my Father:"—and surely such a denial is against our will; but nevertheless it doth not escape punishment, but of it too we have to give account:—both of what we know, and of what we do not know; "For I know nothing by myself," saith one, "yet am I not hereby justified:"—both for what we have done in ignorance, and what in knowledge; "For I bear them record," it is said, "that they have a zeal of God, but not according to knowledge;" but yet this doth not suffice for an excuse for them. And when writing to the Corinthians also he saith, "For I fear, lest by any means, as the serpent beguiled Eve through his subtlety, so your minds should be corrupted from the simplicity that is in Christ."

The things then being so great, for which thou art to give account, dost thou sit laughing and talking wittily, and giving thyself up to luxury? "Why," one may say, "if I did not so, but mourned, what would be the profit?" Very great indeed; even so great, as it is not possible so much as to set it forth by word. For while, before the temporal tribunals, be thy weeping ever so abundant, thou canst not escape punishment after the sentence; here, on the contrary, shouldest thou only sigh, thou hast annulled the sentence, and hast obtained pardon. Therefore it is that Christ discourses to us much of mourning, and blesses them that mourn, and pronounces them that laugh wretched. For this is not the theatre for laughter, neither did we come together for this intent, that we may give way to immoderate mirth, but that we may groan, and by this groaning inherit a kingdom. But thou, when standing by a king, dost not endure so much as merely to smile; having then the Lord of the angels dwelling in thee, dost thou not stand with trembling, and all due self-restraint, but rather laughest, oftentimes when He is displeased? And dost thou not consider that thou provokest Him in this way more than by thy sins? For God is not wont to turn Himself away so much from them that sin, as from those that are not awestruck after their sin.

But for all this, some are of so senseless a disposition, as even after these words to say, "Nay, far be it from me to weep at any time, but may God grant me to laugh and to play all my days." And what can be more childish than this mind? For it is not God that grants to play, but the devil. At least hear, what was the portion of them that played. "The people," it is said, "sat down to eat and drink, and rose up to play." Such were they at Sodom, such were they at the time of the deluge. For touching them of Sodom likewise it is said, that "in pride, and in plenty, and in fullness of bread, they waxed wanton." And they who were in Noah's time, seeing the ark a preparing for so many years, lived on in senseless mirth, forseeing nought of what was coming. For this cause also the flood came and swept them all away, and wrought in that instant the common shipwreck of the world.

Ask not then of God these things, which thou receivest of the devil. For it is God's part to give a contrite and humbled heart, sober, self-possessed, and awestruck, full of repentance and compunction. These are His gifts, forasmuch as it is also of these things that we are most in need. Yes, for a grievous conflict is at hand, and against the powers unseen is our wrestling; against "the spiritual wickednesses" our fight, "against principalities, against powers" our warfare: and it is well for us, if when we are earnest and sober and thoroughly awakened, we can be able to sustain that savage phalanx. But if we are laughing and sporting, and always taking things easily, even before the conflict, we shall be overthrown by our own remissness.

10. It becometh not us then to be continually laughing, and to be dissolute, and luxurious, but it belongs to those upon the stage, the harlot women, the men that are trimmed for this intent, parasites, and flatterers; not them that are called unto heaven, not them that are enrolled into the city above, not them that bear spiritual arms, but them that are enlisted on the devil's side. For it is he, yea, it is he, that even made the thing an art, that he might weaken Christ's soldiers, and soften the nerves of their zeal. For this cause he also built theatres in the cities, and having trained those buffoons, by their pernicious influence he causes that kind of pestilence to light upon the whole city, persuading men to follow those things which Paul bade us flee, "foolish talking and jesting." And what is yet more grievous than these things is the subject of the laughter. For when they that act those absurd things utter any word of blasphemy or filthiness, then many among the more thoughtless laugh and are pleased, applauding in them what they ought to stone them for; and drawing down on their own heads by this amusement the furnace of fire. For they who praise the utterers of such words, it is these above all who induce men so to speak: wherefore they must be more justly accountable for the penalty allotted to these things. For were there no one to be a spectator in such cases, neither would there be one to act; but when they see you forsaking your workshops, and your crafts, and your income from these, and in short everything, for the sake of continuing there, they derive hence a greater forwardness, and exert a greater diligence about these things.

And this I say, not freeing them from reproof, but that ye may learn that it is you chiefly who supply the principle and root of such lawlessness; ye who consume your whole day on these matters, and profanely exhibit the sacred things of marriage, and make an open mock of the great mystery. For not even he who acts these things is so much the offender, as thou art before him; thou who biddest him make a play on these things, or rather who not only biddest him, but art even zealous about it, taking delight, and laughing, and praising what is done, and in every way gaining strength for such workshops of the devil.

Tell me then, with what eyes wilt thou after this look upon thy wife at home, having seen her insulted there? Or how dost thou not blush being put in mind of the partner of thy home, when thou seest nature herself put to an open shame? Nay, tell me not, that what is done is acting; for this acting hath made many adulterers, and subverted many families. And it is for this most especially that I grieve, that what is done doth not so much as seem evil, but there is even applause and clamor, and much laughter, at commission of so foul adultery. What sayest thou? that what is done is acting? Why, for this selfsame reason they must be worthy of ten thousand deaths, that what things all laws command men to flee, they have taken pains to imitate. For if the thing itself be bad, the imitation thereof also is bad. And I do not yet say how many adulterers they make who act these scenes of adultery, how they render the spectators of such things bold and shameless; for nothing is more full of whoredom and boldness than an eye that endures to look at such things.

And thou in a market-place wouldest not choose to see a woman stripped naked, or rather not even in a house, but callest such a thing an outrage. And goest thou up into the theatre, to insult the common nature of men and women, and disgrace thine own eyes? For say not this, that she that is stripped is an harlot; but that the nature is the same, and they are bodies alike, both that of the harlot, and that of the free-woman. For if this be nothing amiss, what is the cause that if thou were to see this done in a market place, thou wouldest both hasten away thyself, and drive thence her who was behaving herself unseemly? Or is it that when we are apart, then such a thing is outrageous, but when we are assembled and all sitting together, it is no longer equally shameful? Nay, this is absurdity and a disgrace, and words of the utmost madness; and it were better to besmear the eyes all over with mud and mire than to be a spectator of such a transgression. For surely mire is not so much an hurt to an eye, as an unchaste sight, and the spectacle of a woman stripped naked. Hear, for example, what it was that caused nakedness at the beginning, and read the occasion of such disgrace. What then did cause nakedness? Our disobedience, and the devil's counsel. Thus, from the first, even from the very beginning, this was his contrivance. Yet they were at least ashamed when they were naked, but ye take a pride in it; "having," according to that saying of the apostle, "your glory in your shame."

How then will thy wife thenceforward look upon thee, when thou art returned from such wickedness? how receive thee? how speak to thee, after thou hast so publicly put to shame the common nature of woman, and art made by such a sight the harlots' captive and slave?

Now if ye grieve at hearing these things, I thank you much, for "who is he that maketh me glad, but he which is made sorry by me?" Do not then ever cease to grieve and be vexed for them, for the sorrow that comes of such things will be to you a beginning of a change for the better. For this cause I also have made my language the stronger, that by cutting deeper I might free you from the venom of them that intoxicate you; that I might bring you back to a pure health of soul; which God grant we may all enjoy by all means, and attain unto the rewards laid up for these good deeds; by the grace and love towards man of our Lord Jesus Christ, to whom be glory and dominion forever and ever. Amen.

HOMILY VII

MATT. II. 4, 5

"And when he had gathered all the chief priests and scribes of the people together, he demanded of them where Christ should be born. And they said unto him, in Bethlehem of Judaea."

Seest thou how all things are done to convict the Jews? how, as long as He was out of their sight, the envy had not yet laid hold of them, and they rehearsed the testimonies of Him with truth; but when they saw the glory that arose from the miracles, a grudging spirit possessed them, and thenceforth they betrayed the truth.

However, the truth was exalted by all things, and strength was the more gathered for it even by its enemies. See for example in this very case, how wonderful and beyond expectation are the results secretly provided for. For both the barbarians and the Jews do the same time alike learn something more of one another, and teach one another. Thus the Jews, for their part, heard from the wise men, that a star also had proclaimed Him in the land of the Persians; the wise men, in their turn, were informed by the Jews that this Man, whom the star proclaimed, prophets also had made known from a long time of old. And the ground of their inquiry was made to both an occasion of setting forth clearer and more perfect instruction; and the enemies of the truth are compelled even against their will to read the writings in favor of the truth, and to interpret the prophecy; although not all of it. For having spoken of Bethlehem, and how that out of it He shall come that should rule Israel, they proceed not afterwards to add what follows, out of flattery to the king. And what was this? That "His goings forth are from of old, from everlasting."

2. "But why," one may say, "if He was to come from thence, did He live in Nazareth after the birth, and obscure the prophecy?" Nay, He did not obscure it, but unfolded it the more. For the fact, that while His mother had her constant residence in the one place, He was born in the other, shows the thing to have been done by a Divine dispensation.

And for this cause, let me add, neither did He remove from thence straightway after His birth, but abode forty days, giving opportunity to them that were disposed to be inquisitive to examine all things accurately. Because there were in truth many things to move them to such an inquiry, at least if they had been disposed to give heed to them. Thus at the coming of the wise men the whole city was in a flutter, and together with the city the king, and the prophet was brought forward, and a court of high authority was summoned; and many other things too were done there, all which Luke relates minutely. Such were what concerns Anna, and Simeon, and Zacharias, and the angels, and the shepherds; all which things were to the attentive sufficient to give hints for ascertaining what had taken place. For if the wise men, who came from Persia, were not ignorant of the place, much more might they, whose abode it was, acquaint themselves with these things.

He manifested Himself then from the beginning by many miracles, but when they would not see, He hid Himself for a while, to be again revealed from another more glorious beginning. For it was no longer the wise men, nor the star, but the Father from above that proclaimed Him at the streams of Jordan; and the Spirit likewise came upon Him, guiding that voice to the head of Him just baptized; and John, with all plainness of speech, cried out everywhere in Judaea, till inhabited and waste country alike were filled with that kind of doctrine; and the witness too of the miracles, and earth, and sea, and the whole creation, uttered in His behalf a distinct voice. But at the time of the birth, just so many things happened as were fitted quietly to mark out Him that was come. Thus, in order that the Jews might not say, "We know not when He was born, nor whereabouts," both all these events in which the wise men were concerned were brought about by God's providence, and the rest of the things which we have mentioned; so that they would have no excuse to plead, for not having inquired into that which had come to pass.

But mark also the exactness of the prophecy. For it does not say, "He will abide" in Bethlehem, but "He will come out" thence. So that this too was a subject of prophecy, His being simply born there.

Some of them, however, being past shame, say that these things were spoken of Zerubbabel. But how can they be right? For surely "his goings forth" were not "from of old, from everlasting." And how can that suit him which is said at the beginning, "Out of thee shall He come forth:" Zorobabel not having been born in Judaea, but in Babylon, whence also he was called Zorobabel, because he had his origin there? And as many as know the Syrians' language know what I say.

And together with what hath been said, all the time also since these things is sufficient to establish the testimony. For what saith he? "Thou art not the least among the princes of Judah," and he adds the cause of the pre-eminence, saying, "out of thee shall He come." But no one else hath made that place illustrious or eminent, excepting Him alone. For example: since that birth, men come from the ends of the earth to see the manger, and the site of the shed. And this the prophet foretold aloud from the first, saying, "Thou art not the least among the princes of Judah;" that is, among the heads of tribes. By which expression he comprehended even Jerusalem. But not even so have they given heed, although the advantage passes on to themselves. Yea, and because of this the prophets at the beginning discourse nowhere so much of His dignity, as touching the benefit which accrued to them by Him. For so, when the Virgin was bearing the child, he saith, "Thou shalt call His name Jesus;" and he gives the reason saying, "for He shall save His people from their sins." And the wise men too said not, "Where is the Son of God?" but "He that is born King of the Jews." And here again it is not affirmed, "Out of thee shall come forth" the Son of God, but "a Governor, that shall feed my people Israel." For it was needful to converse with them at first, setting out in a tone of very exceeding condescension, lest they should be offended; and to preach what related to their salvation in particular, that hereby they might be the rather won over. At any rate, all the testimonies that are first cited, and for which it was the season immediately at the time of the birth, say nothing great, nor lofty concerning Him, nor such as those subsequent to the manifestation of the miracles; for these discourse more distinctly concerning His dignity. For instance, when after many miracles children were singing hymns unto Him, hear what saith the prophet, "Out of the mouth of babes and sucklings Thou hast perfected praise." And again, "I will consider the Heavens, the works of Thy fingers;" which signifies Him to be Maker of the universe. And the testimony too, which was produced after the ascension, manifests His equality with the Father; thus saying, "The Lord said unto my Lord, Sit Thou on my right hand." And Isaiah too saith, "He that riseth up to rule over the Gentiles, in Him shall the Gentiles trust."

But how saith he that Bethlehem is "not the least among the princes of Judah?" for not in Palestine alone, but in the whole world, the village hath become conspicuous. Why, so far he was speaking to Jews; wherefore also he added, "He shall feed my people Israel." And yet He fed the whole world; but as I have said, He is fain not to offend as yet, by revealing what He hath to say touching the Gentiles.

But how was it, one may say, that He did not feed the Jewish people? I answer, first, this too is accomplished: for by the term Israel in this place, he figuratively meant such as believed on Him from among the Jews. And Paul interpreting this, saith, "For they are not all Israel, which are of Israel," but as many as have been born by faith and promise. And if He did not feed them all, this is their own fault and blame. For when they ought to have worshipped with the wise men, and have glorified God that such a time was come, doing away all their sins (for not a word was spoken to them of judgments set, or of accounts to be given, but of a mild and meek Shepherd); they for their part do just the contrary, and are troubled, and make disturbance, and go on continually framing plots without end.

3. "Then Herod, when he had privily called the wise men, inquired of them diligently what time the star appeared:"

Attempting to slay that which was born,—an act of extreme idiotcy not of madness only; since what had been said and done was enough to have withholden him from any such attempt. For those occurrences were not after the manner of man. A star, I mean, calling the wise men from on high; and barbarians making so long a pilgrimage, to worship Him that lay in swaddling clothes and a manger; and prophets too from of old, proclaiming beforehand all this;—these and all the rest were more than human events: but nevertheless, none of these things restrained him. For such a thing is wickedness. It falls foul of itself, and is ever attempting impossibilities. And mark his utter folly. If on the one hand he believed the prophecy, and accounted it to be unchangeable, it was quite clear that he was attempting impossibilities; if again he disbelieved, and did not expect that those sayings would come to pass, he need not have been in fear and alarm, nor have formed any plot on that behalf. So that in either way his craft was superfluous.

And this too came of the utmost folly, to think that the wise men would make more account of him than of the Child that was born, for the sake of which they had come so long a journey. For if, before they saw, they were so inflamed with longing for Him; after they had seen with their eyes, and been confirmed by the prophecy, how hoped he to persuade them to betray the young Child to him?

Nevertheless, many as were the reasons to withhold him, he made the attempt; and having "privily called the wise men, he inquired of them." Because he thought that Jews would be concerned in favor of the Child, and he never could expect that they would fall away unto such madness as to be willing to give up to His enemies their Protector and Saviour, and Him who was come for the deliverance of their nation. On account of this he both calls them privily, and seeks the time not of the Child, but of the star: thereby marking out the object of his chase so as to include far more than it. For the star, I think, must have appeared a long time before. It was a long time which the wise men had to spend on their journey. In order, therefore, that they might present themselves just after His birth (it being meet for Him to be worshipped in His very swaddling clothes, that the marvellous and strange nature of the thing might appear), the star, a long time before, makes itself visible. Whereas if at the moment of His birth in Palestine, and not before, it had been seen by them in the East, they, consuming a long time in their journey, would not have seen Him in swaddling clothes on their arrival. As to his slaying the children "from two years old and under," let us not marvel; for his wrath and dread, for the sake of a fuller security, added very much to the time, so that not one might escape.

Having therefore called them, he saith, "Go and search diligently for the young Child; and when ye have found Him, bring me word again, that I may come and worship Him also."

Seest thou his extreme folly? Why, if thou sayest these things in sincerity, wherefore dost thou inquire privily? But if intending to plot against Him, how is it thou dost not perceive, that from the fact of their being asked secretly the wise men will be able to perceive thy craft? But as I have already said, a soul taken captive by any wickedness becomes more utterly senseless than any thing.

And he said not, "go and learn concerning the King," but "concerning the young Child;" for he could not even endure to call Him by the name of His dominion.

4. But the wise men perceive nothing of this, by reason of their exceeding reverence (for they never could have expected that he could have gone on to so great wickedness, and would have attempted to form plots against a dispensation so marvellous): and they depart suspecting none of these things, but from what was in themselves auguring all that would be in the rest of mankind.

"And, lo! the star, which they saw in the east, went before them."

For therefore only was it hidden, that having lost their guide, they might come to be obliged to make inquiry of the Jews, and so the matter might be made evident to all. Since after they have made inquiries, and have had His enemies for informants, it appears to them again. And mark how excellent was the order; how in the first place after the star the people of the Jews receives them, and the king, and these bring in the prophecy to explain what had appeared: how next, after the prophet, an angel again took them up and taught them all things; but for a time they journey from Jerusalem to Bethlehem by the guidance of the star, the star again journeying with them from that place also; that hence too thou mightest learn, that this was not one of the ordinary stars, for there is not so much as one star that hath this nature. And it not merely moved, but "went before them," drawing and guiding them on in mid-day.

"But what need of this star any more," one may ask, "when the place was ascertained?" In order that the Child also might be seen. For there was not anything to make Him manifest, since the house was not conspicuous, neither was His mother glorious, or distinguished. There was need then of the star, to set them by the place. Wherefore it re-appears on their coming out of Jerusalem, and stays not, before it hath reached the manger.

And marvel was linked on to marvel; for both were strange things, as well the magi worshipping, as the star going before them; and enough to attract even such as were made all of stone. For if the wise men had said, they had heard prophets say these things, or that angels had discoursed with them in private, they might have been disbelieved; but now, when the vision of the star appeared on high, even they that were exceeding shameless had their mouths stopped.

Moreover, the star, when it stood over the young Child, stayed its course again: which thing itself also was of a greater power than belongs to a star, now to hide itself, now to appear, and having appeared to stand still. Hence they too received an increase of faith. For this cause they rejoiced also, that they had found what they were seeking, that they had proved messengers of truth, that not without fruit had they come so great a journey; so great a longing (so to speak) had they for Christ. For first it came and stood over His very head, showing that what is born is Divine; next standing there, it leads them to worship Him; being not simply barbarians, but the wiser sort amongst them.

Seest thou, with how great fitness the star appeared? Why; because even after the prophecy, and after the interpretation of the chief priests and scribes, they still had their minds turned towards it.

5. Shame upon Marcion, shame upon Paul of Samosata, for refusing to see what those wise men saw,—the forefathers of the Church; for I am not ashamed so to call them. Let Marcion be ashamed, beholding God worshipped

in the flesh. Let Paul be ashamed, beholding Him worshipped as not being merely a man. As to His being in the flesh, that first is signified by the swaddling clothes and the manger; as to their not worshipping Him as a mere man, they declare it, by offering Him, at that unripe age, such gifts as were meet to be offered to God. And together with them let the Jews also be ashamed, seeing themselves anticipated by barbarians and magi, whilst they submit not so much as to come after them. For indeed what happened then was a type of the things to come, and from the very beginning it was shown that the Gentiles would anticipate their nation.

"But how was it," one may ask, "that not at the beginning, but afterwards, He said, Go ye, and make disciples of all nations'"? Because the occurrence was a type, as I said, of the future, and a sort of declaration of it beforehand. For the natural order was that Jews should come unto Him first; but forasmuch as they of their own choice gave up their proper benefit, the order of things was inverted. Since not even in this instance should the wise men have come before the Jews, nor should persons from so great a distance have anticipated those who were settled about the very city, nor should those who had heard nothing have prevented them that were nurtured in so many prophecies. But because they were exceedingly ignorant of their own blessings, those from Persia anticipate those at Jerusalem. And this indeed is what Paul also saith: "It was necessary that the word of the Lord should first have been spoken to you, but seeing ye have judged yourselves unworthy, lo, we turn to the Gentiles." For even though before they did not obey, at any rate when they heard it from the wise men, they ought to have made all haste; but they would not. Therefore, while those are slumbering, these run before.

6. Let us then also follow the magi, let us separate ourselves from our barbarian customs, and make our distance therefrom great, that we may see Christ, since they too, had they not been far from their own country, would have missed seeing Him. Let us depart from the things of earth. For so the wise men, while they were in Persia, saw but the star, but after they had departed from Persia, they beheld the Sun of Righteousness. Or rather, they would not have seen so much as the star, unless they had readily risen up from thence. Let us then also rise up; though all men be troubled, let us run to the house of the young Child; though kings, though nations, though tyrants interrupt this our path, let not our desire pass away. For so shall we thoroughly repel all the dangers that beset us. Since these too, except they had seen the young Child, would not have escaped their danger from the king. Before seeing the young Child, fears and dangers and troubles pressed upon them from every side; but after the adoration, it is calm and security; and no longer a star but an angel

receives them, having become priests from the act of adoration; for we see that they offered gifts also.

Do thou therefore likewise leave the Jewish people, the troubled city, the blood-thirsty tyrant, the pomp of the world, and hasten to Bethlehem, where is the house of the spiritual Bread. For though thou be a shepherd, and come hither, thou wilt behold the young Child in an inn: though thou be a king, and approach not here, thy purple robe will profit thee nothing; though thou be one of the wise men, this will be no hindrance to thee; only let thy coming be to honor and adore, not to spurn the Son of God; only do this with trembling and joy: for it is possible for both of these to concur in one.

But take heed that thou be not like Herod, and say, "that I may come and worship Him," and when thou art come, be minded to slay Him. For him do they resemble, who partake of the mysteries unworthily: it being said, that such a one "shall be guilty of the Body and Blood of the Lord." Yes; for they have in themselves the tyrant who is grieved at Christ's kingdom, him that is more wicked than Herod of old, even Mammon. For he would fain have the dominion, and sends them that are his own to worship in appearance, but slaying while they worship. Let us fear then, lest at any time, while we have the appearance of suppliants and worshippers, we should in deed show forth the contrary.

And let us cast everything out of our hands when we are to worship; though it be gold that we have, let us offer it unto him and not bury it. For if those barbarians then offered it for honor, what will become of thee, not giving even to Him that hath need? If those men journeyed so far to see Him newly born, what sort of excuse wilt thou have, not going out of thy way one alley's length, that thou mayest visit Him sick or in bonds? And yet when they are sick or in bonds, even our enemies have our pity; thine is denied even to thy Benefactor and Lord. And they offered gold, thou hardly givest bread. They saw the star and were glad, thou, seeing Christ Himself a stranger and naked, art not moved.

For which of you, for Christ's sake, hath made so long a pilgrimage, you that have received countless benefits, as these barbarians, or rather, these wiser than the wisest philosophers? And why say I, so long a journey? Nay, many of our women are so delicate, that they go not over so much as one crossing of the streets to behold Him on the spiritual manger, unless they can have mules to draw them. And others being able to walk, yet prefer to their attendance here, some a crowd of worldly business, some the theatres. Whereas the barbarians accomplished so great a journey for His sake, before seeing Him; thou not even after thou hast seen Him dost emulate them, but forsakest Him after seeing Him, and runnest to see the stage player. (For I touch again on the same subjects, as I did also of late.) And seeing Christ lying in the manger, thou leavest Him, that thou mayest see women on the stage.

7. What thunderbolts do not these things deserve? For tell me, if any one were to lead thee into a palace, and show thee the king on his throne, wouldest thou indeed choose to see the theatre instead of those things? And yet even in the palace there is nothing to gain; but here a spiritual well of fire gushes up out of this table. And thou leavest this, and runnest down to the theatre, to see women swimming, and nature put to open dishonor, leaving Christ sitting by the well? Yes: for now, as of old, He sits down by the well, not discoursing to a Samaritan woman, but to a whole city. Or perchance now too with a Samaritan woman only. For neither now is any one with Him; but some with their bodies only, and some not even with these. But nevertheless, He retires not, but remains, and asks of us to drink, not water, but holiness, for "His holy things He gives unto the holy." For it is not water that He gives us from this fountain, but living blood; and it is indeed a symbol of death, but it is become the cause of life.

But thou, leaving the fountain of blood, the awful cup, goest thy way unto the fountain of the devil, to see a harlot swim, and to suffer shipwreck of the soul. For that water is a sea of lasciviousness, not drowning bodies, but working shipwreck of souls. And whereas she swims with naked body, thou beholding, art sunk into the deep of lasciviousness. For such is the devil's net; it sinks, not them that go down into the water itself, but them that sit above more than such as wallow therein; and it chokes them more grievously than Pharaoh, who was of old sunk in the sea with his horses and his chariots. And if souls could but be seen, I could show you many floating on these waters, like the bodies of the Egyptians at that time. But what is still more grievous is this, that they even call such utter destruction a delight, and they term the sea of perdition a channel for a pleasure voyage. Yet surely one might easier pass over in safety the AEgean or the Tuscan sea, than this spectacle. For in the first place, through a whole night the devil preoccupies their souls with the expectation of it; then having shown them the expected object, he binds them at once, and makes them captives. For think not, because thou hast not been joined unto the harlot, thou art clean from the sin; for in the purpose of thine heart thou hast done it all. Since if thou be taken by lust, thou hast kindled the flame up higher; if thou feel nothing at what thou seest, thou deservest a heavier charge, for being a scandal to others, by encouraging them in these spectacles, and for polluting thine own eye-sight, and together with thine eye-sight, thy soul.

However, not merely to find fault, come let us devise a mode of correction too. What then will the mode be? I would commit you to your own wives, that they may instruct you. It is true, according to Paul's law, you ought to be the teachers. But since that order is reversed by sin, and the body has come to be above, and the head beneath, let us even take this way.

But if thou art ashamed to have a woman for thy teacher, fly from sin, and thou wilt quickly be able to mount up on the throne which God hath given thee. Since so long as thou sinnest the Scripture sends thee not to a woman only, but even to things irrational, and those of the viler sort; yea, it is not ashamed to send thee who art honored with reason, as a disciple to the ant. Plainly this is no charge against the Scripture, but against them that so betray their own nobility of race. This then we will do likewise; and for the present we will commit thee to thy wife; but if thou despise her, we will send thee away to the school of the very brutes, and will point out to thee how many birds, fishes, four-footed beasts, and creeping things are found more honorable, and chaster than thou.

If now thou art ashamed, and dost blush at the comparison, mount up to thine own nobility, and fly the sea of hell, and the flood of fire, I mean the pool in the theatre. For this pool introduces to that sea, and kindles that abyss of flame. Since if "he that looketh on a woman to lust after her hath already committed adultery," he who is forced even to see her naked, how doth he not become ten thousandfold a captive? The flood in the days of Noah did not so utterly destroy the race of men as these swimming women drown all that are there with great disgrace. For as to that rain, though it wrought indeed a death of the body, yet did it repress the wickedness of the soul; but this hath the contrary effect; while the bodies remain, it destroys the soul. And ye, when there is a question of precedence, claim to take place of the whole word, forasmuch as our city first crowned itself with the name of Christian; but in the competition of chastity, ye are not ashamed to be behind the rudest cities.

8. "Well," saith one, "and what dost thou require us to do? to occupy the mountains, and become monks?" Why it is this which makes me sigh, that ye think them alone to be properly concerned with decency and chastity; and yet assuredly Christ made His laws common to all. Thus, when He saith, "if any one look on a woman to lust after her," He speaks not to the solitary, but to him also that hath a wife; since in fact that mount was at that time filled with all kinds of persons of that description. Form then in thy mind an image of that amphitheatre, and hate thou this, which is the devil's. Neither do thou condemn the severity of my speech. For I neither "forbid to marry," nor hinder thy taking pleasure; but I would have this be done in chastity, not with shame,

and reproach, and imputations without end. I do not make it a law that you are to occupy the mountains and the deserts, but to be good and considerate and chaste, dwelling in the midst of the city. For in fact all our laws are common to the monks also, except marriage; yea rather, even with respect to this, Paul commands us to put ourselves altogether on a level with them; saying, "For the fashion of this world passeth away:" that "they that have wives be as though they had none."

"Wherefore" (so he speaks) "I do not bid you take possession of the summits of the mountains; it is true I could wish it, since the cities imitate the things that were done in Sodom; nevertheless, I do not enforce this. Abide, having house and children and wife; only do not insult thy wife, nor put thy children to shame, neither bring into thine house the infection from the theatre." Hearest thou not Paul saying, "The husband hath not power of his own body, but the wife," and setting down laws common to both? But thou, if thy wife be continually thrusting herself into a public assembly, art severe in blaming her; but thyself, spending whole days on public shows, thou dost not account worthy of blame. Yea, touching thy wife's modesty thou art so strict as even to go beyond necessity or measure, and not to allow her so much as indispensable absences; but to thyself thou deemest all things lawful. Yet Paul allows thee not, who gives the wife likewise the same authority, for thus he speaks: "Let the husband render unto the wife due honor." What sort of honor then is this, when thou insultest her in the chiefest things, and givest up her body to harlots (for thy body is hers); when thou bringest tumults and wars into thine house, when thou doest in the market place such things, as being related by thyself to thy wife at home, overwhelm her with shame, and put to shame also thy daughter if present, and more than them, surely, thyself? For thou must necessarily either be silent, or behave thyself so unseemly, that it would be just for thy very servants to be scourged for it. What plea then wilt thou have, I pray thee, beholding, as thou dost, with great eagerness, things which even to name is disgraceful; preferring to all sights these, which even to recount is intolerable?

Now then for a season, in order not to be too burdensome, I will here bring my discourse to an end. But if ye continue in the same courses, I will make the knife sharper, and the cut deeper; and I will not cease, till I have scattered the theatre of the devil, and so purified the assembly of the Church. For in this way we shall both be delivered from the present disgrace, and shall reap the fruit of the life to come, by the grace and love towards man of our Lord Jesus Christ, to whom be glory and might for ever and ever. Amen.

HOMILY VIII

MATT. II. 2

"And when they were come into the house, they saw the young Child with Mary His mother."

How then saith Luke, that He was lying in the manger? Because at the birth indeed she presently laid Him there (for, as was not unlikely, in that large assemblage for the taxing, they could find no house; which Luke also signifies, by saying, "Because there was no room, she laid Him" there); but afterwards she took Him up, and held Him on her knees. For no sooner was she arrived at Bethlehem than she brought her pangs to an end, that thou mayest thence also learn the whole dispensation, and that these things were not done at random, or by chance, but that they all were in course of accomplishment, according to some Divine foreknowledge, and prophetic order.

But what was it that induced them to worship? For neither was the Virgin conspicuous, nor the house distinguished, nor was any other of the things which they saw apt to amaze or attract them. Yet they not only worship, but also "open their treasures," and "offer gifts;" and gifts, not as to a man, but as to God. For the frankincense and the myrrh were a symbol of this. What then was their inducement? That which wrought upon them to set out from home and to come so long a journey; and this was both the star, and the illumination wrought of God in their mind, guiding them by little and little to the more perfect knowledge. For, surely, had it not been so, all that was in sight being ordinary, they would not have shown so great honor. Therefore none of the outward circumstances was great in that instance, but it was a manger, and a shed, and a mother in poor estate; to set before thine eyes, naked and bare, those wise men's love of wisdom, and to prove to thee, that not as mere man they approached Him, but as a God, and Benefactor. Wherefore neither were they offended by ought of what they saw outwardly, but even worshipped, and brought gifts; gifts not only free from Judaical grossness, in that they sacrificed not sheep and calves, but also coming nigh to the self-devotion of the Church, for it was knowledge and obedience and love that they offered unto Him.

"And being warned of God in a dream that they should not return unto Herod, they departed into their own country another way."

See from this also their faith, how they were not offended, but are docile, and considerate; neither are they troubled, nor reason with themselves, saying, "And yet, if this Child be great, and hath any might, what need of flight, and of a clandestine retreat? and wherefore can it be, that when we have come openly and with boldness, and have stood against so great a people, and against a king's madness, the angel sends us out of the city as runaways and fugitives?" But none of these things did they either say or think. For this most especially belongs to faith, not to seek an account of what is enjoined, but merely to obey the commandments laid upon us.

2. "And when they were departed, behold, an angel appeareth to Joseph in a dream, saying, Arise, and take the young Child and His mother, and flee into Egypt."

There is something here worth inquiring into, both touching the magi, and touching the Child; for if even they were not troubled, but received all with faith, it is worthy of examination on our part, why they and the young Child are not preserved, continuing there, but they as fugitives go into Persia, He with His mother into Egypt. But what? should He have fallen into the hands of Herod, and having fallen, not have been cut off? Nay, He would not have been thought to have taken flesh upon Him; the greatness of the Economy would not have been believed.

For if, while these things are taking place, and many circumstances are being ordered mysteriously after the manner of men, some have dared to say that His assumption of our flesh is a fable; in what degree of impiety would they not have been wrecked had He done all in a manner becoming His Godhead, and according to His own power?

As to the wise men, He sends them off quickly, at once both commissioning them as teachers to the land of the Persians, and at the same time intercepting the madness of the king, that he might learn that he was attempting things impossible, and might quench his wrath, and desist from this his vain labor. For not alone openly to subdue His enemies, but also to deceive them with ease, is worthy of His power. Thus, for example, He deceived the Egyptians also in the case of the Jews, and having power to transfer their wealth openly into the hands of the Hebrews, He bids them do this secretly and with craft; and this surely, not less than the other miracles, made Him an object of terror to His enemies. At least, they of Ascalon, and all the rest, when they had taken the ark, and being smitten, did after that devise their countrymen not to fight, nor to set themselves against Him, with the other miracles brought this also forward, saying, "Wherefore harden ye your hearts, as Egypt and Pharaoh hardened? when He had mocked them, did He not after that send forth His people, and they departed?" Now this they said, as accounting this fresh one not inferior to those other signs that had been done openly, towards the demonstration of His power, and of His greatness. And the like ensued on this occasion too; a thing sufficient to astonish the tyrant. For consider what it was natural for Herod to feel, and how his very breath would be stopped, deceived as he was by the wise men, and thus laughed to scorn. For what, if he did not become better? It is not His fault, who marvellously ordered all this, but it is the excess of Herod's madness, not yielding even to those things which had virtue to have persuaded him, and deterred him from his wickedness, but going on still further, to receive a yet sharper punishment for folly so great.

3. But wherefore, it may be said, is the young Child sent into Egypt? In the first place, the evangelist himself hath mentioned the cause, saying, "That it might be fulfilled, Out of Egypt have I called my Son." And at the same time beginnings of fair hopes were thenceforth proclaimed before to the world. That is, since Babylon and Egypt, most in the whole earth, were burnt up with the flame of ungodliness, He, signifying from the first that He means to correct and amend both, and inducing men hereby to expect His bounties in regard of the whole world likewise, sent to the one the wise men, the other He Himself visited with His mother.

And besides what I have said, there is another lesson also, which we are hereby taught, tending not slightly to true self-command in us. Of what kind then is it? To look from the beginning for temptations and plots. See, for instance, how this was the case even at once from His swaddling clothes. Thus you see at His birth, first a tyrant raging, then flight ensuing, and departure beyond the border; and for no crime His mother is exiled into the land of the barbarians: that thou, hearing these things (supposing thee thought worthy to minister to any spiritual matter, and then to see thyself suffering incurable ills, and enduring countless dangers), shouldest not be greatly troubled, nor say, "What can this be? yet surely I ought to be crowned and celebrated, and be glorious and illustrious for fulfilling the Lord's commandment:" but that having this example, thou mightest bear all things nobly, knowing that this especially is the order of all things spiritual, to have everywhere temptations in the same lot with them. See at least how this is the case not only with regard to the mother of the young Child, but also of those barbarians; since they for their part retire secretly in the condition of fugitives; and she again, who had never passed over the threshold of her house, is commanded to undergo so long a journey of affliction, on account of this wonderful birth, and her spiritual travail.

And behold a wonder again. Palestine plots, and Egypt receives and preserves Him that is the object of the plots. For, as it appears, not only in the instance of the sons of the patriarch did types take place, but also in our Lord's own case. In many instances, we are sure, His doings at that time were prophetic declarations of what was to happen afterwards; as, for example, in the matter of the ass and the colt.

4. Now the angel having thus appeared, talks not with Mary, but with Joseph; and what saith he? "Arise, and take the young Child and His mother." Here, he saith not any more, "thy wife," but "His mother." For after that the birth had taken place, and the suspicion was done away, and the husband appeased, thenceforth the angel talks openly, calling neither child nor wife his, but "take the young Child and His mother, and flee into Egypt;" and he mentions the cause of the flight: "For Herod," saith he, "will seek the young Child's life."

Joseph, when he had heard these things, was not offended, nether did he say, "The thing is hard to understand: Didst thou not say just now, that He should save His people?' and now He saves not even Himself: but we must fly, and go far from home, and be a long time away: the facts are contrary to the promise." Nay, none of these things doth he say (for the man was faithful): neither is he curious about the time of his return; and this though the angel had put it indefinitely thus: "Be thou there until I tell thee." But nevertheless, not even at this did he shudder, but submits and obeys, undergoing all the trials with joy.

And this because God, who is full of love to man, did with these hardships mingle things pleasant also; which indeed is His way with regard to all the saints, making neither their dangers nor their refreshment continual, but weaving the life of all righteous men, out of both the one and the other. This very thing He did here also: for consider, Joseph saw the Virgin with child; this cast him into agitation and the utmost trouble, for he was suspecting the damsel of adultery. But straightway the angel was at hand to do away his suspicion, and remove his fears; and seeing the young child born, he reaped the greatest joy. Again, this joy no trifling danger succeeds, the city being troubled, and the king in his madness seeking after Him that was born. But this trouble was again succeeded by another joy; the star, and the adoration of the wise men. Again, after this pleasure, fear and danger; "For Herod," saith he, "is seeking the young Child's life," and He must needs fly and withdraw Himself as any mortal might: the working of miracles not being seasonable as yet. For if from His earliest infancy He had shown forth wonders, He would not have been accounted a Man.

Because of this, let me add, neither is a temple framed at once; but a regular conception takes place, and a time of nine months, and pangs, and a delivery, and giving suck, and silence for so long a space, and He awaits the age proper to manhood; that by all means acceptance might be won for the mystery of His Economy.

"But wherefore then," one may say, "were even these signs wrought at the beginning?" For His mother's sake; for the sake of Joseph and of Simeon, who was presently to depart; for the sake of the shepherds and of the wise men; for the sake of the Jews. Since they, had they been willing to mind diligently what was taking place, would from this event also have reaped no small advantage in regard of what was to come.

But if the prophets do not mention what relates to the wise men, be not troubled; for they neither foretold all things, nor were they silent touching all. For as without any warning to see those things coming to pass, would naturally occasion much astonishment and trouble; so also to have been informed of all would dispose the hearer to sleep, and would have left nothing for the evangelists to add.

5. And if the Jews should raise a question touching the prophecy, and say, that the words, "Out of Egypt have I called my Son," were uttered concerning themselves; we would tell them, This is a law of prophecy, that in many cases much that is spoken of one set of persons is fulfilled in another; of which kind is that which is said touching Simeon and Levi, "I will divide them," saith He, "in Jacob, and scatter them in Israel." And yet not in themselves did this come to pass, but in their descendants; and Noah's saying again about Canaan, came to pass in the Gibeonites, Canaan's descendants. And that concerning Jacob one may see to have so come to pass; for those blessings which say, "Be lord over thy brother, and let thy father's sons worship thee," had no accomplishment in himself (how could they, he being in fear and trembling, and worshipping his brother over and over again?), but in his offspring they had. The very same may be said in this case also. For which may be called the truer son of God, he that worships a calf, and is joined to Baalpeor and sacrifices his sons to devils? or He that is a Son by nature, and honors Him that begat Him? So that, except this man had come, the prophecy would not have received, its due fulfillment. It is worth observing, too, that the evangelist intimates the same by the phrase, "that it might be fulfilled;" implying that it would not have been fulfilled, unless He had come.

And this makes the Virgin also in no common degree glorious and distinguished; that the very thing which was the whole people's special endowment in the way of praise, she also might thenceforth have for her own. I mean, that whereas they were proud of their coming up from Egypt, and used to boast of it (which indeed the prophet also was hinting at, when he said, "Have I not brought up the strangers from Cappadocia, and the Assyrians from the pit"), He makes this pre-eminence belong to the Virgin likewise.

Rather, however, both the people and the patriarch, going down thither, and coming up thence, were together completing the type of this His return. Thus, as they went down to avoid death by famine, so He death by conspiracy. But whereas they on their arrival were for the time delivered from the famine, this man, when He had gone down, sanctified the whole land, by setting His foot thereon.

At least it is observable how, in the midst of His humiliations, the tokens of His Godhead are disclosed. Thus, first of all, the angel saying, "Flee into Egypt," did not promise to journey with them, either in their descent or return; intimating that they have a great fellow-traveller, the Child that had been born; such an one as actually changed all things immediately on His appearing, and wrought so that His enemies should minister in many ways to this Economy. Thus magi and barbarians, leaving the superstition of their fathers, are come to worship: thus Augustus ministers to the birth at Bethlehem by the decree for the taxing; Egypt receives and preserves Him, driven from His home, and plotted against, and obtains a sort of first impulse towards her union unto Him; so that when in after-time she should hear Him preached by the apostles, she might have this at least to glory of, as having received Him first. And yet this privilege did belong unto Palestine alone; but the second proved more fervent than the first.

6. And now, shouldest thou come unto the desert of Egypt, thou wilt see this desert become better than any paradise, and ten thousand choirs of angels in human forms, and nations of martyrs, and companies of virgins, and all the devil's tyranny put down, while Christ's kingdom shines forth in its brightness. And the mother of poets, and wise men, and magicians, were but inventions of sottish old women, but the real philosophy, and worthy of heaven, is this, which was declared unto them by the fishermen. And for this very cause, together with their so great exactness in doctrine, they exhibit also by their life that extreme seriousness. For when they have stripped themselves of all that they have, and are crucified to the whole world, they urge their course on again yet farther, using the labor of their body for the nourishment of them that be in need. For neither, because they fast and watch, do they think it meet to be idle by day; but their nights they spend in the holy hymns and in vigils, and their days in prayers, and at the same time in laboring with their own hands imitating the zeal of the apostle. For if he when the whole world was looking unto him for the sake of nourishing them that were in need, both occupied a workshop, and practised a craft, and being thus employed did not so much as sleep by night; how much more, say they, is it meet that we, who have taken

up our abode in the wilderness, and have nothing to do with the turmoils in the cities, should use the leisure of our quiet for spiritual labors!

Let us then be ashamed all of us, both they that are rich, and they that are poor, when those having nothing at all but a body only and hands, force their way on and strive eagerly to find thence a supply for the poor; while we, having endless stores within, touch not even our superfluities for these objects. What kind of plea shall we have then, I pray thee? and what sort of excuse?

Yet further consider, how of old these Egyptians were both avaricious, and gluttonous, together with their other vices. For there were the flesh-pots which the Jews remember; there, the great tyranny of the belly. Nevertheless, having a willing mind, they changed: and having caught fire from Christ, they set off at once on their voyage towards heaven; and though more ardent than the rest of mankind, and more headstrong, both in anger, and in bodily pleasures, they imitate the incorporeal powers in meekness, and in the rest of that freedom from passions which pertains unto self-denial.

7. Now if any man hath been in the country, he knows what I say. But if he have never entered those tabernacles, let him call to mind him who even until now is in the mouths of all men,—him whom, after the apostles, Egypt brought forth,—the blessed and great Antony; and let him put it to himself, "This man, too, was born in the same country with Pharaoh; nevertheless he was not thereby damaged, but both had a divine vision vouchsafed him, and showed forth such a life as the laws of Christ require." And this any man shall know perfectly, when he hath read the book that contains the history of that man's life; in which also he will perceive much prophecy. I allude to his prediction about those infected with the errors of Arius, and his statement of the mischief that would arise from them; God even then having shown them to him, and sketched out before his eyes all that was coming. A thing which most especially (among the rest) serves to demonstrate the truth, that no person, belonging to the heresies without, hath such a man to mention. But, not to depend on us for this information, look earnestly into what is written in that book, and ye will learn all exactly, and thence be instructed in much self-denial.

And this advice I give, that we not merely peruse what is written there, but that we also emulate it, and make neither place, nor education, nor forefathers' wickedness an excuse. For if we will take heed to ourselves, none of these things shall be an hindrance to us, since even Abraham had an ungodly father, but he inherited not his wickedness; and Hezekiah, Ahaz: yet nevertheless he became dear to God. And Joseph too when in the midst of Egypt, adorned himself with the crowns of temperance; and the Three Children no less in the midst of Babylon, and of the palace, when a table like those at Sybaris was set before them, showed the highest self-denial; and Moses also in Egypt, and Paul in the whole world; but nothing was to any one of these an hindrance in the race of virtue.

Let us then, bearing in mind all these things, put out of the way these our superfluous pleas and excuses, and apply ourselves to those toils which the cause of virtue requires. For thus shall we both attract to ourselves more favor from God, and persuade Him to assist us in our struggles, and we shall obtain the eternal blessings; unto which God grant that we may all attain, by the grace and love towards man of our Lord Jesus Christ, to whom be glory and victory for ever and ever. Amen.

HOMILY IX

MATT. II. 16

"Then Herod, when he saw that he was mocked of the wise men, was exceeding wroth."

Yet surely it was a case not for anger, but for fear and awe: he ought to have perceived that he was attempting impossible things. But he is not refrained. For when a soul is insensible and incurable, it yields to none of the medicines given by God. See for example this man following up his former efforts, and adding many murders to one, and hurried down the steep any whither. For driven wild by this anger, and envy, as by some demon, he takes account of nothing, but rages even against nature herself, and his anger against the wise men who had mocked him he vents upon the children that had done no wrong: venturing then in Palestine upon a deed akin to the things that had been done in Egypt. For he "sent forth," it is said, "and slew all the children that were in Bethlehem, and in all the coasts thereof, from two years old and under, according to the time which he had diligently inquired of the wise men."

Here attend to me carefully. Because many things are uttered by many very idly touching these children, and the course of events is charged with injustice, and some of these express their perplexity about it in a more moderate way, others with more of audaciousness and frenzy. In order then that we may free these of their madness and those of their perplexity, suffer us to discourse a little upon this topic. Plainly, then, if this be their charge, that the children were left to be slain, they should find fault likewise with the slaughter of the soldiers that kept Peter. For as here, when the young child had fled, other children are massacred in the place of Him who was sought; even so then, too,

Peter having been delivered from his prison and chains by the angel, one of like name with this tyrant, and like temper too, when he had sought him, and found him not, slew instead of him the soldiers that kept him.

"But what is this?" it may be said; "why this is not a solution, but an enhancement of our difficulty." I know it too, and for this intent I bring forward all such cases, that to all I may adduce one and the same solution. What then is the solution of these things? or what fair account of them can we give? That Christ was not the cause of their slaughter, but the king's cruelty; as indeed neither was Peter to those others, but the madness of Herod. For if he had seen the wall broken through, or the doors overthrown, he might, perhaps, have had ground to accuse the soldiers that kept the apostle, of neglect; but now when all things continued in due form, and the doors were thrown wide open, and the chains fastened to the hands of them that kept him (for in fact they were bound unto him), he might have inferred from these things (that is, if he had been strictly doing a judge's office on the matters before him), that the event was not of human power or craft, but of some divine and wonder-working power; he might have adored the doer of these things, instead of waging war with the sentinels. For God had so done all that He did, that so far from exposing the keepers, He was by their means leading the king unto the truth. But if he proved senseless, what signifies to the skillful Physician of Souls, managing all things to do good, the insubordination of him that is diseased?

And just this one may say in the present case likewise. For, wherefore art thou wroth, O Herod, at being mocked of the wise men? didst thou not know that the birth was divine? didst thou not summon the chief priests? didst thou not gather together the scribes? did not they, being called, bring the prophet also with them into thy court of judgment, proclaiming these things beforehand from of old? Didst thou not see how the old things agreed with the new? Didst thou not hear that a star also ministered to these men? Didst thou not reverence the zeal of the barbarians? Didst thou not marvel at their boldness? Wast thou not horror-struck at the truth of the prophet? Didst thou not from the former things perceive the very last also? Wherefore didst thou not reason with thyself from all these things, that this event was not of the craft of the wise men, but of a Divine Power, duly dispensing all things? And even if thou wert deceived by the wise men, what is that to the young children, who have done no wrong?

2. "Yea," saith one, "Herod thou hast full well deprived of excuse, and proved him blood-thirsty; but thou hast not yet solved the question about the injustice of what took place. For if he did unjustly, wherefore did God permit

it?" Now, what should we say to this? That which I do not cease to say continually, in church, in the market-place and everywhere; that which I also wish you carefully to keep in mind, for it is a sort of rule for us, suited to every such perplexity. What then is our rule, and what our saying? That although there be many that injure, yet is there not so much as one that is injured. And in order that the riddle may not disturb you too much, I add the solution too with all speed. I mean, that what we may suffer unjustly from any one, it tells either to the doing away of our sins, God so putting that wrong to our account; or unto the recompense of rewards.

And that what I may say may be clearer, let us conduct our argument in the way of illustration. As thus: suppose a certain servant who owes much money to his master, and then that this servant has been despitefully used by unjust men, and robbed of some of his goods. If then the master, in whose power it was to stay the plunderer and wrong doer, should not indeed restore that same property, but should reckon what was taken away towards what was owed him by his servant, is the servant then injured? By no means. But what if he should repay him even more? Has he not then even gained more than he has lost? Every one, I suppose, perceives it.

Now this same reckoning we are to make in regard of our own sufferings. For as to the fact, that in consideration of what we may suffer wrongfully, we either have sins done away, or receive more glorious crowns, if the amount of our sins be not so great: hear what Paul says concerning him that had committed fornication, "Deliver ye such a one to Satan for the destruction of the flesh, that the spirit may be saved." "But what is this?" you may say, "for the discourse was about them that were injured by others, not about them that are corrected by their teachers." I might answer, that there is no difference; for the question was, whether to suffer evil be not an indignity to the sufferer. But, to bring my argument nearer the very point inquired of; remember David, how, when he saw Shimei at a certain time assailing him, and trampling on his affliction, and pouring on him revilings without end, his captains desiring to slay him, he utterly forbade them, saying, "Let him curse, that the Lord may look upon mine abasement, and that he may requite me good for this cursing this day." And in the Psalms too in his chanting, he said, "Consider mine enemies, that they are multiplied, and they hate me with unjust hatred," and "forgive all my sins." And Lazarus again for the same cause enjoyed remission, having in this life suffered innumerable evils. They therefore who are wronged, are not wronged if they bear nobly all that they suffer, yea, rather they gain even more abundantly, whether they be smitten of God, or scourged by the devil.

3. "But what kind of sin had these children," it may be said, "that they should do it away? for touching those who are of full age, and have been guilty of many negligences, one might with show of reason speak thus: but they who so underwent premature death, what sort of sins did they by their sufferings put away?" Didst thou not hear me say, that though there were no sins, there is a recompense of rewards hereafter for them that suffer ill here? Wherein then were the young children hurt in being slain for such a cause, and borne away speedily into that waveless harbor? "Because," sayest thou, "they would in many instances have achieved, had they lived, many and great deeds of goodness." Why, for this cause He lays up for them beforehand no small reward, the ending their lives for such a cause. Besides, if the children were to have been any great persons, He would not have suffered them to be snatched away beforehand. For if they that eventually will live in continual wickedness are endured by Him with so great long-sufferings, much more would He not have suffered these to be so taken off had He foreknown they would accomplish any great things.

And these are the reasons we have to give; yet these are not all; but there are also others more mysterious than these, which He knoweth perfectly, who Himself ordereth these things. Let us then give up unto Him the more perfect understanding of this matter, and apply ourselves to what follows, and in the calamities of others let us learn to bear all things nobly. Yea, for it was no little scene of woe, which then befell Bethlehem, the children were snatched from their mother's breast, and dragged unto this unjust slaughter.

And if thou art yet faint-hearted, and not equal to controlling thyself in these things, learn the end of him who dared all this, and recover thyself a little. For very quickly was he overtaken by punishment for these things; and he paid the due penalty of such an abominable act, ending his life by a grievous death, and more pitiable than that which he now dared inflict; suffering also countless additional ills, which ye may know of by perusing Josephus' account of these events. But, lest we should make our discourse long, and interrupt its continuity, we have not thought it necessary to insert that account in what we are saying.

4. "Then was fulfilled that which was spoken by Jeremy the prophet, saying, In Rama was there a voice heard, Rachel weeping for her children, and would not be comforted, because they are not."

Thus having filled the hearer with horror by relating these things: the slaughter so violent and unjust, so extremely cruel and lawless; he comforts him again, by saying, Not from God's wanting power to prevent it did all this take place, nor from any ignorance of His, but when He both knew it, and foretold it, and that loudly by His prophet. Be not troubled then, neither despond, looking unto His unspeakable providence, which one may most clearly see, alike by what He works, and by what He permits. And this He intimated in another place also, when discoursing to His disciples. I mean where, having forewarned them of the judgment seats, and executions, and of the wars of the world, and of the battle that knows no truce, to uphold their spirit and to comfort them He saith, "Are not two sparrows sold for a farthing? and one of them shall not fall on the ground without your Father which is in Heaven." These things He said, signifying that nothing is done without His knowledge, but while He knows all, yet not in all doth He act. "Be not then troubled," He saith, "neither be disturbed." For if He know what ye suffer, and hath power to hinder it, it is quite clear that it is in His providence and care for you that He doth not hinder it. And this we ought to bear in mind in our own temptations also, and great will be the consolation we shall thence receive.

But what, it may be said, hath Rachel to do with Bethlehem? For it saith, "Rachel weeping for her children." And what hath Rama to do with Rachel? Rachel was the mother of Benjamin, and on his death, they buried her in the horse-course that was near this place. The tomb then being near, and the portion pertaining unto Benjamin her infant (for Rama was of the tribe of Benjamin), from the head of the tribe first, and next from the place of her sepulture, He naturally denominates her young children who were massacred. Then to show that the wound that befell her was incurable and cruel, He saith, "she would not be comforted because they are not."

Hence again we are taught this, which I mentioned before, never to be confounded when what is happening is contrary to the promise of God. Behold, for instance, when He was come for the salvation of the people, or rather for the salvation of the world, of what kind were His beginnings. His mother, first, in flight; His birth-place is involved in irremediable calamities, and a murder is perpetrated of all murders the bitterest, and there is lamentation and great mourning, and wailings everywhere. But be not troubled; for He is wont ever to accomplish His own dispensations by their contraries, affording us from thence a very great demonstration of His power.

Thus did He lead on His own disciples also, and prepared them to do all their duty, bringing about things by their contraries, that the marvel might be greater. They, at any rate, being scourged and persecuted, and suffering terrors without end, did in this way get the better of them that were beating and persecuting them.

5. "But when Herod was dead, behold, an angel of the Lord appeareth in a dream to Joseph saying, Arise, and take the young Child and His mother, and go into the land of Israel."

He no more saith "fly," but "go." Seest thou again after the temptation refreshment? then after the refreshment danger again? in that he was freed indeed from his banishment, and came back again to his own country; and beheld the murderer of the children brought to the slaughter; but when he hath set foot on his own country, he finds again a remnant of the former perils, the son of the tyrant living, and being king.

But how did Archelaus reign over Judaea, when Pontius Pilate was governor? Herod's death had recently taken place, and the kingdom had not yet been divided into many parts; but as he had only just ended his life, the son for a while kept possession of the kingdom "in the room of his father Herod;" his brother also bearing this name, which is the reason why the evangelist added, "in the room of his father Herod."

It may be said, however, "if he was afraid to settle in Judaea on account of Archelaus, he had cause to fear Galilee also on account of Herod." I answer, By his changing the place, the whole matter was thenceforward thrown into shade; for the whole assault was upon "Bethlehem and the coasts thereof." Therefore now that the slaughter had taken place, the youth Archelaus had no other thought, but that the whole was come to an end, and that amongst the many, He that was sought had been destroyed. And besides, his father having come to such an end of his life before his eyes, he became for the future more cautious about farther proceedings, and about urging on that course of iniquity.

Joseph therefore comes to Nazareth, partly to avoid the danger, partly also delighting to abide in his native place. To give him the more courage, he receives also an oracle from the angel touching this matter. Luke, however, doth not say that he came there by Divine warning, but that when they had fulfilled all the purification, they returned to Nazareth. What then may one say? That Luke is giving an account of the time before the going down to Egypt, when he saith these things. For He would not have brought them down thither before the purification, in order that nothing should be done contrary to the law, but he waited for her to be purified, and to go to Nazareth, and that then they should go down to Egypt. Then, after their return, He bids them go to Nazareth. But before this they were not warned of God to go thither, but yearning after their native place, they did so of their own accord. For since they had gone up for no other cause but on account of the taxing, and had not so much as a place where to stay, when they had fulfilled that for which they had come up, they went down to Nazareth.

6. We see here the cause why the angel also, putting them at ease for the future, restores them to their home. And not even this simply, but he adds to it a prophecy, "That it might be fulfilled," saith he, "which was spoken by the prophets, He shall be called a Nazarene."

And what manner of prophet said this? Be not curious, nor overbusy. For many of the prophetic writings have been lost; and this one may see from the history of the Chronicles. For being negligent, and continually falling into ungodliness, some they suffered to perish, others they themselves burnt up and cut to pieces. The latter fact Jeremiah relates; the former, he who composed the fourth book of Kings, saying, that after a long time the book of Deuteronomy was hardly found, buried somewhere and lost. But if, when there was no barbarian there, they so betrayed their books, much more when the barbarians had overrun them. For as to the fact, that the prophet had foretold it, the apostles themselves in many places call Him a Nazarene.

"Was not this then," one may say, "casting a shade over the prophecy touching Bethlehem?" By no means: rather this very fact was sure greatly to stir up men, and to awaken them to the search of what was said of Him. Thus, for example, Nathanael too enters on the inquiry concerning Him, saying, "Can there any good thing come out of Nazareth?" For the place was of little esteem; or rather not that place only, but also the whole district of Galilee. Therefore the Pharisees said, "Search and look, for out of Galilee ariseth no prophet." Nevertheless, He is not ashamed to be named even from thence, signifying that He needs not ought of the things of men; and His disciples also He choses out of Galilee; everywhere cutting off the pretexts of them who are disposed to be remiss, and giving tokens that we have no need of outward things, if we practise virtue. For this cause He doth not choose for Himself so much as a house; for "the Son of Man," saith He, "hath not where to lay His head;" and when Herod is plotting against Him, He fleeth, and at His birth is laid in a manger, and abides in an inn, and takes a mother of low estate; teaching us to think no such thing a disgrace, and from the first outset trampling under foot the haughtiness of man, and bidding us give ourselves up to virtue only.

7. For why dost thou pride thyself on thy country, when I am commanding thee to be a stranger to the whole world? (so He speaks); when thou hast leave to become such as that all the universe shall not be worthy of thee? For these things are so utterly contemptible, that they are not thought worthy of any consideration even amongst the philosophers of the Greeks, but are called Externals, and occupy the lowest place.

"But yet Paul," one may say, "allows them, saying on this wise, As touching the election, they are beloved for the fathers' sake.'" But tell me, when, and of what things was he discoursing, and to whom? Why, to those of Gentile origin, who were puffing themselves up on their faith, and exalting themselves against the Jews, and so breaking them off the more: to quell the swelling pride of the one, and to win over the others, and thoroughly excite them to the same emulation. For when he is speaking of those noble and great men, hear how he saith, "They that say these things, show plainly that they seek a country; and truly if they had been mindful of that from whence they came out, they might have had opportunity to have returned: but now they desire another, a better country." And again, "These all died in faith, not having obtained the promises, but having seen them afar off, and embraced them." And John too said unto those that were coming to him, "Think not to say, We have Abraham to our father." And Paul again, "For they are not all Israel, which are of Israel; neither they, which are the children of the flesh, are they the children of God." For what were the sons of Samuel advantaged, tell me, by their father's nobleness, when they were not heirs of their father's virtue? And what profit had Moses' sons, not having emulated his perfection? Therefore neither did they inherit the dominion; but whilst they enrolled him as their father, the rule of the people passed away to another, to him who had become his son in the way of virtue. And what harm was it to Timothy, that he was of a Greek father? Or what on the other hand again was Noah's son profited by the virtue of his father, when he became a slave instead of free? Seest thou, how little the nobleness of a father avails his children in the way of advocacy? For the wickedness of Ham's disposition overcame the laws of nature, and cast him not only out of the nobility which he had in respect of his father, but also out of his free estate. And what of Esau? Was he not son of Isaac, and had he not his father to stand his friend? Yea, his father too endeavored and desired that he should partake of the blessings, and he himself for the sake of this did all that was commanded him. Nevertheless, because he was untoward, none of these things profited him; but although he was by birth first, and had his father on his side doing everything for this object, yet not having God with him, he lost all.

But why do I speak of men? The Jews were sons of God, and gained nothing by this their high birth. Now if a man, having become a son of God, but failing to show forth an excellency meet for this noble birth, is even punished the more abundantly; why dost thou bring me forward the nobleness of ancestors remote or near? For not under the old covenant only, but even under the new, one may find this rule to have held. For "as many as received Him," it is said "to them gave He power to become the sons of God." And yet many of these children Paul hath affirmed to be nothing profited by their father; "For if ye be circumcised," saith he, "Christ shall profit you nothing." And if Christ be no help to those who will not take heed to themselves, how shall a man stand up in their behalf?

8. Let us not therefore pride ourselves either on high birth, or on wealth, but rather despise them who are so minded: neither let us be dejected at poverty. But let us seek that wealth, which consists in good works; let us flee that poverty, which causes men to be in wickedness, by reason of which also that rich man was poor; wherefore he had not at his command so much as a drop of water, and that, although he made much entreaty. Whereas, who can be so poor amongst us, as to want water enough even for comfort? There is none such. For even they that are pining with extreme hunger, may have the comfort of a drop of water; and not of a drop only, but of refreshment too far more abundant. Not so that rich man, but he was poor even to this degree: and what was yet more grievous, he could not so much as soothe his poverty from any source. Why then do we gape after riches, since they bring us not into Heaven?

For tell me, if any king among those upon earth had said, It is impossible for him that is rich to be distinguished at court, or to enjoy any honor; would ye not have thrown away every one his riches with contempt? So then, if they cast us out from such honor as is in the palaces below, they shall be worthy of all contempt: but, when the King of Heaven is day by day crying aloud and saying, "It is hard with them, to set foot on that sacred threshold;" shall we not give up all, and withdraw from our possessions, that with boldness we may enter into the kingdom? And of what consideration are we worthy, who are at great pains to encompass ourselves with the things that obstruct our way thither; and to hide them not only in chests, but even in the earth, when we might entrust them to the guard of the very Heavens? Since now surely thou art doing the same, as if any husbandman, having gotten wheat wherewith to sow a rich land, was to leave the land alone, and bury all the wheat in a pit, so as neither to enjoy it himself, nor for the wheat to come to ought, but decay and waste. But what is their common plea, when we accuse them of these things? It gives no little comfort, say they, to know that all is laid up for us in safety at home. Nay, rather not to know of its being laid up is a comfort. For even if thou art not afraid of famine, yet other more grievous things, on account of this store, must needs be a terror to thee: deaths, wars, plots laid against thee. And if a famine should ever befall us, the people again, constrained by the belly, takes weapon in hand against thy house. Or rather, in so doing, thou art first of all bringing famine into our cities, and next thou art forming for thine own house this gulf, more grievous than famine. For by stress of famine I know not any who have come to a speedy end; there being in fact many means in many quarters which may be devised to assuage that evil:

but for possessions and riches, and the pursuits connected with them, I can show many to have come by their ruin, some in secret, some openly. And with many such instances the highways abound, with many the courts of law, and the market-places. But why speak I of the highways, the courts of law and the market-places? Why, the very sea thou mayest behold filled with their blood. For not over the land only, as it seems, hath this tyranny prevailed, but over the ocean also hath walked in festal procession with great excess. And one makes a voyage for gold, another, again, is stabbed for the same; and the same tyrannical power hath made one a merchant, the other a murderer.

What then can be less trustworthy than Mammon, seeing that for his sake one travels, and ventures, and is slain? "But who," it is said, "will pity a charmer that is bitten with a serpent?" For we ought, knowing its cruel tyranny, to flee that slavery, and destroy that grievous longing. "But how," saith one, "is this possible?" By introducing another longing, the longing for Heaven. Since he that desires the kingdom will laugh covetousness to scorn; he that is become Christ's slave is no slave of mammon, but rather his lord; for him that flieth from him, he is wont to follow, and to fly from him that pursues. He honors not so much his pursuer as his despiser; no one doth he so laugh to scorn, as them that desire him; nor doth he only laugh them to scorn, but wraps round them also innumerable bonds.

Be it ours then, however late, to loose these grievous chains. Why bring thy reasonable soul into bondage to brute matter, to the mother of those untold evils? But, oh the absurdity! that while we are warring against it in words, it makes war with us by deeds, and leads and carries us everywhere about, insulting us as purchased with money, and meet for the lash; and what can be more disgraceful and dishonorable than this?

Again: if we do not get the better of senseless forms of matter, how shall we have the advantage of the incorporeal powers? If we despise not vile earth and abject stones, how shall we bring into subjection the principalities and authorities? How shall we practise temperance? I mean, if silver dazzle and overpower us, when shall we be able to hurry by a fair face? For, in fact, some are so sold under this tyranny, as be moved somehow even at the mere show of the gold, and in playfulness to say, that the very eyes are the better for a gold coin coming in sight. But make not such jests, whoever thou art; for nothing so injures the eyes, both those of the body and those of the soul, as the lust of these things. For instance; it was this grievous longing that put out the lamps of those virgins, and cast them out of the bride chamber. This sight, which (as thou saidst) "doeth good to the eyes," suffered not the wretched Judas to hearken unto the Lord's voice, but led him even to the halter, made him burst asunder in the midst; and, after all that, conducted him on to hell.

What then can be more lawless than this? what more horrible? I do not mean the substance of riches, but the unseasonable and frantic desire of them? Why, it even drops human gore, and looks murder, and is fiercer than any wild beast, tearing in pieces them that fall in its way, and what is much worse, it suffers them not even to have any sense of being so mangled. For reason would that those who are so treated should stretch forth their hand to them that pass by, and call them to their assistance, but these are even thankful for such rendings of their flesh, than which what can be more wretched?

Let us then, bearing in mind all these things, flee the incurable disease; let us heal the wounds it hath made, and withdraw ourselves from such a pest: in order that both here we may live a secure and untroubled life, and attain to the future treasure; unto which God grant that we may all attain, by the grace and love towards man of our Lord Jesus Christ, with whom unto the Father together with the Holy Ghost be glory, might, honor, now and ever, and world without end. Amen.

HOMILY X

MATT. III. 1, 2

"In those days cometh John the Baptist, preaching in the wilderness of Judaea, and saying, Repent ye: for the kingdom of Heaven is at hand."

How "in those days"? For not then, surely, when He was a child, and came to Nazareth, but thirty years after, John cometh; as Luke also testifies. How then is it said, "in those days"? The Scripture is always wont to use this manner of speech, not only when it is mentioning what occurs in the time immediately after, but also of things which are to come to pass many years later. Thus also, for example, when His disciples came unto Him as He sat on the Mount of Olives, and sought to learn about His coming, and the taking of Jerusalem: and yet ye know how great is the interval between those several periods. I mean, that having spoken of the subversion of the mother city, and completed His discourse on that subject, and being about to pass to that on the consummation, he inserted, "Then shall these things also come to pass;" not bringing together the times by the word then, but indicating that time only in which these things were to happen. And this sort of thing he doth now also, saying, "In those days." For this is not put to signify the days that come immediately after, but those in which these things were to take place, which he was preparing to relate.

"But why was it after thirty years," it may be said, "that Jesus came unto His baptism"? After this baptism He was thenceforth to do away with the law: wherefore even until this age, which admits of all sins, He continues fulfilling it all; that no one might say, that because He Himself could not fulfill it, He did it away. For neither do all passions assail us at all times; but while in the first age of life there is much thoughtlessness and timidity, in that which comes after it, pleasure is more vehement, and after this again the desire of wealth. For this cause he awaits the fullness of His adult age, and throughout it all fulfills the law, and so comes to His baptism, adding it as something which follows upon the complete keeping of all the other commandments.

To prove that this was to Him the last good work of those enjoined by the law, hear His own words: "For thus it becometh us to fulfill all righteousness." Now what He saith is like this: "We have performed all the duties of the law, we have not transgressed so much as one commandment. Since therefore this only remains, this too must be added, and so shall we "fulfill all righteousness." For He here calls by the name of "righteousness" the full performance of all the commandments.

2. Now that on this account Christ came to His baptism, is from this evident. But wherefore was this baptism devised for Him? For that not of himself did the son of Zacharias proceed to this, but of God who moved him,—this Luke also declares, when he saith, "The word of the Lord came unto him," that is, His commandment. And he himself too saith, "He that sent me to baptize with water, the same said to me, upon whom thou shalt see the Spirit descending like a dove, and remaining on Him, the same is He which baptizeth with the Holy Ghost." Wherefore then was he sent to baptize? The Baptist again makes this also plain to us, saying, "I knew Him not, but that He should be made manifest to Israel, therefore am I come baptizing with water."

And if this was the only cause, how saith Luke, that "he came into the country about Jordan, preaching the baptism of repentance for the remission of sins?" And yet it had not remission, but this gift pertained unto the baptism that was given afterwards; for in this "we are buried with Him," and our old man was then crucified with Him, and before the cross there doth not appear remission anywhere; for everywhere this is imputed to His blood. And Paul too saith, "But ye are washed, but ye are sanctified," not by the baptism of John, but "in the name of our Lord Jesus Christ, and by the Spirit of our God." And elsewhere too he saith, "John verily preached a baptism of repentance," (he saith not "of remission,") "that they should believe on Him that should come after him." For when the sacrifice was not yet offered, neither had the spirit yet come down, nor sin was put away, nor the enmity removed, nor the curse destroyed; how was remission to take place?

What means then, "for the remission of sins?"

The Jews were senseless, and had never any feeling of their own sins, but while they were justly accountable for the worst evils, they were justifying themselves in every respect; and this more than anything caused their destruction, and led them away from the faith. This, for example, Paul himself was laying to their charge, when he said, that "they being ignorant of God's righteousness, and going about to establish their own, had not submitted themselves unto the righteousness of God." And again: "What shall we say then? That the Gentiles, which followed not after righteousness, have attained to righteousness; but Israel, which followed after the law of righteousness, hath not attained unto the law of righteousness. Wherefore? Because they sought it not by faith, but as it were by works."

Since therefore this was the cause of their evils, John cometh, doing nothing else but bringing them to a sense of their own sins. This, among other things, his very garb declared, being that of repentance and confession. This was indicated also by what he preached, for nothing else did he say, but "bring forth fruits meet for repentance." Forasmuch then as their not condemning their own sins, as Paul also hath explained, made them start off from Christ, while their coming to a sense thereof would set them upon longing to seek after their Redeemer, and to desire remission; this John came to bring about, and to persuade them to repent, not in order that they might be punished, but that having become by repentance more humble, and condemning themselves, they might hasten to receive remission.

But let us see how exactly he hath expressed it; how, having said, that he "came preaching the baptism of repentance in the wilderness of Judaea," he adds, "for remission," as though he said, For this end he exhorted them to confess and repent of their sins; not that they should be punished, but that they might more easily receive the subsequent remission. For had they not condemned themselves, they could not have sought after His grace; and not seeking, they could not have obtained remission.

Thus that baptism led the way for this; wherefore also he said, that "they should believe on Him which should come after him;" together with that which hath been mentioned setting forth this other cause of His baptism. For neither would it have been as much for him to have gone about to their houses, and to have led Christ around, taking Him by the hand, and to have said, "Believe in This Man;" as for that blessed voice to be uttered, and all those other things performed in the presence and sight of all.

On account of this He cometh to the baptism. Since in fact both the credit of him that was baptizing, and the purport of the thing itself, was attracting the whole city, and calling it unto Jordan; and it became a great spectacle.

Therefore he humbles them also when they are come, and persuades them to have no high fancies about themselves; showing them liable to the utmost evils, unless they would repent, and leaving their forefathers, and all vaunting in them, would receive Him that was coming.

Because in fact the things concerning Christ had been up to that time veiled, and many thought He was dead, owing to the massacre which took place at Bethlehem. For though at twelve years old He discovered Himself, yet did He also quickly veil Himself again. And for this cause there was need of that splendid exordium and of a loftier beginning. Wherefore also then for the first time he with clear voice proclaims things which the Jews had never heard, neither from prophets, nor from any besides; making mention of Heaven, and of the kingdom there, and no longer saying anything touching the earth.

But by the kingdom in this place he means His former and His last advent.

3. "But what is this to the Jews?" one may say, "for they know not even what thou sayest." "Why, for this cause," saith he, "do I so speak, in order that being roused by the obscurity of my words, they may proceed to seek Him, whom I preach." In point of fact, he so excited them with good hopes when they came near, that even many publicans and soldiers inquired what they should do, and how they should direct their own life; which was a sign of being thenceforth set free from all worldly things, and of looking to other greater objects, and of foreboding things to come. Yea, for all, both the sights and the words of that time, led them unto lofty thoughts.

Conceive, for example, how great a thing it was to see a man after thirty years coming down from the wilderness, being the son of a chief priest, who had never known the common wants of men, and was on every account venerable, and had Isaiah with him. For he too was present proclaiming him, and saying, "This is he who I said should come crying, and preaching throughout the whole wilderness with a clear voice." For so great was the earnestness of the prophets touching these things, that not their own Lord only, but him also who was to minister unto Him, they proclaimed a long time beforehand, and they not only mentioned him, but the place too in which he was to abide, and the manner of the doctrine which he had to teach when he came, and the good effect that was produced by him.

See, at least, how both the prophet and the Baptist go upon the same ideas, although not upon the same words.

Thus the prophet saith that he shall come saying, "Prepare ye the way of the Lord, make his paths straight." And he himself when he was come said, "Bring forth fruits meet for repentance," which corresponds with, "Prepare ye the way of the Lord." Seest thou that both by the words of the prophet, and by his own preaching, this one thing is manifested alone; that he was come, making a way and preparing beforehand, not bestowing the gift, which was the remission, but ordering in good time the souls of such as should receive the God of all?

But Luke expresses somewhat further: not repeating the exordium, and so passing on, but setting down likewise all the prophecy. "For every valley," saith he, "shall be filled; and every mountain and hill shall be brought low; and the crooked shall be made straight, and the rough ways smooth; and all flesh shall see the salvation of God." Dost thou perceive how the prophet hath anticipated all by his words; the concourse of the people, the change of things for the better, the easiness of that which was preached, the first cause of all that was occurring, even if he hath expressed it rather as in figure, it being in truth a prophecy which he was uttering? Thus, when he saith, "Every valley shall be filled, and every mountain and hill shall be brought low, and the rough ways shall be made smooth;" he is signifying the exaltation of the lowly, the humiliation of the self-willed, the hardness of the law changed into easiness of faith. For it is no longer toils and labors, saith he, but grace, and forgiveness of sins, affording great facility of salvation. Next he states the cause of these things, saying, "All flesh shall see the salvation of God;" no longer Jews and proselytes only, but also all earth and sea, and the whole race of men. Because by "the crooked things" he signified our whole corrupt life, publicans, harlots, robbers, magicians, as many as having been perverted before afterwards walked in the right way: much as He Himself likewise said, "publicans and harlots go into the kingdom of God before you," because they believed. And in other words also again the prophet declared the self-same thing, thus saying, "Then wolves and lambs shall feed together." For like as here by the hills and valleys, he meant that incongruities of character are blended into one and the same evenness of self-restraint, so also there, by the characters of the brute animals indicating the different dispositions of men, he again spoke of their being linked in one and the same harmony of godliness. Here also, as before, stating the cause. That cause is, "There shall be He that riseth to reign over the Gentiles, in Him shall the Gentiles trust:" much the same as here too he said, "All flesh shall see the salvation of God," everywhere declaring that the power and knowledge of these our Gospels would be poured out to the ends of the world, converting the human race, from a brutish disposition and a fierce temper to something very gentle and mild.

4. "And the same John had his raiment of camel's hair, and a leathern girdle about his loins."

Observe, how the prophets foretold some things, others they left to the evangelists. Wherefore also Matthew both sets down the prophecies, and adds his own part, not accounting even this superfluous, to speak of the dress of the righteous man.

For indeed it was a marvellous and strange thing to behold so great austerity in a human frame: which thing also particularly attracted the Jews, seeing in him the great Elijah, and guided by what they then beheld, to the memory of that blessed man; or rather, even to a greater astonishment. For the one indeed was brought up in cities and in houses, the other dwelt entirely in the wilderness from his very swaddling clothes. For it became the forerunner of Him who was to put away all the ancient ills, the labor, for example, the curse, the sorrow, the sweat; himself also to have certain tokens of such a gift, and to come at once to be above that condemnation. Thus he neither ploughed land, nor opened furrow, he ate not his bread by the sweat of his face, but his table was hastily supplied, and his clothing more easily furnished than his table, and his lodging yet less troublesome than his clothing. For he needed neither roof, nor bed, nor table, nor any other of these things, but a kind of angel's life in this our flesh did he exhibit. For this cause his very garment was of hair, that by his dress he might instruct men to separate themselves from all things human, and to have nothing in common with the earth, but to hasten back to their earlier nobleness, wherein Adam was before he wanted garments or robe. Thus that garb bore tokens of nothing less than a kingdom, and of repentance.

And do not say to me, "Whence had he a garment of hair and a girdle, dwelling as he did in the wilderness?" For if thou art to make a difficulty of this, thou wilt also inquire into more things besides; how in the winters, and how in the heats of summer, he continued in the wilderness, and this with a delicate body, and at an immature age? how the nature of his infant flesh endured such great inconstancy of weather, and a diet so uncommon, and all the other hardships arising from the wilderness?

Where now are the philosophers of the Greeks, who at random and for nought emu lated the shamelessness of the Cynics (for what is the profit of being shut up in a tub, and afterwards running into such wantonness)? they who encompassed themselves with rings and cups, and men servants and maid servants, and with much pomp besides, falling into either extreme. But this man was not so; but he dwelt in the wilderness as in Heaven, showing forth all strictness of self-restraint. And from thence, like some angel from Heaven, he went down unto the cities, being a champion of godliness, and a crowned victor over the world, and a philosopher of that philosophy which is worthy of the heavens. And these things were, when sin was not yet put away, when the law had not yet ceased, when death was not yet bound, when the brazen gates were not yet broken up, but while the ancient polity still was in force.

Such is the nature of a noble and thoroughly vigilant soul, for it is everywhere springing forward, and passing beyond the limits set to it; as Paul also did with respect to the new polity.

But why, it may be asked, did he use a girdle with his raiment? This was customary with them of old time, before men passed into this soft and loose kind of dress. Thus, for instance, both Peter appears to have been "girded," and Paul; for it saith, "the man that owneth this girdle." And Elijah too was thus arrayed, and every one of the saints, because they were at work continually, laboring, and busying themselves either in journeyings, or about some other necessary matter; and not for this cause only, but also with a view of trampling under foot all ornaments, and practising all austerity. This very kind of thing accordingly Christ declares to be the greatest praise of virtue, thus saying, "What went ye out for to see? a man clothed in soft raiment? behold, they that wear soft clothing are in king's houses."

But if he, who was so pure, and more glorious than the heaven, and above all prophets, than whom none greater was born, and who had such great boldness of speech, thus exercised himself in austerity, scorning so exceedingly all dissolute delicacy, and training himself to this hard life; what excuse shall we have, who after so great a benefit, and the unnumbered burdens of our sins, do not show forth so much as the least part of his penance, but are drinking and surfeiting, and smelling of perfumes, and in no better trim than the harlot women on the stage, and are by all means softening ourselves, and making ourselves an easy prey to the devil?

5. "Then went out to him all Judea, and Jerusalem, and all the region round about Jordan, and were baptized of him, confessing their sins."

Seest thou how great power was in the coming of the prophet? how he stirred up all the people; how he led them to a consideration of their own sins? For it was indeed worthy of wonder to behold him in human form showing forth such things and using so great freedom of speech, and rising up in condemnation of all as children, and having his great grace beaming out from his countenance. And, moreover, the appearance of a prophet after the great interval of time contributed to their amazement, because the gift had failed them, and returned to them after a long time. And the nature of his preaching too was strange and unusual. For they heard of none of those things to which they were accustomed; such as wars and battles and victories below, and famine and pestilence, and Babylonians and Persians, and the taking of the city, and the other things with which they were familiar, but of Heaven and of the kingdom there, and of the punishment in hell. And it was for this cause, let me add, that although they that committed revolt in the wilderness, those in the company of Judas, and of Theudas, had been all of them slain no great while before, yet they were not the more backward to go out thither. For neither was it for the same objects that he summoned them, as for dominion, or revolt, or revolution; but in order to lead them by the hand to the kingdom on high. Wherefore neither did he keep them in the wilderness to take them about with him, but baptizing them, and teaching them the rules concerning self-denial, he dismissed them; by all means instructing them to scorn whatever things are on earth, and to raise themselves up to the things to come, and press on every day.

6. This man then let us also emulate, and forsaking luxury and drunkenness let us go over unto the life of restraint. For this surely is the time of confession both for the uninitiated and for the baptized; for the one, that upon their repentance they may partake of the sacred mysteries; for the others, that having washed away their stain after baptism, they may approach the table with a clean conscience. Let us then forsake this soft and effeminate way of living. For it is not, it is not possible at once both to do penance and to live in luxury. And this let John teach you by his raiment, by his food, by his abode. What then? dost thou require us, you may say, to practise such self-restraint as this? I do not require it, but I advise and recommend it. But if this be not possible to you, let us at least, though in cities, show forth repentance, for the judgment is surely at our doors. But even if it were further off, we ought not even so to be emboldened, for the term of each man's life is the end of the world virtually to him that is summoned. But that it is even at the doors, hear Paul saying, "The night is far spent, the day is at hand;" and again, "He that cometh will come, and will not tarry."

For the signs too are now complete, which announce that day. For "this Gospel of the Kingdoms," saith He, "shall be preached in all the world for a witness unto all nations; and then shall the end come." Attend with care to what is said. He said not, "when it hath been believed by all men," but "when it hath been preached to all." For this cause he also said, "for a witness to the nations," to show, that He doth not wait for all men to believe, and then for Him to come. Since the phrase, "for a witness," hath this meaning, "for accusation," "for reproof," "for condemnation of them that have not believed."

But we, while hearing these things and seeing them, slumber, and see dreams, sunk in a lethargy, as in some very deepest night. For the things present are nothing better than dreams, whether they be prosperous, or whether they be painful. Wherefore I entreat you now at length to be awakened, and to look another way, unto the Sun of Righteousness. For no man while sleeping can see the sun, nor delight his eyes with the beauty of its beams; but whatever he may see, he beholds all as in a dream. For this cause we need much penance, and many tears; both as being in a state of insensibility while we err, and because our sins are great, and beyond excuse. And that I lie not, the more part of them that hear me are witnesses. Nevertheless, although they be beyond excuse, let us repent, and we shall receive crowns.

7. But by repentance I mean, not only to forsake our former evil deeds, but also to show forth good deeds greater than those. For, "bring forth," saith he, "fruits meet for repentance." But how shall we bring them forth? If we do the opposite things: as for instance, hast thou seized by violence the goods of others? henceforth give away even thine own. Hast thou been guilty of fornication for a long time? abstain even from thy wife for certain appointed days; exercise continence. Hast thou insulted and stricken such as were passing by? Henceforth bless them that insult thee, and do good to them that smite thee. For it sufficeth not for our health to have plucked out the dart only, but we must also apply remedies to the wound. Hast thou lived in self-indulgence, and been drunken in time past? Fast, and take care to drink water, in order to destroy the mischief that hath so grown up within thee. Hast thou beheld with unchaste eyes beauty that belonged to another? Henceforth do not so much as look upon a woman at all, that thou mayest stand in more safety. For it is said, "Depart from evil, and do good;" and again, "Make thy tongue to cease from evil, and thy lips that they speak no guile." "But tell me the good too." "Seek peace, and pursue it:" I mean not peace with man only, but also peace with God. And he hath well said, "pursue" her: for she is driven away, and cast out; she hath left the earth, and is gone to sojourn in Heaven. Yet shall we be able to bring her back again, if we will put away pride and boasting, and whatsoever things stand in her way, and will follow this temperate and frugal life. For nothing is more grievous than wrath and fierce anger. This renders men both puffed up and servile, by the former making them ridiculous, by the other hateful; and bringing in opposite vices, pride and flattery, at the same time. But if we will cut off the greediness of this passion, we shall be both lowly with exactness, and exalted with safety. For in our bodies too all distempers arise from excess; and when the elements thereof leave their proper limits, and go on beyond moderation, then all these countless diseases are generated, and griev-

ous kinds of death. Somewhat of the same kind one may see take place with respect to the soul likewise.

8. Let us therefore cut away excess, and drinking the salutary medicine of moderation, let us abide in our proper temperament, and give careful heed to our prayers. Though we receive not, let us persevere that we may receive; and if we do receive, then because we have received. For it is not at all His wish to defer giving, but by such delay He is contriving for us to persevere. With this intent He doth also lengthen out what is good for us better than we do, and loves us more ardently than those who gave us birth. And let both these considerations be a charm for us to chant to ourselves in every terror that occurs, that so we may quell our despondency, and in all things glorify Him, who on our behalf doeth and ordereth all, even God.

For so we shall both easily repulse all hostile devices, and attain unto the incorruptible crowns: by the grace and love towards man of our Lord Jesus Christ, with whom be unto the Father glory, might, and honor, together with the Holy Ghost, now, and always, even for ever and ever. Amen.

HOMILY XI

MATT. III. 7

"But when he saw many of the Pharisees and Sadducees come to his baptism, he said unto them, O generation of vipers, who hath warned you to flee from the wrath to come?"

How then doth Christ say, that they did not believe John? Because this was not believing, to decline receiving Him whom he preached. For so they thought they regarded their prophets and their lawgiver, nevertheless He said they had not regarded them, forasmuch as they received not Him, that was foretold by them. "For if ye had believed Moses," saith He, "ye would have believed Me." And after this again, being asked by Christ, "The baptism of John, whence is it?" they said, "If we shall say, Of earth, we fear the people; if we shall say, From heaven, He will say unto us, How then did ye not believe him?"

So that from all these things it is manifest that they came indeed and were baptized, yet they did not abide in the belief of that which was preached. For John also points out their wickedness, by their sending unto the Baptist, and saying, "Art thou Elias? Art thou Christ?" wherefore he also added, "they which were sent were of the Pharisees."

"What then? were not the multitudes also of this same mind"? one may say. Nay, the multitudes in simplicity of mind had this suspicion, but the Pharisees, wishing to lay hold of Him. For since it was acknowledged that Christ comes out of the village of David, and this man was of the tribe of Levi, they laid a snare by the question, in order that if he should say any such thing they might quickly come upon him. This at any rate he hath declared by what follows; for on his not acknowledging any of the things which they expected, even so they take hold of him, saying, "Why baptizest thou then, if thou be not the Christ?"

And to convince thee that the Pharisees came with one mind, and the people with another, hear how the evangelist hath declared this too; saying of the people, "that they came and were baptized of him, confessing their sins;" but concerning the Pharisees, no longer like that, but that "when he saw many of the Pharisees and Sadducees coming, he said, O generation of vipers, who hath warned you to flee from the wrath to come?" O greatness of mind! How doth he discourse unto men ever thirsting after the blood of the prophets, and in disposition no better than serpents! how doth he disparage both themselves and their progenitors with all plainness!

2. "Yea," saith one; "he speaks plainly enough, but the question is if there be any reason in this plainness. For he did not see them sinning, but in the act of change; wherefore they did not deserve blame, but rather praise and approbation, for having left city and houses, and making haste to hear his preaching."

What then shall we say? That he had not things present, and even now doing, in his view, but he knew the secrets of their mind, God having revealed this. Since then they were priding themselves on their forefathers, and this was like to prove the cause of their destruction, and was casting them into a state of carelessness, he cuts away the roots of their pride. For this cause Isaiah also calls them, "rulers of Sodom," and "people of Gomorrah;" and another prophet saith, "Are ye not as children of the Ethiopians;" and all withdraw them from this way of thinking, bringing down their pride, which had caused them unnumbered evils.

"But the prophets," you will say, "naturally did so; for they saw them sinning: but in this case, with what view and for what cause doeth he the same, seeing them obey him." To make them yet more tender-hearted.

But if one accurately mark his words, he hath also tempered his rebuke with commendation. For he spake these things, as marveling at them, that they were become able, however late, to do what seemed almost an impossibility for them. His rebuke, you see, is rather that of one bringing them over, and working upon them to arouse themselves. For in that he appears amazed, he implies both their former wickedness to be great, and their conversion marvellous and beyond expectation. Thus, "what hath come to pass," saith he, "that being children of those men, and brought up so badly, they have repented? Whence hath come so great a change? Who hath softened down the harshness of their spirit? Who corrected that which was incurable?"

And see how straightway from the beginning he alarmed them, by laying first, for a foundation, his words concerning hell. For he spake not of the usual topics: "Who hath warned you to flee from wars, from the inroads of the barbarians, from captivities, from famines, from pestilences?" but concerning another sort of punishment, never before made manifest to them, he was striking the first preparatory note, saying thus, "Who hath warned you to flee from the wrath to come?"

And full well did he likewise call them, "generation of vipers." For that animal too is said to destroy the mother that is in travail with her, and eating through her belly, thus to come forth unto light; which kind of thing these men also did being "murderers of fathers, and murderers of mothers," and destroying their instructors with their own hands.

3. However, he stops not at the rebuke, but introduces advice also. For, "Bring forth," says he, "fruits meet for repentance."

For to flee from wickedness is not enough, but you must show forth also great virtue. For let me not have that contradictory yet ordinary case, that refraining yourselves for a little while, ye return unto the same wickedness. For we are not come for the same objects as the prophets before. Nay, the things that are now are changed, and are more exalted, forasmuch as the Judge henceforth is coming, His very self, the very Lord of the kingdom, leading unto greater self-restraint, calling us to heaven, and drawing us upward to those abodes. For this cause do I unfold the doctrine also touching hell, because both the good things and the painful are for ever. Do not therefore abide as ye are, neither bring forward the accustomed pleas, Abraham, Isaac, Jacob, the noble race of your ancestors."

And these things he said, not as forbidding them to say that they were sprung from those holy men, but as forbidding them to put confidence in this, while they were neglecting the virtue of the soul; at once bringing forward publicly what was in their minds, and foretelling things to come. Because after this they are found to say, "We have Abraham to our father, and were never in bondage to any man." Since then it was this, which most of all lifted them up with pride and ruined them, he first puts it down.

And see how with his honor paid to the patriarch he combines his correction touching these things. Namely, having said, "Think not to say, We have Abraham to our father," he said not, "for the patriarch shall not be able to profit you anything," but somehow in a more gentle and acceptable manner he intimated the self-same thing, by saying,

"For God is able of these stones to raise up children to Abraham."

Now some say, that concerning the Gentiles he saith these things, calling them stones, metaphorically; but I say, that the expression hath also another meaning. But of what kind is this? Think not, saith he, that if you should perish, you would make the patriarch childless. This is not, this is not so. For with God it is possible, both out of stones to give him men, and to bring them to that relationship; since at the beginning also it was so done. For it was like the birth of men out of stones, when a child came forth from that hardened womb.

This accordingly the prophet also was intimating, when he said, "Look unto the hard rock, whence ye are hewn, and to the hole of the pit, whence ye are digged: look unto Abraham your father, and unto Sarah that bare you." Now of this prophecy, you see, he reminds them, showing that if at the beginning he made him a father, as marvellously as if he had made him so out of stones, it was possible for this now also to come to pass. And see how he both alarms them, and cuts them off: in that he said not, "He had already raised up," lest they should despair of themselves, but that He "is able to raise up:" and he said not, "He is able out of stones to make men," but what was a much greater thing, "kinsmen and children of Abraham."

Seest thou how for the time he drew them off from their vain imagination about things of the body, and from their refuge in their forefathers; in order that they might rest the hope of their salvation in their own repentance and continence? Seest thou how by casting out their carnal relationship, he is bringing in that which is of faith?

4. Mark then how by what follows also he increases their alarm, and adds intensity to their agonizing fear.

For having said that "God is able of these stones to raise up children unto Abraham," he added, "And now also the axe is laid unto the root of the trees," by all means making his speech alarming. For as he from his way of life had much freedom of speech, so they needed his severe rebuke, having been left barren now for a long time. For "why do I say" (such are his words) "that ye are on the point of falling away from your relationship to the patriarch and of seeing others, even those that are of stones, brought in to your pre-eminence? Nay, not to this point only will your penalty reach, but your punishment will proceed further. "For now," saith he, "the axe is laid unto the root of the trees." There is nothing more terrible than this turn of his discourse. For it is no longer "a flying sickle," nor "the taking down of a hedge," nor "the treading under foot of the vineyard;" but an axe exceeding sharp, and what is worse, it is even at the doors. For inasmuch as they continually disbelieved the prophets, and used to say, "Where is the day of the Lord:" and "let the counsel of the Holy One of Israel come, that we may know it," by reason that it was many years before what they said came to pass; to lead them off from this encouragement also, he sets the terrors close to them. And this he declared by saying "now," and by his putting it to "the root." "For the space between is nothing now," saith he, "but it is laid to the very root." And he said not, "to the branches," nor "to the fruits," but "to the root." Signifying, that if they were negligent, they would have incurable horrors to endure, and not have so much as a hope of remedy. It being no servant who is now come, as those before Him were, but the very Lord of all, bringing on them His fierce and most effectual vengeance.

Yet, although he hath terrified them again, he suffers them not to fall into despair; but as before he said not "He hath raised up," but "He is able to raise up children to Abraham" (at once both alarming and comforting them); even so here also he did not say that "it hath touched the root," but "it is laid to the root, and is now hard by it, and shows signs of no delay." However, even though He hath brought it so near, He makes its cutting depend upon you. For if ye change and become better men, this axe will depart without doing anything; but if ye continue in the same ways, He will tear up the tree by the roots. And therefore, observe, it is neither removed from the root, nor applied as it is doth it cut at all: the one, that ye may not grow supine, the other to let you know that it is possible even in a short time to be changed and saved. Wherefore he doth also from all topics heighten their fear, thoroughly awakening and pressing them on to repentance. Thus first their falling away from their forefathers; next, others being introduced instead; lastly, those terrors being at their doors, the certainty of suffering incurable evils (both which he declared by the root and the axe), was sufficient to rouse thoroughly those even that were very supine, and to make them full of anxiety. I may add, that Paul too was setting forth the same, when he said, "A short word will the Lord make upon the whole world."

But be not afraid; or rather, be afraid, but despair not. For thou hast yet a hope of change; the sentence is not quite absolute, neither did the axe come to cut (else what hindered it from cutting, close as it was to the root?); but on purpose by this fear to make thee a better man, and to prepare thee to bring forth fruit. For this cause he added, "Therefore every tree, which bringeth not forth good fruit, is hewn down, and cast into the fire." Now by the word "every," he rejects again the privilege which they had from their noble descent;

"Why, if thou be Abraham's own descendant," saith he, "if thou have thousands of patriarchs to enumerate, thou wilt but undergo a double punishment, abiding unfruitful."

By these words he alarmed even publicans, the soldiers' mind was startled by him, not casting them into despair, yet ridding them of all security. For along with the terror, there is also much encouragement in what he saith; since by the expression, "which bringeth not forth good fruit," he signified that what bears fruit is delivered from all vengeance.

5. "And how," saith one, "shall we be able to bring forth fruit, when the edge is being applied, and the time so strait, and the appointed season cut short." "Thou wilt be able," saith he, "for this fruit is not of the same kind as that of common trees, waiting a long time, and in bondage to the necessities of seasons, and requiring much other management; but it is enough to be willing, and the tree at once hath put forth its fruit. For not the nature of the root only, but also the skill of the husbandman contributes the most to that kind of fruit-bearing."

For (let me add) on account of this,—lest they should say, "Thou art alarming and pressing, and constraining us, applying an axe, and threatening us with being cut down, yet requiring produce in time of punishment,"—he hath added, to signify the ease of bearing that fruit, "I indeed baptize you with water, but He that cometh after me is mightier than I, the latchet of whose shoe I am not worthy to unloose; He shall baptize you with the Holy Ghost and with fire:" implying hereby that consideration only is needed and faith, not labors and toils; and as it is easy to be baptized, so is it easy to be converted, and to become better men. So having stirred their mind by the fear of God's judgment, and the expectation of His punishment, and by the mention of the axe, and by the loss of their ancestors, and by the bringing in of those other children, and by the double vengeance of cutting off and burning, and having by all means softened their hardness, and brought them to desire deliverance from so great evils; then he brings in what he hath to say touching Christ; and not simply, but with a declaration of His great superiority. Then in setting forth the difference between himself and Him, lest he should seem to say this out of favor, he establishes the fact by comparison of the gifts bestowed by each of them. For he did not at once say, "I am not worthy to unloose the latchet of His shoe;" but when he had first set forth the little value of his own baptism, and had shown that it hath nothing more than to lead them to repentance (for he did not say with water of remission, but of repentance), he sets forth Christ's also, which is full of the unspeakable gift. Thus he seems to say, "Lest, on being told that He cometh after me, thou shouldest despise Him as having come later; learn thou the virtue of His gift, and thou wilt clearly know that I uttered nothing worthy nor great, when I said, "I am not worthy to unloose the latchet of His shoe." So too when thou art told, "He is mightier than I," do not think I said this in the way of making a comparison. For I am not worthy to be ranked so much as among His servants, no, not even the lowest of His servants, nor to receive the least honored portion of His ministry." Therefore He did not merely say, "His shoes," but not even "the latchet," which kind of office was counted the last of all. Then to hinder thy attributing what he had said to humility, he adds also the proof from the facts: "For He shall baptize you," saith he, "with the Holy Ghost and with fire."

6. Seest thou how great is the wisdom of the Baptist? how, when He Himself is preaching, He saith everything to alarm, and fill them with anxiety; but when He is sending men to Him, whatever was mild and apt to recover them: not bringing forward the axe, nor the tree that is cut down and burnt, and cast into the fire, nor the wrath to come, but remission of sins, and removing of punishment, and righteousness, and sanctification, and redemption, and adoption, and brotherhood, and a partaking of the inheritance, and an abundant supply of the Holy Ghost. For all these things he obscurely denoted, when he said, "He shall baptize you with the Holy Ghost;" at once, by the very figure of speech, declaring the abundance of the grace (for he said not, "He will give you the Holy Ghost," but "He will baptize you with the Holy Ghost"); and by the specification of fire on the other hand indicating the vehement and uncontrollable quality of His grace.

Imagine only what sort of men it was meet for the hearers to become, when they considered that they were at once to be like the prophets, and like those great ones. For it was on this account, you see, that he made mention at all of fire; that he might lead them to reflect on the memory of those men. Because, of all the visions that appeared unto them, I had almost said, the more part appeared in fire; thus God discoursed with Moses in the bush, thus with all the people in the mount Sinai, thus with Ezekiel on the cherubim.

And mark again how he rouses the hearer, by putting that first which was to take place after all. For the Lamb was to be slain, and sin to be blotted out, and the enmity to be destroyed, and the burial to take place, and the resurrection, and then the Spirit to come. But none of these things doth he mention as yet, but that first which was last, and for the sake of which all the former were done, and which was fittest to proclaim His dignity; so that when the hearer should be told that he was to receive so great a Spirit he might search with himself, how and in what manner this shall be, while sin so prevails; that finding him full of thought and prepared for that lesson, he might thereupon introduce what he had to say touching the Passion, no man being any more offended, under the expectation of such a gift.

Wherefore he again cried out, saying, "Behold the Lamb of God, which beareth the sin of the world." He did not say, "which remitteth," but, that which implies a more guardian care, "which heareth it." For it is not all one, simply to remit, and to take it upon Himself. For the one was to be done without peril, the other with death.

And again, he said, "He is Son of God." But not even this declared His rank openly to the hearers (for they did not so much as know yet how to conceive of Him as a true Son): but by so great a gift of the Spirit that also was established. Therefore the Father also in sending John gave him, as you know, this as a first token of the dignity of Him that was come, saying, "Upon whom thou shalt see the Spirit descending and remaining, the same is He which baptizeth with the Holy Ghost." Wherefore himself too saith, "I saw and bare record that this is the Son of God;" as though the one were to all time the clear evidence of the other.

7. Then, as having uttered the gentler part of his message, and soothed and relaxed the hearer, he again binds him up, that he may not become remiss. For such was the nature of the Jewish nation; by all encouraging things they were easily puffed up, and corrupted. Wherefore he again adduces his terrors, saying, "Whose fan is in His hand."

Thus, as before he had spoken of the punishment, so here he points out the Judge likewise, and introduces the eternal vengeance. For "He will burn the chaff," saith he, "with unquenchable fire." Thou seest that He is Lord of all things, and that He is Himself the Husbandman; albeit in another place He calls His Father the same. For "My Father," saith He, "is the Husbandman." Thus, inasmuch as He had spoken of an axe, lest thou shouldest suppose that the thing needed labor, and the separation was hard to make; by another comparison he suggests the easiness of it, implying that all the world is His; since He could not punish those who were not His own. For the present, it is true, all are mingled together (for though the wheat appears gleaming through, yet it lies with the chaff, as on a threshing floor, not as in a garner), but then, great will be the separation.

Where now are they by whom hell-fire is disbelieved? Since surely here are two points laid down, one, that He will baptize with the Holy Ghost, the other, that He will burn up the disobedient. If then that is credible, so is this too, assuredly. Yea, this is why the two predictions are put by him in immediate connection, that by that which hath taken place already, he might accredit the other, as yet unaccomplished. For Christ too Himself in many places doth so, often of the same things, and often of opposites, setting down two prophecies; the one of which He performs here, the other He promises in the future; that such as are too contentious may, from the one which has already come to pass, believe the other also, which is not yet accomplished. For instance, to them that strip themselves of all that they have for His sake He promised to give an hundred fold in the present world, and life eternal in that which is to come; by the things already given making the future also credible. Which, as we see, John likewise hath done in this place; laying down two things, that He shall both baptize with the Holy Ghost, and burn up with unquenchable fire. Now then, if He had not baptized with the Spirit the apostles, and all every day who are willing, thou mightest have doubts concerning those other things too; but if that which seems to be greater and more difficult, and which transcends all reason, hath been done, and is done every day; how deniest thou that to be true, which is easy, and comes to pass according to reason? Thus having said, "He shall baptize with the Holy Ghost and with fire," and having thence promised great blessings; lest thou, released wholly from the former things, grow supine, he hath added the fan, and the judgment thereby declared. Thus, "think not at all," saith he, "that your baptism suffices, if ye become ordinary persons hereafter:" for we need both virtue, and plenty of that known self-restraint. Therefore as by the axe he urges them unto grace, and unto the font, so after grace he terrifies them by the fan, and the unquenchable fire. And of the one sort, those yet unbaptized, he makes no distinction, but saith in general, "Every tree that bringeth not forth good fruit is hewn down," punishing all the unbelievers. Whereas after baptism He works out a kind of division, because many of them that believed would exhibit a life unworthy of their faith.

Let no man then become chaff, let no one be tossed to and fro, nor lie exposed to wicked desires, blown about by them easily every way. For if thou continue wheat, though temptation be brought on thee, thou wilt suffer nothing dreadful; nay, for in the threshing floor, the wheels of the car, that are like saws, do not cut in pieces the wheat; but if thou fall away into the weakness of chaff, thou wilt both here suffer incurable ills, being smitten of all men, and there thou wilt undergo the eternal punishment. For all such persons both before that furnace become food for the irrational passions here, as chaff is for the brute animal: and there again they are material and food for the flame.

Now to have said directly that He will judge men's doings, would not so effectually procure acceptance for His doctrine: but to blend with it the parable, and so establish it all, was apter to persuade the hearer, and attract him by a more ample encouragement. Wherefore also Christ Himself for the most part so discourses with them; threshing floor, and harvest, and vineyard, and winepress, and field, and net, and fishing, and all things familiar, and among which they were busied He makes ingredients in His discourses. This kind of thing then the Baptist likewise did here, and offered an exceeding great demonstration of his words, the giving of the Spirit. For "He who hath so great power, as both to forgive sins, and to give the Spirit, much more will these things also be within His power:" so he speaks.

Seest thou how now in due order the mystery came to be laid as a foundation, before the resurrection and judgment?

"And wherefore," it may be said, "did he not mention the signs and wonders which were straightway to be done by Him?" Because this was greater than all, and for its sake all those were done. Thus, in his mention of the chief thing, he comprehended all; death dissolved, sins abolished, the curse blotted out, those long wars done away; our entrance into paradise, our ascent into heaven, our citizenship with the angels, our partaking of the good things to come: for in truth this is the earnest of them all. So that in mentioning this, he hath mentioned also the resurrection of our bodies, and the manifestation of His miracles here, and our partaking of His kingdom, and the good things, which "eye hath not seen, nor ear heard, neither have entered into the heart of man." For all these things He bestowed on us by that gift. It was therefore superfluous to speak of the signs that were immediately to ensue, and which sight can judge of; but those were meet to be discoursed on, whereof they doubted; as for instance, that He is the Son of God; that He exceeds John beyond comparison; that He "beareth the sin of the world;" that He will require an account of all that we do; that our interests are not limited to the present, but elsewhere every one will undergo the due penalty. For these things were not as yet proveable by sight.

8. Therefore, knowing these things, let us use great diligence, while we are in the threshing floor; for it is possible while we are here, to change even out of chaff into wheat, even as on the other hand many from wheat have become chaff. Let us not then be supine, nor be carried about with every wind; neither let us separate ourselves from our brethren, though they seem to be small and mean; forasmuch as the wheat also compared with the chaff is less in measure, but better in nature. Look not therefore to the forms of outward pomp, for they are prepared for the fire, but to this godly humility, so firm and indissoluble, and which cannot be cut, neither is burnt by the fire. It being for their sake that He bears long with the very chaff, that by their intercourse with them they may become better. Therefore judgment is not yet, that we may be all crowned together, that from wickedness many may be converted unto virtue.

Let us tremble then at hearing this parable. For indeed that fire is unquenchable. "And how," it may be said, "is it unquenchable?" Seest thou not this sun ever burning, and never quenched? didst thou not behold the bush burning, and not consumed? If then thou also desirest to escape the flame, lay up alms beforehand, and so thou wilt not even taste of that fire. For if, while here, thou wilt believe what is told thee, thou shalt not so much as see this furnace, after thy departure into that region; but if thou disbelieve it now, thou shalt know it there full well by experience, when no sort of escape is possible. Since in truth no entreaty shall avert the punishment from them who have not shown forth an upright life. For believing surely is not enough, since even the devils tremble at God, but for all that they will be punished.

9. Wherefore our care of our conduct hath need to be great. Why, this is the very reason of our continually assembling you here; not simply that ye should enter in, but that ye should also reap some fruit from your continuance here. But if ye come indeed constantly, but go away again reaping no fruit from thence, ye will have no advantage from your entering in and attendance in this place.

For if we, when sending children to teachers, should we see them reaping no benefit thereby, begin to be severe in blaming the teachers, and remove them often to others; what excuse shall we have for not bestowing upon virtue even so much diligence as upon these earthly things, but forever bringing our tablets home empty? And yet our teachers here are more in number and greater. For no less than prophets and apostles and patriarchs, and all righteous men, are by us set over you as teachers in every Church. And not even so is there any profit, but if you have joined in chanting two or three Psalms, and making the accustomed prayers at random and anyhow, are so dismissed, ye think this enough for your salvation. Have ye not heard the prophet, saying (or rather God by the prophet), "This people honoreth me with their lips, but their heart is far from me?"

Therefore, lest this be our case too, wipe thou out the letters, or rather the impressions, which the devil hath engraven in thy soul; and bring me a heart set free from worldly tumults, that without fear I may write on it what I will. Since now at least there is nothing else to discern, except his letters;—rapines, covetings, envy, jealousy. Wherefore of course, when I receive your tablets, I am not able so much as to read them. For I find not the letters, which we every Lord's day inscribe on you, and so let you go; but others, instead of these, unintelligible and misshapen. Then, when we have blotted them out, and have written those which are of the Spirit, ye departing, and giving up your hearts to the works of the devil, give him again power to substitute his own characters in you. What then will be the end of all this, even without any words of mine, each man's own conscience knoweth. For I indeed will not cease to do my part, and to write in you the right letters. But if ye mar our diligence, for our part our reward is unaltered, but your danger is not small.

Now, though I would fain say nothing to disgust you, yet I beseech again and entreat you, imitate at least the little children's diligence in these matters. For so they first learn the form of the letters, after that they practise themselves in distinguishing them put out of shape, and then at last in their reading they proceed orderly by means of them. Just so let us also do; let us divide virtue, and learn first not to swear, nor to forswear ourselves, nor to speak evil; then proceeding to another row, not to envy, not to lust, not to be gluttonous, not to be drunken, not fierce, not slothful, so that from these we may pass on again to the things of the Spirit, and practise continence, and neglect of the belly, temperance, righteousness, to be above glory, and gentle and contrite in mind; and let us join these one with another, and write them upon our soul.

10. And all these let us practise at home, with our own friends, with our wife, with our children. And, for the present, let us begin with the things that come first, and are easier; as for instance, with not swearing; and let us practise this one letter continually at home. For, in truth, there are many at home to hinder this our practice; sometimes a man's servant provoking him, sometimes his wife annoying and angering him, sometimes an indocile and disorderly child urges him on to threatening and swearing. If now at home, when thus continually galled, thou shouldest attain not to be tempted into swearing, thou wilt in the market-place also have power with ease to abide unconquered.

Yea, and in like sort, thou wilt attain to keep thyself from insulting any, by not insulting thy wife, nor thy servants, nor any one else among those in thy house. For a man's wife too not seldom, praising this or that person, or bemoaning herself, stirs him up to speak evil of that other. But do not thou let thyself be constrained to speak evil of him that is praised, but bear it all nobly. And if thou shouldest perceive thy servants praising other masters, be not perturbed, but stand nobly. Let thy home be a sort of lists, a place of exercise for virtue, that having trained thyself well there, thou mayest with entire skill encounter all abroad.

Do this with respect to vainglory also. For if thou train thyself not to be vainglorious in company of thy wife and thy servants, thou wilt not ever afterwards be easily caught by this passion with regard to any one else. For though this malady be in every case grievous and tyrannical, yet is it so especially when a woman is present. If we therefore in that instance put down its power, we shall easily master it in the other cases also.

And with respect to the other passions too, let us do this self-same thing, exercising ourselves against them at home, and anointing ourselves every day.

And that our exercise may be easier, let us further enact a penalty for ourselves, upon our transgressing any of our purposes. And let the very penalty again be such as brings with it not loss, but reward,—such as procures some very great gain. And this is so, if we sentence ourselves to intenser fastings, and to sleeping often on the bare ground, and to other like austerity. For in this way will much profit come unto us from every quarter; we shall both live the sweet life of virtue here, and we shall attain unto the good things to come and be perpetually friends of God.

But in order that the same may not happen again,—that ye may not, having here admired what is said, go your way, and cast aside at random, wherever it may chance, the tablet of your mind, and so allow the devil to blot out these things;—let each one, on returning home, call his own wife, and tell her these things, and take her to help him; and from this day let him enter into that noble school of exercise, using for oil the supply of the Spirit. And though thou fall once, twice, many times in thy training, despair not, but stand again, and wrestle; and do not give up until thou hast bound on thee the glorious crown of triumph over the devil, and hast for the time to come stored up the riches of virtue in an inviolable treasure-house.

For if thou shouldest establish thyself in the habits of this noble self-restraint, then, not even when remiss, wilt thou be able to transgress any of the commandments, habit imitating the solidity of nature. Yea, as to sleep is easy, and to eat, and to drink, and to breathe, so also will the deeds of virtue be easy to us, and we shall reap to ourselves that pure pleasure, resting in a harbor without a wave, and enjoying continual calm, and with a great freight bringing our vessel into haven, in that City, on that day; and we shall attain unto the undecaying crowns, unto which may we all attain, by the grace and love towards man of our Lord Jesus Christ, to whom be all glory and might, now and always, and world without end. Amen.

HOMILY XII

MATT. III. 13

"Then cometh Jesus from Galilee to Jordan," etc.

With the servants the Lord, with the criminals the Judge, cometh to be baptized. But be not thou troubled; for in these humiliations His exaltation doth most shine forth. For He who vouchsafed to be borne so long in a Virgin's womb, and to come forth thence with our nature, and to be smitten with rods, and crucified, and to suffer all the rest which He suffered;—why marvellest thou if He vouchsafed also to be baptized, and to come with the rest to His servant. For the amazement lay in that one thing, that being God, He would be made Man; but the rest after this all follows in course of reason.

For this cause, let me add, John also by way of anticipation said all that he had said before, that he "was not worthy to unloose the latchet of His shoe;" and all the rest, as for instance, that He is Judge, and rewards every man according to his desert, and that He will bestow His Spirit abundantly on all; in order that when thou shouldest see Him coming to the baptism, thou mightest not suspect anything mean. Therefore he forbids Him, even when He was come, saying,

"I have need to be baptized of Thee, and comest Thou to me." For, because the baptism was "of repentance," and led men to accuse themselves for their offenses, lest any one should suppose that He too "cometh to Jordan" in this sort of mind, John sets it right beforehand, by calling Him both Lamb, and Redeemer from all the sin that is in the world. Since He that was able to take away the sins of the whole race of men, much more was He Himself without sin. For this cause then he said not, "Behold, He that is without sin," but what was much more, He "that beareth the sin of the world," in order that together with this truth thou mightest receive that other with all assurance, and having received it mightest perceive, that in the conduct of some further economy He cometh to the baptism. Wherefore also he said to Him when He came, "I have need to be baptized of Thee, and comest Thou to me?"

And he said not, "And art Thou baptized of me?" nay, for this he feared to say: but what? "And comest Thou to me?" What then doth Christ? What He did afterwards with respect to Peter, this did He then also. For so he too would have forbidden Him to wash his feet, but when he had heard, "What I do thou knowest not now, but thou shalt know hereafter," and "thou hast no part with me," he speedily withdrew from his determination, and went over to the contrary. And this man again in like manner, when he had heard, "Suffer it to be so now, for thus it becometh us to fulfill all righteousness," straightway obeyed. For they were not unduly contentious, but they manifested both love and obedience, and made it their study to be ruled by their Lord in all things.

And mark how He urges him on that very ground which chiefly caused him to look doubtfully on what was taking place; in that He did not say, "thus it is just," but "thus it becometh." For, inasmuch as the point unworthy of Him was in his mind chiefly this, His being baptized by His servant, He stated this rather than anything else, which is directly opposed to that impression: as though He had said, "Is it not as unbecoming that thou avoidest and forbid-dest this? nay, for this self-same cause I bid thee suffer it, that it is becoming, and that in the highest degree."

And He did not merely say, "suffer," but He added, "now." "For it will not be so forever," saith He, "but thou shalt see me such as thou desirest; for the present, however, endure this." Next He shows also how this "becometh" Him. How then doth it so? "In that we fulfill the whole law;" and to express this He said, "all righteousness." For righteousness is the fulfilling of the commandments. "Since then we have performed all the rest of the commandments," saith He, "and this alone remains, it also must be added: because I am come to do away the curse that is appointed for the transgression of the law. I must therefore first fulfill it all, and having delivered you from its condemnation, in this way bring it to an end. It becometh me therefore to fulfill the whole law, by the same rule that it becometh me to do away the curse that is written against you in the law: this being the very purpose of my assuming flesh, and coming hither."

2. "Then he suffereth Him. And Jesus, when He was baptized, went up straightway out of the water; and, lo, the heavens were opened unto Him, and he saw the Spirit of God descending like a dove, and lighting upon Him."

For inasmuch as many supposed that John was greater than He, because John had been brought up all his time in the wilderness, and was son of a chief priest, and was clothed with such raiment, and was calling all men unto his baptism, and had been born of a barren mother; while Jesus, first of all, was of a damsel of ordinary rank (for the virgin birth was not yet manifest to all); and besides, He had been brought up in an house, and held converse with all men, and wore this common raiment; they suspected Him to be less than John, knowing as yet nothing of those secret things;—and it fell out moreover that He was baptized of John, which thing added support to this surmise, even if none of those mentioned before had existed; for it would come into their mind that this man was one of the many (for were He not one of the many, He would not have come with the many to the baptism), but that John was greater than He and far more admirable:—in order therefore that this opinion might not prevail with the multitude, the very heavens are opened, when He is baptized, and the Spirit comes down, and a voice with the Spirit, proclaiming the dignity of the Only Begotten. For since the voice that said, "This is my beloved Son," would seem to the multitude rather to belong to John, for It added not, "This that is baptized," but simply This, and every hearer would conceive it to be said concerning the baptizer, rather than the baptized, partly on account of the Baptist's own dignity, partly for all that hath been mentioned; the Spirit came in form of a dove, drawing the voice towards Jesus, and making it evident to all, that This was not spoken of John that baptized, but of Jesus who was baptized.

And how was it, one may say, that they did not believe, when these things came to pass? Because in the days of Moses also many wonderful works were done, albeit not such as these; and after all those, the voices, and the trumpets, and the lightnings, they both forged a calf, and "were joined unto Baal-peor." And those very persons too, who were present at the time, and saw Lazarus arise, so far from believing in Him, who had wrought these things, repeatedly attempted even to slay Him. Now if seeing before their eyes one rise from the dead, they were so wicked, why marvel at their not receiving a voice wafted from above? Since when a soul is uncandid and perverse, and possessed by the disease of envy, it yields to none of these things; even as when it is candid it receives all with faith, and hath no great need of these.

Speak not therefore thus, "They believed not," but rather inquire, "Did not all things take place which ought to have made them believe?" For by the prophet also God frames this kind of defense of His own ways in general. That is, the Jews being on the point of ruin, and of being given over to extreme punishment; lest any from their wickedness should calumniate His providence, He saith, "What ought I to have done to this vineyard, that I have not done?" Just so here likewise do thou reflect; "what ought to have been done, and was not done?" And indeed whensoever arguments arise on God's Providence, do thou make use of this kind of defense, against those who from the wickedness of the many try to raise a prejudice against it. See, for instance, what astonishing things are done, preludes of those which were to come; for it is no more paradise, but Heaven that is opened.

But let our argument with the Jews stand over unto some other time; for the present, God working with us, we would direct our discourse to what is immediately before us.

3. "And Jesus, when He was baptized, went up straightway out of the water; and lo! the heavens were opened unto Him."

Wherefore were the heavens opened? To inform thee that at thy baptism also this is done, God calling thee to thy country on high, and persuading thee to have nothing to do with earth. And if thou see not, yet never doubt it. For so evermore at the beginnings of all wonderful and spiritual transactions, sensible visions appear, and such-like signs, for the sake of them that are somewhat dull in disposition, and who have need of outward sight, and who cannot at all conceive an incorporeal nature, but are excited only by the things that are seen: that so, though afterward no such thing occur, what hath been declared by them once for all at the first may be received by thy faith.

For in the case of the apostles too, there was a "sound of a mighty wind," and visions of fiery tongues appeared, but not for the apostles' sake, but because of the Jews who were then present. Nevertheless, even though no sensible signs take place, we receive the things that have been once manifested by them. Since the dove itself at that time therefore appeared, that as in place of a finger (so to say) it might point out to them that were present, and to John, the Son of God. Not however merely on this account, but to teach thee also, that upon thee no less at thy baptism the Spirit comes. But since then we have no need of sensible vision, faith sufficing instead of all. For signs are "not for them that believe, but for them that believe not."

But why in the fashion of a dove? Gentle is that creature, and pure. Forasmuch then as the Spirit too is "a Spirit of meekness," He therefore appears in this sort. And besides, He is reminding us of an ancient history. For so, when once a common shipwreck had overtaken the whole world, and our race was in danger of perishing, this creature appeared, and indicated the deliverance from the tempest, and bearing an olive branch, published the good tidings of the common calm of the whole world; all which was a type of the things to come. For in fact the condition of men was then much worse, and they deserved a much sorer punishment. To prevent thy despairing, therefore, He reminds thee of that history. Because then also, when things were desperate, there was a sort of deliverance and reformation; but then by punishment, now, on the contrary, by grace and an unspeakable gift. Therefore the dove also appears, not bearing an olive branch, but pointing out to us our Deliverer from all evils, and suggesting the gracious hopes. For not from out of an ark doth she lead one man only, but the whole world she leads up into heaven at her appearing, and instead of a branch of peace from an olive, she conveys the adoption to all the world's offspring in common.

Reflect now on the greatness of the gift, and do not account His dignity the less for His appearing in such a likeness. For I actually hear some saying, that "such as is the difference between a man and a dove, so great is that between Christ and the Spirit: since the one appeared in our nature, the other in the likeness of a dove." What must we say then to these things? That the Son of God did indeed take upon Him the nature of man, but the Spirit took not on Him the nature of a dove. Therefore the evangelist also said not, "in the nature of a dove," but "in the form of a dove." Accordingly, never after did He so much as appear in this fashion, but at that moment only. And if on this account thou affirmest His dignity to be less, the cherubim too will be made out by this reasoning much His superior, even as much so as an eagle is to a dove: because they too were figured into that visible shape. And the angels too superior again, for they no less have many times appeared in the fashion of men. But these things are not so, indeed they are not. For the truth of an economy is one thing, and the condescension of a temporary vision another.

Do not now, I pray thee, become unthankful towards thy Benefactor nor with the very contraries requite Him that hath bestowed on thee the fountain of blessedness. For where adoption is vouchsafed, there is also the removing of evils, and the giving of all good things.

4. On this very account the Jewish baptism ceases, and ours takes its beginning. And what was done with regard to the Passover, the same ensues in the baptism also. For as in that case too, He acting with a view to both, brought the one to an end, but to the other He gave a beginning: so here, having fulfilled the Jewish baptism, He at the same time opens also the doors of that of the Church; as on one table then, so in one river now, He had both sketched out the shadow, and now adds the truth. For this baptism alone hath the grace of the Spirit, but that of John was destitute of this gift. For this very cause in the case of the others that were baptized no such thing came to pass, but only in the instance of Him who was to hand on this; in order that, besides what we have said, thou mightest learn this also, that not the purity of the baptizer, but the power of the baptized, had this effect. Not until then, assuredly, were either the heavens opened, nor did the Spirit make His approach. Because henceforth He leads us away from the old to the new polity, both opening to us the gates on high, and sending down His Spirit from thence to call us to our country there; and not merely to call us, but also with the greatest mark of dignity. For He hath not made us angels and archangels, but He hath caused us to become "sons of God," and "beloved," and so He draws us on towards that portion of ours.

Having then all this in thy mind, do thou show forth a life worthy of the love of Him who calls thee, and of thy citizenship in that world, and of the honor that is given thee. Crucified as thou art to the world, and having crucified it to thyself, show thyself with all strictness a citizen of the city of the heavens. And do not, because thy body is not translated unto heaven, suppose that thou hast anything to do with the earth; for thou hast thy Head abiding above. Yea with this very purpose the Lord, having first come here and having brought His angels, did then, taking thee with Him, depart thither; that even before thy going up to that place, thou mightest understand that it is possible for thee to inhabit earth as it were heaven.

Let us then keep watch over that noble birth, which we received from the beginning; and let us every day seek more and more the palaces there, and account all that is here to be a shadow and a dream. For so, had any king among those on earth, finding thee poor and a beggar, made thee suddenly his son, never wouldest thou have thought upon thy cottage, and thy cottage's mean appointments. Yet surely in that case the difference is not much. Do not then either in this case take account of any of the former things, for thou art called unto much greater. For both He who calls is the Lord of the angels, and the good things that are given surpass all both word and thought. Since not from earth to earth doth He remove thee, as the king doth, but from earth to heaven, and from a mortal nature to an immortal, and to glory unspeakable, then only possible to be properly manifested, when we shall actually enjoy it.

Now then, having to partake of such blessings, do I see thee minding money, and clinging to the pomp which is here? And dost thou not esteem all that is seen to be more vile than beggars rags? And how wilt thou appear worthy of this honor? And what excuse wilt thou have to plead? or rather, what punishment wilt thou not have to suffer, who after so great a gift art running to thy former vomit? For no longer art thou punished merely as a man, but as a son of God that hath sinned; and the greatness of thy honor becomes a mean of bringing a sorer punishment on thee. Since we too punish not equally slaves that do wrong, and sons committing the same offense; and most of all when they have received some great kindness from us.

For if he who had paradise for his portion, for one disobedience underwent such dreadful things after his honor; we, who have received Heaven, and are become joint heirs with the Only Begotten, what excuse shall we have, for running to the serpent after the dove? For it will be no longer, "Dust thou art, and unto dust shalt thou return," and thou "tillest the ground," and those former words, that will be said to us; but what is far more grievous than these, the "outer darkness," the bonds that may not be burst, the venomous worm, the "gnashing of teeth;" and this with great reason. For he that is not made better even by so great a benefit, would justly suffer the most extreme, and a yet more grievous punishment. Elias once opened and shut Heaven, but that was to bring down rain, and restrain it; whereas to thee the heaven is not so opened, but in order for thee to ascend thither; and what is yet more, not to ascend only, but to lead up others also, if thou wilt; such great confidence and power hath He bestowed on thee in all that is His.

5. Forasmuch then as our house is there, there let us store up all, and leave nothing here, lest we lose it. For here, though thou put a lock on it, and doors, and bars, and set thousands of servants to watch it; though thou get the better of all the crafty ones, though thou escape the eyes of the envious, the worms, the wasting that comes of time; which is impossible;—death at any rate thou wilt never escape, but wilt be deprived of all those things in one moment of

time; and not deprived of them only, but wilt have to transfer them into the hands often of thy very enemies. Whereas if thou wouldest transfer them into that house, thou wilt be far above all. For there is no need to apply either key, or doors, or bars; such is the virtue of that city, so inviolable is this place, and by nature inaccessible to corruption and all wickedness.

How then is it not of the utmost folly, where destruction and waste is the lot of all that is stored, there to heap up all, but where things abide untouched and increase, there not to lay up even the least portion; and this, when we are to live there forever? For this cause the very heathens disbelieve the things that we say, since our doings, not our sayings, are the demonstration which they are willing to receive from us; and when they see us building ourselves fine houses, and laying out gardens and baths, and buying fields, they are not willing to believe that we are preparing for another sort of residence away from our city.

"For if this were so," say they, "they would turn to money all they have here, and lay them up beforehand there;" and this they divine from the things that are done in this world. For so we see those who are very rich getting themselves houses and fields and all the rest, chiefly in those cities in which they are to stay. But we do the contrary; and with all earnest zeal we get possession of the earth, which we are soon after to leave; giving up not money only, but even our very blood for a few acres and tenements: while for the purchase of Heaven we do not endure to give even what is beyond our wants, and this though we are to purchase it at a small price, and to possess it forever, provided we had once purchased it.

Therefore I say we shall suffer the utmost punishment, departing thither naked and poor; or rather it will not be for our own poverty that we shall undergo these irremediable calamities, but also for our making others to be such as ourselves. For when heathens see them that have partaken of so great mysteries earnest about these matters, much more will they cling themselves to the things heaping much fire upon our head. For when we, who ought to teach them to despise all things that appear, do ourselves most of all urge them to the lust of these things; when shall it be possible for us to be saved, having to give account for the perdition of others? Hearest thou not Christ say, that He left us to be for salt and for lights in this world, in order that we may both brace up those that are melting in luxury, and enlighten them that are darkened by the care of wealth? When therefore we even cast them into more thorough darkness, and make them more dissolute, what hope shall we have of salvation? There is none at all; but wailing and gnashing our teeth, and bound hand and foot, we shall depart into the fire of hell, after being full well worn down by the cares of riches.

Considering then all these things, let us loose the bands of such deceit, that we may not at all fall into those things which deliver us over to the unquenchable fire. For he that is a slave to money, the chains both here and there will have him continually liable to them; but he that is rid of this desire will attain to freedom from both. Unto which that we also may attain, let us break in pieces the grievous yoke of avarice, and make ourselves wings toward Heaven; by the grace and love towards man of our Lord Jesus Christ, to whom be glory and might forever and ever. Amen.

HOMILY XIII

MATT. IV. 1

"Then was Jesus led up of the Spirit into the wilderness, to be tempted of the devil."

Then. When? After the descent of the Spirit, after the voice that was borne from above, and said, "This is My Beloved Son, in whom I am well pleased." And what was marvellous, it was of the Holy Spirit; for this, he here saith, led Him up. For since with a view to our instruction He both did and underwent all things; He endures also to be led up thither, and to wrestle against the devil: in order that each of those who are baptized, if after his baptism he have to endure greater temptations may not be troubled as if the result were unexpected, but may continue to endure all nobly, as though it were happening in the natural course of things.

Yea, for therefore thou didst take up arms, not to be idle, but to fight. For this cause neither doth God hinder the temptations as they come on, first to teach thee that thou art become much stronger; next, that thou mayest continue modest neither be exalted even by the greatness of thy gifts, the temptations having power to repress thee; moreover, in order that that wicked demon, who is for a while doubtful about thy desertion of him, by the touchstone of temptations may be well assured that thou hast utterly forsaken and fallen from him; fourthly, that thou mayest in this way be made stronger, and better tempered than any steel; fifthly, that thou mayest obtain a clear demonstration of the treasures entrusted to thee.

For the devil would not have assailed thee, unless he had seen thee brought to greater honor. Hence, for example, from the beginning, he attacked Adam, because he saw him in the enjoyment of great dignity. For this reason he arrayed himself against Job, because he saw him crowned and proclaimed by the God of all.

How then saith He, "Pray that ye enter not into temptation." For this cause he doth not show thee Jesus simply going up, but "led up" according to the principle of the Economy; signifying obscurely by this, that we ought not of ourselves to leap upon it, but being dragged thereto, to stand manfully.

And see whither the Spirit led Him up, when He had taken Him; not into a city and forum, but into a wilderness. That is, He being minded to attract the devil, gives him a handle not only by His hunger, but also by the place. For then most especially doth the devil assail, when he sees men left alone, and by themselves. Thus did he also set upon the woman in the beginning, having caught her alone, and found her apart from her husband. Just as when he sees us with others and banded together, he is not equally confident, and makes no attack. Wherefore we have the greatest need on this very account to be flocking together continually, that we may not be open to the devil's attacks.

2. Having then found Him in the wilderness, and in a pathless wilderness (for that the wilderness was such, Mark hath declared, saying, that He "was with the wild beasts"), behold with how much craft he draws near, and wickedness; and for what sort of opportunity he watches. For not in his fast, but in his hunger he approaches Him; to instruct thee how great a good fasting is, and how it is a most powerful shield against the devil, and that after the font, men should give themselves up, not to luxury and drunkenness, and a full table, but to fasting. For, for this cause even He fasted, not as needing it Himself, but to instruct us. Thus, since our sins before the font were brought in by serving the belly: much as if any one who had made a sick man whole were to forbid his doing those things, from which the distemper arose; so we see here likewise that He Himself after the font brought in fasting. For indeed both Adam by the incontinence of the belly was cast out of paradise; and the flood in Noah's time, this produced; and this brought down the thunders on Sodom. For although there was also a charge of whoredom, nevertheless from this grew the root of each of those punishments; which Ezekiel also signified when he said, "But this was the iniquity of Sodom, that she waxed wanton in pride and in fullness of bread, and in abundance of luxury." Thus the Jews also per petrated the greatest wickedness, being driven upon transgression by their drunkenness and delicacy.

On this account then even He too fasts forty days, pointing out to us the medicines of our salvation; yet proceeds no further, lest on the other hand, through the exceeding greatness of the miracle the truth of His Economy should be discredited. For as it is, this cannot be, seeing that both Moses and Elias, anticipating Him, could advance to so great a length of time, strengthened by the power of God. And if He had proceeded farther, from this among other things His assumption of our flesh would have seemed incredible to many.

Having then fasted forty days and as many nights,

"He was afterwards an hungered; " affording him a point to lay hold of and approach, that by actual conflict He might show how to prevail and be victorious. Just so do wrestlers also: when teaching their pupils how to prevail and overcome, they voluntarily in the lists engage with others, to afford these in the persons of their antagonists the means of seeing and learning the mode of conquest. Which same thing then also took place. For it being His will to draw him on so far, He both made His hunger known to him, and awaited his approach, and as He waited for him, so He dashed him to earth, once, twice, and three times, with such ease as became Him.

3. But that we may not, by hurrying over these victories, mar your profit, let us begin from the first assault, and examine each with exact care.

Thus, after He was an hungered, it is said, "The tempter came, and said unto Him, If Thou be Son of God, command that these stones be made bread."

For, because he had heard a voice borne from above, and saying, "This is My beloved Son;" and had heard also John bearing so large witness concerning Him, and after that saw Him an hungered; he was thenceforth in perplexity, and neither could believe that He was a mere man, because of the things spoken concerning Him; nor on the other hand receive it that He was Son of God, seeing Him as he did in hunger. Whence being in perplexity he utters ambiguous sounds. And much as when coming to Adam at the beginning, he feigns things that are not, that he may learn the things that are; even so here also, not knowing clearly the unutterable mystery of the Economy, and who He may be that is come, he attempts to weave other nets, whereby he thought to know that which was hidden and obscure. And what saith he? "If Thou be Son of God, command that these stones be made bread." He said not, because thou art an hungered, but, "if Thou be Son of God;" thinking to cheat Him with his compliments. Wherefore also he was silent touching the hunger, that he might not seem to be alleging it, and upbraiding Him. For not knowing the greatness of the Economy which was going on, he supposed this to be a reproach to Him. Wherefore flattering Him craftily, he makes mention of His dignity only.

What then saith Christ? To put down his pride, and to signify that there was nothing shameful in what had happened, nor unbecoming His wisdom; that which the other had passed over in silence to flatter Him, He brings forward and sets it forth, saying, "Man shall not live by bread alone."

So that He begins with the necessity of the belly. But mark, I pray thee, the craft of that wicked demon, and whence he begins his wrestlings, and how he doth not forget his proper art. For by what means he cast out also the first man, and encompassed him with thousands of other evils, with the same means here likewise he weaves his deceit; I mean, with incontinence of the belly. So too even now one may hear many foolish ones say their bad words by thousands because of the belly. But Christ, to show that the virtuous man is not compelled even by this tyranny to do anything that is unseemly, first hungers, then submits not to what is enjoined Him; teaching us to obey the devil in nothing. Thus, because the first man did hereby both offend God, and transgress the law, as much and more doth He teach thee:—though it be no transgression which he commands, not even so to obey.

And why say I, "transgression"? "Why, even though something expedient be suggested by the devils, do not thou," saith He, "even so give heed unto them." Thus, for instance, He stopped the mouths of those devils also, proclaiming Him Son of God. And Paul too again rebuked them, crying this selfsame thing; and yet what they said was profitable; but he more abundantly dishonoring them, and obstructing their plot against us, drove them away even when doctrines of salvation were preached by them, closing up their mouths, and bidding them be silent.

And therefore neither in this instance did He consent to what was said. But what saith He? "Man shall not live by bread alone." Now His meaning is like this: "God is able even by a word to nourish the hungry man;" bringing him a testimony out of the ancient Scripture, and teaching us, though we hunger, yea, whatever we suffer, never to fall away from our Lord.

But if a man say, "still He should have displayed Himself;" I would ask him, with what intent, and for what reason? For not at all that he might believe did the other so speak, but that he might, as he thought, over-argue Him into unbelief. Since the first of mankind were in this way beguiled and over-argued by him, not putting earnest faith in God. For the contrary of what God had said he promised them, and puffed them up with vain hopes, and brought them to unbelief, and so cast them out of the blessings they actually possessed. But Christ signifies Himself not to have consented, either to him then or afterwards to the Jews his partisans, in their demand of signs: invariably instructing us, whatever we may have power to do, yet to do nothing vainly and at random; nor even when want urges to obey the devil.

4. What then doth this accursed one? Overcome, and unable to persuade Him to do his bidding, and that when pressed by such violent hunger, he proceeds to another thing, saying,

"If Thou be Son of God, cast Thyself down; for it is written, He shall give His angels charge concerning Thee, and in their hands they shall bear Thee up."

What can the reason be, that at each temptation He adds this, "If Thou be Son of God?" Much the same as he did in that former case, he doth also at this time. That is, as he then slandered God, saying, "In the day ye eat, your eyes shall be opened;" thereby intending to signify, that they were beguiled and overreached, and had received no benefit; even so in this case also he insinuates this same thing, saying, "in vain God hath called Thee Son, and hath beguiled Thee by His gift; for, if this be not so, afford us some clear proof that Thou art of that power." Then, because Christ had reasoned with him from Scripture, he also brings in a testimony of the prophet.

How then doth Christ? He is not indignant, nor provoked, but with that extreme gentleness He reasons with him again from the Scriptures, saying, "Thou shalt not tempt the Lord thy God:" teaching us that we must overcome the devil, not by miracles, but by forbearance and long-suffering, and that we should do nothing at all for display and vainglory.

But mark thou his folly, even by the very testimony which he produced. For while the testimonies cited by the Lord were both of them spoken with exceeding fitness: his, on the other hand, were chance and random sayings, neither did he bring forward on his part that which applied to the matter in hand. For that it is written, "He shall give His angels charge concerning Thee," this surely is not advice to dash and toss one's self down headlong; and moreover, this was not so much as spoken concerning the Lord. However, this for the time He did not expose, although there was both insult in his manner of speech, and great inconsistency. For of God's Son no man requires these things: but to cast one's self down is the part of the devil, and of demons. Whereas God's part is to raise up even them that are down. And if He ought to have displayed His own power, it would not have been by casting and tossing Himself down at random, but by saving others. But to cast ourselves down precipices, and into pits, pertains properly to his troop. Thus, for example, the juggler among them doth everywhere.

But Christ, even when these things are said, doth not yet reveal Himself, but as man for a while discourses with him. For the sayings, "Man shall not live by bread alone;" and, "Thou shalt not tempt the Lord thy God," suited one not greatly revealing Himself, but representing Himself as one of the many.

But marvel thou not, if he in reasoning with Christ oftentimes turn himself about. For as pugilists, when they have received deadly blows, reel about, drenched in much blood, and blinded; even so he too, darkened by the first and the second blow, speaks at random what comes uppermost: and proceeds to his third assault.

5. "And he leadeth Him up into a high mountain, and showeth Him all the kingdoms, and saith, All these things will I give Thee, if Thou wilt fall down and worship me. Then saith He, Get thee behind me, Satan, for it is written, Thou shalt worship the Lord thy God, and Him only shalt thou serve."

For since he was now come to sinning against the Father, saying, that all that is the Father's was his, and was endeavoring to make himself out to be God, as artificer of the universe; He then rebuked him: but not even then with vehemence, but simply, "Get thee hence, Satan;" which itself had in it something of command rather than of rebuke. For as soon as He had said to him, "Get thee hence," He caused him to take to flight; since he brought not against Him any other temptations.

And how saith Luke, that "he ended all temptation." To me it seems that in mentioning the chief of the temptations, he had spoken of all, as though the rest too were included in these. For the things that form the substance of innumerable evils are these: to be a slave to the belly, to do anything for vainglory, to be in subjection to the madness of riches. Which accordingly that accursed one considering, set last the most powerful of all, I mean the desire of more: and though originally, and from the beginning, he was travailing to come to this, yet he kept it for the last, as being of more force than the rest. For in fact this is the manner of his wrestling, to apply those things last, which seem more likely to overthrow. And this sort of thing he did with respect to Job likewise. Wherefore in this instance too, having begun with the motives which seem to be viler and weaker, he goes on to the more prevailing.

How then are we to get the better of him? In the way which Christ that taught us, by fleeing to God for refuge; and neither to be depressed in famine, as believing in God who is able to feed even with a word; nor amidst whatever good things we may receive to tempt Him who gave them, but to be content with the glory which is from above, making no account of that which is of men, and on every occasion to despise what is beyond our need. For nothing doth so make us fall under the power of the devil, as longing for more, and loving covetousness. And this we may see even by what is done now. For now also there are those who say, "All these things will we give thee, if thou wilt fall down and worship;" who are indeed men by nature, but have become his instruments. Since at that time too he approached Him, not by himself only, but also by others. Which Luke also was declaring, when he said, that "he departed from Him for a season;" showing that hereafter he approached Him by his proper instruments.

"And, behold, angels came and ministered unto Him." For when the assault was going on, He suffered them not to appear, that He might not thereby drive away the prey; but after He had convicted him in all points, and caused him to take to flight, then they appear: that thou also mayest learn, that after thy victories which are copied from His, angels will receive thee also, applauding thee, and waiting as guards on thee in all things. Thus, for example, angels take Lazarus away with them, after the furnace of poverty and of famine and of all distress. For as I have already said, Christ on this occasion exhibits many things, which we ourselves are to enjoy.

6. Forasmuch then as all these things have been done for thee, do thou emulate and imitate His victory. And should any one approach thee of those who are that evil spirit's servants, and savor the things that be of him, upbraiding thee and saying, "If thou art marvellous and great, remove the mountain;" be not troubled, nor confounded, but answer with meekness, and say some such thing as thou hast heard thy Lord say: "Thou shalt not tempt the Lord thy God."

Or should he, offering glory and dominion, and an endless amount of wealth, enjoin thee to worship him, do thou stand again manfully. For neither did the devil deal so with the common Lord of us all only, but every day also he brings these his machinations to bear on each of His servants, not in mountains only and in wildernesses, nor by himself: but in cities likewise, in marketplaces, and in courts of justice, and by means of our own kindred, even men. What then must we do? Disbelieve him altogether, and stop our ears against him, and hate him when he flatters, and when he proffers more, then so much the more shun him. Because in Eve's case also, when he was most lifting her up with hopes, then he cast her down, and did her the greatest evils. Yea, for he is an implacable enemy, and hath taken up against us such war as excludes all treaty. And we are not so earnest for our own salvation, as he is for our ruin. Let us then shun him, not with words only, but also with works; not in mind only, but also in deed; and let us do none of the things which he approves, for so shall we do all those which God approves. Yea, for he makes also many promises, not that he may give, but that he may take. He promises by rapine, that he may deprive us of the kingdom, and of righteousness; and sets treasures in the earth as a kind of gins or traps, that he may deprive us both of these and of the treasures in Heaven, and he would have us be rich here, that we may not be rich there.

And if he should not be able by wealth to cast us out of our portion there, he comes another way, the way of poverty; as he did with respect to Job. That is, when he saw that wealth did him no harm, he weaves his toils by poverty, expecting on that side to get the better of him. But what could be more foolish than this? Since he that hath been able to bear wealth with moderation, much more will he bear poverty with manliness; and he who desires not riches when present, neither will he seek them when absent; even as that blessed man did not, but by his poverty, on the other hand, he became still more glorious. For of his possessions that wicked demon had power indeed to deprive him, but his love toward God he not only could not take away, but made it even stronger, and when he had stripped him of all, he caused him to abound with more blessings; wherefore also he was in perplexity. For the more plagues he brought upon him, the more mighty he then saw him become. And therefore, as you know, when he had gone through all, and had thoroughly tried his metal, because he made no way, he ran to his old weapon, the woman, and assumes a mask of concern, and makes a tragical picture of his calamities in most pitiable tone, and feigns that for removal of his evil he is introducing that deadly counsel. But neither so did he prevail; nay, for his bait was perceived by that wondrous man, who with much wisdom stopped the mouth of the woman speaking at his instigation.

Just so we likewise must act: though it be a brother, a tried friend, a wife, whom you will of those nearest to us, whom he hath entered into, and so utters something not convenient, we must not receive the counsel for the person of him who so speaks, but for the deadly counsel turn away from the speaker. Since in fact now also he doth many such things, and puts before him a mask of sympathy, and while he seems to be friendly, he is instilling his pernicious words, more grievous than poisons. Thus, as to flatter for evil is his part, so to chastise for our good, is God's.

7. Let us not then be deceived, neither let us by every mean seek after the life of ease. For "whom the Lord loveth," it is said, "He chasteneth." Wherefore when we enjoy prosperity, living in wickedness, then most of all should we grieve. For we ought ever to be afraid while we sin, but especially when we suffer no ill. For when God exacts our penalties by little and little, he makes our payment for these things easy to us; but when he is long-suffering for each of our negligences, He is storing us up, if we continue in such things, unto a great punishment. Since, if for the well-doers affliction be a necessary thing, much more for them that sin.

See for instance how much long-suffering Pharaoh met with, and afterwards underwent for all most extreme punishment: in how many things Nebuchadnezzar offended, yet at the end expiated all; and the rich man, because he had suffered no great ill here, for this very cause chiefly became miserable, for that having lived in luxury in the present life, he departed to pay the penalty of all these things there, where he could not obtain anything at all to soothe his calamity.

Yet for all this some are so cold and senseless, as to be always seeking only the things that are here, and uttering those absurd sayings, "Let me enjoy all things present for a time, and then I will consider about things out of sight: I will gratify my belly, I will be a slave to pleasures, I will make full use of the present life; give me to-day, and take tomorrow." Oh excess of folly! Why, wherein do they who talk so differ from goats and swine? For if the prophet permits not them to be accounted men, that "neigh after their neighbors wife," who shall blame us for esteeming these to be goats and swine, and more insensible than asses, by whom those things are held uncertain, which are more evident than what we see? Why, if thou believest nothing else, attend to the devils in their scourging, to them who had our hurt for their object in all their practice, both in word and deed. For thou wilt not, I am sure, contradict this, that they do all to increase our security, and to do away with the fear of hell, and to breed disbelief of the tribunals in that world. Nevertheless, they that are so minded, by cryings and wailings do oftentimes proclaim the torments that are there. Whence is it then that they so speak, and utter things contrary to their own will? From no other cause, but because they are under the pressure of stronger compulsion. For they would have not been minded of their own accord to confess either that they are tormented by dead men, or that they at all suffer anything dreadful.

Wherefore now have I said this? Because evil demons confess hell, who would fain have hell disbelieved; but thou who enjoyest honor so great, and hast been a partaker in unutterable mysteries, dost not so much as imitate them, but art become more hardened even than they.

8. "But who," one will say, "hath come from those in hell, and hath declared these things?" Why, who hath arrived here from heaven, and told us that there is a God who created all things? And whence is it clear that we have a soul? For plainly, if thou art to believe the things only that are in sight, both God and angels, and mind and soul, will be matter of doubting to thee, and in this way thou wilt find all the doctrines of the truth gone.

Yet surely, if thou art willing to believe what is evident, the things invisible ought to be believed by thee, rather than those which are seen. Even though what I say be a paradox, nevertheless it is true, and among men of understanding is fully acknowledged. For whereas the eyes are often deceived, not in the things unseen only (for of those they do not so much as take cognizance), but even in those which men think they actually see, distance and atmosphere, and absence of mind, and anger, and care, and ten thousand other things impeding their accuracy; the reasoning power of the soul on the other hand, if it receive the light of the divine Scriptures, will prove a more accurate, an unerring standard of realities.

Let us not then vainly deceive ourselves, neither in addition to the carelessness of our life, which is the offspring of such doctrines as these, heap up to ourselves, for the very doctrines themselves, a more grievous fire. For if there be no judgment, and we are not to give account of our deeds, neither shall we receive rewards for our labors. Observe which way your blasphemies tend, when ye say, that God, who is righteous, and loving, and mild, overlooks so great labors and toils. And how can this be reasonable? Why, if by nothing else, at any rate by the circumstances of thine own house, I bid thee weigh these things, and then thou wilt see the absurdity. For though thou wert thyself savage and inhuman beyond measure, and wilder than the very wild beasts, thou wouldest not choose at thy death to leave unhonored the servant that had been affectionate to thee, but requitest him both with freedom, and with a gift of money; and forasmuch as in thine own person hereafter, having departed, thou wilt be able to do him no good, thou givest charge concerning him to the future inheritors of thy substance, beseeching, exhorting, doing everything, so that he may not remain unrewarded.

So then thou, who art evil, art so kind and loving towards thy servant; and will the Infinite Goodness, that is, God, the Unspeakable Love to man, the kindness so vast: will He overlook and leave uncrowned His own servants, Peter and Paul, and James, and John, those who every day for His sake suffered hunger, were bound, were scourged, were drowned in the sea, were given up to wild beasts, were dying, were suffering so great things as we cannot so much as reckon up? And whereas the Olympic judge proclaims and crowns the victor, and the master rewards the servant, and the king the soldier, and each in general him that hath done him service, with what good things he can; shall God alone, after those so great toils and labors, repay them with no good thing great or small? shall those just and pious men, who have walked in every virtue, lie in the same state with adulterers, and parricides, and manslayers, and violators of tombs? And in what way can this be reasonable? Since, if there be nothing after our departure hence, and our interests reach no further than things present, those are in the same case with these, or rather not so much as in the same. For what though hereafter, as thou sayest, they fare alike? yet here, the whole of their time, the wicked have been at ease, the righteous in chastisement. And this what sort of tyrant, what savage and relentless man did ever so devise, touching his own servants and subjects?

Didst thou mark the exceeding greatness of the absurdity, and in what this argument issues? Therefore if thou wilt not any other way, yet by these reasonings be instructed to rid thyself of this wicked thought, and to flee from vice, and cleave to the toils which end in virtue: and then shalt thou know certainly that our concerns are not bounded by the present life. And if any one ask thee, "Who hath come from thence and brought word what is there?" say unto him, "of men not one; for surely he would have been often disbelieved, as vaunting, and exaggerating the thing; but the Lord of the angels hath brought word with exactness of all those things. What need then have we of any man, seeing He, that will demand account of us, crieth aloud every day, that He hath both made ready a hell, and prepared a kingdom; and affords us clear demonstrations of these things? For if He were not hereafter to judge, neither would he have exacted any penalty here.

9. "Well, but as to this very point how can it be reasonable? that of the wicked some should be punished, others not? I mean, if God be no respecter of persons, as surely He is not, why can it be that of one He exacts a penalty, but another He suffers to go away unpunished? Why, this is again more inexplicable than the former."

Yet if you are willing to hear what we say with candor, we will solve this difficulty also.

What then is the solution? He neither exacts penalty of all here, lest thou shouldest despair of the resurrection, and lose all expectation of the judgment, as though all were to give account here; nor doth He suffer all to go away unpunished, lest on the other hand thou shouldest account all to be without His providence; but He both punishes and abstains from punishing: by those whom He punishes, signifying that in that world also He will exact a penalty of such as are unpunished here; and by those whom He doth not punish, working upon thee to believe that there is some fearful trial after our departure hence.

But if He were altogether indifferent about our former deeds, He neither would have punished any here, nor have conferred benefits. But now thou seest Him for thy sake stretching out the heaven, kindling the sun, founding the earth, pouring forth the sea, expanding the air, and appointing for the moon her courses, setting unchangeable laws for the seasons of the years, and all other things too performing their own courses exactly at a sign from Him. For both our nature, and that of creatures irrational, of them that creep, that walk, that fly, that swim, in marshes, in springs, in rivers, in mountains, in forests, in houses, in the air, in plains; plants also, and seeds, and trees, both wild and cultivated, both fruitful and unfruitful; and all things in general, moved by that unwearied Hand, make provision for our life, affording to us of themselves their ministry, not for our need only, but also for our feeling of high station.

Seeing therefore order so great and fair (and yet we have not mentioned so much as the least portion thereof), darest thou say, that He who for thy sake hath wrought things so many and great will overlook thee in the most critical points, and suffer thee when dead to lie with the asses and swine: and that having honored thee with so great a gift, that of godliness, whereby He hath even equaled thee with the angels, He will overlook thee after thy countless labors and toils?

And how can this be reasonable? Why, these things, if we be silent "the stones will immediately cry out;" so plain are they, and manifest, and more lucid than the sunbeam itself.

Having then considered all these things, and having convinced our own soul, that after our departure hence, we shall both stand at the fearful judgment-seat, and give account of all that we have done, and shall bear our penalty, and submit to our sentence, if we continue in our negligences; and shall receive crowns and unutterable blessings, if we are willing to give a little heed to ourselves; let us both stop the mouths of them who gainsay these things, and ourselves choose the way of virtue; that with due confidence departing to that tribunal, we may attain unto the good things that are promised us, by the grace and love towards man of our Lord Jesus Christ, to whom be glory and dominion, now and ever, world without end. Amen.

HOMILY XIV

MATT. IV. 12

"Now when Jesus had heard that John was delivered up, He departed into Galilee."

1. Wherefore doth He depart? Again instructing us not to go to meet temptations, but to give place and withdraw ourselves. For it is no reproach, the not casting one's self into danger, but the failing to stand manfully when fallen into it. To teach us this accordingly, and to soothe the envy of the Jews, He retires to Capernaum; at once fulfilling the prophecy, and making haste to catch the teachers of the world: for they, as you know, were abiding there, following their craft.

But mark, I pray thee, how in every case when He is about to depart unto the Gentiles, He hath the occasion given Him by Jews. For so in this instance, by plotting against His forerunner, and casting him into prison, they thrust out Christ into the Galilee of the Gentiles. For to show that He neither speaks of the Jewish nation by a part of it, nor signifies obscurely all the tribes; mark how the Prophet distinguishes that place, saying "The land of Nephthalim, by the way of the sea, beyond Jordan, Galilee of the Gentiles, the people which sat in darkness, saw great light:" by darkness here not meaning that which is sensible, but men's errors and ungodliness. Wherefore he also added, "They which sat in the region and shadow of death, to them light is sprung up." For that thou mightest learn that neither the light nor the darkness which he speaks of are sensible, in discoursing of the light, he called it not merely light, but "a great light" which elsewhere he expresses by the word, True: and in describing the darkness, he termed it, "a shadow of death."

Then implying that they did not of themselves seek and find, but that God showed Himself to them from above, he saith to them, "Light is sprung up;" that is, the light of itself sprang up and shone forth: it was not that they first ran to the light. For in truth the condition of men was at the worst before Christ's coming. Since they more than "walked in darkness;" they "sat in darkness;" a kind of sign that they did not even hope to be delivered. For as persons not even knowing where to put a step forward, so they sat, overtaken by the darkness, not being able so much as to stand any more.

2. "From that time Jesus began to preach and to say, Repent; for the kingdom of heaven is at hand."

"From that time:" what time? After John was cast into prison. And wherefore did He not preach to them from the beginning? Indeed what occasion for John at all, when the witness of His works was proclaiming Him?

That hence also thou mightest learn His dignity; namely, that as the Fathers, so He too hath prophets; to which purpose Zacharias also spake; "And thou, child, shalt be called a prophet of the Highest." And that he might leave no occasion to the shameless Jews; which motive He himself alleged, saying, "John came neither eating nor drinking, and they say, he hath a devil. The Son of Man came eating and drinking, and they say, Behold a man gluttonous and a winebibber, a friend of publicans and sinners. But wisdom is justified of her children."

And moreover it was necessary that what concerned Him should be spoken by another first and not by Himself. For if even after both testimonies and demonstrations so many and so great, they said, "Thou bearest record of Thyself, Thy record is not true:" had He, without John's saying anything, come into the midst, and first borne record Himself; what would they not have said? For this cause, neither did He preach before John, nor did He work miracles, until John was cast into prison; lest in this way the multitude should be divided. Therefore also John did no miracle at all; that by this means also might give over the multitude to Jesus, His miracles drawing them unto Him.

Again, if even after so many divine precautions, John's disciples, both before and after his imprisonment, were jealously disposed towards Him, and the people too suspected not Him but John to be the Christ; what would not the result have been, had none of these things taken place? For this cause both Matthew distinctly notes, that "from that time He began to preach;" and when He began His preaching, He Himself also taught this same doctrine, which the other used to preach; and no word as yet concerning Himself doth the doctrine which he preached say. Because it was for the time a great thing even for this to be received, forasmuch as they had not as yet the proper opinion about Him. Therefore also at the beginning He puts nothing severe or grievous, as the other did, mentioning an axe, and a tree cut down; a fan, and a threshing-floor, and unquenchable fire; but His preludes are gracious: the Heavens and the kingdom there are the good tidings which he declares to His hearers.

3. "And walking by the sea of Galilee, He saw two brethren, Simon that was surnamed Peter, and Andrew his brother, casting a net into the sea; for they were fishers. And He saith unto them, Come ye after me, and I will make you fishers of men. And they left their nets, and followed Him."

And yet John saith that they were called in another manner. Whence it is evident that this was a second call; and from many things one may perceive this. For there it is said, that they came to Him when "John was not yet cast into prison;" but here, after he was in confinement. And there Andrew calls Peter, but here Jesus calls both. And John saith, Jesus seeing Simon coming, saith, "Thou art Simon, the Son of Jona, thou shalt be called Cephas, which is by interpretation, a stone." But Matthew saith that he was already called by that name; for his words are, "Seeing Simon that was called Peter." And from the place whence they were called, and from many other things, one may perceive this; and from their ready obedience, and abandonment of all. For now they were well instructed beforehand. Thus, in the other case, Andrew is seen coming into His house, and hearing many things; but here, having heard one bare word, they followed immediately. Since neither was it unnatural for them to follow Him at the beginning, and then leave Him again and return anew to their own craft, when they saw both John thrown into prison, and Himself departing. Accordingly you see that He finds them actually fishing. But He neither forbad them at the first when minded to withdraw, nor having withdrawn themselves, did He let them go altogether; but He gave way when they started aside from Him, and comes again to win them back; which kind of thing is the great point in fishing.

But mark both their faith, and their obedience. For though they were in the midst of their work (and ye know how greedy a thing fishing is), when they heard His command, they delayed not, they procrastinated not, they said not, "let us return home, and converse with our kinsfolk," but "they forsook all and followed," even as Elisha did to Elijah." Because such is the obedience which Christ seeks of us, as that we delay not even a moment of time, though something absolutely most needful should vehemently press on us. Wherefore also when some other had come unto Him, and was asking leave to bury his own father, not even this did He permit him to do; to signify that before all we ought to esteem the following of Himself.

But if thou should say, "the promise is very great;" even for this do I most admire them, for that when they had not as yet seen any sign, they believed in so great a reach of promise, and accounted all but second to that attendance. And this, because they believed that by what words they were caught, by the same they would be able to catch others also.

To these, then, such was His promise: but to James and John He saith no such thing. For the obedience of those that had gone before had by this time paved the way for these. And besides they had also heard many things before concerning Him.

And see how he doth with exact care intimate unto us their poverty also: in that He found them sewing up their nets. So exceeding great was their poverty, that they were mending what was worn out, not being able to buy others. And this too was for the time no small proof of virtue, their beating poverty with ease, their supporting themselves by honest labor, their being bound one to another by the power of love, their having their father with them, and attending upon them.

4. When therefore He had caught them, then He begins in their presence to work miracles, by His deeds confirming the words of John concerning Him. And He was continually frequenting their synagogues, even by this instructing them that He was not a sort of adversary of God and deceiver, but that He was come in accordance with the Father.

And while frequenting them, He did not preach only, but also showed forth miracles. And this, because on every occasion, whensoever anything is done strange and surprising, and any polity is introduced, God is wont to work miracles as pledges of his power, which He affords to them that are to receive His laws. Thus, for instance, when He was about to make man, He created a whole world, and then gave him that law which he had in Paradise. And when He was to give laws to Noah, He showed forth anew great miracles, in that He reduced again the whole creation to its elements, and made that fearful sea to prevail for a full year; and in that, amid so great a tempest, He preserved that righteous man. And in the time of Abraham too He vouchsafed many signs; as his victory in the war, the plague upon Pharaoh, his deliverance from dangers. And when about to legislate for the Jews, He showed forth those marvellous and great prodigies, and then gave the law. Just so in this case also, being to introduce a certain high polity, and to tell them what they had never heard, by the display of the miracles He confirms what He saith.

Thus because the kingdom He was preach ing appeared not, by the things that appear, He makes it, though invisible, manifest.

And mark the evangelist's care to avoid superfluity of words; how he tells us not of every one of them that are healed, but in a few words speeds over showers of miracles.

For "they brought unto Him," saith he, "all that were sick with divers diseases, and torments, and those which were possessed with devils, and those which were lunatic, and those that had the palsy, and He healed them."

But our inquiry is this; why it can have been that He demanded faith of none of them? For He said not, what we find Him saying after this, "Believe ye that I am able to do this?" because He had not as yet given proof of His power. And besides, the very act of approaching Him, and of bringing others to Him, exhibited no common faith. For they brought them even from far; whereas they would never have brought them, unless they had persuaded themselves of great things concerning Him.

Now then, let us too follow Him; for we also have many diseases of our soul, and these especially He would fain heal. Since with this intent He corrects that other sort, that He may banish these out of our soul.

5. Let us therefore come unto Him, and let us ask nothing pertaining to this life, but rather remission of sins. For indeed He gives it even now, if we be in earnest. Since as then "His fame went out into Syria," so now into the whole world. And they indeed ran together on hearing that He healed persons possessed: and thou, after having much more and greater experience of His power, dost thou not rouse thyself and run?

But whereas they left both country, and friends, and kinsfolk; endurest thou not so much as to leave thy house for the sake of drawing near, and obtaining far greater things? Or rather we do not require of thee so much as this, but leave thy evil habits only, and thou canst easily be made whole, remaining at home with thy friends.

But as it is, if we have any bodily ailment, we do and contrive everything to be rid of what pains us; but when our soul is indisposed, we delay, and draw back. For which cause neither from the other sort are we delivered: since the things that are indispensable are becoming to us secondary, and the secondary indispensable; and letting alone the fountain of our ills, we would fain cleanse out the streams.

For that our bodily ills are caused by the wickedness of the soul, is shown both by him that had the palsy thirty and eight years, and by him that was let down through the roof, and by Cain also before these; and from many other things likewise one may perceive this. Let us do away then with the well-spring of our evils, and all the channels of our diseases will be stayed. For the disease is not palsy only, but also our sin; and this more than that, by how much a soul is better than a body.

Let us therefore now also draw nigh unto Him; let us entreat Him that He would brace our paralyzed soul, and leaving all things that pertain to this life, let us take account of the things spiritual only. Or if thou cleave unto these also, yet think of them after the other.

Neither must thou think lightly of it, because thou hast no pain in sinning; rather on this very account most of all do thou lament, that thou feelest not the anguish of thine offenses. For not because sin bites not, doth this come to pass, but because the offending soul is insensible. Regard with this view them that have a feeling of their own sins, how they wail more bitterly than such as are being cut, or burned; how many things they do, how many suffer, how greatly they mourn and lament, in order to be delivered from their evil conscience. They would not do any such thing, unless they were exceedingly pained in soul.

The best thing then is, to avoid sin in the first instance: the next to it, is to feel that we sin, and thoroughly amend ourselves. But if we have not this, how shall we pray to God, and ask forgiveness of our sins, we who take no account of these matters? For when thou thyself who hast offended art unwilling to know so much as this very fact, that thou hast sinned; for what manner of offenses will thou entreat God for pardon? For what thou knowest not? And how wilt thou know the greatness of the benefit? Tell therefore thine offenses in particular, that thou mayest learn for what thou receivest forgiveness, that so thou mayest become grateful towards thy Benefactor.

But thou, when it is a man whom thou hast provoked, entreatest friends, neighbors, and door-keepers, and spendest money, and consumest many days in visiting and petitioning, and though he that is provoked utterly reject thee once, twice, ten thousand times over, thou despondest not, but becoming more earnest thou makest the more entreaty; but when the God of all is provoked, we gape, and throw ourselves back, and live in luxury and in drunkenness, and do all things as usual. And when shall we be able to propitiate Him? and how shall we by this very thing fail to provoke Him so much the more? For not so much sinning, as signing without even pain, causes in Him indignation and wrath. Wherefore it were meet after all this to sink into the very earth, and not so much as to behold this sun, nor to breathe at all, for that having so placable a Master, we provoke Him first, and then have no remorse for provoking Him. And yet He assuredly, even when He is wroth, doeth not so as hating and turning away from us, but in order that in this way at least He may win us over to Himself. For if He continued after insult befriending thee, thou wouldest the more despise Him. Therefore in order that this may not be, He turns away for a little while, to have thee ever with Himself.

6. Let us now, I pray you, take courage at His love to man, and let us show forth an anxious repentance, before the day come on, which permits us not to profit thereby. For as yet all depends on us, but then He that judges hath alone control over the sentence. "Let us therefore come before His face with confession;" let us bewail, let us mourn. For if we should be able to prevail upon the Judge before the appointed day to forgive us our sins, then we need not so much as enter into the court; as on the other hand, if this be not done, He will hear us publicly in the presence of the world, and we shall no longer have any hope of pardon. For no one of those who have not done away with their sins here, when he hath departed thither shall be able to escape his account for them; but as they who are taken out of these earthly prisons are brought in their chains to the place of judgment, even so all souls, when they have gone away hence bound with the manifold chains of their sins, are led to the awful judgment-seat. For in truth our present life is nothing better than a prison. But as when we have entered into that apartment, we see all bound with chains; so now if we withdraw ourselves from outward show, and enter into each man's life, into each man's soul, we shall see it bound with chains more grievous than iron: and this most especially if thou enter into the souls of them that are rich. For the more men have about them, so much the more are they bound. As therefore with regard to the prisoner, when thou seest him with irons on his back, on his hands, and often on his feet too, thou dost therefore most of all account him miserable; so also as to the rich man, when thou seest him encompassed with innumerable affairs, let him not be therefore rich, but rather for these very things wretched, in thine account. For together with these bonds, he hath a cruel jailor too, the wicked love of riches; which suffers him not to pass out of this prison, but provides for him thousands of fetters, and

guards, and doors, and bolts; and when he hath cast him into the inner prison, persuades him even to feel pleasure in these bonds; that he may not find so much as any hope of deliverance from the evils which press on him.

And if in thought thou wert to lay open that man's soul, thou wouldest see it not bound only, but squalid, and filthy, and teeming with vermin. For no better than vermin are the pleasures of luxury, but even more abominable, and destroy the body more, together with the soul also; and upon the one and upon the other they bring ten thousand scourges of sickness.

On account then of all these things let us entreat the Redeemer of our souls, that He would both burst asunder our bands, and remove this our cruel jailor, and having set us free from the burden of those iron chains, He would make our spirits lighter than any wing. And as we entreat Him, so let us contribute our own part, earnestness, and consideration, and an excellent zeal. For thus we shall be able both in a short time to be freed from the evils which now oppress us, and to learn in what condition we were before, and to lay hold on the liberty which belongs to us; unto which God grant we may all attain, by the grace and love towards man of our Lord Jesus Christ, to whom be glory and power forever and ever. Amen.

HOMILY XV

MATT. V. 1, 2

"And Jesus seeing the multitudes went up into the mountain, and when He was set, His disciples came unto Him. And He opened His mouth, and taught them saying, Blessed," etc.

See how unambitious He was, and void of boasting: in that He did not lead people about with Him, but whereas, when healing was required, He had Himself gone about everywhere, visiting both towns and country places; now when the multitude is become very great, He sits in one spot: and that not in the midst of any city or forum, but on a mountain and in a wilderness; instructing us to do nothing for display, and to separate ourselves from the tumults of ordinary life, and this most especially, when we are to study wisdom, and to discourse of things needful to be done.

But when He had gone up into the mount, and "was set down, His disciples came unto Him." Seest thou their growth in virtue? and how in a moment they became better men? Since the multitude were but gazers on the miracles, but these from that hour desired also to hear some great and high thing. And indeed this it was set Him on His teaching, and made Him begin this discourse.

For it was not men's bodies only that He was healing, but He was also amending their souls; and again from the care of these He would pass to attendance on the other. Thus He at once varied the succor that He gave, and likewise mingled with the instruction afforded by His words, the manifestation of His glory from His works; and besides, He stopped the shameless mouths of the heretics, signifying by this His care of both parts of our being, that He Himself is the Maker of the whole creation. Therefore also on each nature He bestowed abundant providence, now amending the one, now the other.

And in this way He was then employed. For it is said, that "He opened His mouth, and taught them." And wherefore is the clause added, "He opened His mouth"? To inform thee that in His very silence He gave instruction, and not when He spoke only: but at one time by "opening His mouth," at another uttering His voice by the works which He did.

But when thou hearest that He taught them, do not think of Him as discoursing with His disciples only, but rather with all through them.

For since the multitude was such as a multitude ever is, and consisted moreover of such as creep on the ground, He withdraws the choir of His disciples, and makes His discourse unto them: in His conversation with them providing that the rest also, who were yet very far from the level of His sayings, might find His lesson of self-denial no longer grievous unto them. Of which indeed both Luke gave intimation, when he said, that He directed His words unto them: and Matthew too, clearly declaring the same, wrote, "His disciples came unto Him, and He taught them." For thus the others also were sure to be more eagerly attentive to Him, than they would have been, had He addressed Himself unto all.

2. Whence then doth He begin? and what kind of foundations of His new polity doth He lay for us?

Let us hearken with strict attention unto what is said. For though it was spoken unto them, it was written for the sake also of all men afterwards. And accordingly on this account, though He had His disciples in His mind in His public preaching, yet unto them He limits not His sayings, but applies all His words of blessing without restriction. Thus He said not, "Blessed are ye, if ye become poor," but "Blessed are the poor." And I may add that even if He had spoken of them, the advice would still be common to all. For so, when He saith, "Lo! I am with you always, even unto the end of the world," He is discoursing not with them only, but also, through them, with all the world. And in pronouncing them blessed, who are persecuted, and chased, and suffer all intolerable things; not for them only, but also for all who arrive at the same excellency, He weaves His crown.

However, that this may be yet plainer, and to inform thee that thou hast great interest in His sayings, and so indeed hath all mankind, if any choose to give heed; hear how He begins these wondrous words.

"Blessed are the poor in spirit; for theirs is the kingdom of Heaven."

What is meant by "the poor in spirit?" The humble and contrite in mind. For by "spirit" He hath here designated the soul, and the faculty of choice. That is, since many are humble not willingly, but compelled by stress of circumstances; letting these pass (for this were no matter of praise), He blesses them first, who by choice humble and contract themselves.

But why said he not, "the humble," but rather "the poor?" Because this is more than that. For He means here them who are awestruck, and tremble at the commandments of God. Whom also by His prophet Isaiah God earnestly accepting said, "To whom will I look, but to him who is meek and quiet, and trembleth at My words?" For indeed there are many kinds of humility: one is humble in his own measure, another with all excess of lowliness. It is this last lowliness of mind which that blessed prophet commends, picturing to us the temper that is not merely subdued, but utterly broken, when he saith, "The sacrifice for God is a contrite spirit, a contrite and an humble heart God will not despise." And the Three Children also offer this unto God as a great sacrifice, saying, "Nevertheless, in a contrite soul, and in a spirit of lowliness, may we be accepted." This Christ also now blesses.

3. For whereas the greatest of evils, and those which make havoc of the whole world, had their entering in from pride:—for both the devil, not being such before, did thus become a devil; as indeed Paul plainly declared, saying, "Lest being lifted up with pride, he fall into the condemnation of the devil:"—and the first man, too, puffed up by the devil with these hopes, was made an example of, and became mortal (for expecting to become a god, he lost even what he had; and God also upbraiding him with this, and mocking his folly, said, "Behold, Adam is become as one of us" ; and each one of those that came after did hereby wreck himself in impiety, fancying some equality with God:—since, I say, this was the stronghold of our evils, and the root and fountain of all wickedness, He, preparing a remedy suitable to the disease, laid this law first as a strong and safe foundation. For this being fixed as a base, the builder in security lays on it all the rest. But if this be taken away, though a man reach to the Heavens in his course of life, it is all easily undermined, and issues in a grievous end. Though fasting, prayer, almsgiving, temperance, any other good thing whatever, be gathered together in thee; without humility all fall away and perish.

It was this very thing that took place in the instance of the Pharisee. For even after he had arrived at the very summit, he "went down" with the loss of all, because he had not the mother of virtues: for as pride is the fountain of all wickedness, so is humility the principle of all self-command. Wherefore also He begins with this, pulling up boasting by the very root out of the soul of His hearers.

"And what," one may ask, "is this to His disciples, who were on every account humble? For in truth they had nothing to be proud of, being fishermen, poor, ignoble, and illiterate." Even though these things concerned not His disciples, yet surely they concerned such as were then present, and such as were hereafter to receive the disciples, lest they should on this account despise them. But it were truer to say that they did also concern His disciples. For even if not then, yet by and by they were sure to require this help, after their signs and wonders, and their honor from the world, and their confidence towards God. For neither wealth, nor power, nor royalty itself, had so much power to exalt men, as the things which they possessed in all fullness. And besides, it was natural that even before the signs they might be lifted up, at that very time when they saw the multitude, and all that audience surrounding their Master; they might feel some human weakness. Wherefore He at once represses their pride.

And He doth not introduce what He saith by way of advice or of commandments, but by way of blessing, so making His word less burthensome, and opening to all the course of His discipline. For He said not, "This or that person," but "they who do so, are all of them blessed." So that though thou be a slave, a beggar, in poverty, a stranger, unlearned, there is nothing to hinder thee from being blessed, if thou emulate this virtue.

4. Now having begun, as you see, where most need was, He proceeds to another commandment, one which seems to be opposed to the judgment of the whole world. For whereas all think that they who rejoice are enviable, those in dejection, poverty, and mourning, wretched, He calls these blessed rather than those; saying thus,

"Blessed are they that mourn."

Yet surely all men call them miserable. For therefore He wrought the miracles beforehand, that in such enactments as these He might be entitled to credit.

And here too again he designated not simply all that mourn, but all that do so for sins: since surely that other kind of mourning is forbidden, and that earnestly, which relates to anything of this life. This Paul also clearly declared, when he said, "The sorrow of the world worketh death, but godly sorrow worketh repentance unto salvation, not to be repented of."

These then He too Himself calls blessed, whose sorrow is of that kind; yet not simply them that sorrow did He designate, but them that sorrow intensely. Therefore He did not say, "they that sorrow," but "they that mourn." For this commandment again is fitted to teach us entire self-control. For if those who grieve for children, or wife, or any other relation gone from them, have no fondness for gain or pleasure during that period of their sorrow; if they aim not at glory, are not provoked by insults, nor led captive by envy, nor beset by any other passion, their grief alone wholly possessing them; much more will they who mourn for their own sins, as they ought to mourn, show forth a self-denial greater than this.

Next, what is the reward for these? "For they shall be comforted," saith He.

Where shall they be comforted! tell me. Both here and there. For since the thing enjoined was exceeding burthensome and galling, He promised to give that, which most of all made it light. Wherefore, if thou wilt be comforted, mourn: and think not this a dark saying. For when God doth comfort, though sorrows come upon thee by thousands like snow-flakes, thou wilt be above them all. Since in truth, as the returns which God gives are always far greater than our labors; so He hath wrought in this case, declaring them that mourn to be blessed, not after the value of what they do, but after His own love towards man. For they that mourn, mourn for misdoings, and to such it is enough to enjoy forgiveness, and obtain wherewith to answer for themselves. But forasmuch as He is full of love towards man, He doth not limit His recompense either to the removal of our punishments, or to the deliverance from our sins, but He makes them even blessed, and imparts to them abundant consolation.

But He bids us mourn, not only for our own, but also for other men's misdoings. And of this temper were the souls of the saints: such was that of Moses, of Paul, of David; yea, all these many times mourned for evils not their own.

5. "Blessed are the meek, for they shall inherit the earth." Tell me, what kind of earth? Some say a figurative earth, but it is not this, for nowhere in Scripture do we find any mention of an earth that is merely figurative. But what can the saying mean? He holds out a sensible prize; even as Paul also doth, in that when he had said, "Honor thy father and thy mother," he added, "For so shalt thou live long upon the earth." And He Himself unto the thief again, "Today shalt thou be with me in Paradise."

Thus He doth not incite us by means of the future blessings only, but of the present also, for the sake of the grosser sort of His hearers, and such as before the future seek those others.

Thus, for example, further on also He said, "Agree with thine adversary." Then He appoints the reward of such self-command, and saith, "Lest at any time the adversary deliver thee to the judge, and the judge to the officer." Seest thou whereby He alarmed us? By the things of sense, by what happens before our eyes. And again, "Whosoever shall say to his brother, Raca, shall be in danger of the council."

And Paul too sets forth sensible rewards at great length, and uses things present in his exhortations; as when he is discoursing about virginity. For having said nothing about the heavens there, for the time he urges it by things present, saying, "Because of the present distress," and, "But I spare you," and, "I would have you without carefulness."

Thus accordingly Christ also with the things spiritual hath mingled the sensible. For whereas the meek man is thought to lose all his own, He promises the contrary, saying, "Nay, but this is he who possesses his goods in safety, namely, he who is not rash, nor boastful: while that sort of man shall often lose his patrimony, and his very life."

And besides, since in the Old Testament the prophet used to say continually, "The meek shall inherit the earth;" He thus weaves into His discourse the words to which they were accustomed, so as not everywhere to speak a strange language.

And this He saith, not as limiting the rewards to things present, but as joining with these the other sort of gifts also. For neither in speaking of any spiritual thing doth He exclude such as are in the present life; nor again in promising such as are in our life, doth He limit his promise to that kind. For He saith, "Seek ye the kingdom of God, and all these things shall be added unto you." And again: "Whosoever hath left houses or brethren, shall receive an hundred fold in this world, and in the future shall inherit everlasting life."

6. "Blessed are they which do hunger and thirst after righteousness."

What sort of righteousness? He means either the whole of virtue, or that particular virtue which is opposed to covetousness. For since He is about to give commandment concerning mercy, to show how we must show mercy, as, for instance, not of rapine or covetousness, He blesses them that lay hold of righteousness.

And see with what exceeding force He puts it. For He said not, "Blessed are they which keep fast by righteousness," but, "Blessed are they which do hunger and thirst after righteousness:" that not merely anyhow, but with all desire we may pursue it. For since this is the most peculiar property of covetousness, and we are not so enamored of meat and drink, as of gaining, and compassing ourselves with more and more, He bade us to transfer this desire to a new object, freedom from covetousness.

Then He appoints the prize, again from things sensible; saying, "for they shall be filled." Thus, because it is thought that the rich are commonly made such by covetousness, "Nay," saith He, "it is just contrary: for it is righteousness that doeth this. Wherefore, so long as thou doest righteously, fear not poverty, nor tremble at hunger. For the extortioners, they are the very persons who lose all, even as he certainly who is in love with righteousness, possesses himself the goods of all men in safety."

But if they who covet not other men's goods enjoy so great abundance, much more they who give up their own.

"Blessed are the merciful."

Here He seems to me to speak not of those only who show mercy in giving of money, but those likewise who are merciful in their actions. For the way of showing mercy is manifold, and this commandment is broad. What then is the reward thereof? "For they shall obtain mercy."

And it seems indeed to be a sort of equal recompence, but it is a far greater thing than the act of goodness. For whereas they themselves show mercy as men, they obtain mercy from the God of all; and it is not the same thing, man's mercy, and God's; but as wide as is the interval between wickedness and goodness, so far is the one of these removed from the other.

"Blessed are the pure in heart, for they shall see God."

Behold again the reward is spiritual. Now He here calls "pure," either those who have attained unto all virtue, and are not conscious to themselves of any evil; or those who live in temperance. For there is nothing which we need so much in order to see God, as this last virtue. Wherefore Paul also said, "Follow peace with all men, and holiness, without which no man shall see the Lord." He is here speaking of such sight as it is possible for man to have.

For because there are many who show mercy, and who commit no rapine, nor are covetous, who yet are guilty of fornication and uncleanness; to signify that the former alone suffices not, He hath added this, much in the same sense as Paul, writing to the Corinthians, bore witness of the Macedonians, that they were rich not only in almsgiving, but also in all other virtue. For having spoken of the noble spirit they had shown in regard of their goods, he saith, "They gave also their own selves to the Lord, and to us."

7. "Blessed are the peace-makers."

Here He not only takes away altogether our own strife and hatred amongst ourselves, but He requires besides this something more, namely, that we should set at one again others, who are at strife.

And again, the reward which He annexes is spiritual. Of what kind then is it.

"For they shall be called the children of God."

Yea, for this became the work of the Only Begotten, to unite the divided, and to reconcile the alienated.

Then, lest thou shouldest imagine peace in all cases a blessing, He hath added,

"Blessed are they which are persecuted for righteousness' sake."

That is, for virtue's sake, for succor given to others, and for godliness: it being ever His wont to call by the name of "righteousness" the whole practical wisdom of the soul.

"Blessed are ye, when men shall revile you and persecute you, and say all manner of evil against you falsely, for my sake. Rejoice, and be exceeding glad."

As if He said, "Though they should call you sorcerers, deceivers, pestilent persons, or whatever else, blessed are ye:" so He speaks. What could be newer than these injunctions? wherein the very things which all others avoid, these He declares to be desirable; I mean, being poor, mourning, persecution, evil report. But yet He both affirmed this, and convinced not two, nor ten, nor twenty, nor an hundred, nor a thousand men, but the whole world. And hearing things so grievous and galling, so contrary to the accustomed ways of men, the multitudes "were astonished." So great was the power of Him who spake.

However, lest thou shouldest think that the mere fact of being evil spoken of makes men blessed, He hath set two limitations; when it is for His sake, and when the things that are said are false: for without these, he who is evil spoken of, so far from being blessed, is miserable.

Then see the prize again: "Because your reward is great in heaven." But thou, though thou hear not of a kingdom given in each one of the blessings, be not discouraged. For although He give different names to the rewards, yet He brings all into His kingdom. Thus, both when He saith, "they that mourn shall be comforted;" and, "they that show mercy shall obtain mercy;" and, "the pure in heart shall see God;" and, the peacemakers "shall be called the children of God;" nothing else but the Kingdom doth He shadow out by all these sayings. For such as enjoy these, shall surely attain unto that. Think not therefore that this reward is for the poor in spirit only, but for those also who hunger after righteousness, for the meek, and for all the rest without exception.

Since on this account He hath set His blessing on them all, that thou mightest not look for anything sensible: for that man cannot be blessed, who is crowned with such things as come to an end with this present life, and hurry by quicker than a shadow.

8. But when He had said, "your reward is great," he added also another consolation, saying, "For so persecuted they the prophets which were before you."

Thus, since that first, the promise of the Kingdom, was yet to come, and all in expectation, He affords them comfort from this world; from their fellowship with those who before them had been ill-treated.

For "think not," saith He, "that for something inconsistent in your sayings and enactments ye suffer these things: or, as being teachers of evil doctrines, ye are to be persecuted by them; the plots and dangers proceed not of any wickedness in your sayings, but of the malice of those who hear you. Wherefore neither are they any blame to you who suffer wrong, but to them who do the wrong. And to the truth of these things all preceding time bears witness. For against the prophets they did not even bring any charge of transgressing the law, and of sentiments of impiety, that they stoned some, chased away others, encompassed others with innumerable afflictions. Wherefore let not this trouble you, for of the very same mind they do all that is done now." Seest thou how He raised up their spirits, by placing them near to the company of Moses and Elias?

Thus also Paul writing to the Thessalonians, saith, "For ye became followers of the Churches of God, which are in Judea; for ye also have suffered the same things of your own fellow-countrymen, even as they have of the Jews: who both killed the Lord Jesus, and their own prophets, and have driven us out; and they please not God, and are contrary to all men." Which same point here also Christ hath established.

And whereas in the other beatitudes, He said, "Blessed are the poor," and "the merciful;" here He hath not put it generally, but addresses His speech unto themselves, saying, "Blessed are ye, when they shall revile you, and persecute you, and say every evil word:" signifying that this is an especial privilege of theirs; and that beyond all others, teachers have this for their own.

At the same time He here also covertly signifies His own dignity, and His equality in honor with Him who begat Him. For "as they on the Father's account," saith He, "so shall ye also for me suffer these things." But when He saith, "the prophets which were before you," He implies that they were also by this time become prophets.

Next, declaring that this above all profits them, and makes them glorious, He did not say, "they will calumniate and persecute you, but I will prevent it." For not in their escaping evil report, but in their noble endurance thereof, and in refuting them by their actions, He will have their safety stand: this being a much greater thing than the other; even as to be struck and not hurt, is much greater than escaping the blow.

9. Now in this place He saith, "Your reward is great in heaven." But Luke reports Him to have spoken this, both earnestly, and with more entire consolation; for He not only, as you know, pronounces them blessed, who are evil spoken of for God's sake, but declares them likewise wretched, who are well spoken of by all men. For, "Woe unto you," saith He, "when all men shall speak well of you." And yet the apostles were well spoken of, but not by all men. Wherefore He said not, "Woe unto you, when men shall speak well of you," but, "when all men" shall do so: for it is not even possible that those who live in the practice of virtue should be well spoken of by all men.

And again He saith, "When they shall cast out your name as evil, rejoice ye, and leap for joy." For not only of the dangers they underwent, but of the calumny also, He appoints the recompence to be great. Wherefore He said not, "When they shall persecute, and kill you," but, "When they shall revile you, and say all manner of evil." For most assuredly, men's evil reports have a sharper bite than their very deeds. For whereas, in our dangers, there are many things that lighten the toil, as to be cheered by all, to have many to applaud, to crown, to proclaim our praise; here in our reproach even this consolation is destroyed. Because we seem not to have achieved anything great; and this galls the combatant more than all his dangers: at least many have gone on even to hang themselves, not bearing evil report. And why marvellest thou at the others? since that traitor, that shameless and accursed one, he who had ceased to blush for anything whatever, was wrought upon by this chiefly to hurry to the halter. And Job again, all adamant as he was, and firmer than a rock; when he had been robbed of all his possessions, and was suffering those incurable ills, and had become on a sudden childless, and when he saw his body pouring out worms like a fountain, and his wife attacking him, he repelled it all with ease; but when he saw his friends reproaching and trampling upon him, and entertaining an evil opinion of him, and saying that he suffered those things for some sins, and was paying the penalty of wickedness: then was there trouble, then commotion, even in that great and noble-hearted man.

And David also, letting pass all that he had suffered, sought of God a retribution for the calumny alone. For, "Let him curse," saith he, "for the Lord hath bidden him: that the Lord may see my humiliation, and requite me for this cursing of his on this day."

And Paul too proclaims the triumph not of those only who incur danger, or are deprived of their goods, but of these also, thus saying, "Call to remembrance the former days, in which after ye were illuminated ye endured a great fight of afflictions; partly whilst ye were made a gazing stock by reproaches, and afflictions." On this account then Christ hath appointed the reward also to be great.

After this, lest any one should say, "Here thou givest no redress, nor stoppest men's mouths; and dost thou assign a reward there?" He hath put before us the prophets, to show that neither in their case did God give redress. And if, where the rewards were at hand, He cheered them with things to come; much more now, when this hope is become clearer, and self-denial is increased.

And observe too, after how many commandments He hath put this, for surely He did it not without reason, but to show that it is not possible for one unprovided, and unarmed with all those other virtues, to go forth unto these conflicts. Therefore, you see, in each instance, by the former precept making way for the following one, He hath woven a sort of golden chain for us. Thus, first, he that is "humble," will surely also "mourn" for his own sins: he that so "mourns," will be both "meek," and "righteous," and "merciful;" he that is "merciful," and "righteous," and "contrite" will of course be also "pure in heart:" and such a one will be "a peacemaker" too: and he that hath attained unto all these, will be moreover arrayed against dangers, and will not be troubled when evil is spoken of him, and he is enduring grievous trials innumerable.

10. Now then, after giving them due exhortation, He refreshes them again with praises. As thus: the injunctions being high, and far surpassing those in the Old Testament; lest they should be disturbed and confounded, and say, "How shall we be able to achieve these things?" hear what He saith: "Ye are the salt of the earth." Implying, that of absolute necessity He enjoins all this. For "not for your own life apart," saith He, "but for the whole world, shall your account be. For not to two cities, nor to ten or twenty, nor to a single nation am I sending you, as I sent the prophets; but to earth, and sea, and the whole world; and that in evil case." For by saying, "Ye are the salt of the earth," He signified all human nature to have "lost its savor," and to be decayed by our sins. For which cause, you see, He requires of them such virtues, as are most necessary and useful for the superintendence of the common sort. For first, the meek, and yielding, and merciful, and righteous, shuts not up his good deeds unto himself only, but also provides that these good fountains should run over for the benefit of others. And he again who is pure in heart, and a peacemaker, and is persecuted for the truth's sake; he again orders his way of life for the common good. "Think not then," He saith, "that ye are drawn on to ordinary

conflicts, or that for some small matters you are to give account." "Ye are the salt of the earth."

What then? did they restore the decayed? By no means; for neither is it possible to do any good to that which is already spoilt, by sprinkling it with salt. This therefore they did not. But rather, what things had been before restored, and committed to their charge, and freed from that ill savor, these they then salted, maintaining and preserving them in that freshness, which they had received of the Lord. For that men should be set free from the rottenness of their sins was the good work of Christ; but their not returning to it again any more was the object of these men's diligence and travail.

Seest thou how by degrees He indicates their superiority to the very prophets? in that He saith they are teachers, not of Palestine, but of the whole world; and not simply teachers, but awful ones too. For this is the marvellous thing, that not by flattering, nor soothing, but by sharply bracing them, as salt, even so they became dear to all men.

"Now marvel not," saith He, "if leaving all others, I discourse to you, and draw you on to so great dangers. For consider over how many cities, tribes, and nations, I am to send you to preside. Wherefore I would have you not only be prudent yourselves, but that you should also make others the same. And such persons have great need to be intelligent, in whom the salvation of the rest is at stake: they ought so much to abound in virtue, as to impart of the profit to others also. For if ye do not become such as this, ye will not suffice even for your own selves.

"Be not then impatient, as though my sayings were too burdensome. For while it is possible for others who have lost their savor to return by your means, you, if you should come to this, will with yourselves destroy others also. So that in proportion as the matters are great, which ye have put into your hands, you need so much the greater diligence." Therefore He saith,

"But if the salt have lost its savor, wherewith shall it be salted? it is thenceforth good for nothing, but to be cast out, and to be trodden under foot of men."

For other men, though they fall never so often, may possibly obtain indulgence: but the teacher, should this happen to him, is deprived of all excuse, and will suffer the most extreme vengeance. Thus, lest at the words, "When they shall revile you, and persecute you, and say all manner of evil against you," they should be too timid to go forth: He tells them, "unless ye are prepared to combat with all this, ye have been chosen in vain." For it is not evil report that ye should fear, but lest ye should prove partners in dissimulation. For then, "Ye will lose your savor, and be trodden under foot:" but if ye continue sharply to brace them up, and then are evil spoken of, rejoice; for this is the very use of salt, to sting the corrupt, and make them smart. And so their censure follows of course, in no way harming you, but rather testifying your firmness. But if through fear of it you give up the earnestness that becomes you, ye will have to suffer much more grievously, being both evil spoken of, and despised by all. For this is the meaning of "trodden under foot."

11. After this He leads on to another, a higher image.

"Ye are the light of the world."

"Of the world" again; not of one nation, nor of twenty states, but of the whole inhabited earth. And "a light" to the mind, far better than this sunbeam: like as they were also a spiritual salt. And before they are salt, and now light; to teach thee how great is the gain of these strict precepts, and the profit of that grave discipline: how it binds, and permits not to become dissolute; and causes clear sight, leading men on to virtue.

"A city that is set on a hill cannot be hid, neither do men light a candle, and put it under the bushel."

Again, by these words He trains them to strictness of life, teaching them to be earnest in their endeavors, as set before the eyes of all men, and contending in the midst of the amphitheatre of the world. For, "look not to this," He saith, "that we are now sitting here, that we are in a small portion of one corner. For ye shall be as conspicuous to all as a city set on the ridge of a hill, as a candle in a house on the candlestick, giving light."

Where now are they who persevere in disbelieving the power of Christ? Let them hear these things, and let them adore His might, amazed at the power of the prophecy. For consider how great things he promised to them, who were not known even in their own country: that earth and sea should know them, and that they should by their fame reach to the limits of the inhabited world; or rather, not by their fame, but by the working of the good they wrought. For it was not fame that bearing them everywhere made them conspicuous, but also the actual demonstration by their works. Since, as though they had wings, more vehemently than the sunbeam did they overrun the whole earth, sowing the light of godliness.

But here He seems to me to be also training them to boldness of speech. For to say, "A city set on a hill cannot be hid," is to speak as declaring His own powers. For as that city can by no means be hidden, so it was impossible that what they preached should sink into silence and obscurity. Thus, since He had spoken of persecutions and calumnies, of plots and wars, for fear they might think that these would have power to stop their mouths; to encourage them,

He saith, that so far from being hid, it should over-shine the whole world; and that on this very account they should be illustrious and renowned.

By this then He declares His own power. In what follows, He requires that boldness of speech which was due on their part; thus saying,

"Neither do men light a candle and put it under the bushel, but on the candlestick, and it giveth light unto all that are in the house. Let your light so shine before men, that they may see your good works, and glorify your Father which is in Heaven."

"For I," saith He, "it is true, have kindled the light, but its continuing to burn, let that come of your diligence: not for your own sakes alone, but also for their sake, who are to profit by these rays, and to be guided unto the truth. Since the calumnies surely shall not be able to obscure your brightness, if you be still living a strict life, and as becomes those who are to convert the whole world. Show forth therefore a life worthy of His grace; that even as it is everywhere preached, so this light may everywhere accompany the same.

Next He sets before them another sort of gain, besides the salvation of mankind, enough to make them strive earnestly, and to lead them unto all diligence. As thus, "Ye shall not only," saith He, "amend the world, if ye live aright, but ye will also give occasion that God shall be glorified; even as if ye do the contrary, ye will both destroy men, and make God's name to be blasphemed."

And how, it may be asked, shall God be glorified through us, if at least men are to speak evil of us? Nay, not all men, and even they themselves who in envy do this, will in their conscience admire and approve you; even as the outward flatterers of such as live in wickedness do in mind accuse them.

What then? Dost thou command us to live for display and vain glory? Far from it; I say not this; for I did not say, "Give ye diligence to bring forward your own good deeds," neither did I say, "Show them;" but "Let your light shine." That is, "Let your virtue be great, and the fire abundant, and the light unspeakable." For when virtue is so great, it cannot lie hid, though its pursuer shade it over ten thousand fold. Present unto them an irreprehensible life, and let them have no true occasion of evil speaking; and then, though there be thousands of evil-speakers, no man shall be able to cast any shade upon you. And well did He say, "your light," for nothing makes a man so illustrious, how manifold soever his will to be concealed, as the manifestation of virtue. For as if he were clad with the very sunbeam, so he shines, yet brighter than it; not spending his rays on earth, but surmounting also Heaven itself.

Hence also He comforts them more abundantly. For, "What though the slander pain you," saith He; "yet shall ye have many to honor God on your account. And in both ways your recompence is gathering, as well because God is glorified through you, as because ye are defamed for God's sake. Thus, lest we should on purpose seek to be reproached, on hearing that there is a reward for it: first, He hath not expressed that sentiment simply, but with two limitations, namely, when what is said is false, and when it is for God's sake:—and next He signifies how not that only, but also good report, hath its great profit, the glory of it passing on to God. And He holds out to them those gracious hopes. "For," saith He, "the calumny of the wicked avails not so much as to put all others in the dark, in respect of seeing your light. For then only when you have "lost your savor" shall they tread you under foot; but not when you are falsely accused, doing right. Yea, rather then shall there be many admiring, not you only, but for your sake your Father also." And He said not "God," but "your Father;" already sowing beforehand the seeds of that noble birth, which was about to be bestowed upon them. Moreover, indicating His parity in honor, as He said above, "Grieve not when ye are evil spoken of, for it is enough for you that for my sake you are thus spoken of;" so here He mentions the Father: every where manifesting His equality.

12. Since then we know the gain that arises from this earnestness, and the danger of indolence (for if our Lord be blasphemed because of us, that were far worse than our perdition), let us "give none offense, neither to the Jews, nor to the Gentiles, nor to the Church of God." And while the life which we present before them is brighter than the sun, yet if any one will speak evil of us, let us not grieve at being defamed, but only if we be defamed with justice.

For, on the one hand, if we live in wickedness, though there be none to speak ill of us, we shall be the most wretched of all men: on the other hand, if we apply ourselves to virtue, though the whole world speak evil of us, at that very time we shall be more enviable than any. And we shall draw on to follow us all who choose to be saved, for not the calumny of the wicked, but our good life, will draw their attention. For indeed no trumpet is so clear as the proof that is given by our actions: neither is the light itself so transparent as a pure life, though our calumniators be beyond number.

I say, if all the above-mentioned qualities be ours; if we be meek and lowly and merciful; if we be pure, and peacemakers; if hearing reproach, we revile not again, but rather rejoice; then shall we attract all that observe us no less than the miracles do. And all will be kindly disposed towards us, though one be a wild beast, a demon, or what you will.

Or if there should even be some who speak evil of thee, be not thou at all troubled thereat, nor because they revile thee in public, regard it; but search into their conscience, and thou shalt see them applauding and admiring thee, and numbering up ten thousand praises.

See, for instance, how Nebuchadnezzar praises the children in the furnace; yet surely he was an adversary and an enemy. But upon seeing them stand nobly, he proclaims their triumph, and crowns them: and that for nought else, but because they disobeyed him, and hearkened unto the law of God. For the devil, when he sees himself effecting nothing, from that time departs, fearing lest he should be the cause of our winning more crowns. And when he is gone, even one who is abominable and depraved will recognize virtue, that mist being withdrawn. Or if men still argue perversely, thou shalt have from God the greater praise and admiration.

Grieve not now, I pray thee, neither despond; since the very apostles were to some a "savor of death;" to others, a "savor of life." And if there be nothing to lay hold of in thyself, thou art rid of all their charges; or rather, thou art become the more blessed. Shine out therefore in thy life, and take no account of them who speak evil of thee. For it cannot, it cannot be, that one careful of virtue, should not have many enemies. However, this is nothing to the virtuous man. For by such means his brightness will increase the more abundantly.

Let us then, bearing these things in mind, look to one object only; how to order our own life with strictness. For thus we shall also guide to the life that is there, such as are now sitting in darkness. For such is the virtue of that light, as not only to shine here, but also to conduct its followers thither. For when men see us despising all things present, and preparing ourselves for that which is to come, our actions will persuade them sooner than any discourse. For who is there so senseless, that at sight of one, who within a day or two was living in luxury and wealth, now stripping himself of all, and putting on wings, and arrayed to meet both hunger and poverty, and all hardship, and dangers, and blood, and slaughter, and everything that is counted dreadful; will not from this sight derive a clear demonstration of the things which are to come?

But if we entangle ourselves in things present, and plunge ourselves in them more and more, how will it be possible for them to be persuaded that we are hastening to another sojourn?

And what excuse after this shall we have, if the fear of God avail not so much with us, as human glory availed with the Greek philosophers? For some of them did really both lay aside wealth, and despised death, that they might make a show before men; wherefore also their hopes became vain. What plea then shall deliver us, when with so great things set before us, and with so high a rule of self-denial laid open to us, we are not able even to do as they did, but ruin both ourselves and others besides? For neither is the harm so great when a heathen commits transgression, as when a Christian doeth the same. Of course not; for their character is already lost, but ours, by reason of the grace of God, is even among the ungodly venerable and glorious. Therefore when they would most revile us, and aggravate their evil speech, they add some such taunt as, "Thou Christian:" a taunt which they would not utter, did they not secretly entertain a great opinion of our doctrine.

Hast thou not heard how many, and how great precepts Christ enjoined? Now when wilt thou be able to fulfill one of those commandments, while thou leavest all, and goest about gathering interest, tacking together usuries, setting on foot transactions of business, buying herds of slaves, procuring silver vessels, purchasing houses, fields, goods without end? And I would this were all. But when to these unseasonable pursuits, thou addest even injustice, removing landmarks, taking away houses by violence, aggravating poverty, increasing hunger, when wilt thou be able to set thy foot on these thresholds?

13. But sometimes thou showest mercy to the poor. I know it as well as thou. But even in this again great is the mischief. For thou doest this either in pride or in vainglory, so as not to profit even by thy good deeds. What can be more wretched than this, to be making thy shipwreck in the very harbor? To prevent this, when thou hast done any good action, seek not thanks from me, that thou mayest have God thy debtor. For, "Lend," saith He, "unto them from whom ye do not expect to receive."

Thou hast thy Debtor; why leave Him, and require it of me, a poor and wretched mortal? What? is that Debtor displeased, when the debt is required of Him? What? is He poor? Is He unwilling to pay? Seest thou not His unspeakable treasures? Seest thou not His indescribable munificence? Lay hold then on Him, and make thy demand; for He is pleased when one thus demands the debt of Him. Because, if He see another required to pay for what He Himself owes, He will feel as though He were insulted, and repay thee no more; nay, He justly finds fault, saying, "Why, of what ingratitude hast thou convicted me? what poverty dost thou know to be in me, that thou hastenest by me, and resortest unto others? Hast thou lent to One, and dost thou demand the debt of another?"

For although man received it, it was God that commanded thee to bestow; and His will is to be Himself, and in the original sense, debtor, and surety, affording thee ten thousand occasion to demand the debt of Him from every quarter. Do not thou then let go so great facility and abundance, and seek to receive of me who have nothing. Why, to what end dost thou display to me thy mercy shown to the poor. What! was it I that said to thee, Give? was it from me that thou didst hear this; that thou shouldest demand it back of me?

He Himself hath said, "He that hath pity upon the poor lendeth to God." Thou hast lent to God: put it to His account.

"But He doth not repay the whole now." Well, this too He doth for thy good. For such a debtor is He: not as many, who are anxious simply to repay that which is lent; whereas He manages and doeth all things, with a view of investing likewise in security that which hath been given unto Him. Therefore some, you see, He repays here: some He assigns in the other place.

14. Knowing therefore as we do these things, let us make our mercifulness abundant, let us give proof of much love to man, both by the use of our money, and by our actions. And if we see any one ill-treated and beaten in the market-place, whether we can pay down money, let us do it: or whether by words we may separate them, let us not be backward. For even a word has its re ward, and still more have sighs. And this the blessed Job said; "But I wept for every helpless one, and I sighed when I saw a man in distress." But if there be a reward for tears and sighs; when words also, and an anxious endeavor, and many things besides are added, consider how great the recompence becomes. Yea, for we too were enemies to God, and the Only-begotten reconciled us, casting himself between, and for us receiving stripes, and for us enduring death.

Let us then likewise do our diligence to deliver from countless evils such as are incurring them; and not as we now do, when we see any beating and tearing one another: we are apt to stand by, finding pleasure in the disgrace of others, and forming a devilish amphitheatre around: than which what can be more cruel? Thou seest men reviled, tearing each other to pieces, rending their clothes, smiting each other's faces, and dost thou endure to stand by quietly?

What! is it a bear that is fighting? a wild beast? a serpent? It is a man, one who hath in every respect fellowship with thee: a brother, a member. Look not on, but separate them. Take no pleasure, but amend the evil. Stir not up others to the shameful sight, but rather drive off and separate those who are assembled. It is for shameless persons, and born slaves, to take pleasure in such calamities; for those that are mere refuse, for asses without reason.

Thou seest a man behaving himself unseemly, and dost thou not account the unseemliness thine own? Dost thou not interpose, and scatter the devil's troop, and put an end to men's miseries?

"That I may receive blows myself," saith one; "is this also thy bidding?" Thou wilt not have to suffer even this; but if thou shouldest, the thing would be to thee a sort of martyrdom; for thou didst suffer on God's behalf. And if thou art slow to receive blows, consider that thy Lord was not slow to endure the cross for thee.

Since they for their part are drunken in darkness; wrath being their tyrant and commander; and they need some one who is sound to help them, both the wrong-doer, and he who is injured; the one that he may be delivered from suffering evil, the other that he may cease to do it. Draw nigh, therefore, and stretch forth the hand, thou that art sober to him that is drunken. For there is a drunkenness of wrath too, and that more grievous than the drunkenness of wine.

Seest thou not the seamen, how, when they see any meeting with shipwreck, they spread their sails, and set out with all haste, to rescue those of the same craft out of the waves? Now, if partakers in an art show so much care one for another, how much more ought they who are partakers of the same nature to do all these things! Because in truth here too is a shipwreck, a more grievous one than that; for either a man under provocation blasphemes, and so throws all away: or he forswears himself under the sway of his wrath, and that way falls into hell: or he strikes a blow and commits murder, and thus again suffers the very same shipwreck. Go thou then, and put a stop to the evil; pull out them that are drowning, though thou descend into the very depth of the surge; and having broken up the theatre of the devil, take each one of them apart, and admonish him to quell the flame, and to lull the waves.

But if the burning pile wax greater, and the furnace more grievous, be not thou terrified; for thou hast many to help thee, and stretch forth the hand, if thou furnish but a beginning; and above all thou surely hast with thee the God of peace. And if thou wilt first turn aside the flames, many others also will follow, and of what they do well, thou wilt thyself receive the reward.

Hear what precept Christ gave to the Jews, creeping as they did upon the earth: "If thou see," saith He, "thine enemy's beast of burden falling down, do not hasten by, but raise it." And thou must see that to separate and reconcile men that are fighting is a much lighter thing than to lift up the fallen beast. And if we ought to help in raising our enemies' ass, much more our friends' souls: and most when the fall is more grievous; for not into mire do these fall, but into the fire of hell, not bearing the burden of their wrath. And thou, when thou seest thy brother lying under the load, and the devil standing by, and kindling the pile, thou runnest by, cruelly and unmercifully; a kind of thing not safe to do, even where brutes are concerned.

And whereas the Samaritan, seeing a wounded man, unknown, and not at all appertaining to him, both staid, and set him on a beast, and brought him home to the inn, and hired a physician, and gave some money, and promised more: thou, seeing one fallen not among thieves, but amongst a band of demons, and beset by anger; and this not in a wilderness, but in the midst of the forum; not having to lay out money, nor to hire a beast, nor to bring him on a long way, but only to say some words:—art thou slow to do it? and holdest back, and hurriest by cruelly and unmercifully? And how thinkest thou, calling upon God, ever to find Him propitious?

15. But let me speak also to you, who publicly disgrace yourselves: to him who is acting despitefully, and doing wrong. Art thou inflicting blows? tell me; and kicking, and biting? art thou become a wild boar, and a wild ass? and art thou not ashamed? dost thou not blush at thus being changed into a wild beast, and betraying thine own nobleness? For though thou be poor, thou art free; though thou be a working man, thou art a Christian.

Nay, for this very reason, that thou art poor, thou shouldest be quiet. For fightings belong to the rich, not to the poor; to the rich, who have many causes to force them to war. But thou, not having the pleasure of wealth, goest about gathering to thyself the evils of wealth, enmities, and strifes, and fightings; and takest thy brother by the throat, and goest about to strangle him, and throwest him down publicly in the sight of all men: and dost thou not think that thou art thyself rather disgraced, imitating the violent passions of the brutes; nay rather, becoming even worse than they? For they have all things in common; they herd one with another, and go about together: but we have nothing in common, but all in confusion: fightings, strifes, revilings, and enmities, and insults. And we neither reverence the heaven, unto which we are called all of us in common; nor the earth, which He hath left free to us all in common; nor our very nature; but wrath and the love of money sweeps all away.

Hast thou not seen him who owed the ten thousand talents, and then, after he was forgiven that debt, took his fellow-servant by the throat for an hundred pence, what great evils he underwent, and how he was delivered over to an endless punishment? Hast thou not trembled at the example? Hast thou no fear, lest thou too incur the same? For we likewise owe to our Lord many and great debts: nevertheless, He forbears, and suffers long, and neither urges us, as we do our fellow-servants, nor chokes and takes us by the throat; yet surely had he been minded to exact of us but the least part thereof, we had long ago perished.

16. Let us then, beloved, bearing these things in mind, be humbled, and feel thankful to those who are in debt to us. For they become to us, if we command ourselves, an occasion of obtaining most abundant pardon; and giving a little, we shall receive much. Why then exact with violence, it being meet, though the other were minded to pay, for thee of thine accord to excuse him, that thou mayest receive the whole of God? But now thou doest all things, and art violent, and contentious, to have none of thy debts forgiven

thee; and whilst thou art thinking to do despite unto thy neighbor, thou art thrusting the sword into thyself, so increasing thy punishment in hell: whereas if thou wilt show a little self-command here, thou makest thine own accounts easy. For indeed God therefore wills us to take the lead in that kind of bounty, that He may take occasion to repay us with increase.

As many therefore as stand indebted to thee, either for money, or for trespasses, let them all go free, and require of God the recompense of such thy magnanimity. For so long as they continue indebted to thee, thou canst not have God thy debtor. But if thou let them go free, thou wilt be able to detain thy God, and to require of Him the recompense of so great self-restraint in bountiful measure. For suppose a man had come up and seeing thee arresting thy debtor, had called upon thee to let him go free, and transfer to himself thy account with the other: he would not choose to be unfair after such remission, seeing he had passed the whole demand to himself: how then shall God fail to repay us manifold, yea, ten thousand fold, when for His commandment's sake, if any be indebted to us, we urge no complaint against them, great or small, but let them go exempt from all liability? Let us not then think of the temporary pleasure that springs up in us by exacting of our debtors, but of the loss, rather, how great! which we shall thereby sustain hereafter, grievously injuring ourselves in the things which are eternal. Rising accordingly above all, let us forgive those who must give account to us, both their debts and their offenses; that we may make our own accounts prove indulgent, and that what we could not reach by all virtue besides, this we may obtain by not bearing malice against our neighbors; and thus enjoy the eternal blessings, by the grace and love towards man of our Lord Jesus Christ, to whom be glory and might now and always, even forever and ever. Amen.

HOMILY XVI

MATT. V. 17

"Think not that I am come to destroy the Law or the Prophets."

Why, who suspected this? or who accused Him, that He should make a defense against this charge? Since surely from what had gone before no such suspicion was generated. For to command men to be meek, and gentle, and merciful, and pure in heart, and to strive for righteousness, indicated no such design, but rather altogether the contrary.

Wherefore then can He have said this? Not at random, nor vainly: but inasmuch as He was proceeding to ordain commandments greater than those of old, saying, "It was said to them of old time, Thou shalt not kill; but I say unto you, Be not even angry;" and to mark out a way for a kind of divine and heavenly conversation; in order that the strangeness thereof might not disturb the souls of the hearers, nor dispose them quite to mutiny against what He said He used this means of setting them right beforehand.

For although they fulfilled not the law, yet nevertheless they were possessed with much conscientious regard to it; and whilst they were annulling it every day by their deeds, the letters thereof they would have remain unmoved, and that no one should add anything more to them. Or rather, they bore with their rulers adding thereto, not however for the better, but for the worse. For so they used to set aside the honor due to our parents by additions of their own, and very many others also of the matters enjoined them, they would free themselves of by these unseasonable additions.

Therefore, since Christ in the first place was not of the sacredotal tribe, and next, the things which He was about to introduce were a sort of addition, not however lessening, but enhancing virtue; He knowing beforehand that both these circumstances would trouble them, before He wrote in their mind those wondrous laws, casts out that which was sure to be harboring there. And what was it that was harboring there, and making an obstacle?

2. They thought that He, thus speaking, did so with a view to the abrogation of the ancient institutions. This suspicion therefore He heals; nor here only doth He so, but elsewhere also again. Thus, since they accounted Him no less than an adversary of God, from this sort of reason, namely, His not keeping the sabbath; He, to heal such their suspicion, there also again sets forth His pleas, of which some indeed were proper to Himself; as when He saith, "My Father worketh, and I work;" but some had in them much condescension, as when He brings forward the sheep lost on the sabbath day, and points out that the law is disturbed for its preservation, and makes mention again of circumcision, as having this same effect.

Wherefore we see also that He often speaks words somewhat beneath Him, to remove the semblance of His being an adversary of God.

For this cause He who had raised thousands of the dead with a word only, when He was calling Lazarus, added also a prayer; and then, lest this should make Him appear less than Him that begat Him, He, to correct this suspicion, added, "I said these things, because of the people which standeth by, that they may believe that thou hast sent me." And neither doth He work all things as one who acted by His own power, that He might thoroughly correct their weakness; nor doth He all things with prayer, lest He should leave matter of evil suspicion to them that should follow, as though He were without strength or power: but He mingles the latter with the former, and those again with these. Neither doth He this indiscriminately, but with His own proper wisdom. For while He doeth the greater works authoritatively, in the less He looks up unto Heaven. Thus, when absolving sins, and revealing His secrets, and opening Paradise, and driving away devils, and cleansing lepers, and bridling death, and raising the dead by thousands, He did all by way of command: but when, what was much less than these, He was causing many loaves to spring forth out of few, then He looked up to Heaven: signifying that not through weakness He doth this. For He who could do the greater with authority, how in the lesser could He need prayer? But as I was saying, He doeth this to silence their shamelessness. The same reckoning, then, I bid thee make of His words also, when thou hearest Him speak lowly things. For many in truth are the causes both for words and for actions of that cast: as, for instance, that He might not be supposed alien from God; His instructing and waiting on all men; His teaching humility; His being encompassed with flesh; the Jews' inability to hear all at once; His teaching us to utter no high word of ourselves. For this cause many times, having in His own person said much that is lowly of Himself, the great things He leaves to be said by others. Thus He Himself indeed, reasoning with the Jews, said, "Before Abraham was, I Am:" but His disciple not thus, but, "In the beginning was the Word, and the Word was with God, and the Word was God."

Again, that He Himself made Heaven, and earth, and sea, and all things visible and invisible, in His own person He nowhere expressly said: but His disciple, speaking plainly out, and suppressing nothing, affirms this once, twice, yea often: writing that "all things were made by Him;" and, "without Him was not one thing made;" and, He was in the world, and the world was made by Him."

And why marvel, if others have said greater things of Him than He of Himself; since (what is more) in many cases, what He showed forth by His deeds, by His words He uttered not openly? Thus that it was Himself who made mankind He showed clearly even by that blind man; but when He was speaking of our formation at the beginning, He said not, "I made," but "He who made them, made them male and female." Again, that He created the world and all things therein, He demonstrated by the fishes, by the wine, by the loaves, by the calm in the sea, by the sunbeam which He averted on the Cross; and by very many things besides: but in words He hath nowhere said this plainly, though His disciples are continually declaring it, both John, and Paul, and Peter.

For if they who night and day hear Him discourse, and see Him work marvels; to whom He explained many things in private, and gave so great power as even to raise the dead; whom He made so perfect, as to forsake all things for Him: if even they, after so great virtue and self-denial, had not strength to bear it all, before the supply of the Spirit; how could the people of the Jews, being both void of understanding, and far behind such excellency, and only by hazard present when He did or said anything, how could they have been persuaded but that He was alien from the God of all, unless he had practised such great condescension throughout?

For on this account we see that even when He was abrogating the sabbath, He did not as of set purpose bring in such His legislation, but He puts together many and various pleas of defense. Now if, when He was about to cause one commandment to cease, He used so much reserve in His language, that He might not startle the hearers; much more, when adding to the law, entire as it was, another entire code of laws, did He require much management and attention, not to alarm those who were then hearing Him.

For this same cause, neither do we find Him teaching everywhere clearly concerning His own Godhead. For if His adding to the law was sure to perplex them so greatly, much more His declaring Himself God.

3. Wherefore many things are uttered by Him, far below His proper dignity, and here when He is about to proceed upon His addition to the law, He hath used abundance for correction beforehand. For neither was it once only that He said, "I do not abrogate the law," but He both repeated it again, and added another and a greater thing; in that, to the words, "Think not that I am come to destroy," He subjoined, "I am not come to destroy, but to fulfill."

Now this not only obstructs the obstinacy of the Jews, but stops also the mouths of those heretics, who say that the old covenant is of the devil. For if Christ came to destroy his tyranny, how is this covenant not only not destroyed, but even fulfilled by Him? For He said not only, "I do not destroy it;" though this had been enough; but "I even fulfill it:" which are the words of one so far from opposing himself, as to be even establishing it.

And how, one may ask, did He not destroy it? in what way did He rather fulfill either the law or the prophets? The prophets He fulfilled, inasmuch as He confirmed by His actions all that had been said concerning Him; wherefore also the evangelist used to say in each case, "That it might be fulfilled which was spoken by the prophet." Both when He was born, and when the children sung that wondrous hymn to Him, and when He sat on the ass, and in very many more instances He worked this same fulfillment: all which things must have been unfulfilled, if He had not come.

But the law He fulfilled, not in one way only, but in a second and third also. In one way, by transgressing none of the precepts of the law. For that He did fulfill it all, hear what He saith to John, "For thus it becometh us to fulfill all righteousness." And to the Jews also He said, "Which of you convinceth me of sin." And to His disciples again, "The prince of this world cometh, and findeth nothing in me." And the prophet too from the first had said that "He did no sin."

This then was one sense in which He fulfilled it. Another, that He did the same through us also; for this is the marvel, that He not only Himself fulfilled it, but He granted this to us likewise. Which thing Paul also declaring said, "Christ is the end of the law for righteousness to every one that believeth." And he said also, that "He judged sin in the flesh, that the righteousness of the law might be fulfilled in us who walk not after the flesh." And again, "Do we then make void the law through faith? God forbid! yea, we establish the law." For since the law was laboring at this, to make man righteous, but had not power, He came and brought in the way of righteousness by faith, and so established that which the law desired: and what the law could not by letters, this He accomplished by faith. On this account He saith, "I am not come to destroy the law."

4. But if any one will inquire accurately, he will find also another, a third sense, in which this hath been done. Of what sort is it then? In the sense of that future code of laws, which He was about to deliver to them.

For His sayings were no repeal of the former, but a drawing out, and filling up of them. Thus, "not to kill," is not annulled by the saying, Be not angry, but rather is filled up and put in greater security: and so of all the others.

Wherefore, you see, as He had before unsuspectedly cast the seeds of this teaching; so at the time when from His comparison of the old and new commandments, He would be more distinctly suspected of placing them in opposition, He used His corrective beforehand. For in a covert way He had indeed already scattered those seeds, by what He had said. Thus, "Blessed are the poor," is the same as that we are not to be angry; and, "Blessed are the pure in heart," as not to "look upon a woman for lust;" and the "not laying up treasures on earth," harmonizes with, "Blessed are the merciful;" and "to mourn" also, "to be persecuted" and "reviled," coincide with "entering in at the strait gate;" and, "to hunger and thirst after righteousness," is nothing else than that which He saith afterwards, "Whatsoever ye would that men should do to you, do ye also to them." And having declared "the peace-maker blessed," He again almost said the same, when He gave command "to leave the gift," and hasten to reconciliation with him that was grieved, and about "agreeing with our adversary."

But there He set down the rewards of them that do right, here rather the punishments of them who neglect practice. Wherefore as in that place He said, "The meek shall inherit earth;" so here, "He who calleth his brother fool, shall be in danger of hell-fire;" and there, "The pure in heart shall see God;" here, he is a complete adulterer who looks unchastely. And having there called "the peace-makers, sons of God;" here He alarms us from another quarter, saying, "Lest at any time the adversary deliver thee to the judge." Thus also, whereas in the former part He blesses them that mourn, and them that are persecuted; in the following, establishing the very same point, He threatens destruction to them that go not that way; for, "They that walk in the broad way,' saith He, make their end there.'" And, "Ye cannot serve God and mammon," seems to me the same with, "Blessed are the merciful," and, "those that hunger after righteousness."

But as I said, since He is going to say these things more clearly, and not only more clearly, but also to add again more than had been already said (for He no longer merely seeks a merciful man, but bids us give up even our coat; not simply a meek person, but to turn also the other cheek to him that would smite us): therefore He first takes away the apparent contradiction.

On this account, then, as I have already stated, He said this not once only, but once and again; in that to the words, "Think not that I am come to destroy," He added, "I am not come to destroy, but to fulfill."

"For verily I say unto you, Till Heaven and earth pass, one jot or one tittle shall in no wise pass from the law, till all come to pass."

Now what He saith is like this: it cannot be that it should remain unaccomplished, but the very least thing therein must needs be fulfilled. Which thing He Himself performed, in that He completed it with all exactness.

And here He signifies to us obscurely that the fashion of the whole world is also being changed. Nor did He set it down without purpose, but in order to arouse the hearer, and indicate, that He was with just cause introducing another discipline; if at least the very works of the creation are all to be transformed, and mankind is to be called to another country, and to a higher way of practising how to live.

5. "Whosoever therefore shall break one of these least commandments, and shall teach men so, he shall be called least in the kingdom of Heaven."

Thus, having rid Himself of the evil suspicion, and having stopped the mouths of them who would fain gainsay, then at length He proceeds to alarm, and sets down a heavy, denunciation in support of the enactments He was entering on.

For as to His having said this in behalf not of the ancient laws, but of those which He was proceeding to enact, listen to what follows, "For I say unto you," saith He, "Except your righteousness shall exceed the righteousness of the Scribes and Pharisees, ye shall in no case enter into the kingdom of Heaven."

For if He were threatening with regard to the ancient laws, how said He, "except it shall exceed?" since they who did just the same as those ancients, could not exceed them on the score of righteousness.

But of what kind was the required excess? Not to be angry, not even to look upon a woman unchastely.

For what cause then doth He call these commandments "least," though they were so great and high? Because He Himself was about to introduce the enactment of them; for as He humbled Himself, and speaks of Himself frequently with measure, so likewise of His own enactments, hereby again teaching us to be modest in everything. And besides, since there seemed to be some suspicion of novelty, He ordered His discourse for a while with reserve.

But when thou hearest, "least in the kingdom of Heaven," surmise thou nothing but hell and torments. For He was used to mean by "the kingdom," not merely the enjoyment thereof, but also the time of the resurrection, and that awful coming. And how could it be reasonable, that while he who called his brother fool, and trangressed but one commandment, falls into hell; the breaker of them all, and instigator of others to the same, should be within the kingdom. This therefore is not what He means, but that such a one will be at that time least, that is, cast out, last. And he that is last will surely then fall into hell. For, being God, He foreknew the laxity of the many, He foreknew that some would think these sayings were merely hyperbolical, and would argue about the laws, and say, What, if any one call another a fool, is he punished? If one merely look on a woman, doth he become an adulterer? For this very cause He, destroying such insolence beforehand, hath set down the strongest denunciation against either sort, as well them who transgress, as them who lead on others so to do.

Knowing then His threat as we do, let us neither ourselves transgress, nor discourage such as are disposed to keep these things.

"But whosoever shall do and teach," saith He, "shall be called great."

For not to ourselves alone, should we be profitable, but to others also; since neither is the reward as great for him who guides himself aright, as for one who with himself adds also another. For as teaching without doing condemns the teacher (for "thou which teachest another," it is said, "teachest thou not thyself" ?) so doing but not guiding others, lessens our reward. One ought therefore to be chief in either work, and having first set one's self right, thus to proceed also to the care of the rest. For on this account He Himself hath set the doing before the teaching; to intimate that so most of all may one be able to teach, but in no other way. For one will be told, "Physician, heal thyself." Since he who cannot teach himself, yet attempts to set others right, will have many to ridicule him. Or rather such a one will have no power to teach at all, his actions uttering their voice against him. But if he be complete in both respects, "he shall be called great in the kingdom of Heaven."

6. "For I say unto you, Except your righteousness shall exceed the righteousness of the Scribes and Pharisees, ye shall in no case enter into the kingdom of Heaven."

Here by righteousness He means the whole of virtue; even as also discoursing of Job, He said, "He was a blameless man, righteous." According to the same signification of the word, Paul also called that man "righteous" for whom, as he said, no law is even set. "For," saith he, "a law is not made for a righteous man." And in many other places too one might find this name standing for virtue in general.

But observe, I pray thee, the increase of grace; in that He will have His newly-come disciples better than the teachers in the old covenant. For by "Scribes and Pharisees" here, He meant not merely the lawless, but the well-doers. For, were they not doing well, He would not have said they have a righteousness; neither would He have compared the unreal to the real.

And observe also here, how He commends the old law, by making a comparison between it and the other; which kind of thing implies it to be of the same tribe and kindred. For more and less, is in the same kind. He doth not, you see, find fault with the old law, but will have it made stricter. Whereas, had it been evil, He would not have required more of it; He would not have made it more perfect, but would have cast it out.

And how one may say, if it be such, doth it not bring us into the Kingdom? It doth not now bring in them who live after the coming of Christ, favored as they are with more strength, and bound to strive for greater things: since as to its own foster-children, them it doth bring in one and all. Yea, for "many shall come," saith He, "from east and west, and shall lie down in the bosoms of Abraham, Isaac, and Jacob." And Lazarus also receiving the great prize, is shown dwelling in Abraham's bosom. And all, as many as have shone forth with excellency in the old dispensation, shone by it, every one of them. And Christ Himself, had it been in anything evil or alien from Him, would not have fulfilled it all when He came. For if only to attract the Jews He was doing this, and not in order to prove it akin to the new law, and concurrent therewith; wherefore did He not also fulfill the laws and customs of the Gentiles, that He might attract the Gentiles also?

So that from all considerations it is clear, that not from any badness in itself doth it fail to bring us in, but because it is now the season of higher precepts.

And if it be more imperfect than the new, neither doth this imply it to be evil: since upon this principle the new law itself will be in the very same case. Because in truth our knowledge of this, when compared with that which is to come, is a sort of partial and imperfect thing, and is done away on the coming of that other. "For when," saith He, "that which is perfect is come, then that which is in part shall be done away:" even as it befell the old law through the new. Yet we are not to blame the new law for this, though that also gives place on our attaining unto the Kingdom: for "then," saith He, "that which is in part shall be done away:" but for all this we call it great.

Since then both the rewards thereof are greater, and the power given by the Spirit more abundant, in reason it requires our graces to be greater also. For it is no longer "a land that floweth with milk and honey," nor a comfortable old age, nor many children, nor corn and wine, and flocks and herds: but Heaven, and the good things in the Heavens, and adoption and brotherhood with the Only-Begotten, and to partake of the inheritance and to be glorified and to reign with Him, and those unnumbered rewards. And as to our having received more abundant help, hear thou Paul, when he saith, "There is therefore no condemnation now to them which are in Christ Jesus, who walk not after the flesh, but after the Spirit: for the law of the Spirit of life hath made me free from the law of sin and death."

7. And now after threatening the transgressors, and setting great rewards for them that do right, and signifying that He justly requires of us something beyond the former measures; He from this point begins to legislate, not simply, but by way of comparison with the ancient ordinances, desiring to intimate these two things: first, that not as contending with the former, but rather in great harmony with them, He is making these enactments; next, that it was meet and very seasonable for Him to add thereto these second precepts.

And that this may be made yet clearer, let us hearken to the words of the Legislator. What then doth He Himself say?

"Ye have heard that it was said to them of old time, Thou shalt not kill."

And yet it was Himself who gave those laws also, but so far He states them impersonally. For if on the one hand He had said, "Ye have heard that I said to them of old," the saying would have been hard to receive, and would have stood in the way of all the hearers. If again, on the other hand, after having said, "Ye have heard that it was said to them of old by my Father," He had added, "But I say," He would have seemed to be taking yet more on Himself.

Wherefore He hath simply stated it, making out thereby one point only; the proof that in fitting season He had come saying these things. For by the words, "It was said to them of old," He pointed out the length of the time, since they received this commandment. And this He did to shame the hearer, shrinking from the advance to the higher class of His commandments; as though a teacher should say to a child that was indolent, "Knowest thou not how long a time thou hast consumed in learning syllables?" This then He also covertly intimates by the expression, "them of old time," and thus for the future summons them on to the higher order of His instructions: as if He had said, "Ye are learning these lessons long enough, and you must henceforth press on to such as are higher than these."

And it is well that He doth not disturb the order of the commandments, but begins first with that which comes earlier, with which the law also began. Yea, for this too suits with one showing the harmony between them.

"But I say unto you, that whosoever is angry with his brother without a cause, shall be in danger of the judgment."

Seest thou authority in perfection? Seest thou a bearing suited to a legislator? Why, which among prophets ever spake on this wise? which among righteous men? which among patriarchs? None; but, "Thus saith the Lord." But the Son not so. Because they were publishing their Master's commands, He His Father's. And when I say, "His Father's," I mean His own. "For mine," saith He, "are thine, and thine are mine." And they had their fellow-servants to legislate for, He His own servants.

Let us now ask those who reject the law, "is, Be not angry' contrary to Do no murder'? or is not the one commandment the completion and the development of the other?" Clearly the one is the fulfilling of the other, and that is greater on this very account. Since he who is not stirred up to anger, will much more refrain from murder; and he who bridles wrath will much more keep his hands to himself. For wrath is the root of murder. And you see that He who cuts up the root will much more remove the branches; or rather, will not permit them so much as to shoot out at all. Not therefore to abolish the law did He make these enactments, but for the more complete observation of it. For with what design did the law enjoin these things? Was it not, that no one might slay his neighbor? It follows, that he who was opposing the law would have to enjoin murder. For to murder, were the contrary to doing no murder. But if He doth not suffer one even to be angry, the mind of the law is established by Him more completely. For he that studies to avoid murder will not refrain from it equally with him that hath put away even anger; this latter being further removed from the crime.

8. But that we may convict them in another way also, let us bring forward all their allegations. What then do they affirm? They assert that the God who made the world, who "makes His sun to rise on the evil and on the good, who sends the rain on the just and on the unjust," is in some sense an evil being. But the more moderate (forsooth) among them, though declining this, yet while they affirm Him to be just, they deprive Him of being good. And some other one, who is not, nor made any of the things that are, they assign for a Father to Christ. And they say that he, who is not good, abides in his own, and preserves what are his own; but that He, that is good, seeks what are another's, and desires of a sudden to become a Saviour to them whose Creator He was not. Seest thou the children of the devil, how they speak out of the fountain of their father, alienating the work of creation from God: while John cries out, "He came unto His own," and, "The world was made by Him?"

In the next place, they criticise the law in the old covenant, which bids put out "an eye for an eye," and "a tooth for a tooth;" and straightway they insult and say, "Why, how can He be good who speaks so?"

What then do we say in answer to this? That it is the highest kind of philanthropy. For He made this law, not that we might strike out one another's eyes, but that fear of suffering by others might restrain us from doing any such thing to them. As therefore He threatened the Ninevites with overthrow, not that He might destroy them, (for had that been His will, He ought to have been silent), but that He might by fear make them better, and so quiet His wrath: so also hath He appointed a punishment for those who wantonly assail the eyes of others, that if good principle dispose them not to refrain from such cruelty, fear may restrain them from injuring their neighbors' sight.

And if this be cruelty, it is cruelty also for the murderer to be restrained, and the adulterer checked. But these are the sayings of senseless men, and of those that are mad to the extreme of madness. For I, so far from saying that this comes of cruelty, should say, that the contrary to this would be unlawful, according to men's reckoning. And whereas, thou sayest, "Because He commanded to pluck out "an eye for an eye," therefore He is cruel;" I say, that if He had not given this commandment, then He would have seemed, in the judgment of most men, to be that which thou sayest He is.

For let us suppose that this law had been altogether done away, and that no one feared the punishment ensuing thereupon, but that license had been given to all the wicked to follow their own disposition in all security, to adulterers, and to murderers, to perjured persons, and to parricides; would not all things have been turned upside down? would not cities, market-places, and houses, sea and land, and the whole world, have been filled with unnumbered pollutions and murders? Every one sees it. For if, when there are laws, and fear, and threatening, our evil dispositions are hardly checked; were even this security taken away, what is there to prevent men's choosing vice? and what degree of mischief would not then come revelling upon the whole of human life?

The rather, since cruelty lies not only in allowing the bad to do what they will, but in another thing too quite as much; to overlook, and leave uncared for, him who hath done no wrong, but who is without cause or reason suffering ill. For tell me; were any one to gather together wicked men from all quarters, and arm them with swords, and bid them go about the whole city, and massacre all that came in their way, could there be anything more like a wild beast than he? And what if some other should bind, and confine with the utmost strictness those whom that man had armed, and should snatch from those lawless hands them, who were on the point of being butchered; could anything be greater humanity than this?

Now then, I bid thee transfer these examples to the law likewise; for He that commands to pluck out "an eye for an eye," hath laid the fear as a kind of strong chain upon the souls of the bad, and so resembles him, who detains those assassins in prison; whereas he who appoints no punishment for them, doth all but arm them by such security, and acts the part of that other, who was putting the swords in their hands, and letting them loose over the whole city.

Seest thou not, how the commandments, so far from coming of cruelty, come rather of abounding mercy? And if on account of these thou callest the Lawgiver grievous, and hard to bear with; tell me which sort of command is the more toilsome and grievous, "Do no murder," or, "Be not even angry"? Which is more in extreme, he who exacts a penalty for murder, or for mere anger? He who subjects the adulterer to vengeance after the fact, or he who enjoins a penalty even for the very desire, and that penalty everlasting? See ye not how their reasoning comes round to the very contrary? how the God of the old covenant, whom they call cruel, will be found mild and meek: and He of the new, whom they acknowledged to be good, will be hard and grievous, according to their madness? Whereas we say, that there is but one and the same Legislator of either covenant, who dispensed all meetly, and adapted to the difference of the times the difference between the two systems of law. Therefore neither are the first commandments cruel, nor the second hard and grievous, but all of one and the same providential care.

For that He Himself gave the old covenant also, hear the affirmation of the prophet, or rather (so we must speak), of Him who is both the one and the other: "I will make a covenant with you, not according to the covenant which I made with your fathers."

But if he receive not this, who is diseased with the Manichaean doctrines, let him hear Paul saying the very same in another place, "For Abraham had two sons, one by the bondmaid, and another by the freewoman; and these are two covenants." As therefore in that case the wives are different, the husband the same; so here too the covenants are two, the Lawgiver one.

And to prove to thee that it was of one and the same mildness; in the one He saith, "An eye for an eye," but in this other,

"If one smite thee on thy right cheek, turn to him the other also."

For as in that case He checks him that doth the wrong with the fear of this suffering, even so also in this. "How so," it may be said, "when He bids turn to him the other cheek also?" Nay, what of that? Since not to take away his fear did He enjoin this, but as charging yourself to allow him to take his fill entirely. Neither did He say, that the other continues unpunished, but, "do not thou punish;" at once both enhancing the fear of him that smiteth, if he persist, and comforting him who is smitten.

9. But these things we have said, as one might say them incidentally, concerning all the commandments. Now we must go on to that which is before us, and keep to the thread of what had been affirmed. "He that is angry with his brother without a cause shall be in danger of the judgment:" so He speaks. Thus He hath not altogether taken the thing away: first, because it is not possible, being a man, to be freed from passions: we may indeed get the dominion over them, but to be altogether without them is out of the question.

Next, because this passion is even useful, if we know how to use it at the suitable time. See, for instance, what great good was wrought by that anger of Paul, which he felt against the Corinthians, on that well-known occasion; and how, as it delivered them from a grievous pest, so by the same means again he recovered the people of the Galatians likewise, which had fallen aside; and others too beside these. What then is the proper time for anger? When we are not avenging ourselves, but checking others in their lawless freaks, or forcing them to attend in their negligence.

And what is the unsuitable time? When we do so as avenging ourselves: which Paul also forbidding, said "Avenge not yourselves, dearly beloved, but rather give place unto wrath." When we are contending for riches: yea, for this hath he also taken away, where he saith, "Why do ye not rather take wrong? why do ye not rather suffer yourselves to be defrauded?" For as this last sort is superfluous, so is the first necessary and profitable. But most men do the contrary; becoming like wild beasts when they are injured themselves, but remiss and cowardly when they see despite done to another: both which are just opposite to the laws of the Gospel.

Being angry then is not a transgression, but being so unseasonably. For this cause the prophet also said, "Be ye angry, and sin not."

10. "And whosoever shall say to his brother, Raca, shall be in danger of the council."

By the council in this place He means the tribunal of the Hebrews: and He hath mentioned this now, on purpose that He might not seem everywhere to play the stranger and innovator.

But this word, "Raca," is not an expression of a great insolence, but rather of some contempt and slight on the part of the speaker. For as we, giving orders either to our servants, or to any very inferior person, say, "Away with thee; you here, tell such an one:" so they who make use of the Syrians' language say, "Raca," putting that word instead of "thou." But God, the lover of man, roots up even the least faults, commanding us to behave to one another in seemly manner, and with due respect; and this with a view of destroying hereby also the greater.

"But whosoever shall say, Thou fool, shall be in danger of hell fire."

To many this commandment hath appeared grievous and galling, if for a mere word we are really to pay so great a penalty. And some even say that it was spoken rather hyperbolically. But I fear lest, when we have deceived ourselves with words here, we may in deeds there suffer that extreme punishment.

For wherefore, tell me, doth the commandment seem overburdensome? Knowest thou not that most punishments and most sins have their beginning from words? Yea, for by words are blasphemies, and denials are by words, and revilings, and reproaches, and perjuries, and bearing false witness. Regard not then its being a mere word, but whether it have not much danger, this do thou inquire. Art thou ignorant that in the season of enmity, when wrath is inflamed, and the soul kindled, even the least thing appears great, and what is not very reproachful is counted intolerable? And often these little things have given birth even to murder, and overthrown whole cities. For just as where friendship is, even grievous things are light, so where enmity lies beneath, very trifles appear intolerable. And however simply a word be spoken, it is surmised to have been spoken with an evil meaning. And as in fire: if there be but a small spark, though thousands of planks lie by, it doth not easily lay hold of them; but if the flame have waxed strong and high, it readily seizes not planks only, but stones, and all materials that fall in its way; and by what things it is usually quenched, by the same it is kindled the more (for some say that at such a time not only wood and tow, and the other combustibles, but even water darted forth upon it doth but fan its power the more); so is it also with anger; whatever any one may say, becomes food in a moment for this evil conflagration. All which kind of evils Christ checking beforehand, had condemned first him that is angry without a cause to the judgment, (this being the very reason why He said, "He that is angry shall be in danger of the judgment"); then him that saith "Raca," to the council. But as yet these are no great things; for the punishments are here. Therefore for him who calleth "fool" He hath added the fire of hell, now for the first time mentioning the name of hell. For having before discoursed much of the kingdom, not until then did He mention this; implying, that the former comes of His own love and indulgence towards man, this latter of our negligence.

11. And see how He proceeds by little and little in His punishments, all but excusing Himself unto thee, and signifying that His desire indeed is to threaten nothing of the kind, but that we drag Him on to such denunciations. For observe: "I bade thee," saith He, "not be angry for nought, because thou art in danger of the judgment. Thou hast despised the former commandment: see what anger hath produced; it hath led thee on straightway to insult, for thou hast called thy brother Raca.' Again, I set another punishment, the council.' If thou overlook even this, and proceed to that which is more grievous, I visit thee no longer with these finite punishments, but with the undying penalty of hell, lest after this thou shouldest break forth even to murder." For there is nothing, nothing in the world more intolerable than insolence; it is what hath very great power to sting a man's soul. But when the word too which is spoken is in itself more wounding than the insolence, the blaze becomes twice as great. Think it not then a light thing to call another "fool." For when of that which separates us from the brutes, and by which especially we are human beings, namely, the mind and the understanding,—when of this thou hast robbed thy brother, thou hast deprived him of all his nobleness.

Let us not then regard the words merely, but realizing the things themselves, and his feeling, let us consider how great a wound is made by this word, and unto how much evil it proceeds. For this cause Paul likewise cast out of the kingdom not only "the adulterous" and "the effeminate," but "the revilers" also. And with great reason: for the insolent man mars all the beauty of charity, and casts upon his neighbor unnumbered ills, and works up lasting enmities, and tears asunder the members of Christ, and is daily driving away that peace which God so desires: giving much vantage ground unto the devil by his injurious ways, and making him the stronger. Therefore Christ Himself, cutting out the sinews of the devil's power, brought in this law.

For indeed He makes much account of love: this being above all things the mother of every good, and the badge of His disciples, and the bond which holds together our whole condition. With reason therefore doth He remove with great earnestness the roots and the sources of that hatred which utterly spoils it.

Think not therefore that these sayings are in any wise hyperbolical, but consider the good done by them, and admire the mildness of these laws. For there is nothing for which God takes so much pains, as this; that we should be united and knit together one with another. Therefore both in His own person, and by His disciples, as well those in the Old, as in the New Testament, He makes so much account of this commandment; and is a severe avenger and punisher of those who despise the duty. For in truth nothing so effectually gives entrance and root to all wickedness, as the taking away of love. Wherefore He also said, "When iniquity abounds, the love of the many shall wax cold." Thus Cain became his brother's murderer; thus Esau; thus Joseph's brethren; thus our unnumbered crimes have come revelling in, this bond being dissevered. You see why He Himself also roots out whatever things injure this, on every side, with great exactness.

12. Neither doth He stop at those precepts only which have been mentioned, but adds also others more than those: whereby He signifies how much account He makes thereof. Namely, having threatened by "the council," by "the judgment," and by "hell," He added other sayings again in harmony with the former, saying thus:

"If thou bring thy gift to the altar, and there rememberest that thy brother hath ought against thee; leave there thy gift before the altar, and go away; first be reconciled to thy brother, and then come and offer thy gift."

O goodness! O exceeding love to man! He makes no account of the honor due unto Himself, for the sake of our love towards our neighbor; implying that not at all from any enmity, nor out of any desire to punish, had He uttered those former threatenings, but out of very tender affection. For what can be milder than these sayings? "Let my service," saith he, "be interrupted, that thy love may continue; since this also is a sacrifice, thy being reconciled to thy brother." Yea, for this cause He said not, "after the offering," or "before the offering;" but, while the very gift lies there, and when the sacrifice is already beginning, He sends thee to be reconciled to thy brother; and neither after removing that which lies before us, nor before presenting the gift, but while it lies in the midst, He bids thee hasten thither.

With what motive then doth He command so to do, and wherefore? These two ends, as it appears to me, He is hereby shadowing out and providing for. First, as I have said, His will is to point out that He highly values charity, and considers it to be the greatest sacrifice: and that without it He doth not receive even that other; next, He is imposing such a necessity of reconciliation, as admits of no excuse. For whoso hath been charged not to offer before he be reconciled, will hasten, if not for love of his neighbor, yet, that this may not lie unconsecrated, to run unto him who hath been grieved, and do away the enmity. For this cause He hath also expressed it all most significantly, to alarm and thoroughly to awaken him. Thus, when He had said, "Leave thy gift," He stayed not at this, but added, "before the altar" (by the very place again causing him to shudder); "and go away." And He said not merely, "Go away," but He added, "first, and then come and offer thy gift." By all these things making it manifest, that this table receives not them that are at enmity with each other.

Let the initiated hear this, as many as draw nigh in enmity: and let the uninitiated hear too: yea, for the saying hath some relation to them also. For they too offer a gift and a sacrifice: prayer, I mean, and alms-giving. For as to this also being a sacrifice, hear what the prophet saith: "A sacrifice of praise will glorify me;" and again, "Sacrifice to God a sacrifice of praise;" and, "The lifting up of mine hands is an evening sacrifice." So that if it be but a prayer, which thou art offering in such a frame of mind, it were better to leave thy prayer, and become reconciled to thy brother, and then to offer thy prayer.

For to this end were all things done: to this end even God became man, and took order for all those works, that He might set us at one.

And whereas in this place He is sending the wrong doer to the sufferer, in His prayer He leads the sufferer to the wrong doer, and reconciles them. For as there He saith, "Forgive men their debts;" so here, "If he hath ought against thee, go thy way unto him."

Or rather, even here too He seems to me to be sending the injured person: and for some such reason He said not, "Reconcile thyself to thy brother," but, "Be thou rec onciled." And while the saying seems to pertain to the aggressor, the whole of it really pertains to him that is aggrieved. Thus, "If thou art reconciled to him," saith Christ, "through thy love to him thou wilt have me also propitious, and wilt be able to offer thy sacrifice with great confidence. But if thou art still irritated, consider that even I readily command that which is mine to be lightly esteemed, that ye may become friends; and let these thoughts be soothing to thine anger."

And He said not, "When thou hast suffered any of the greater wrongs, then be reconciled; but, "Though it be some trifle that he hath against thee." And

He added not, "Whether justly or unjustly;" but merely, "If he hath ought against thee." For though it be justly, not even in that case oughtest thou to protract the enmity; since Christ also was justly angered with us, yet nevertheless He gave Himself for us to be slain, "not imputing those trespasses."

For this cause Paul also, when urging us in another way to reconciliation, said, "Let not the sun go down upon your wrath." For much as Christ by this argument of the sacrifice, so there Paul by that of the day, is urging us on to the self-same point. Because in truth he fears the night, lest it overtake him that is smitten alone, and make the wound greater. For whereas in the day there are many to distract, and draw him off; in the night, when he is alone, and is thinking it over by himself, the waves swell, and the storm becomes greater. Therefore Paul, you see, to prevent this, would fain commit him to the night already reconciled, that the devil may after that have no opportunity, from his solitude, to rekindle the furnace of his wrath, and make it fiercer. Thus also Christ permits not, though it be ever so little delay, lest, the sacrifice being accomplished, such an one become more remiss, procrastinating from day to day: for He knows that the case requires very speedy treatment. And as a skillful physician exhibits not only the preventives of our diseases, but their correctives also, even so doth He likewise. Thus, to forbid our calling "fool," is a preventive of enmity; but to command reconciliation is a means of removing the diseases that ensue on the enmity.

And mark how both commands are set forth with earnestness. For as in the former case He threatened hell, so here He receives not the gift before the reconciliation, indicating great displeasure, and by all these methods destroying both the root and the produce.

And first of all He saith, "Be not angry;" and after that, "revile not." For indeed both these are augmented, the one by the other: from enmity is reviling, from reviling enmity. On this account then He heals now the root, and now the fruit; hindering indeed the evil from ever springing up in the first instance: but if perchance it may have sprouted up and borne its most evil fruit, then by all means He burns it down the more.

13. Therefore, you see, having mentioned, first the judgment, then the council, then hell, and having spoken of His own sacrifice, He adds other topics again, thus speaking:

"Agree with thine adversary quickly, whilst thou art in the way with him."

That is, that thou mayest not say, "What then, if I am injured;" "what if I am plundered, and dragged too before the tribunal?" even this occasion and excuse He hath taken away: for He commands us not even so to be at enmity. Then, since this injunction was great, He draws His advice from the things present, which are wont to restrain the grosser sort more than the future. "Why, what sayest thou?" saith He. "That thine adversary is stronger, and doeth thee wrong? Of course then he will wrong thee more, if thou do not make it up, but art forced to go into court. For in the former case, by giving up some money, thou wilt keep thy person free; but when thou art come under the sentence of the judge, thou wilt both be bound, and pay the utmost penalty. But if thou avoid the contest there, thou wilt reap two good results: first, not having to suffer anything painful: and secondly, that the good done will be thereafter thine own doing, and no longer the effect of compulsion on his part. But if thou wilt not be ruled by these sayings, thou wrongest not him, so much as thyself."

And see here also how He hastens him; for having said, "Agree with thine adversary," He added, "quickly;" and He was not satisfied with this, but even of this quickness He hath required a further increase, saying, "Whilst thou art in the way with him;" pressing and hastening him hereby with great earnestness. For nothing doth so much turn our life upside down, as delay and procrastination in the performance of our good works. Nay, this hath often caused us to lose all. Therefore, as Paul for his part saith, "Before the sun set, do away the enmity;" and as He Himself had said above, "Before the offering is completed, be reconciled;" so He saith in this place also, "Quickly, whilst thou art in the way with him," before thou art come to the doors of the court; before thou standest at the bar and art come to be thenceforth under the sway of him that judgeth. Since, before entering in, thou hast all in thine own control; but if thou set thy foot on that threshold, thou wilt not by ever so earnest efforts be able to arrange thy matters at thy will, having come under the constraint of another.

But what is it "to agree?" He means either, "consent rather to suffer wrong?" or, "so plead the cause, as if thou wert in the place of the other;" that thou mayest not corrupt justice by self-love, but rather, deliberating on another's cause as thine own, mayest so proceed to deliver thy vote in this matter. And if this be a great thing, marvel not; since with this view did He set forth all those His blessings, that having beforehand smoothed and prepared the hearer's soul, he might render it apter to receive all His enactments.

Now some say that He obscurely signifies the devil himself, under the name of the adversary; and bids us have nothing of his, (for this, they say, is to "agree" with him): no compromise being possible after our departure hence, nor anything awaiting us, but that punishment, from which no prayers can deliver. But to me He seems to be speaking of the judges in this world, and of the way to the court of justice, and of this prison.

For after he had abashed men by higher things, and things future, he alarms them also by such as are in this life. Which thing Paul also doth, using both the future and the present to sway his hearer: as when, deterring from wickedness, he points out to him that is inclined to evil, the ruler armed: thus saying, "But if thou do that which is evil, be afraid; for he beareth not the sword in vain; for he is a minister of God." And again, enjoining us to be subject unto him, he sets forth not the fear of God only, but the threatening also of the other party, and his watchful care. "For ye must needs be subject, not only for wrath, but also for conscience sake." Because the more irrational, as I have already said, are wont to be sooner corrected by these things, things which appear and are at hand. Wherefore Christ also made mention, not of hell only, but also of a court of justice, and of being dragged thither, and of the prison, and of all the suffering there; by all these means destroying the roots of murder. For he who neither reviles, nor goes to law, nor prolongs enmity, how will he ever commit murder? So that from hence also it is evident, that in the advantage of our neighbor stands our own advantage. For he that agrees with his adversary, will benefit himself much more; becoming free, by his own act, from courts of law, and prisons, and the wretchedness that is there.

14. Let us then be obedient to His sayings; let us not oppose ourselves, nor be contentious; for first of all, even antecedently to their rewards, these injunctions have their pleasure and profit in themselves. And if to the more part they seem to be burdensome, and the trouble which they cause, great; have it in thy mind that thou art doing it for Christ's sake, and the pain will be pleasant. For if we maintain this way of reckoning at all times, we shall experience nothing burdensome, but great will be the pleasure we reap from every quarter; for our toil will no longer seem toil, but by how much it is enhanced, so much the sweeter and pleasanter doth it grow.

When therefore the custom of evil things, and the desire of wealth, keep on bewitching thee; do thou war against them with that mode of thinking which tells us, "Great is the reward we shall receive, for despising the pleasure which is but for a season;" and say to thy soul; "Art thou quite dejected because I defraud thee of pleasure? Nay, be of good cheer, for I am introducing thee into Heaven. Thou doest it not for man's sake, but for God's. Be patient therefore a little while, and thou shalt see how great is the gain. Endure for the present life, and thou shalt receive an unspeakable confidence." For if we would thus discourse with our own soul, and not only consider that which is burdensome in virtue, but take account also of the crown that comes thereof, we shall quickly withdraw it from all wickedness.

For if the devil, holding out pleasure for a season, but pain for ever, is yet strong, and prevails; seeing our case is just the reverse in these matters, the labor temporary, the pleasure and profit immortal, what plea shall we have, if we follow not virtue after so great encouragement? Why, the object of our labors is enough to set against all, and our clear persuasion that for God's sake we are enduring all this. For if one having the king his debtor, thinks he hath sufficient security for all his life; consider how great will he be, who hath made the Gracious and Everlasting God a debtor to himself, for good deeds both small and great. Do not then allege to me labors and sweats; for not by the hope only of the things to come, but in another way also, God hath made virtue easy, assisting us everywhere, and putting His hand to our work. And if thou wilt only contribute a little zeal, everything else follows. For to this end He will have thee too to labor a little, even that the victory may be thine also. And just as a king would have his own son present indeed in the array; he would have him shoot with the bow, and show himself, that the trophy may be reckoned his, while he achieves it all Himself: even so doth God in our war against the devil: He requires of thee one thing alone, that thou show forth a sincere hatred against that foe. And if thou contribute this to Him, He by Himself brings all the war to an end. Though thou burn with anger, with desire of riches, with any tyrannical passion whatever; if He see thee only stripping thyself and prepared against it, He comes quickly to thee, and makes all things easy, and sets thee above the flame, as He did those children of old in the Babylonian furnace: for they too carried in with them nought but their good will.

In order then that we also may extinguish all the furnace of disordered pleasure here, and so escape the hell that is there, let these each day be our counsels, our cares, and our practice, drawing towards us the favor of God, both by our full purpose concerning good works, and by our frequent prayers. For thus even those things which appear insupportable now, will be most easy, and light, and lovely. Because, so long as we are in our passions, we think virtue rugged and morose and arduous, vice desirable and most pleasing; but if we would stand off from these but a little, then both vice will appear abominable and unsightly, and virtue easy, mild, and much to be desired. And this you may learn plainly from those who have done well. Hear, for instance, how of those passions Paul is ashamed, even after his deliverance from them, saying, "For what fruit had ye then in those things, whereof ye are now ashamed?" But virtue, even after his labor, he affirms to be light, calling the laboriousness of our affliction momentary and "light," and rejoicing in his sufferings, and glorying in his tribulations, and taking a pride in the marks wherewith he had been branded for Christ's sake.

In order then that we too may establish ourselves in this habit, let us order ourselves each day by what hath been said, and "forgetting those things which are behind, and reaching forth unto those things which are before, let us press on towards the prize of the high calling:" unto which God grant that we may all attain, by the grace and love towards man of our Lord Jesus Christ, to whom be glory and power for ever and ever. Amen.

HOMILY XVII

MATT. V. 27, 28

"Ye have heard that it was said to them of old time, Thou shalt not commit adultery; but I say unto you, that every one who looketh upon a woman to lust after her, hath committed adultery with her already in his heart."

Having now finished the former commandment, and having extended it unto the height of self-denial, He, advancing in course and order, proceeds accordingly unto the second, herein too obeying the law.

"And yet," it may be said, "this is not the second, but the third; for neither is the first, "Thou shalt not kill," but "The Lord thy God is one Lord."

Wherefore it is worth inquiring too, why He did not begin with that. Why was it then? Because, had He begun from thence, He must have enlarged it also, and have brought in Himself together with His Father. But it was not as yet time to teach any such thing about Himself.

And besides, He was for a while practising His moral doctrine only, being minded from this first, and from His miracles, to convince the hearers that He was the Son of God. Now, if He had said at once, before He had spoken or done anything, "Ye have heard that it was said to them of old time, "I am the Lord thy God, and there is none other but me," but I say unto you, Worship me even as Him; this would have made all regard Him as a madman. For if, even after His teaching, and His so great miracles, while not even yet was He saying this openly, they called Him possessed with a devil; had He before all these attempted to say any such thing, what would they not have said? what would they not have thought?

But by keeping back at the proper season His teaching on these subjects, He was causing that the doctrine should be acceptable to the many. Wherefore now He passed it by quickly, but when He had everywhere established it by His miracles, and by His most excellent teaching, He afterwards unveiled it in words also.

For the present, however, by the manifestation of His miracles, and by the very manner of His teaching, He unfolds it on occasion, gradually and quietly. For His enacting such laws, and such corrections of laws, with authority, would lead on the attentive and understanding hearer, by little and little, unto the word of His doctrine. For it is said, "they were astonished at Him, because He taught not as their Scribes."

2. For beginning from those passions, which most belong to our whole race, anger, I mean, and desire (for it is these chiefly that bear absolute sway within us, and are more natural than the rest); He with great authority, even such as became a legislator, both corrected them, and reduced them to order with all strictness. For He said not that the adulterer merely is punished; but what He had done with respect to the murderer, this He doth here also, punishing even the unchaste look: to teach thee wherein lies what He had more than the scribes. Accordingly, He saith, "He that looketh upon a woman to lust after her hath already committed adultery with her:" that is, he who makes it his business to be curious about bright forms, and to hunt for elegant features, and to feast his soul with the sight, and to fasten his eyes on fair countenances. For He came to set free from all evil deeds not the body only, but the soul too before the body. Thus, because in the heart we receive the grace of the Spirit, He cleanses it out first.

"And how," one may say, "is it possible to be freed from desire?" I answer, first, if we were willing, even this might be deadened, and remain inactive.

In the next place, He doth not here take away desire absolutely, but that desire which springs up in men from sight. For he that is curious to behold fair countenances, is himself chiefly the enkindler of the furnace of that passion, and makes his own soul a captive, and soon proceeds also to the act.

Thus we see why He said not, "whosoever shall lust to commit adultery," but, "whosoever shall look to lust." And in the case of anger He laid down a certain distinction, saying, "without a cause," and "for nought;" but here not so; rather once for all He took away the desire. Yet surely both are naturally implanted, and both are set in us for our profit; both anger, and desire: the one that we may chastise the evil, and correct those who walk disorderly; the other that we may have children, and that our race may be recruited by such successions.

Why then did He not make a distinction here also? Nay, very great is the distinction which, if thou attend, thou wilt see here also included. For He said not simply, "whosoever shall desire," since it is possible for one to desire even when sitting in the mountains; but, "Whosoever shall look to lust;" that is to say, he who gathers in lust unto himself; he who, when nothing compels him, brings in the wild beast upon his thoughts when they are calm. For this comes no longer of nature, but of self-indulgence. This even the ancient Scripture corrects from the first, saying, "Contemplate not beauty which is another's." And then, lest any one should say, "what then, if I contemplate, and be not taken captive," He punishes the look, lest confiding in this security thou shouldest some time fall into sin. "What then," one may say, "if I should look, and desire indeed, but do no evil?" Even so thou art set among the adulterers. For the Lawgiver hath pronounced it, and thou must not ask any more questions. For thus looking once, twice, or thrice, thou wilt perhaps have power to refrain; but if thou art continually doing this, and kindling the furnace, thou wilt assuredly be taken; for thy station is not beyond that nature which is common to men. As we then, if we see a child holding a knife, though we do not see him hurt, beat him, and forbid his ever holding it; so God likewise takes away the unchaste look even before the act, lest at any time thou shouldest fall in act also. For he who hath once kindled the flame, even when the woman whom he hath beheld is absent, is forming by himself continually images of shameful things, and from them often goes on even to the deed. For this cause Christ takes away even that embrace which is in the heart only.

What now can they say, who have those virgin inmates? Why, by the tenor of this law they must be guilty of ten thousand adulteries, daily beholding them with desire. For this cause the blessed Job also laid down this law from the beginning, blocking out from himself on all sides this kind of gazing.

For in truth greater is the struggle on beholding, and not possessing the object of fondness: nor is the pleasure so great which we reap from the sight, as the mischief we undergo from increasing this desire; thus making our opponent strong, and giving more scope to the devil, and no longer able to repulse him, now that we have brought him into our inmost parts, and have thrown our mind open unto him. Therefore He saith, "commit no adultery with thine eyes, and thou wilt commit none with thy mind."

For one may indeed behold in another way, such as are the looks of the chaste; wherefore he did not altogether prohibit our seeing, but that seeing which is accompanied with desire. And if He had not meant this, He would have said simply, "He who looketh on a woman." But now He said not thus, but, "He who looketh to lust," "he who looketh to please his sight."

For not at all to this end did God make thee eyes, that thou shouldest thereby introduce adultery, but that, beholding His creatures, thou shouldest admire the Artificer.

Just then as one may feel wrath at random, so may one cast looks at random; that is, when thou doest it for lust. Rather, if thou desirest to look and find pleasure, look at thine own wife, and love her continually; no law forbids that. But if thou art to be curious about the beauties that belong to another, thou art injuring both thy wife by letting thine eyes wander elsewhere, and her on whom thou hast looked, by touching her unlawfully. Since, although thou hast not touched her with the hand, yet hast thou caressed her with thine eyes; for which cause this also is accounted adultery, and before that great penalty draws after it no slight one of its own. For then all within him is filled with disquiet and turmoil, and great is the tempest, and most grievous the pain, and no captive nor person in chains can be worse off than a man in this state of mind. And oftentimes she who hath shot the dart is flown away, while the wound even so remains. Or rather, it is not she who hath shot the dart, but thou gavest thyself the fatal wound, by thine unchaste look. And this I say to free modest women from the charge: since assuredly, should one deck herself out, and invite towards herself the eyes of such as fall in her way; even though she smite not him that meets with her, she incurs the utmost penalty: for she mixed the poison, she prepared the hemlock, even though she did not offer the cup. Or rather, she did also offer the cup, though no one were found to drink it.

3. "Why then doth He not discourse with them also?" it may be said. Because the laws which He appoints are in every case common, although He seem to address Himself unto men only. For in discoursing with the head, He makes His admonition common to the whole body also. For woman and man He knows as one living creature, and nowhere distinguishes their kind.

But if thou desirest to hear also His rebuke for them in particular, listen to Isaiah, in many words inveighing against them, and deriding their habit, their aspect, their gait, their trailing garments, their tripping feet, their drooping necks. Hear with him the blessed Paul also, setting many laws for them; and both about garments, and ornaments of gold, and plaiting of hair, and luxurious living, and all other such things, vehemently rebuking this sex. And Christ too, by what follows next, obscurely intimated this very same; for when He saith, "pluck out and cut off the eye that offendeth thee," He speaks as indicating His anger against them.

3. Wherefore also He subjoins,

"If thy right eye offend thee, pluck it out, and cast it from thee."

Thus, lest thou shouldest say, "But what if she be akin to me? what if in any other way she belong to me?" therefore He hath given these injunctions; not discoursing about our limbs;—far from it,—for nowhere doth He say that our flesh is to be blamed for things, but everywhere it is the evil mind that is accused. For it is not the eye that sees, but the mind and the thought. Often, for instance, we being wholly turned elsewhere, our eye sees not those who are present. So that the matter does not entirely depend upon its working. Again, had He been speaking of members of the body, He would not have said it of one eye, nor of the right eye only, but of both. For he who is offended by his right eye, most evidently will incur the same evil by his left also. Why then did He mention the right eye, and add the hand? To show thee that not of limbs is He speaking, but of them who are near unto us. Thus, "If," saith He, "thou so lovest any one, as though he were in stead of a right eye; if thou thinkest him so profitable to thee as to esteem him in the place of a hand, and he hurts thy soul; even these do thou cut off." And see the emphasis; for He saith not, "Withdraw from him," but to show the fullness of the separation, "pluck it out," saith He, "and cast it from thee."

Then, forasmuch as His injunction was sharp, He shows also the gain on either hand, both from the benefits and from the evils, continuing in the metaphor.

"For it is profitable for thee," saith He, "that one of thy members should perish, and not that thy whole body should be cast into hell."

For while he neither saves himself, nor fails to destroy thee too, what kindness is it for both to sink, whereas if they were separated, one at least might have been preserved?

But why did Paul then, it may be said, choose to become accursed? Not on condition of gaining nothing, but with a view to the salvation of others. But in this case the mischief pertains to both. And therefore He said not, "pluck out" only, but also "cast from thee:" to receive him again no more, if he continue as he is. For so shalt thou both deliver him from a heavier charge, and free thyself from ruin.

But that thou mayest see yet more clearly the profit of this law; let us, if you please, try what hath been said, in the case of the body itself, by way of supposition. I mean, if choice were given, and thou must either, keeping thine eye, be cast into a pit and perish, or plucking it out, preserve the rest of thy body; wouldest thou not of course accept the latter? It is plain to everyone. For this were not to act as one hating the eye, but as one loving the rest of the body. This same reckoning do thou make with regard to men also and women: that if he who harms thee by his friendship should continue incurable, his being thus cut off will both free thee from all mischief, and he also will himself be delivered from the heavier charges, not having to answer for thy destruction along with his own evil deeds.

Seest thou how full the law is of gentleness and tender care, and that which seems to men in general to be severity, how much love towards man it discloses?

Let them hearken to these things, who hasten to the theatres, and make themselves adulterers every day. For if the law commands to cut off him, whose connexion with us tends to our hurt; what plea can they have, who, by their haunting those places, attract towards them daily those even that have not yet become known to them, and procure to themselves occasions of ruin without number?

For henceforth, He not only forbids us to look unchastely, but having signified the mischief thence ensuing, He even straitens the law as He goes on, commanding to cut off, and dissever, and cast somewhere far away. And all this He ordains, who hath uttered words beyond number about love, that in either way thou mightest learn His providence, and how from every source He seeks thy profit.

4. "Now it hath been said, Whosoever shall put away his wife, let him give her a writing of divorcement. But I say unto you, Whosoever shall put away his wife, saving for the cause of fornication, causeth her to commit adultery; and whosoever marrieth her that is put away, committeth adultery."

He goes not on to what lies before Him, until He have well cleared out the former topics. For, lo, He shows us yet another kind of adultery. And what is this? There was an ancient law made, that he who hated his wife, for whatever kind of cause, should not be forbidden to cast her out, and to bring home another instead of her. The law however did not command him simply to do this, but after giving the woman a writing of divorcement, that it might not be in her power to return to him again; that so at least the figure of the marriage might remain.

For if He had not enjoined this, but it were lawful first to cast her out, and take another, then afterwards to take back the former, the confusion was sure to be great, all men continually taking each others' wives; and the matter thenceforth would have been direct adultery. With a view to this, He devised, as no small mitigation, the writing of divorcement.

But these things were done by reason of another, a far greater wickedness; I mean, had He made it necessary to keep in the house her even that was hated, the husband, hating, would have killed her. For such was the race of the Jews. For they who did not spare children, who slew prophets, and "shed blood as water," much more would they have showed no mercy to women. For this cause He allowed the less, to remove the greater evil. For that this was not a primary law, hear Him saying, "Moses wrote these things according to the hardness of your hearts," that ye might not slay them in the house, but rather put them out. But forasmuch as He had taken away all wrath, having forbidden not murder only, but even the mere feeling of anger, He with ease introduces this law likewise. With this view also He is ever bringing to mind the former words, to signify that His sayings are not contrary to them, but in agreement: that He is enforcing, not overthrowing them; perfecting, not doing them away.

And observe Him everywhere addressing His discourse to the man. Thus, "He that putteth away his wife," saith He, "causeth her to commit adultery, and he that marrieth a woman put away, committeth adultery." That is, the former, though he take not another wife, by that act alone hath made himself liable to blame, having made the first an adulteress; the latter again is become an adulterer by taking her who is another's. For tell me not this, "the other hath cast her out;" nay, for when cast out she continues to be the wife of him that expelled her. Then lest He should render the wife more self-willed, by throwing it all upon him who cast her out, He hath shut against her also the doors of him who was afterwards receiving her; in that He saith, "He who marrieth her that is put away committeth adultery;" and so makes the woman chaste even though unwilling, and blocks up altogether her access to all, and suffers her not to give an occasion for jealousy. For she who hath been made aware that she positively must either keep the husband, who was originally allotted to her, or being cast out of that house, not have any other refuge;—she even against her will was compelled to make the best of her consort.

And if He discourse not at all unto her concerning these things, marvel not; for the woman is rather a weak creature. For this cause letting her go, in his threatening against the men He fully corrects her remissness. Just as if any one who had a prodigal child, leaving him, should rebuke those who make him such, and forbid them to have intercourse, or to approach him. And if that be galling, call to mind, I pray thee, His former sayings, on what terms He had blessed His hearers; and thou wilt see that it is very possible and easy. For he that is meek, and a peacemaker, and poor in spirit, and merciful, how shall he cast out his wife? He that is used to reconcile others, how shall he be at variance with her that is his own?

And not thus only, but in another way also He hath lightened the enactment: forasmuch as even for him He leaves one manner of dismissal, when He saith, "Except for the cause of fornication;" since the matter had else come round again to the same issue. For if He had commanded to keep her in the house, though defiling herself with many, He would have made the matter end again in adultery.

Seest thou how these sayings agree with what had gone before? For he who looks not with unchaste eyes upon another woman, will not commit whoredom; and not committing whoredom, he will give no occasion to the husband to cast out his wife.

Therefore, you see, after this He presses the point without reserve, and builds up this fear as a bulwark, urging on the husband the great danger, if he do cast her out, in that he makes himself accountable for her adultery. Thus, lest thou being told, "pluck out the eye," shouldest suppose this to be said even of a wife: He added in good time this corrective, in one way only giving leave to cast her out, but no otherwise.

5. "Again, ye have heard that it was said to them of old time, Thou shalt not forswear thyself, but shalt perform unto the Lord thine oaths. But I say unto you, swear not at all."

Why did He go straightway not to theft, but to false witness, passing over that commandment? Because he that steals, doth upon occasion swear also; but he that knows not either swearing or speaking falsehood, much less will he choose to steal. So that by this He hath overthrown the other sin likewise: since falsehood comes of stealing.

But what means, "Thou shalt perform unto the Lord thine oaths?" It is this, "thou shalt be true in swearing." "But I say unto you, swear not at all."

Next, to lead them farther away from swearing by God, He saith, "Neither by Heaven, for it is God's throne, nor by the earth, for it is the footstool of His feet; nor by Jerusalem, for it is the city of the great King:" still speaking out of the prophetical writings, and signifying Himself not to be opposed to the ancients. This was because they had a custom of swearing by these objects, and he intimates this custom near the end of his Gospel.

But mark, I pray thee, on what ground He magnifies the elements; not from their own nature, but from God's relation to them, such as it had been in condescension declared. For because the tyranny of idolatry was great, that the elements might not be thought worthy of honor for their own sake, He hath assigned this cause, which we have mentioned, which again would pass on to the glory of God. For He neither said, "because Heaven is beautiful and great," nor, "because earth is profitable;" but "because the one is God's throne, the other His footstool;" on every side urging them on towards their Lord.

"Neither by thy head," saith He, "because thou canst not make one hair white or black."

Here again, not as wondering at man, hath He withdrawn him from swearing by his head (for so man himself would be worshipped), but as referring the glory to God, and signifying that thou art not master even of thyself, and of course therefore not of the oaths made by thy head. For if no one would give up his own child to another, much more will not God give up His own work to thee. For though it be thy head, yet is it the property of another; and so far from being master thereof, thou shalt not be able to do with it, no not the least thing of all. For He said not, "Thou canst not make one hair grow;" but, "Not so much as change its quality."

"But what," it may be said, "if any one should require an oath, and apply constraint?" Let the fear of God be more powerful than the constraint: since, if thou art to bring forward such excuses, thou wilt keep none of the things which are enjoined.

Yea, for first with respect to thy wife thou wilt say, "what if she be contentious and extravagant;" and then as to the right eye, "what if I love it, and am quite on fire?" and of the unchaste look, "what then, if I cannot help seeing?" and of our anger against a brother, "what if I be hasty, and not able to govern my tongue?" and in general, all His sayings thou mayest on this wise trample under foot. Yet surely with regard to human laws thou darest not in any case use this allegation, nor say, "what then if this or that be the case," but, willing or unwilling, thou receivest what is written.

And besides, thou wilt never have compulsion to undergo at all. For he that hath hearkened unto those former blessings, and hath framed himself to be such as Christ enjoined, will have no such constraint to endure from any, being held in reverence and veneration by all.

"But let your yea, be yea; and your nay, nay: for that which exceedeth these cometh of the evil one."

What is it then that "exceeds yea" and "nay"? it is the oath, not the perjury. For this latter is quite acknowledged, and no man needs to learn that it is of the evil one; and it is not an excess, but an opposite: whereas an excess means something more, and added over and above: which kind of thing swearing is.

"What then," saith one, "was it of the evil one? and if it was of the evil one, how was it a law?" Well, this same thing thou wilt say concerning the wife also; how is that now accounted adultery, which was before permitted?

What now may one reply to this? That the precepts then uttered had reference to the weakness of them who were receiving the laws; since also to be worshipped with the vapor of sacrifice is very unworthy of God, just as to lisp is unworthy of a philosopher. That kind of thing accordingly was now laid down to be adultery, and swearing to be of the evil one, now that the principles of virtue have advanced. But if these things had been, from the first, laws of the devil, they would not have attained to so great goodness. Yea, for had those not been forerunners in the first place, these which we now have would not have been so easily received. Do not thou then require their excellency now, when their use is past: but then, when the time was calling for them. Or rather, if thou wilt, even now: yea, for now also is their virtue shown: and most of all for the very cause, by reason of which we find fault with them. For their appearing such now, is the greatest commendation of them. For had they not brought us up well, and made us meet for the reception of the greater precepts, they would not have appeared such.

Therefore as the breast, when it hath fulfilled all its part, and is dismissing the child to the more manly diet, after that appears useless; and the parents who before thought it necessary for the babe, now abuse it with ten thousand mockeries (and many even not content with words of abuse, anoint it also with bitter drugs; that when their words have not power to remove the child's unseasonable propensity towards it, the real things may quench their longing): so also Christ saith, that they are of the evil one, not to indicate that the old law is of the devil, but in order that with most exceeding earnestness He might lead them away from their ancient poverty. And to them He saith these things; but with regard to the Jews, who were insensible and persevered in the same ways, He hath anointed their city all round with the terror of captivity, as with some bitter drug, and made it inaccessible. But since not even this had power to restrain them, but they desired to see it again, running to it, just as a child to the breast, He hid it from them altogether; both pulling it down, and leading away the more part of them far from it: as it is with our cattle; many, by shutting out the calves, in time induce them to forego their old familiar use of the milk.

But if the old law had belonged to the devil, it would not have led people away from idolatry, but rather would have drawn them on and cast them into it; for this did the devil desire. But now we see the opposite effect produced by the old law. And indeed this very thing, the oath, was ordained of old for this cause, that they might not swear by the idols. For "ye shall swear," saith He, "by the true God." They were then no small advantages which the law effected, but rather very great. For that they came unto the "strong meat," was the work of its care.

"What then," it may be said, "is not swearing of the evil one?" Yes, indeed it is altogether of the evil one; that is, now, after so high a rule of self-restraint; but then not so.

"But how," one may say, "should the same thing become at one time good, at another time not good?" Nay, I say the very contrary: how could it help becoming good and not good, while all things are crying aloud, that they are so: the arts, the fruits of the earth, and all things else?

See it, for example, taking place first in our own kind. Thus, to be carried, in the earliest age of life, is good, but afterwards pernicious; to eat food that hath been softened in the mouth, in the first scene of our life, is good, but afterwards it is full of disgust; to be fed upon milk and to fly to the breast, is at first profitable and healthful, but tends afterwards to decay and harm. Seest thou how the same actions, by reason of the times, appear good, and again not so? Yea, and to wear the robe of a child is well as long as you are a boy, but contrariwise, when you are become a man, it is disgraceful. Wouldest thou learn of the contrary case too, how to the child again the things of the man are unsuited? Give the boy a man's robe, and great will be the laughter; and greater the danger, he being often upset in walking after that fashion. Allow him to handle public affairs, and to traffic, and sow, and reap, and great again will be the laughter.

And why do I mention these things? when killing, which among all is acknowledged to be an invention of the evil one, killing, I say, having found its proper occasion, caused Phinehas, who committed it, to be honored with the priesthood. For that killing is a work of him whom I just now mentioned, hear what Christ saith; "Ye will do the works of your Father; he was a manslayer from the beginning." But Phinehas became a manslayer, and "it was counted unto him" (so He speaks) "for righteousness:" and Abraham again on becoming not a man-slayer only, but (which was far worse) the slayer of his child, won more and more approbation. And Peter too wrought a twofold slaughter, nevertheless what he did was of the Spirit.

Let us not then examine simply the acts, but the season too, and the causes, and the mind, and the difference of persons, and whatsoever else may accompany them, these let us search out with all exactness: for there is no arriving at the truth otherwise.

And let us be diligent, if we would attain unto the kingdom, to show forth something more than the old commandments; since we cannot otherwise lay hold of the things of Heaven. For if we arrive but at the same measure, that of the ancients, we shall stand without that threshold; for "except your righteousness shall exceed the righteousness of the Scribes and Pharisees, ye cannot enter into the kingdom of Heaven."

6. Yet, although so heavy a threat is set down, there are some who so far from over-passing this righteousness, even come short of it; so far from shunning oaths, they even swear falsely; so far from avoiding an unchaste gaze, they even fall into the very act of wickedness. And all the rest of the things which are forbidden, they dare to do, as though past feeling: waiting for one thing only, the day of punishment, and the time when they are to pay the most

extreme penalty for their misdoings. And this is the portion of those only who have ended their lives in wickedness. For these have reason to despair, and thenceforth to expect nothing else but punishment; whereas they who are yet here, may have power both to renew the fight and to conquer and be crowned with ease.

Despond not therefore, O man, neither put away thy noble earnestness; for in truth the things are not grievous, which are enjoined. What trouble is it, I pray thee, to shun an oath? What, does it cost any money? Is it sweat and hardship? It is enough to have willed only, and the whole is done.

But if you allege to me thine habit; for this very reason most of all do I say, that thy doing right is easy. For if thou bring thyself to another habit, thou hadst effected all.

Consider, for example, how among the Greeks, in many instances, persons lisping have entirely cured by much practice their halting tongue; while others, who were used to shrug up their shoulders in an unseemly way, and to be continually moving them, by putting a sword over them, have broken themselves of it.

For since you are not persuaded out of the Scriptures, I am compelled to shame you by them that are without. This God also did unto the Jews, when He said, "Go ye forth unto the Isles of Chittim, and send unto Kedar, and know if nations will change their gods; which yet are no gods." And to the brutes likewise He sends us oftentimes, saying on this wise, "Go to the ant, thou sluggard, and emulate her ways:" and "go forth to the bee."

This therefore I also now say unto you; consider the philosophers of the Greeks; and then ye will know of how great punishment we are worthy, who disobey the laws of God: in that they for seemliness before men have taken exceeding pains, and you bestow not the same diligence, no, not for the things of Heaven.

But if thou shouldest reply, "Habit has a wonderful power to beguile even those who are very much in earnest:" this I likewise acknowledge; however, there is another thing which I say with it; that as it is powerful to beguile, so also is it easy to be corrected. For if thou wilt set over thyself at home many to watch thee, such as thy servant, thy wife, thy friend, thou wilt easily break off from the bad habits, being hard pressed and closely restrained by all. If thou succeed in doing this for ten days only, thou wilt after that no longer need any further time, but all will be secured to thee, rooted anew in the firmness of the most excellent habit.

When therefore thou art beginning to correct this, though thou shouldest transgress thy law a first, a second, a third, a twentieth time, do not despair, but rise up again, and resume the same diligence, and thou wilt surely prevail.

For perjury surely is no trifling mischief. If to swear is of the evil one, how great the penalty which false swearing will bring! Did ye give praise to what hath been said? Nay, I want not applause, nor tumults, nor noise. One thing only do I wish, that quietly and intelligently listening, you should do what is said. This is the applause, this the panegyric for me. But if thou praisest what I say, but doest not what thou applaudest, greater is the punishment, more aggravated the accusation: and to us it is shame and ridicule. For the things here present are no dramatic spectacle; neither do ye now sit gazing on actors, that ye may merely applaud. This place is a spiritual school. Wherefore also there is but one thing aimed at, duly to perform the things that have been spoken, and to show forth our obedience by our works. For then only shall we have obtained all. Since as things are, to say the truth, we have fairly given up in despair. For I have not ceased giving these admonitions either to those whom I meet in private, or in discourse with you all in common. Yet I see no advantage at all gained, but you are still clinging to the former rude beginnings, which thing is enough to fill the teacher with weariness.

See, for example, Paul himself, hardly bearing it, because his scholars were delaying a long time in their earlier lessons: "For when for the time," saith he, "ye ought to be teachers, ye have need to be taught again which be the first principles of the oracles of God. "

Wherefore we too mourn and lament. And if I see you persisting, I will forbid you for the future to set foot on this sacred threshold, and partake of the immortal mysteries; as we do fornicators and adulterers, and persons charged with murder. Yea, for it is better to offer our accustomed prayers, with two or three, who keep the laws of God, than to sweep together a multitude of trangressors and corrupters of others.

Let me have no rich man, no potentate, puffing at me here, and drawing up his eyebrows; all these things are to me a fable, a shade, a dream. For no one of those who are now rich, will stand up for me there, when I am called to account and accused, as not having thoroughly vindicated the laws of God, with all due earnestness. For this, this ruined even that admirable old man, though in his own life giving no handle for blame; yet for all that, because he overlooked the treading under foot of God's laws, he was chastised with his children, and paid that grievous penalty. And if, where the absolute authority of nature was so great, he who failed to treat his own children with due firmness endured so grievous a punishment; what indulgence shall we have, freed as we are from that dominion, and yet ruining all by flattery?

In order therefore that ye may not destroy both us and your own selves with us, be persuaded, I entreat you; set very many to watch over you, and call you to account, and so free yourselves from the habit of oaths; that going on orderly from thence, ye may both with all facility succeed in attaining unto all other virtue, and may enjoy the good things to come; which God grant that we may all win, by the grace and love towards man of our Lord Jesus Christ, to whom be glory and might now and always, even for ever and ever. Amen.

HOMILY XVIII

MATT. V. 38, 39, 40

"Ye have heard that it hath been said, An eye for an eye, and a tooth for a tooth. But I say unto you, that ye resist not the evil: but whosoever shall smite thee on the right cheek, turn to him the other also. And if any man will sue thee at the law, and take away thy coat, let him have thy cloak also."

Seest thou that it was not of an eye that He was speaking before, when He made the law to pluck out the offending eye, but of him who by his friendship is harming us, and casting us into the gulf of destruction? For He who in this place uses so great strength of expression, and who, not even when another is plucking out your eye, permits you to strike out his; how should He have made it a law to strike out one's own?

But if any one accuses the ancient law, because it commands such retaliation, he seems to me very unskillful in the wisdom that becomes a legislator, and ignorant of the virtue of opportunities, and the gain of condescension. For if he considered who were the hearers of these sayings, and how they were disposed, and when they received this code of laws, he will thoroughly admit the wisdom of the Lawgiver, and will see that it is one and the same, who made both those laws and these, and who wrote each of them exceeding profitably, and in its due season. Yes, for if at the beginning He had introduced these high and most weighty commandments, men would not have received either these, or the others; but now ordaining them severally in their due time, He hath by the two corrected the whole world.

And besides, He commanded this, not that we might strike out one another's eyes, but that we might keep our hands to ourselves. For the threat of suffering hath effectually restrained our inclination to be doing.

And thus in fact He is silently dropping seed of much self-restraint, at least in that He commands to retaliate with just the same acts. Yet surely he that began such transgression were worthy of a greater punishment, and this the abstract nature of justice demands. But forasmuch as He was minded to mingle mercy also with justice, He condemns him whose offenses were very great to a punishment less than his desert: teaching us even while we suffer to show forth great consideration.

Having therefore mentioned the ancient law, and recognized it all, He signifies again, that it is not our brother who hath done these deeds, but the evil one. For this cause he hath also subjoined, "But I say unto you, that ye resist not the evil one." He did not say, "resist not your brother," but "the evil one," signifying that on his motion men dare so to act; and in this way relaxing and secretly removing most of our anger against the aggressor, by transferring the blame to another.

"What then?" it is said, "ought we not to resist the evil one?" Indeed we ought, but not in this way, but as He hath commanded, by giving one's self up to suffer wrongfully; for thus shalt thou prevail over him. For one fire is not quenched by another, but fire by water. And to show thee that even under the old law he that suffered rather prevails, that he it is who wins the crown; examine just what is done, and thou wilt see that his advantage is great. For as he that hath begun with unjust acts, will have himself destroyed the eyes of both, his neighbor's and his own (wherefore also he is justly hated of all, and ten thousand accusations are aimed at him): so he that hath been injured, even after his equal retaliation, will have done nothing horrible. Wherefore also he hath many to sympathize with him, as being clear from that offense even after he hath retaliated. And though the calamity be equal to both parties, yet the sentence passed on it is not equal, either with God, or with men. It should seem then, that neither is the calamity equal in the end.

Now whereas at the beginning He said, "he that is angry with his brother without a cause," and "he that calleth him fool shall be in danger of hell fire," here He requires yet more entire self-restraint, commanding him that suffers ill not merely to be quiet, but even to be more exceedingly earnest in his turn, by offering the other cheek.

And this He saith, not as legislating about such a blow as this only, but as teaching also what forbearance we should practise in all our other trials. For just as when He saith, "whoso calleth his brother fool, is in danger of hell," He speaks not of this word only, but also of all reviling; even so here also He is making a law, not so much for our bearing it manfully, when smitten, as that we should be undisturbed, whatever we suffer. Because of this He both there singled out the extremest insult, and here hath set down that which seems to be of all blows most opprobrious, the blow on the cheek, so full of all insolence. And He commands this as having regard both of him that strikes and of him that is stricken. Since both he that is insulted will not think that he suffers any harm, being thus framed to self-restraint (nay, he will not even have any sense of the insult, as striving rather for a prize than as receiving a blow); and he that is offering the affront will be made ashamed, and not add a second blow, though he be fiercer than any wild beast, yea, rather will condemn himself heartily for the former. For nothing so restrains the wrong doers, as when the injured bear what is done with gentleness. And it not only restrains them from rushing onward, but works upon them also to repent for what has gone before, and in wonder at such forbearance to draw back. And it makes them more our own, and causes them to be slaves, not merely friends, instead of haters and enemies; even as avenging one's self does just the contrary: for it both disgraces each of the two, and makes them worse, and their anger it heightens into a greater flame; yea, often no less than death itself is the end of it, going on from bad to worse. Wherefore He not only forbade thee to be angry when smitten, but even enjoined thee to satiate the other's desire, that so neither may the former blow appear to have befallen thee against thy will. For thus, lost as he may be to shame, thou wilt be able to smite him with a mortal blow, rather than if thou hadst smitten him with thine hand; or if his shamelessness be still greater, thou wilt make him gentle in proportion.

2. "And if any man will sue thee at the law, and take away thy coat, let him have thy cloak also."

For not in the matter of blows only, but of our goods also, He would have such forbearance exhibited. Wherefore He again employs the same strong figure. That is, as in the other case He commands to overcome in suffering, so here again, by allowing ourselves to be deprived of more than the wrong doer expected. However, He did not put it so merely, but with something to enhance it: not saying, "give thy cloak to him that asketh," but "to him that would sue thee at the law," that is, "if he drag thee into court, and give thee trouble."

And just as, after He had bidden not to call another fool, nor to be angry without cause, He went on and required more, in that He commanded to offer the right cheek also; even so here, having said, "Agree with thine adversary," He again amplifies the precept. For now He orders us not only to give what the other would have, but even to show forth a greater liberality.

"What then!" one may say, "am I to go about naked?" We should not be naked, if we obeyed these sayings with exactness; rather more abundantly than any should we be clothed. For first, no one would attack men of this disposition; and next, if there chanced to be any one so savage and ungentle, as to proceed even so far, yet many more would be found to clothe him, who acted with such self-denial, not with garments only, but even with their own flesh, if it were possible.

Further: even though one were of necessity to go about naked on account of this sort of self-denial, neither so were it any disgrace. Since Adam too was "naked" in paradise, "and was not ashamed;" and Isaiah was "naked, and barefoot," and more glorious than all the Jews; and Joseph also, when he stripped himself, did then more than ever shine forth. For to be thus naked is no evil, but to be so clad, as we now are, with costly garments, this is both disgraceful and ridiculous. For this cause, you see, those had praise of God, but these He blames, both by prophets and by apostles.

Let us not therefore suppose His injunctions impossible. Nay, for besides their expediency, they are very easy, if we are sober-minded; and the profit of them is so great as to be an exceeding help, not to ourselves only, but to those also who are using us despitefully. And in this chiefly stands their excellence, that while they induce us to suffer wrong, they by the same means teach them also that do the wrong to control themselves. For while he on his part thinks it a great thing to take what belongs to others, but thou signifiest to him, that to thee it is easy to give even what he doth not ask: while thou bringest in liberality for a counterpoise to his meanness, and a wise moderation to his covetousness: consider what a lesson he will get, being taught not by sayings, but by actual deeds, to scorn vice and to seek after virtue.

For God will have us profitable not to ourselves alone, but to all our neighbors as well. Now if thou givest, and abstainest from suing, thou hast sought thine own advantage only; but if thou give him some other thing, thou hast made him too better, and so sent him away. Of this nature is salt, which is what He would have them to be; seeing it both recruits itself, and keeps all other bodies with which it may associate: of this nature is light; for it shows objects both to a man's self and to all others. Forasmuch then as He hath set thee in the rank of these things, help thou likewise him who is sitting in darkness, and teach him that neither before did he take any thing by force: persuade him that he hath done no despite. Yea, for thus thou thyself also wilt be had in more respect and reverence, if thou signify that thou gavest freely and wert not robbed. Make therefore his sin, through thy moderation, an instance of thine own bounty.

3. And if thou think this a great thing, wait, and thou wilt see clearly, that neither yet hast thou attained to perfection. For not even here doth He stop with thee, who is laying down the laws of patient endurance, but He proceeds even further, thus saying,

"If any one shall compel thee to go one mile, go with him twain."

Seest thou the height of self-denial? in this at least, that after giving thy coat, and thy cloak, not even if thine enemy should wish to use thy naked body for hardships and labors, not even so (saith He), must thou forbid him. For He would have us possess all things in common, both our bodies and our goods, as with them that are in need, so with them that insult us: for the latter comes of manliness, the former of mercifulness.

Because of this, He said, "If any one shall compel thee to go one mile, go with him twain:" again leading thee higher up, and commanding thee to show forth the same kind of ambition.

For if the things of which He spake at the beginning, being far less than these, have so great blessings pronounced on them; consider what sort of portion awaits them, who duly perform these, and what they become even before their rewards, in a human and passible body winning entire freedom from passion. Since when neither insult, nor blows, nor the spoiling of their property, galls them; while they give way to no such thing, but rather add in large measure to their endurance; reflect what kind of training their soul is undergoing.

On this account then, as in regard of blows, as in regard of our goods, so in this case also, He hath bidden us act. "For why," saith He, "do I mention insult, and property? Though he should want to make use of thy very own limbs for toil and weary work, and this unjustly, do thou again conquer and overpass His unjust desire."

For "to compel" is this, to drag unjustly and without any reason, and by way of despite. Nevertheless, for this also be thou ready in thy station, so as to suffer more than the other would fain do to thee.

"Give to him that asketh thee, and from him that would borrow of thee, turn not thou away."

These last are less than what went before; but marvel not, for this He is ever wont to do, mingling the small with the great. And if these be little in comparison with those, let them hearken, who take the goods of others, who distribute their own among harlots, and kindle to themselves a double fire, both by the unrighteous income, and by the pernicious outlay.

But by "borrowing," here, He means not the compact with usury, but the use merely. And elsewhere He even amplifies it, saying that we should give to them, from whom we do not expect to receive.

4. "Ye have heard that it hath been said, Thou shalt love thy neighbor, and hate thine enemy. But I say unto you, love your enemies, and pray for them which despitefully use you: bless them that curse you, do good to them that

hate you. That ye may become like your Father which is in Heaven; for He maketh His sun to rise on the evil and on the good, and sendeth rain on the just and on the unjust."

See how He hath set the highest pinnacle on our good deeds. For this is why He teaches not only to endure a blow, but to offer the right cheek also; not only to add the cloak to the coat, but to travel also two miles with him who compels thee to go one; in order that thou mightest receive with all facility that which is much more than these. "But what," one may say, "is more than these?" Not even to count as an enemy him who is doing these things: or rather even somewhat else more than this. For He said not, "do not hate," but "love;" He said not, "do not injure," but "do good."

And if any one should examine accurately, he will see that even to these things somewhat is added, much greater than they are. For neither did He simply command to love, but to pray.

Seest thou how many steps He hath ascended, and how He hath set us on the very summit of virtue? Nay, mark it, numbering from the beginning. A first step is, not to begin with injustice: a second, after he hath begun, to vindicate one's self by equal retaliation; a third, not to do unto him that is vexing us the same that one hath suffered, but to be quiet; a fourth, even to give one's self up to suffer wrongfully; a fifth, to give up yet more than the other, who did the wrong, wishes; a sixth, not to hate him who hath done so; a seventh, even to love him; an eighth, to do him good also; a ninth, to entreat God Himself on his behalf. Seest thou, what height of self-command? Wherefore glorious too, as we see, is the reward which it hath. That is, because the thing enjoined was great, and needed a fervent soul, and much earnestness, He appoints for it also such a reward, as for none of the former. For He makes not mention here of earth, as with respect to the meek; nor of comfort and mercy, as with regard to the mourners and the merciful; nor of the kingdom of Heaven; but of that which was more thrilling than all; our becoming like God, in such wise as men might become so. For He saith, "That ye may become like unto your Father which is in Heaven."

And observe, I pray thee, how neither in this place, nor in the preceding parts, doth He call Him His own Father, but in that instance, "God," and "a great King," when He was discoursing about oaths, and here, "their Father." And this He doth, as reserving for the proper season what He had to say touching these points.

5. Then, bringing the likeness yet closer, He saith,

"Because He maketh His sun to rise on the evil and on the good, and sendeth rain upon just and unjust."

"For He too, so far from hating," so He speaks, "even pours benefits on those that insult Him." Yet surely in no respect is the case parallel, not only because of the surpassing nature of His benefits, but also by reason of the excellence of His dignity. For thou indeed art despised by thy fellow-slave, but He by His slave, who hath also received ten thousand benefits from Him: and thou indeed givest words, in praying for him, but He, deeds, very great and marvellous, kindling the sun, and giving the annual showers. "Nevertheless, even so I grant thee to be mine equal, in such wise as it is possible for a man so to be."

Hate not then the man that doeth thee wrong, who is procuring thee such good things, and bringing thee to so great honor. Curse not him that uses thee despitefully; for so hast thou undergone the labor, but art deprived of the fruit; thou wilt bear the loss, but lose the reward; which is of the utmost folly, having borne the more grievous, not to bear what is less than it. "But how," saith one, "is it possible for this to take place?" Having seen God become man, and descend so far, and suffer so much for thy sake, dost thou still inquire and doubt, how it is possible to forgive thy fellow-servants their injuriousness? Hearest thou not Him on the cross, saying, "Forgive them, for they know not what they do?" Hearest thou not Paul, when he saith, "He who is gone up on high, and is sitting on the right hand intercedeth for us?" Seest thou not that even after the cross, and after He had been received up, He sent the apostles unto the Jews that had slain Him, to bring them His ten thousand blessings, and this, though they were to suffer ten thousand terrors at their hands?

6. But hast thou been greatly wronged? Nay, what hast thou endured like thy Lord, bound, beaten with whips, with rods, spit upon by servants, enduring death, and that death, which is of all deaths the most shameful, after ten thousand favors shown? And even if thou hast been greatly wronged, for this very cause most of all do thou do him good, that thou mayest both make thine own crown more glorious, and set thy brother free from the worst infirmity. For so too the physicians, when they are kicked, and shamefully handled by the insane, then most of all pity them, and take measures for their perfect cure, knowing that the insult comes of the extremity of their disease. Now I bid thee too have the same mind touching them that are plotting against thee, and do thou so treat them that are injuring thee. For it is they above all that are diseased, it is they who are undergoing all the violence. Deliver him then from this grievous contumely, and grant him to let go his anger, and set him free from that grievous demon, wrath. Yea, for if we see persons possessed by devils, we weep for them; we do not seek to be ourselves also possessed.

Now let us do this too likewise with respect to them that are angry; for in truth the enraged are like the possessed; yea rather, are more wretched than they, being mad with consciousness of it. Wherefore also their frenzy is without excuse. Trample not then on the fallen, but rather pity him. For so, should we see any one troubled with bile, blinded and giddy, and straining to cast up this evil humor, we stretch forth a hand, and continue to support him through his struggles, and though we stain our garments, we regard it not, but seek one thing only, how we may set him free from this grievous distress. This then let us do with respect to the angry also, and continue to bear them up when vomiting and struggling; nor let him go, until he put from him all the bitterness. And then shall he feel toward thee the greatest thankfulness; when he is at rest, then he will know clearly from how great trouble thou hast released him.

But why do I speak of the thanks from him? for God will straightway crown thee, and will requite thee with ten thousand honors, because thou hast freed thy brother from a grievous disease; and that brother too will honor thee as a master, ever reverencing thy forbearance.

Seest thou not the women that are in travail, how they bite those that stand by, and they are not pained? or rather they are pained, but bear it bravely, and sympathize with them who are in sorrow and are torn by those pangs. These do thou too emulate, and prove not softer than women. For after these women have brought forth (for these men are more feeble minded than women), then they will know thee to be a man in comparison. of Heaven?

9. What then can we deserve, who are commanded to emulate God, and are perhaps in a way not so much as to equal the publicans? For if "to love them that love us" be the part of publicans, sinners, and heathens: when we do not even this (and we do it not, so long as we envy our brethren who are in honor), what penalty shall we not incur, commanded as we are to surpass the scribes, and taking our place below the heathens? How then shall we behold the kingdom, I pray thee? how shall we set foot on that holy threshold, who are not surpassing even the publicans? For this He covertly signified, when He said, "Do not even the publicans the same?"

And this thing most especially we may admire in His teaching, that while in each instance He sets down with very great fullness the prizes of the conflicts; such as "to see God," and "to inherit the kingdom of Heaven," and "to become sons of God," and "like God," and "to obtain mercy," and "to be comforted," and "the great reward:" if anywhere He must needs mention things grievous, He doth this in a subdued tone. Thus in the first place, the name of hell He hath set down once only in so many sentences; and in some other instances too, it is with reserve that He corrects the hearer, and as though he were managing His discourse rather in the way of shaming than threatening him; where He saith, "do not even the publicans the same?" and, "if the salt have lost its savor;" and, "he shall be called least in the kingdom of Heaven."

And there are places where He puts down the sin itself by way of punishment, leaving to the hearer to infer the grievousness of the punishment: as when He saith, "he hath committed adultery with her in his heart;" and, "he that putteth away causeth her to commit adultery;" and, "That which is more than these is of the evil one." For to them that have understanding, instead of the mention of the punishment, the very greatness of the sin is sufficient for correction.

Wherefore also He here brings forward the heathens and the publicans, by the quality of the person putting the disciple to shame. Which Paul too did, saying, "Sorrow not, even as the rest which have no hope;" and, "Even as the Gentiles which know not God."

And to signify that He requires nothing very overpowering, but a little more than was accustomed, He saith,

"Do not even the Gentiles the same?" Yet nevertheless He stops not the discourse at this, but makes it end with His rewards, and those good hopes, saying,

"Be ye therefore perfect, as your Heavenly Father."

And He intersperses everywhere abundantly the name of the heavens, by the very place thoroughly elevating their minds. For as yet, I know not how, they were somewhat weak and dull.

10. Let us then, bearing in mind all the things which have been said, show forth great love even towards our enemies; and let us cast away that ridiculous custom, to which many of the more thoughtless give way, waiting for those that meet them to address them first. Towards that which hath a great blessing, they have no zeal; but what is ridiculous, that they follow after.

Wherefore now dost thou not address him first? "Because he is waiting for this," is the reply. Nay, for this very reason most of all thou shouldest have sprung forward to him, that thou mightest win the crown. "No," saith he, "since this was his object." And what can be worse than this folly? That is, "Because this," saith he, "was his object;—to become procurer of a reward for me;—I will not put my hand to what he has thus suggested." Now if he first address thee, thou gainest nothing, even though thou accost him. But if thou be first to spring forward and speak to him, thou hast made thyself profit of his pride, and hast gathered in a manner abundant fruit from his obstinacy. What is it then but the utmost folly, when we are to reap so large fruit from bare words, to give up the gain; and condemning him, to stumble at the very same thing? For if thou blamest him for this, that he first waits to be addressed by another, wherefore dost thou emulate that same thing which thou accusest? That which thou saidst was evil, why art thou to imitate the same as good? Seest thou how that nothing is more senseless than a man who associates with wickedness? Wherefore, I entreat, let us flee this evil and ridiculous practice. Yea, for ten thousand friendships hath this pestilence overthrown, many enmities hath it wrought.

For this cause then let us anticipate them. Since we who are commanded to take blows, and be compelled to journey, and to be stripped by enemies, and to bear it; what kind of indulgence should we deserve, exhibiting so great contentiousness in a mere formal address?

11. "Why," saith one, "we are despised and spit upon, the moment we have given him up this." And in order that man may not despise thee, dost thou offend God? And in order that thy frenzied fellow servant may not despise thee, dost thou despise the Lord, who hath bestowed on thee benefits so great? Nay, if it be amiss that thine equal should despise thee, how much more that thou shouldest despise the God that made thee?

And together with this, consider that other point also; that when he despises thee, he is at that very moment employed in procuring to thee a greater reward. Since for God's sake thou submittest to it, because thou hast hearkened to His laws. And this, to what kind of honor is it not equal? to how many diadems? Be it my portion both to be insulted and despised for God's sake, rather than to be honored by all kings; for nothing, nothing is equal to this glory.

This then let us pursue, in such wise as Himself commanded, and making no account of the things of men, but showing forth perfect self restraint in all things, let us so direct our own lives. For so even now, from this very time, we shall enjoy the good things of the heavens, and of the crowns that are there, walking as angels among men, going about in the earth like the angelic powers, and abiding apart from all lust, from all turmoil.

And together with all these things we shall receive also the unutterable blessings: unto which may we all attain, by the grace and love towards man of our Lord Jesus Christ, to whom be glory, and power, and worship, with the unoriginate Father, and the Holy and Good Spirit, now and always, even forever and ever. Amen.

HOMILY XIX

MATT. VI. 1

"Take heed that ye do not your alms before men, to be seen of them."

He roots out in what remains the most tyrannical passion of all, the rage and madness with respect to vainglory, which springs up in them that do right. For at first He had not at all discoursed about it; it being indeed superfluous, before He had persuaded them to do any of the things which they ought, to teach in which way they should practise and pursue them.

But after He had led them on to self-command, then He proceeds to purge away also the alloy which secretly subsists with it. For this disease is by no means of random birth; but when we have duly performed many of the commandments.

It behooved therefore first to implant virtue, and then to remove the passion which mars its fruit.

And see with what He begins, with fasting, and prayer, and almsgiving: for in these good deeds most especially it is wont to make its haunt. The Pharisee, for instance, was hereby puffed up, who saith, "I fast twice a week, I give tithes of my substance." And he was vainglorious too in his very prayer, making it for display. For since there was no one else present, he pointed himself out to the publican, saying, "I am not as the rest of men, nor even as this publican."

And mark how Christ began, as though He were speaking of some wild beast, hard to catch, and crafty to deceive him who was not very watchful. Thus, "take heed," saith He, "as to your alms." So Paul also speaks to the Philippians; "Beware of dogs." And with reason, for the evil beast comes in upon us secretly, and without noise puffs all away, and unobservedly carries out all that is within.

Forasmuch then as He had made much discourse about almsgiving, and brought forward God, "Who maketh His sun to rise on the evil and the good," and by motives from all quarters had urged them on to this, and had persuaded them to exult in the abundance of their giving; He finishes by taking away also all things that encumber this fair olive tree. For which same cause He saith, "Take heed that ye do not your alms before men," for that which was before mentioned, is "God's" almsgiving.

2. And when He had said, "not to do it before men," He added, "to be seen of them." And though it seems as if the same thing were said a second time, yet if any one give particular attention, it is not the same thing, but one is different from the other; and it hath great security, and unspeakable care and tenderness. For it may be, both that one doing alms before men may not do it to be

seen of them, and again that one not doing it before men may do it to be seen of them. Wherefore it is not simply the thing, but the intent, which He both punishes and rewards. And unless such exactness were employed, this would make many more backward about the giving of alms, because it is not on every occasion altogether possible to do it secretly. For this cause, setting thee free from this restraint, He defines both the penalty and the reward not by the result of the action, but by the intention of the doer.

That is, that thou mayest not say, "What? am I then the worse, should another see?"—"it is not this," saith He, "that I am seeking, but the mind that is in thee, and the tone of what thou doest." For His will is to bring our soul altogether into frame, and to deliver it from every disease. Now having, as you see, forbidden men's acting for display, and having taught them the penalty thence ensuing, namely, to do it vainly, and for nought, He again rouses their spirits by putting them in mind of the Father, and of Heaven, that not by the loss alone He might sting them, but also shame them by the recollection of Him who gave them being.

"For ye have no reward," saith He, "with your Father which is in Heaven."

Nor even at this did He stop, but proceeds yet further, by other motives also increasing their disgust. For as above He set forth publicans and heathens, by the quality of the person shaming their imitators, so also in this place the hypocrites.

"Therefore when thou doest thine alms," saith He, "do not sound a trumpet before thee, as the hypocrites do."

Not that they had trumpets, but He means to display the greatness of their frenzy, by the use of this figure of speech, deriding and making a show of them hereby.

And well hath He called them "hypocrites" for the mask was of mercy, but the spirit of cruelty and inhumanity. For they do it, not because they pity their neighbors, but that they themselves may enjoy credit; and this came of the utmost cruelty; while another was perishing with hunger, to be seeking vainglory, and not putting an end to his suffering.

It is not then the giving alms which is required, but the giving as one ought, the giving for such and such an end.

Having then amply derided those men, and having handled them so, that the hearer should be even ashamed of them, He again corrects thoroughly the mind which is so distempered: and having said how we ought not to act, He signifies on the other hand how we ought to act. How then ought we to do our alms?

"Let not thy left hand know," saith He, "what thy right hand doeth."

Here again His enigmatical meaning is not of the hands, but He hath put the thing hyperbolically. As thus: "If it can be," saith He, "for thyself not to know it, let this be the object of thine endeavor; that, if it were possible, it may be concealed from the very hands that minister." It is not, as some say, that we should hide it from wrong-headed men, for He hath here commanded that it should be concealed from all.

And then the reward too; consider how great it is. For after He had spoken of the punishment from the one, He points out also the honor derived from the other; from either side urging them, and leading them on to high lessons. Yea, for He is persuading them to know that God is everywhere present, and that not by our present life are our interests limited, but a yet more awful tribunal will receive us when we go hence, and the account of all our doings, and honors, and punishments: and that no one will be hid in doing anything either great or small, though he seem to be hid from men. For all this did He darkly signify, when He said,

"Thy Father which seeth in secret shall reward thee openly."

Setting for him a great and august assemblage of spectators, and what He desires, that very thing bestowing on him in great abundance. "For what," saith He, "dost thou wish? is it not to have some to be spectators of what is going on? Behold then, thou hast some; not angels, nor archangels, but the God of all." And if thou desire to have men also as spectators, neither of this desire doth He deprive thee at the fitting season, but rather in greater abundance affords it unto thee. For, if thou shouldest now make a display, thou wilt be able to make it to ten only, or twenty, or (we will say) a hundred persons: but if thou take pains to lie hid now, God Himself will then proclaim thee in the presence of the whole universe. Wherefore above all, if thou wilt have men see thy good deeds, hide them now, that then all may look on them with the more honor, God making them manifest, and extolling them, and proclaiming them before all. Again, whereas now they that behold will rather condemn thee as vainglorious; when they see thee crowned, so far from condemning, they will even admire thee, all of them. When therefore by waiting a little, thou mayest both receive a reward, and reap greater admiration; consider what folly it is to cast thyself out of both these; and while thou art seeking thy reward from God, and while God is beholding, to summon men for the display of what is going on. Why, if display must be made of our love, to our Father above all should we make it; and this most especially, when our Father hath the power both to crown and to punish.

And let me add, even were there no penalty, it were not meet for him who desires glory, to let go this our theatre, and take in exchange that of men. For who is there so wretched, as that when the king was hastening to come and see his achievements, he would let him go, and make up his assembly of spectators of poor men and beggars? For this cause then, He not only commands to make no display, but even to take pains to be concealed: it not being at all the same, not to strive for publicity, and to strive for concealment.

3. "And when ye pray," saith He, "ye shall not be as the hypocrites, for they love to pray standing in the synagogues, and in the corners of the streets. Verily I say unto you, they have their reward."

"But thou, when thou prayest, enter into thy closet, and when thou hast shut thy door, pray to thy Father which is in secret."

These too again He calls "hypocrites," and very fitly; for while they are feigning to pray to God, they are looking round after men; wearing the garb not of suppliants, but of ridiculous persons. For he, who is to do a suppliant's office, letting go all other, looks to him alone, who hath power to grant his request. But if thou leave this one, and go about wandering and casting around thine eyes everywhere, thou wilt depart with empty hands. For this was thine own will. Wherefore He said not, "such shall not receive a reward," but, "they have it out:" that is, they shall indeed receive one, but from those of whom they themselves desire to have it. For God wills not this: He rather for His part was willing to bestow on men the recompence that comes from Himself; but they seeking that which is from men, can be no longer justly entitled to receive from Him, for whom they have done nothing.

But mark, I pray thee, the lovingkindness of God, in that He promises to bestow on us a reward, even for those good things which we ask of Him.

Having then discredited them, who order not this duty as they ought, both from the place and from their disposition of mind, and having shown that they are very ridiculous: He introduces the best manner of prayer, and again gives the reward, saying, "Enter into thy closet."

"What then," it may be said, "ought we not to pray in church?" Indeed we ought by all means, but in such a spirit as this. Because everywhere God seeks the intention of all that is done. Since even if thou shouldest enter into thy closet, and having shut the door, shouldest do it for display, the doors will do thee no good.

It is worth observing in this case also, how exact the definition, which He made when He said, "That they may appear unto men." So that even if thou shut the doors, this He desires thee duly to perform, rather than the shutting of the doors, even to shut the doors of the mind. For as in everything it is good to be freed from vainglory, so most especially in prayer. For if even without this, we wander and are distracted, when shall we attend unto the things which we are saying, should we enter in having this disease also? And if we who pray and beseech attend not, how do we expect God to attend?

4. But yet some there are, who after such and so earnest charges, behave themselves so unseemly in prayer, that even when their person is concealed, they make themselves manifest to all by their voice, crying out disorderly, and rendering themselves objects of ridicule both by gesture and voice. Seest thou not that even in a market place, should any one come up doing like this, and begging clamorously, he wilt drive away him whom he is petitioning; but if quietly, and with the proper gesture, then he rather wins over him that can grant the favor?

Let us not then make our prayer by the gesture of our body, nor by the loudness of our voice, but by the earnestness of our mind: neither with noise and clamor and for display, so as even to disturb those that are near us, but with all modesty, and with contrition in the mind, and with inward tears.

But art thou pained in mind, and canst not help crying aloud? yet surely it is the part of one exceedingly pained to pray and entreat even as I have said. Since Moses too was pained, and prayed in this way and was heard; for this cause also God said unto him, "Wherefore criest thou unto me." And Hannah too again, her voice not being heard, accomplished all she wished, forasmuch as her heart cried out. But Abel prayed not only when silent, but even when dying, and his blood sent forth a cry more clear than a trumpet.

Do thou also then groan, even as that holy one, I forbid it not. "Rend," as the prophet commanded, "thine heart, and not thy garments." Out of deeps call upon God, for it is said, "Out of the depths have I cried to Thee, O Lord." From beneath, out of the heart, draw forth a voice, make thy prayer a mystery. Seest thou not that even in the houses of kings all tumult is put away, and great on all sides is the silence? Do thou also therefore, entering as into a palace,—not that on the earth, but what is far more awful than it, that which is in heaven,—show forth great seemliness. Yea, for thou art joined to the choirs of angels, and art in communion with archangels, and art singing with the seraphim. And all these tribes show forth much goodly order, singing with great awe that mystical strain, and their sacred hymns to God, the King of all. With these then mingle thyself, when thou art praying, and emulate their mystical order.

For not unto men art thou praying, but to God, who is everywhere present, who hears even before the voice, who knows the secrets of the mind. If thou so pray, great is the reward thou shalt receive.

"For thy Father," saith He, "who seeth in secret, shall reward thee openly."

He said not, "shall freely give thee," but, "shall reward thee;" yea, for He hath made Himself a debtor to thee, and even from this hath honored thee with great honor. For because He Himself is invisible, He would have thy prayer be so likewise.

5. Then He speaks even the very words of the prayer.

"When ye pray," saith He, "use no vain repetitions, even as the heathen do."

You see that when He was discoursing of almsgiving, He removed only that mischief which comes of vainglory, and added nothing more; neither did He say whence one should give alms; as from honest labor, and not from rapine nor covetousness: this being abundantly acknowledged among all. And also before that, He had thoroughly cleared up this point, when He blessed them "that hunger after righteousness."

But touching prayer, He adds somewhat over and above; "not to use vain repetitions." And as there He derides the hypocrites, so here the heathen; shaming the hearer everywhere most of all by the vileness of the persons. For since this, in most cases, is especially biting and stinging, I mean our appearing to be likened to outcast persons; by this topic He dissuades them; calling frivolousness, here, by the name of "vain repetition:" as when we ask of God things unsuitable, kingdoms, and glory, and to get the better of enemies, and abundance of wealth, and in general what does not at all concern us.

"For He knoweth," saith He, "what things ye have need of."

And herewith He seems to me to command in this place, that neither should we make our prayers long; long, I mean, not in time, but in the number and length of the things mentioned. For perseverance indeed in the same requests is our duty: His word being, "continuing instant in prayer."

And He Himself too, by that example of the widow, who prevailed with the pitiless and cruel ruler, by the continuance of her intercession; and by that of the friend, who came late at night time, and roused the sleeper from his bed, not for his friendship's, but for his importunity's sake; what did He, but lay down a law, that all should continually make supplication unto Him? He doth not however bid us compose a prayer of ten thousand clauses, and so come to Him and merely repeat it. For this He obscurely signified when He said, "They think that they shall be heard for their much speaking."

"For He knoweth," saith He, "what things ye have need of." And if He know, one may say, what we have need of, wherefore must we pray? Not to instruct Him, but to prevail with Him; to be made intimate with Him, by continuance in supplication; to be humbled; to be reminded of thy sins.

6. "After this manner, therefore, pray ye," saith He: "Our Father, which art in heaven."

See how He straightway stirred up the hearer, and reminded him of all God's bounty in the beginning. For he who calls God Father, by him both remission of sins, and taking away of punishment, and righteousness, and sanctification, and redemption, and adoption, and inheritance, and brotherhood with the Only-Begotten, and the supply of the Spirit, are acknowledged in this single title. For one cannot call God Father, without having attained to all those blessings. Doubly, therefore, doth He awaken their spirit, both by the dignity of Him who is called on, and by the greatness of the benefits which they have enjoyed. But when He saith, "in Heaven," He speaks not this as shutting up God there, but as withdrawing him who is praying from earth, and fixing him in the high places, and in the dwellings above.

He teaches, moreover, to make our prayer common, in behalf of our brethren also. For He saith not, "my Father, which art in Heaven," but, "our Father," offering up his supplications for the body in common, and nowhere looking to his own, but everywhere to his neighbor's good. And by this He at once takes away hatred, and quells pride, and casts out envy, and brings in the mother of all good things, even charity, and exterminates the inequality of human things, and shows how far the equality reaches between the king and the poor man, if at least in those things which are greatest and most indispensable, we are all of us fellows. For what harm comes of our kindred below, when in that which is on high we are all of us knit together, and no one hath aught more than another; neither the rich more than the poor, nor the master than the servant, neither the ruler than the subject, nor the king than the common soldier, nor the philosopher than the barbarian, nor the skillful than the unlearned? For to all hath He given one nobility, having vouchsafed to be called the Father of all alike.

7. When therefore He hath reminded us of this nobility, and of the gift from above, and of our equality with our brethren, and of charity; and when He hath removed us from earth, and fixed us in Heaven; let us see what He commands us to ask after this. Not but, in the first place, even that saying alone is sufficient to implant instruction in all virtue. For he who hath called God Father, and a common Father, would be justly bound to show forth such a conversation, as not to appear unworthy of this nobility, and to exhibit a diligence proportionate to the gift. Yet is He not satisfied with this, but adds, also another clause, thus saying,

"Hallowed be Thy name."

Worthy of him who calls God Father, is the prayer to ask nothing before the glory of His Father, but to account all things secondary to the work of praising Him. For "hallowed" is glorified. For His own glory He hath complete, and ever continuing the same, but He commands him who prays to seek that He may be glorified also by our life. Which very thing He had said before likewise, "Let your light so shine before men, that they may see your good works, and glorify your Father which is in heaven." Yea, and the seraphim too, giving glory, said on this wise, "Holy, holy, holy." So that "hallowed" means this, viz. "glorified." That is, "vouchsafe," saith he, "that we may live so purely, that through us all may glorify Thee." Which thing again appertains unto perfect self-control, to present to all a life so irreprehensible, that every one of the beholders may offer to the Lord the praise due to Him for this.

"Thy kingdom come."

And this again is the language of a right-minded child, not to be rivetted to things that are seen, neither to account things present some great matter; but to hasten unto our Father, and to long for the things to come. And this springs out of a good conscience, and a soul set free from things that are on earth. This, for instance, Paul himself was longing after every day: wherefore he also said, that "even we ourselves, who have the first-fruits of the Spirit, groan, waiting for an adoption, the redemption of our body." For he who hath this fondness, can neither be puffed up by the good things of this life, nor abashed by its sorrows; but as though dwelling in the very heavens, is freed from each sort of irregularity.

"Thy will be done in earth, as it is in Heaven."

Behold a most excellent train of thought! in that He bade us indeed long for the things to come, and hasten towards that sojourn; and, till that may be, even while we abide here, so long to be earnest in showing forth the same conversation as those above. For ye must long, saith He, for heaven, and the things in heaven; however, even before heaven, He hath bidden us make the earth a heaven and do and say all things, even while we are continuing in it, as having our conversation there; insomuch that these too should be objects of our prayer to the Lord. For there is nothing to hinder our reaching the perfection of the powers above, because we inhabit the earth; but it is possible even while abiding here, to do all, as though already placed on high. What He saith therefore is this: "As there all things are done without hindrance, and the angels are not partly obedient and partly disobedient, but in all things yield and obey (for He saith, Mighty in strength, performing His word'); so vouchsafe that we men may not do Thy will by halves, but perform all things as Thou willest."

Seest thou how He hath taught us also to be modest, by making it clear that virtue is not of our endeavors only, but also of the grace from above? And again, He hath enjoined each one of us, who pray, to take upon himself the care of the whole world. For He did not at all say, "Thy will be done" in me, or in us, but everywhere on the earth; so that error may be destroyed, and truth implanted, and all wickedness cast out, and virtue return, and no difference in this respect be henceforth between heaven and earth. "For if this come to pass," saith He, "there will be no difference between things below and above, separated as they are in nature; the earth exhibiting to us another set of angels."

8. "Give us this day our daily bread."

What is "daily bread"? That for one day.

For because He had said thus, "Thy will be done in earth as it is in heaven," but was discoursing to men encompassed with flesh, and subject to the necessities of nature, and incapable of the same impassibility with the angels:—while He enjoins the commands to be practised by us also, even as they perform them; He condescends likewise, in what follows, to the infirmity of our nature. Thus, "perfection of conduct," saith He, "I require as great, not however freedom from passions; no, for the tyranny of nature permits it not: for it requires necessary food." But mark, I pray thee, how even in things that are bodily, that which is spiritual abounds. For it is neither for riches, nor for delicate living, nor for costly raiment, nor for any other such thing, but for bread only, that He hath commanded us to make our prayer. And for "daily bread," so as not to "take thought for the morrow." Because of this He added, "daily bread," that is, bread for one day.

And not even with this expression is He satisfied, but adds another too afterwards, saying, "Give us this day;" so that we may not, beyond this, wear ourselves out with the care of the following day. For that day, the interval before which thou knowest not whether thou shalt see, wherefore dost thou submit to its cares?

This, as He proceeded, he enjoined also more fully, saying, "Take no thought for the morrow." He would have us be on every hand unencumbered and winged for flight, yielding just so much to nature as the compulsion of necessity requires of us.

9. Then forasmuch as it comes to pass that we sin even after the washing of regeneration, He, showing His love to man to be great even in this case, commands us for the remission of our sins to come unto God who loves man, and thus to say,

"Forgive us our debts, as we also forgive our debtors."

Seest thou surpassing mercy? After taking away so great evils, and after the unspeakable greatness of His gift, if men sin again, He counts them such as may be forgiven. For that this prayer belongs to believers, is taught us both by the laws of the church, and by the beginning of the prayer. For the uninitiated could not call God Father. If then the prayer belongs to believers, and they pray, entreating that sins may be forgiven them, it is clear that not even after the laver is the profit of repentance taken away. Since, had He not meant to signify this, He would not have made a law that we should so pray. Now He who both brings sins to remembrance, and bids us ask forgiveness, and teaches how we may obtain remission and so makes the way easy; it is perfectly clear that He introduced this rule of supplication, as knowing, and signifying, that it is possible even after the font to wash ourselves from our offenses; by reminding us of our sins, persuading us to be modest; by the command to forgive others, setting us free from all revengeful passion; while by promising in return for this to pardon us also, He holds out good hopes, and instructs us to have high views concerning the unspeakable mercy of God toward man.

But what we should most observe is this, that whereas in each of the clauses He had made mention of the whole of virtue, and in this way had included also the forgetfulness of injuries (for so, that "His name be hallowed," is the exactness of a perfect conversation; and that "His will be done," declares the same thing again: and to be able to call God "Father," is the profession of a blameless life; in all which things had been comprehended also the duty of remitting our anger against them that have transgressed): still He was not satisfied with these, but meaning to signify how earnest He is in the matter, He sets it down also in particular, and after the prayer, He makes mention of no other commandment than this, saying thus:

"For if ye forgive men their trespasses, your heavenly Father also will forgive you."

So that the beginning is of us, and we ourselves have control over the judgment that is to be passed upon us. For in order that no one, even of the senseless, might have any complaint to make, either great or small, when brought to judgment; on thee, who art to give account, He causes the sentence to depend; and "in what way soever thou hast judged for thyself, in the same," saith He, "do I also judge thee." And if thou forgive thy fellow servant, thou shalt obtain the same favor from me; though indeed the one be not equal to the other. For thou forgivest in thy need, but God, having need of none: thou, thy fellow slave; God, His slave: thou liable to unnumbered charges; God, being without sin. But yet even thus doth He show forth His lovingkindness towards man.

Since He might indeed, even without this, forgive thee all thine offenses; but He wills thee hereby also to receive a benefit; affording thee on all sides innumerable occasions of gentleness and love to man, casting out what is brutish in thee, and quenching wrath, and in all ways cementing thee to him who is thine own member.

For what canst thou have to say? that thou hast wrongfully endured some ill of thy neighbor? (For these only are trespasses, since if it be done with justice, the act is not a trespass.) But thou too art drawing near to receive forgiveness for such things, and for much greater. And even before the forgiveness, thou hast received no small gift, in being taught to have a human soul, and in being trained to all gentleness. And herewith a great reward shall also be laid up for thee elsewhere, even to be called to account for none of thine offenses.

What sort of punishment then do we not deserve, when after having received the privilege, we betray our salvation? And how shall we claim to be heard in the rest of our matters, if we will not, in those which depend on us, spare our own selves?

10. "And lead us not into temptation; but deliver us from the evil one: for Thine is the kingdom, and the power, and the glory, for ever. Amen."

Here He teaches us plainly our own vileness, and quells our pride, instructing us to deprecate all conflicts, instead of rushing upon them. For so both our victory will be more glorious, and the devil's overthrow more to be derided. I mean, that as when we are dragged forth, we must stand nobly; so when we are not summoned, we should be quiet, and wait for the time of conflict; that we may show both freedom from vainglory, and nobleness of spirit.

And He here calls the devil "the wicked one," commanding us to wage against him a war that knows no truce, and implying that he is not such by nature. For wickedness is not of those things that are from nature, but of them that are added by our own choice. And he is so called pre-eminently, by reason of the excess of his wickedness, and because he, in no respect injured by us, wages against us implacable war. Wherefore neither said He, "deliver us from the wicked ones," but, "from the wicked one;" instructing us in no case to entertain displeasure against our neighbors, for what wrongs soever we may suffer at their hands, but to transfer our enmity from these to him, as being himself the cause of all our wrongs.

Having then made us anxious as before conflict, by putting us in mind of the enemy, and having cut away from us all our remissness; He again encourages and raises our spirits, by bringing to our remembrance the King under whom we are arrayed, and signifying Him to be more powerful than all. "For Thine," saith He, "is the kingdom, and the power, and the glory."

Doth it not then follow, that if His be the kingdom, we should fear no one, since there can be none to withstand, and divide the empire with him. For when He saith, "Thine is the kingdom," He sets before us even him, who is warring against us, brought into subjection, though he seem to oppose, God for a while permitting it. For in truth he too is among God's servants, though of the degraded class, and those guilty of offense; and he would not dare set upon any of his fellow servants, had he not first received license from above. And why say I, "his fellow servants?" Not even against swine did he venture any outrage, until He Himself allowed him; nor against flocks, nor herds, until he had received permission from above.

"And the power," saith He. Therefore, manifold as thy weakness may be, thou mayest of right be confident, having such a one to reign over thee, who is able fully to accomplish all, and that with ease, even by thee.

"And the glory, for ever. Amen." Thus He not only frees thee from the dangers that are approaching thee, but can make thee also glorious and illustrious. For as His power is great, so also is His glory unspeakable, and they are all boundless, and no end of them. Seest thou how He hath by every means anointed His Champion, and hath framed Him to be full of confidence?

11. Then, as I said before, meaning to signify, that of all things He most loathes and hates bearing malice, and most of all accepts the virtue which is opposite to that vice; He hath after the prayer also again put us in mind of this same point of goodness; both by the punishment set, and by the reward appointed, urging the hearer to obey this command.

"For if ye forgive men," saith He, "your heavenly Father will also forgive you. But if ye forgive not, neither will He forgive you."

With this view He hath again mentioned heaven also, and their Father; to abash the hearer by this topic likewise; that he of all people, being of such a Father, should be made a wild beast of; and summoned as he is to heaven, should cherish an earthly and ordinary sort of mind. Since not by grace only, you see, ought we to become His children, but also by our works. And nothing makes us so like God, as being ready to forgive the wicked and wrong-doers; even as indeed He had taught before, when He spake of His "making the sun to shine on the evil and on the good."

For this same cause again in every one of the clauses He commands us to make our prayers common, saying, "Our Father," and "Thy will be done in earth as it is in heaven," and "Give us the bread, and forgive us our debts," and "lead us not into temptation," and "deliver us;" everywhere commanding us to use this plural word, that we may not retain so much as a vestige of anger against our neighbor.

How great punishment then must they deserve, who after all this, so far from themselves forgiving, do even entreat God for vengeance on their enemies, and diametrically as it were transgress this law; and this while He is doing and contriving all, to hinder our being at variance one with another? For since love is the root of all that is good, He removing from all sides whatever mars it, brings us together, and cements us to each other. For there is not, there is not one, be he father, or mother, or friend, or what you will, who so loved us as the God who created us. And this, above all things, both His daily benefits and His precepts make manifest. But if thou tell me of the pains, and of the sorrows, and of the evils of life; consider in how many things thou offendest Him every day, and thou wilt no longer marvel, though more than these evils should come upon thee, but if thou shouldest enjoy any good, then thou wilt marvel, and be amazed. But as it is, we look upon the calamities that come upon us, but the offenses, whereby we offend daily, we consider not: therefore we are perplexed. Since if we did but reckon up with strictness our sins of one day only, in that case we should know well how great evils we must be liable to.

And to let pass the other misdoings of which we have been guilty, each one for himself, and to speak of what have been committed this day; although of course I know not in what each of us may have sinned, yet such is the abundance of our misdoings, that not even he who knew all exactly would be able to choose from among these only. Which of us, for instance, hath not been careless in his prayers? Which hath not been insolent, or vainglorious? Who hath not spoken evil of his brother, hath not admitted a wicked desire, hath not looked with unchaste eyes, hath not remembered things with hostile feeling, even till he made his heart swell?

And if while we are in church, and in a short time we have become guilty of so great evils; what shall be when we are gone out from hence? If in the harbor the waves are so high, when we are gone forth into the channel of wickednesses, the forum I mean, and to public business, and our cares at home, shall we indeed be able so much as to know ourselves again?

But yet from our so great and so many sins, God hath given us a short and easy way of deliverance, and one that is free from all toil. For what sort of toil is it to forgive him that hath grieved us? Nay, it is a toil not to forgive, but to keep up our enmity: even as to be delivered from the anger, both works in us a great refreshment, and is very easy to him that is willing. For there is no sea to be crossed, nor long journey to be travelled, nor summits of mountains to be passed over, nor money to be spent, no need to torment thy body; but it suffices to be willing only, and all our sins are done away.

But if so far from forgiving him thyself, thou makest intercession to God against him, what hope of salvation wilt thou then have, if at the very time when thou oughtest rather to appease God, even then thou provokest Him; putting on the garb of a suppliant, but uttering the cries of a wild beast, and darting out against thyself those shafts of the wicked one? Wherefore Paul also, making mention of prayer, required nothing so much as the observance of this commandment; for He saith, "lifting up holy hands without wrath and doubting." And if when thou hast need of mercy, not even then wilt thou let go thine anger, but art rather exceedingly mindful of it, and that, although thou knowest thou art thrusting the sword into thyself; when will it be possible for thee to become merciful, and to spew out the evil venom of this wickedness?

But if thou hast not yet seen this outrageousness in its full extent, suppose it happening among men, and then thou wilt perceive the excess of the insolence. As thus: should one approach thee who are a man, seeking to obtain mercy, and then, in the midst of his lying on the ground, should see an enemy, and leaving off to supplicate thee, begin to beat him; wouldest thou not make thyself more angry with him? This do thou consider as taking place with regard to God also. For so thou likewise, making supplication unto God, leavest thy supplication in the midst, and smitest thine enemy with thy words, and insultest the laws of God. Him who made a law to dismiss all anger, thou art summoning against those that have vexed thee, and requiring Him to do things contrary to His own commandments. Is it not enough for thee in the way of revenge, that thou thyself transgressest the law of God, but entreatest thou Him likewise to do so? What? hath He forgotten what He commanded? What? is He a man who spake these things? It is God, who knows all things, and whose will is, that His own laws be kept with the utmost exactness, and who, so far from doing these things which thou art requiring of Him, doth even regard thee who sayest these things, merely because thou sayest them, with aversion and hatred, and exacts of thee the most extreme penalty. How then seekest thou to obtain of Him things, from which He very seriously bids thee refrain?

Yet some there are, who have come to such a point of brutishness, as not only to make intercession against their enemies, but even to curse their children, and to taste, if only it might be, of their very flesh; or rather they are even tasting thereof. For tell me not this, that thou hast not fixed thy teeth in the body of him that vexed thee; since thou hast done, at least as far as concerned thee, what is much more grievous; in claiming that wrath from above should fall upon him, and that he should be delivered over to undying punishment, and be overthrown with his whole house.

Why, what sort of bites are as ferocious as this? what kind of weapons as bitter? Not so did Christ instruct thee; not so did He command thee to stain thy mouth with blood. Nay, mouths made bloody with human flesh are not so shocking as tongues like these.

How then wilt thou salute thy brother? how wilt thou touch the sacrifice? how taste the Lord's blood, when thou hast so much venom upon thy mind? Since when thou sayest, "Rend him in pieces, and overthrow his house, and destroy all," when thou art imprecating on him ten thousand deaths, thou art in nothing different from a murderer, or rather from a wild beast that devours men.

Let us cease then from this disease and madness, and that kindliness which He com manded let us show forth towards them that have vexed us: that we may become like "our Father which is in heaven." And we shall cease therefrom, if we call to mind our own sins; if we strictly search out all our misdeeds at home, abroad, and in the market, and in church.

12. For if for nothing else, surely for our disrespectfulness here we are worthy to undergo the utmost punishment. For when prophets are chanting, and apostles singing hymns, and God is discoursing, we wander without, and bring in upon us a turmoil of worldly business. And we do not afford to the laws of God so great stillness, even as the spectators in the theatres to the emperor's letters, keeping silence for them. For there, when these letters are being read, deputies at once, and governors, and senate, and people, stand all upright, with quietness hearkening to the words. And if amid that most profound silence any one should suddenly leap up and cry out, he suffers the utmost punishment, as having been insolent to the emperor. But here, when the letters from heaven are being read, great is the confusion on all sides. And yet both He who sent the letters is much greater than this our king, and the assembly more venerable: for not men only, but angels too are in it; and these triumphs, of which the letters bear us the good tidings, are much more awful than those on earth. Wherefore not men only, but angels also and archangels; both the nations of heaven, and all we on the earth, are commanded to give praise. For, "Bless the Lord," it is said, "all His works." Yea, for His are no small achievements, rather they surpass all speech, and thought, and understanding of man.

And these things the prophets proclaim every day, each of them in a different way publishing this glorious triumph. For one saith, "Thou hast gone up on high, Thou hast led captivity captive, and hast received gifts amongst men." And, "The Lord strong and mighty in battle." And another saith, "He shall divide the spoils of the strong." For indeed to this purpose He came, that He might "preach deliverance to captives, and recovery of sight to the blind."

And raising aloud the cry of victory over death, he said, "Where, O Death, is thy victory? Where, O Grave, is thy sting?" And another again, declaring glad tidings of the most profound peace, said, "They shall beat their swords into ploughshares, and their spears into pruning hooks." And while one calls on Jerusalem, saying, "Rejoice greatly, O daughter of Sion, for lo! thy King cometh to thee meek, riding upon an ass, and a young colt;" another proclaims His second coming also, saying on this wise, "The Lord, whom ye seek, will come, and who will abide the day of His coming? Leap ye as calves set free from bonds." And another again, amazed at such things, said, "This is our God; there shall none other be accounted of in comparison of Him."

Yet, nevertheless, while both these and many more sayings than these are being uttered, while we ought to tremble, and not so much as account ourselves to be on the earth; still, as though in the midst of a forum, we make an uproar and disturbance, and spend the whole time of our solemn assembly in discoursing of things which are nothing to us.

When therefore both in little things, and in great, both in hearing, and in doing, both abroad, and at home, in the church, we are so negligent; and together with all this, pray also against our enemies: whence are we to have any hope of salvation, adding to so great sins yet another grievous enhancement, and equivalent to them all, even this unlawful prayer?

Have we then hereafter any right to marvel, if aught befall us of the things which are unexpected and painful? whereas we ought to marvel when no such thing befalls us. For the former is in the natural order of things, but the latter were beyond all reason and expectation. For surely it is beyond reason, that they who are become enemies of God, and are provoking Him to anger, should enjoy sunshine and showers, and all the rest; who being men surpass the barbarity of wild beasts, setting themselves one against another, and by the biting of their neighbors staining their own tongues with blood: after the spiritual table, and His so great benefits, and His innumerable injunctions.

Therefore, considering these things, let us cast up that venom; let us put an end to our enmities, and let us make the prayers that become such as we are. Instead of the brutality of devils, let us take upon us the mildness of angels; and in whatsoever things we may have been injured, let us, consider ing our own case, and the reward appointed us for this commandment, soften our anger; let us assuage the billows, that we may both pass through the present life calmly, and when we have departed thither, may find our Lord such as we have been towards our fellow-servants. And if this be a heavy and fearful thing, let us make it light and desirable; and let us open the glorious gates of confidence towards Him; and what we had not strength to effect by abstaining from sin, that let us accomplish by becoming gentle to them who have sinned against us (for this surely is not grievous, nor burdensome); and let us by doing kindnesses to our enemies, lay up beforehand much mercy for ourselves.

For so both during this present life all will love us, and above all others, God will both befriend and crown us, and will count us worthy of all the good things to come; unto which may we all attain, by the grace and love towards man of our Lord Jesus Christ, to whom be glory and might for ever and ever. Amen.

HOMILY XX

MATT. VI. 16

"And when ye fast, be not as the hypocrites, of a sad countenance. For they disfigure their faces, that they may appear unto men to fast."

Here it were well to sigh aloud, and to wail bitterly: for not only do we imitate the hypocrites, but we have even surpassed them. For I know, yea I know many, not merely fasting and making a display of it, but neglecting to fast, and yet wearing the masks of them that fast, and cloaking themselves with an excuse worse than their sin.

For "I do this," say they, "that I may not offend the many." What sayest thou? There is a law of God which commands these things, and dost thou talk of offense? And thinkest thou that in keeping it thou art offending, in transgressing it, delivering men from offense? And what can be worse than this folly?

Wilt thou not leave off becoming worse than the very hypocrites, and making thine hypocrisy double? And when thou considerest the great excess of this evil, wilt thou not be abashed at the force of the expression now before us? In that He did not say, "they act a part," merely, but willing also to touch them more deeply, He saith, "For they disfigure their faces;" that is, they corrupt, they mar them.

But if this be a disfiguring of the face, to appear pale for vainglory, what should we say concerning the women who corrupt their faces with colorings and paintings to the ruin of the unchaste sort of young men? For while those harm themselves only, these women harm both themselves and them who behold them. Wherefore we should fly both from the one pest and from the other, keeping at distance enough and to spare. For so He not only commanded to make no display, but even to seek to be concealed. Which thing He had done before likewise.

And whereas in the matter of almsgiving, He did not put it simply, but having said, "Take heed not to do it before men," He added, "to be seen of them;" yet concerning fasting and prayer, He made no such limitation. Why could this have been? Because for almsgiving to be altogether concealed is impossible, but for prayer and fasting, it is possible.

As therefore, when He said, "Let not thy left hand know what thy right hand doeth," it was not of hands that He was speaking, but of the duty of being strictly concealed from all; and as when He commanded us to enter into our closet, not there alone absolutely, nor there primarily, did He command us to pray, but He covertly intimated the same thing again; so likewise here, in commanding us "to be anointed," He did not enact that we positively must anoint ourselves; for then we should all of us be found transgressors of this law; and above all, surely, they who have taken the most pains to keep it, the societies of the monks, who have taken up their dwelling on the mountains. It was not this then that He enjoined, but, forasmuch as the ancients had a custom to anoint themselves continually, when they were taking their pleasure and rejoicing (and this one may see clearly from David and from Daniel); He said that we were to anoint ourselves, not that we should positively do this, but that by all means we might endeavor, with great strictness, to hide this our acquisition. And to convince thee that so it is, He Himself, when by action exhibiting what He enjoined in words, having fasted forty days, and fasted in secret, did neither anoint nor wash Himself: nevertheless, though He did not these things, He most assuredly fulfilled the whole without vainglory. It is this then that He enjoins on us likewise, both bringing before us the hypocrites, and by a twice repeated charge dissuading the hearers.

And somewhat else He signified by this name, this of hypocrites, I mean. That is, not only by the ridiculousness of the thing, nor by its bringing an extreme penalty, but also by showing that such deceit is but for a season, doth He withdraw us from that evil desire. For the actor seems glorious just so long as the audience is sitting; or rather not even then in the sight of all. For the more part of the spectators know who it is, and what part he is acting. However, when the audience is broken up, he is more clearly discovered to all. Now this, you see, the vainglorious must in all necessity undergo. For even here they are manifest to the majority, as not being that which they appear to be, but as wearing a mask only; but much more will they be detected hereafter, when all things appear "naked and open."

And by another motive again He withdraws them from the hypocrites, by showing that His injunction is light. For He doth not make the fast more strict, nor command us to practise more of it, but not to lose the crown thereof. So that what seems hard to bear, is common to us and to the hypocrites, for they also fast; but that which is lightest, namely, not to lose the reward after our labors, "this is what I command," saith He; adding nothing to our toils, but gathering our wages for us with all security, and not suffering us to go away unrewarded, as they do. Nay, they will not so much as imitate them that wrestle in the Olympic games, who although so great a multitude is sitting there, and so many princes, desire to please but one, even him who adjudges the victory amongst them; and this, though he be much their inferior. But thou, though thou hast a twofold motive for displaying the victory to Him, first, that He is the person to adjudge it, and also, that He is beyond comparison superior to all that are sitting in the theatre,—thou art displaying it to others, who so far from profiting, do privily work thee the greatest harm.

However, I do not forbid even this, saith He. Only, if thou art desirous to make a show to men, also, wait, and I will bestow on thee this too in fuller abundance, and with great profit. For as it is, this quite breaks thee off from the glory which is with me, even as to despise these things unites thee closely; but then shalt thou enjoy all in entire security; having, even before that last, no little fruit to reap in this world also, namely, that thou hast trodden under foot all human glory, and art freed from the grievous bondage of men, and art become a true worker of virtue. Whereas now, as long at least as thou art so disposed, if thou shouldest be in a desert, thou wilt be deserted by all thy virtue, having none to behold thee. This is to act as one insulting virtue itself, if thou art to pursue it not for its own sake, but with an eye to the ropemaker, and the brazier, and the common people of the baser sort, that the bad and they that are far removed from virtue may admire thee. And thou art calling the enemies of virtue to the display and the sight thereof, as if one were to choose to live continently, not for the excellency of continence, but that he might make a show before prostitutes. Thou also, it would seem, wouldest not choose virtue, but for the sake of virtue's enemies; whereas thou oughtest indeed to admire her on this very ground, that she hath even her enemies to praise her,—yet to admire her (as is meet), not for others, but for her own sake. Since we too, when we are loved not for our own, but for others' sake, account the thing an insult. Just so I bid thee reckon in the case of virtue as well, and neither to follow after her for the sake of others, nor for men's sake to obey God; but men for God's sake. Since if thou do the contrary, though thou seem to follow virtue, thou hast provoked equally with him who follows her not. For just as he disobeyed by not doing, so thou by doing unlawfully.

2. "Lay not up for yourselves treasures upon earth."

Thus, after He hath cast out the disease of vainglory, and not before, He seasonably introduces His discourse of voluntary poverty. For nothing so trains men to be fond of riches, as the fondness for glory. This, for instance, is why men devise those herds of slaves, and that swarm of eunuchs, and their horses with trappings of gold, and their silver tables, and all the rest of it, yet more ridiculous; not to satisfy any wants, nor to enjoy any pleasure, but that they may make a show before the multitude.

Now above He had only said, that we must show mercy; but here He points out also how great mercy we must show, when He saith, "Lay not up treasure." For it not being possible at the beginning to introduce all at once His discourse on contempt of riches, by reason of the tyranny of the passion, He breaks it up into small portions, and having set free the hearer's mind, instills it therein, so as that it shall become acceptable. Wherefore, you see, He said first, "Blessed are the merciful;" and after this, "Agree with thine adversary;" and after that again, "If any one will sue thee at the law and take thy coat, give him thy cloak also;" but here, that which is much greater than all these. For there His meaning was, "if thou see a law-suit impending, do this; since to want and be freed from strife, is better than to possess and strive;" but here, supposing neither adversary nor any one at law with thee, and without all mention of any other such party, He teaches the contempt of riches itself by itself, implying that not so much for their sake who receive mercy, as for the giver's sake, He makes these laws: so that though there be no one injuring us, or dragging us into a court of justice, even so we may despise our possessions, bestowing them on those that are in need.

And neither here hath He put the whole, but even in this place it is gently spoken; although He had in the wilderness shown forth to a surpassing extent His conflicts in that behalf. However He doth not express this, nor bring it forward; for it was not yet time to reveal it; but for a while He searches out for reasons, maintaining the place of an adviser rather than a lawgiver, in His sayings on this subject.

For after He had said, "Lay not up treasures upon the earth," He added, "where moth and rust doth corrupt, and where thieves break through and steal."

For the present He signifies the hurtfulness of the treasure here, and the profit of what is there, both from the place, and from the things which mar it. And neither at this point doth He stop, but adds also another argument.

And first, what things they most fear, from these He urges them. For "of what art thou afraid?" saith He: "lest thy goods should be spent, if thou give alms? Nay, then give alms, and so they will not be spent; and, what is more, so far from being spent, they will actually receive a greater increase; yea, for the things in heaven are added unto them."

However, for a time He saith it not, but puts it afterwards. But for the present, what had most power to persuade them, that He brings forward, namely, that the treasure would thus remain for them unspent.

And on either hand He attracts them. For He said not only, "If thou give alms, it is preserved:" but He threatened also the opposite thing, that if thou give not, it perishes.

And see His unspeakable prudence. For neither did He say, "Thou dost but leave them to others;" since this too is pleasant to men: He alarms them however on a new ground, by signifying that not even this do they obtain: since though men defraud not, there are those which are sure to defraud, "the moth" and "the rust." For although this mischief seem very easy to restrain, it is nevertheless irresistible and uncontrollable, and devise what thou wilt, thou wilt be unable to check this harm.

"What then, doth moth make away with the gold?" Though not moth, yet thieves do. "What then, have all been despoiled?" Though not all, yet the more part.

3. On this account then He adds another argument, which I have already mentioned, saying,

"Where the man's treasure is, there is his heart also."

For though none of these things should come to pass, saith He, thou wilt undergo no small harm, in being nailed to the things below, and in becoming a slave instead of a freeman, and casting thyself out of the heavenly things, and having no power to think on aught that is high, but all about money, usuries and loans, and gains, and ignoble traffickings. Than this what could be more wretched? For in truth such an one will be worse off than any slave, bringing upon himself a most grievous tyranny, and giving up the chiefest thing of all, even the nobleness and the liberty of man. For how much soever any one may discourse unto thee, thou wilt not be able to hear any of those things which concern thee, whilst thy mind is nailed down to money; but bound like a dog to a tomb, by the tyranny of riches, more grievously than by any chain, barking at all that come near thee, thou hast this one employment continually, to keep for others what thou hast laid up. Than this what can be more wretched?

However, forasmuch as this was too high for the mind of His hearers, and neither was the mischief within easy view of the generality, nor the gain evident, but there was need of a spirit of more self-command to perceive either of these; first, He hath put it after those other topics, which are obvious, saying, "Where the man's treasure is, there is his heart also;" and next He makes it clear again, by withdrawing His discourse from the intellectual to the sensible, and saying,

"The light of the body is the eye."

What He saith is like this: Bury not gold in the earth, nor do any other such thing, for thou dost but gather it for the moth, and the rust, and the thieves. And even if thou shouldest entirely escape these evils, yet the enslaving of thine heart, the nailing it to all that is below, thou wilt not escape: "For wheresoever thy treasure may be, there is thine heart also." As then, laying up stores in heaven, thou wilt reap not this fruit only, the attainment of the rewards for these things, but from this world thou already receivest thy recompence, in getting into harbor there, in setting thine affections on the things that are there, and caring for what is there (for where thou hast laid up thy treasures, it is most clear thou transferrest thy mind also); so if thou do this upon earth, thou wilt experience the contrary.

But if the saying be obscure to thee, hear what comes next in order. "The light of the body is the eye; if therefore thine eye be single, thy whole body shall be full of light. But if thine eye be evil, thy whole body shall be full of darkness. But if the light that is in thee be darkness, how great is the darkness!"

He leads His discourse to the things which are more within the reach of our senses. I mean, forasmuch as He had spoken of the mind as enslaved and brought into captivity, and there were not many who could easily discern this, He transfers the lesson to things outward, and lying before men's eyes, that by these the others also might reach their understanding. Thus, "If thou knowest not," saith He, "what a thing it is to be injured in mind, learn it from the things of the body; for just what the eye is to the body, the same is the mind to the soul." As therefore thou wouldest not choose to wear gold, and to be clad in silken garments, thine eyes withal being put out, but accountest their sound health more desirable than all such superfluity (for, shouldest thou lose this health or waste it, all thy life besides will do thee no good): for just as when the eyes are blinded, most of the energy of the other members is gone, their light being quenched; so also when the mind is depraved, thy life will be filled with countless evils:—as therefore in the body this is our aim, namely, to keep the eye sound, so also the mind in the soul. But if we mutilate this, which ought to give light to the rest, by what means are we to see clearly any more? For as he that destroys the fountain, dries up also the river, so he who hath quenched the understanding hath confounded all his doings in this life. Wherefore He saith, "If the light that is in thee be darkness, how great is the darkness?"

For when the pilot is drowned, and the candle is put out, and the general is taken prisoner; what sort of hope will there be, after that, for those that are under command?

Thus then, omitting now to speak of the plots to which wealth gives occasion, the strifes, the suits (these indeed He had signified above, when He said, "The adversary shall deliver thee to the judge, and the judge to the officer"); and setting down what is more grievous than all these, as sure to occur, He so withdraws us from the wicked desire. For to inhabit the prison is not nearly so grievous, as for the mind to be enslaved by this disease; and the former is not sure to happen, but the other is connected as an immediate consequent with the desire of riches. And this is why He puts it after the first, as being a more grievous thing, and sure to happen.

For God, He saith, gave us understanding, that we might chase away all ignorance, and have the right judgment of things, and that using this as a kind of weapon and light against all that is grievous or hurtful, we might remain in safety. But we betray the gift for the sake of things superfluous and useless.

For what is the use of soldiers arrayed in gold, when the general is dragged along a captive? what the profit of a ship beautifully equipped, when the pilot is sunk beneath the waves? what the advantage of a well-proportioned body, when the sight of the eyes is stricken out? As therefore, should any one cast into sickness the physician (who should be in good health, that he may end our diseases), and then bid him lie on a silver couch, and in a chamber of gold, this will nothing avail the sick persons; even so, if thou corrupt the mind (which hath power to put down our passions), although thou set it by a treasure, so far from doing it any good, thou hast inflicted the very greatest loss, and hast harmed thy whole soul.

4. Seest thou how by those very things, through which most especially men everywhere affect wickedness, even by these most of all He deters them from it, and brings them back to virtue? "For with what intent dost thou desire riches?" saith He; "is it not that thou mayest enjoy pleasure and luxury? Why now, this above all things thou wilt fail to obtain thereby, it will rather be just contrary." For if, when our eyes are stricken out, we perceive not any pleasant thing, because of such our calamity; much more will this be our case in the perversion and maiming of the mind.

Again, with what intent dost thou bury it in the earth? That it may be kept in safety? But here too again it is the contrary, saith He.

And thus, as in dealing with him that for vainglory fasts and gives alms and prays, by those very things which he most desires He had allured him not to be vainglorious:—"for with what intent," saith He, "dost thou so pray and give alms? for love of the glory that may be had from men? then do not pray thus," saith He, "and so thou shalt obtain it in the day that is to come:"—so He hath taken captive the covetous man also, by those things for which he was most earnest. Thus: "what wouldest thou?" saith He, "to have thy wealth preserved, and to enjoy pleasure? Both these things I will afford thee in great abundance, if thou lay up thy gold in that place, where I bid thee."

It is true that hereafter He displayed more clearly the evil effect of this on the mind, I mean, when He made mention of the thorns; but for the present, even here He hath strikingly intimated the same, by representing him as darkened who is beside himself in this way.

And as they that are in darkness see nothing distinct, but if they look at a rope, they suppose it to be a serpent, if at mountains and ravines, they are dead with fear; so these also: what is not alarming to them that have sight, that they regard with suspicion. Thus among other things they tremble at poverty: or rather not at poverty only, but even at any trifling loss. Yea, and if they should lose some little matter, those who are in want of necessary food do not so grieve and bewail themselves as they. At least many of the rich have come even to the halter, not enduring such ill fortune: and to be insulted also, and to be despitefully used, seems to them so intolerable, that even because of this again many have actually torn themselves from this present life. For to everything wealth had made them soft, except to the waiting on it. Thus, when it commands them to do service unto itself, they venture on murders, and stripes, and revilings, and all shame. A thing which comes of the utmost wretchedness; to be of all men most effeminate, where one ought to practise self-command, but where more caution was required, in these cases again to become more shameless and obstinate. Since in fact the same kind of thing befalls them, as one would have to endure who had spent all his goods on unfit objects. For such an one, when the time of necessary expenditure comes on, having nothing to supply it, suffers incurable evils, forasmuch as all that he had hath been ill spent beforehand.

And as they that are on the stage, skilled in those wicked arts, do in them go through many things strange and dangerous, but in other necessary and useful things none so ridiculous as they; even so is it with these men likewise. For so such as walk upon a stretched rope, making a display of so much courage, should some great emergency demand daring or courage, they are not able, neither do they endure even to think of such a thing. Just so they likewise that are rich, daring all for money, for self-restraint's sake endure not to submit to anything, be it small or great. And as the former practise both a hazardous and fruitless business; even so do these undergo many dangers and downfalls, but arrive at no profitable end. Yea, they undergo a twofold darkness, both having their eyes put out by the perversion of their mind, and being by the deceitfulness of their cares involved in a great mist. Wherefore neither can they easily so much as see through it. For he that is in darkness, is freed from the darkness by the mere appearance of the sun; but he that hath his eyes mutilated not even when the sun shines; which is the very case of these men: not even now that the Sun of Righteousness hath shone out, and is admonishing, do they hear, their wealth having closed their eyes. And so they have a twofold darkness to undergo, part from themselves, part from disregard to their teacher.

5. Let us then give heed unto Him exactly, that though late we may at length recover our sight. And how may one recover sight? If thou learn how thou wast blinded. How then wast thou blinded? By thy wicked desire. For the love of money, like an evil humor which hath collected upon a clear eyeball, hath caused the cloud to become thick.

But even this cloud may be easily scattered and broken, if we will receive the beam of the doctrine of Christ; if we will hear Him admonishing us, and saying, "Lay not up for yourselves treasures upon earth."

"But," saith one, "what avails the hearing to me, as long as I am possessed by the desire?" Now in the first place, there will be power in the continual hearing to destroy even the desire. Next, if it continue to possess thee, consider that this thing is not really so much as a desire. For what sort of desire is this, to be in grievous bondage, and to be subject to a tyranny, and to be bound on all sides, and to dwell in darkness, and to be full of turmoil, and to endure toils without profit, and to keep thy wealth for others, and often for thy very enemies? with what sort of desire do these things agree? or rather of what flight and aversion are they not worthy? What sort of desire, to lay up treasure in the midst of thieves? Nay, if thou dost at all desire wealth, remove it where it may remain safe and unmolested. Since what you are now doing is the part of one desiring, not riches, surely, but bondage, and affront, and loss, and continual vexation. Yet thou, were any one among men on earth to show thee a place beyond molestation, though he lead thee out into the very desert, promising security in the keeping of thy wealth,—thou art not slow nor backward; thou hast confidence in him, and puttest out thy goods there; but when it is God instead of men who makes thee this promise, and when He sets before thee not the desert, but Heaven, thou acceptest the contrary. Yet surely, how manifold soever be their security below, thou canst never become free from the care of them. I mean, though thou lose them not, thou wilt never be delivered from anxiety lest thou lose. But there thou wilt undergo none of these things: and mark, what is yet more, thou dost not only bury thy gold, but plantest it. For the same is both treasure and seed; or rather it is more than either of these. For the seed remains not for ever, but this abides perpetually. Again, the treasure germinates not, but this bears thee fruits which never die.

6. But if thou tellest me of the time, and the delay of the recompence, I too can point out and tell how much thou receivest back even here: and besides all this, from the very things of this life, I will try to convict thee of making this excuse to no purpose. I mean, that even in the present life thou providest many things which thou art not thyself to enjoy; and should any one find fault, thou pleadest thy children and their children, and so thinkest thou hast found palliation enough for thy superfluous labors. For when in extreme old age thou art building splendid houses, before the completion of which (in many instances) thou wilt have departed; when thou plantest trees, which will bear their fruit after many years; when thou art buying properties and inheritances, the ownership of which thou wilt acquire after a long time, and art eagerly busy in many other such things, the enjoyment whereof thou wilt not reap; is it indeed for thine own sake, or for those to come after, that thou art so employed? How then is it not the utmost folly, here not at all to hesitate at the delay of time; and this though thou art by this delay to lose all the reward of thy labors: but there, because of such waiting to be altogether torpid; and this, although it bring thee the greater gain, and although it convey not thy good things on to others, but procure the gifts for thyself.

But besides this, the delay itself is not long; nay, for those things are at the doors, and we know not but that even in our own generation all things which concern us may have their accomplishment, and that fearful day may arrive, setting before us the awful and incorruptible tribunal. Yea, for the more part of the signs are fulfilled, and the gospel moreover hath been preached in all parts of the world, and the predictions of wars, and of earthquakes, and of famines, have come to pass, and the interval is not great.

But is it that thou dost not see any signs? Why, this self-same thing is a very great sign. For neither did they in Noah's time see any presages of that universal destruction, but in the midst of their playing, eating, marrying, doing all things to which they were used, even so they were overtaken by that fearful judgment. And they too in Sodom in like manner, living in delight, and suspecting none of what befell them, were consumed by those lightnings, which then came down upon them.

Considering then all these things, let us betake ourselves unto the preparation for our departure hence.

For even if the common day of the consummation never overtake us, the end of each one is at the doors, whether he be old or young; and it is not possible for men after they have gone hence, either to buy oil any more, or to obtain pardon by prayers, though he that entreats be Abraham, or Noah, or Job, or Daniel.

While then we have opportunity, let us store up for ourselves beforehand much confidence, let us gather oil in abundance, let us remove all into Heaven, that in the fitting time, and when we most need them, we may enjoy all: by the grace and love towards man of our Lord Jesus Christ, to whom be the glory, and the might, now and always, and forever and ever. Amen.

HOMILY XXI

MATT. VI. 24

"No man can serve two masters, for either he will hate the one and love the other, or else he will hold to one and despise the other."

Seest thou how by degrees He withdraws us from the things that now are, and at greater length introduces what He hath to say, touching voluntary poverty, and casts down the dominion of covetousness?

For He was not contented with His former sayings, many and great as they were, but He adds others also, more and more alarming.

For what can be more alarming than what He now saith, if indeed we are for our riches to fall from the service of Christ? or what more to be desired, if indeed, by despising wealth, we shall have our affection towards Him and our charity perfect? For what I am continually repeating, the same do I now say likewise, namely, that by both kinds He presses the hearer to obey His sayings; both by the profitable, and by the hurtful; much like an excellent physician, pointing out both the disease which is the consequence of neglect, and the good health which results from obedience.

See, for instance, what kind of gain He signifies this to be, and how He establishes the advantage of it by their deliverance from the contrary things. Thus, "wealth," saith He, "hurts you not in this only, that it arms robbers against you, nor in that it darkens your mind in the most intense degree, but also in that it casts you out of God's service, making you captive of lifeless riches, and in both ways doing you harm, on the one hand, by causing you to be slaves of what you ought to command; on the other, by casting you out of God's service, whom, above all things, it is indispensable for you to serve." For just as in the other place, He signified the mischief to be twofold, in both laying up here, "where moth corrupteth," and in not laying up there, where the watch kept is impregnable; so in this place, too, He shows the loss to be twofold, in that it both draws off from God, and makes us subject to mammon.

But He sets it not down directly, rather He establishes it first upon general considerations, saying thus; "No man can serve two masters:" meaning here two that are enjoining opposite things; since, unless this were the case, they would not even be two. For so, "the multitude of them that believed were of one heart and of one soul," and yet were they divided into many bodies; their unanimity however made the many one.

Then, as adding to the force of it, He saith, "so far from serving, he will even hate and abhor:" "For either he will hate the one," saith He, "and love the other, or else he will hold to the one and despise the other." And it seems indeed as if the same thing were said twice over; He did not however choose this form without purpose, but in order to show that the change for the better is easy. I mean, lest thou shouldest say, "I am once for all made a slave; I am brought under the tyranny of wealth," He signifies that it is possible to transfer one's self, and that as from the first to the second, so also from the second one may pass over to the first.

2. Having thus, you see, spoken generally, that He might persuade the hearer to be an uncorrupt judge of His words, and to sentence according to the very nature of the things; when he hath made sure of his assent, then, and not till then, He discovers Himself. Thus He presently adds, "Ye cannot serve God and mammon." Let us shudder to think what we have brought Christ to say; with the name of God, to put that of gold. But if this be shocking, its taking place in our deeds, our preferring the tyranny of gold to the fear of God, is much more shocking.

"What then? Was not this possible among the ancients?" By no means. "How then," saith one, "did Abraham, how did Job obtain a good report?" Tell me not of them that are rich, but of them that serve riches. Since Job also was rich, but he served not mammon, but possessed it and ruled over it, and was a master, not a slave. Therefore he so possessed all those things, as if he had been the steward of another man's goods; not only not extorting from others, but even giving up his own to them that were in need. And what is more, when he had them they were no joy to him: so he also declared, saying, "If I did so much as rejoice when my wealth waxed great:" wherefore neither did he grieve when it was gone. But they that are rich are not now such as he was, but are rather in a worse condition than any slave, paying as it were tribute to some grievous tyrant. Because their mind is as a kind of citadel occupied by the love of money, which from thence daily sends out unto them its commands full of all iniquity, and there is none to disobey. Be not therefore thus over subtle. Nay, for God hath once for all declared and pronounced it a thing impossible for the one service and the other to agree. Say not thou, then, "it is possible." Why, when the one master is commanding thee to spoil by violence, the other to strip thyself of thy possessions; the one to be chaste, the other to commit fornication; the one to be drunken and luxurious, the other to keep the belly in subjection; the one again to despise the things that are, the other to be rivetted to the present; the one to admire marbles, and walls, and roofs, the other to contemn these, but to honor self-restraint: how is it possible that these should agree?

Now He calls mammon here "a master," not because of its own nature, but on account of the wretchedness of them that bow themselves beneath it. So also He calls "the belly a god," not from the dignity of such a mistress, but from the wretchedness of them that are enslaved: it being a thing worse than any punishment, and enough, before the punishment, in the way of vengeance on him who is involved in it. For what condemned criminals can be so wretched, as they who having God for their Lord, do from that mild rule desert to this grievous tyranny, and this when their act brings after it so much harm even here? For indeed their loss is unspeakable by so doing: there are suits, and molestations, and strifes, and toils, and a blinding of the soul; and what is more grievous than all, one falls away from the highest blessings; for such a blessing it is to be God's servant.

3. Having now, as you see, in all ways taught the advantage of contemning riches, as well for the very preservation of the riches, as for the pleasure of the soul, and for acquiring self-command, and for the securing of godliness; He proceeds to establish the practicability of this command. For this especially pertains to the best legislation, not only to enjoin what is expedient, but also to make it possible. Therefore He also goes on to say,

"Take no thought for your life, what ye shall eat."

That is, lest they should say, "What then? if we cast all away, how shall we be able to live?" At this objection, in what follows, He makes a stand, very seasonably. For as surely as if at the beginning He had said, "Take no thought," the word would have seemed burdensome; so surely, now that He hath shown the mischief arising out of covetousness, His admonition coming after is made easy to receive. Wherefore neither did He now simply say, "Take no thought," but He added the reason, and so enjoined this. After having said, "Ye cannot serve God and mammon," He added, "therefore I say unto you, take no thought. Therefore;" for what? Because of the unspeakable loss. For the hurt you receive is not in riches only, rather the wound is in the most vital parts, and in that which is the overthrow of your salvation; casting you as it does out from God, who made you, and careth for you, and loveth you.

"Therefore I say unto you, take no thought." Thus, after He hath shown the hurt to be unspeakable, then and not before He makes the commandment stricter; in that He not only bids us cast away what we have, but forbids to take thought even for our necessary food, saying, "Take no thought for your soul, what ye shall eat." Not because the soul needs food, for it is incorporeal; but He spake according to the common custom. For though it needs not food, yet can it not endure to remain in the body, except that be fed. And in saying this, He puts it not simply so, but here also He brings up arguments, some from those things which we have already, and some from other examples.

From what we have already, thus saying:

"Is not the soul more than meat, and the body more than the raiment?"

He therefore that hath given the greater, how shall He not give the less? He that hath fashioned the flesh that is fed, how shall He not bestow the food? Wherefore neither did He simply say, "Take no thought what ye shall eat," or "wherewithal ye shall be clothed;" but, "for the body," and, "for the soul:" forasmuch as from them He was to make His demonstrations, carrying on His discourse in the way of comparison. Now the soul He hath given once for all, and it abides such as it is; but the body increases every day. Therefore pointing out both these things, the immortality of the one, and the frailty of the other, He subjoins and says,

"Which of you can add one cubit unto his stature?"

Thus, saying no more of the soul, since it receives not increase, He discoursed of the body only; hereby making manifest this point also, that not the food increases it, but the providence of God. Which Paul showing also in other ways, said, "So then, neither is he that planteth any thing, neither he that watereth; but God that giveth the increase."

From what we have already, then, He urges us in this way: and from examples of other things, by saying, "Behold the fowls of the air." Thus, lest any should say, "we do good by taking thought," He dissuades them both by that which is greater, and by that which is less; by the greater, i.e. the soul and the body; by the less, i.e. the birds. For if of the things that are very inferior He hath so much regard, how shall He not give unto you? saith He. And to them on this wise, for as yet it was an ordinary multitude: but to the devil not thus; but how? "Man shall not live by bread alone, but by every word that proceedeth out of the mouth of God." But here He makes mention of the birds, and this in a way greatly to abash them; which sort of thing is of very great value for the purpose of admonition.

4. However, some of the ungodly have come to so great a pitch of madness, as even to attack His illustration. Because, say they, it was not meet for one strengthening moral principle, to use natural advantages as incitements to that end. For to those animals, they add, this belongs by nature. What then shall we say to this? That even though it is theirs by nature, yet possibly we too may attain it by choice. For neither did He say, "behold how the birds fly," which were a thing impossible to man; but that they are fed without taking thought, a kind of thing easy to be achieved by us also, if we will. And this they have proved, who have accomplished it in their actions.

Wherefore it were meet exceedingly to admire the consideration of our Lawgiver, in that, when He might bring forward His illustration from among men, and when He might have spoken of Moses and Elias and John, and others like them, who took no thought; that He might touch them more to the quick, He made mention of the irrational beings. For had He spoken of those righteous men, these would have been able to say, "We are not yet become like them." But now by passing them over in silence, and bringing forward the fowls of the air, He hath cut off from them every excuse, imitating in this place also the old law. Yea, for the old covenant likewise sends to the bee, and to the ant, and to the turtle, and to the swallow. And neither is this a small sign of honor, when the same sort of things, which those animals possess by nature, those we are able to accomplish by an act of our choice. If then He take so great care of them which exist for our sakes, much more of us; if of the servants, much more of the master. Therefore He said, "Behold the fowls," and He said not, "for they do not traffic, nor make merchandise," for these were among the things that were earnestly forbidden. But what? "they sow not, neither do they reap." "What then?" saith one, "must we not sow?" He said not, "we must not sow," but "we must not take thought;" neither that one ought not to work, but not to be low-minded, nor to rack one's self with cares. Since He bade us also be nourished, but not in "taking thought."

Of this lesson David also lays the foundation from old time, saying enigmatically on this wise, "Thou openest Thine hand, and fillest every living thing with bounty;" and again, "To Him that giveth to the beasts their food, and to the young ravens that call upon Him."

"Who then," it may be said, "have not taken thought"? Didst thou not hear how many of the righteous I adduced? Seest thou not with them Jacob, departing from his father's house destitute of all things? Dost thou not hear him praying and saying, "If the Lord give me bread to eat and raiment to put on?"

which was not the part of one taking thought, but of one seeking all of God. This the apostles also attained, who cast away all, and took no thought: also, the "five thousand," and the "three thousand."

5. But if thou canst not bear, upon hearing so high words, to release thyself from these grievous bonds, consider the unprofitableness of the thing, and so put an end to thy care. For

"Which of you by taking thought" (saith He) "can add one cubit unto his stature."

Seest thou how by that which is evident, He hath manifested that also which is obscure? Thus, "As unto thy body," saith He, "thou wilt not by taking thought be able to add, though it be ever so little; so neither to gather food; think as thou mayest otherwise." Hence it is clear that not our diligence, but the providence of God, even where we seem to be active, effects all. So that, were He to forsake us, no care, nor anxiety, nor toil, nor any other such thing, will ever appear to come to anything, but all will utterly pass away.

Let us not therefore suppose His injunctions are impossible: for there are many who duly perform them, even as it is. And if thou knowest not of them, it is nothing marvellous, since Elias too supposed he was alone, but was told, "I have left unto myself seven thousand men." Whence it is manifest that even now there are many who show forth the apostolical life; like as the "three thousand" then, and the "five thousand." And if we believe not, it is not because there are none who do well, but because we are far from so doing. So that just as the drunkard would not easily believe, that there exists any man who doth not taste even water (and yet this hath been achieved by many solitaries in our time); nor he who connects himself with numberless women, that it is easy to live in virginity; nor he that extorts other men's goods, that one shall readily give up even his own: so neither will those, who daily melt themselves down with innumerable anxieties, easily receive this thing.

Now as to the fact, that there are many who have attained unto this, we might show it even from those, who have practised this self-denial even in our generation.

But for you, just now, it is enough to learn not to covet, and that almsgiving is a good thing; and to know that you must impart of what ye have. For these things if thou wilt duly perform, beloved, thou wilt speedily proceed to those others also.

6. For the present therefore let us lay aside our excessive sumptuousness, and let us endure moderation, and learn to acquire by honest labor all that we are to have: since even the blessed John, when he was discoursing with those that were employed upon the tribute, and with the soldiery, enjoined them "to

be content with their wages." Anxious though he were to lead them on to another, and a higher self-command, yet since they were still unfit for this, he speaks of the lesser things. Because, if he had mentioned what are higher than these, they would have failed to apply themselves to them, and would have fallen from the others.

For this very reason we too are practising you in the inferior duties. Yes, because as yet, we know, the burden of voluntary poverty is too great for you, and the heaven is not more distant from the earth, than such self-denial from you. Let us then lay hold, if it be only of the lowest commandments, for even this is no small encouragement. And yet some amongst the heathens have achieved even this, though not in a proper spirit, and have stripped themselves of all their possessions. However, we are contented in your case, if alms are bestowed abundantly by you; for we shall soon arrive at those other duties too, if we advance in this way. But if we do not so much as this, of what favor shall we be worthy, who are bidden to surpass those under the old law, and yet show ourselves inferior to the philosophers among the heathens? What shall we say, who when we ought to be angels and sons of God, do not even quite maintain our being as men? For to spoil and to covet comes not of the gentleness of men, but of the fierceness of wild beasts; nay, worse than wild beasts are the assailers of their neighbor's goods. For to them this comes by nature, but we who are honored with reason, and yet are falling away unto that unnatural vileness, what indulgence shall we receive?

Let us then, considering the measures of that discipline which is set before us, press on at least to the middle station, that we may both be delivered from the punishment which is to come, and proceeding regularly, may arrive at the very summit of all good things; unto which may we all attain, by the grace and love towards man of our Lord Jesus Christ, to whom be glory and dominion for ever and ever. Amen.

HOMILY XXII

MATT. VI. 28, 29

"Consider the lilies of the field, how they grow; they toil not, neither do they spin. And yet I say unto you, That even Solomon in all his glory was not arrayed like one of these."

Having spoken of our necessary food, and having signified that not even for this should we take thought, He passes on in what follows to that which is more easy. For raiment is not so necessary as food.

Why then did He not make use here also of the same example, that of the birds, neither mention to us the peacock, and the swan, and the sheep? for surely there were many such examples to take from thence. Because He would point out how very far the argument may be carried both ways: both from the vileness of the things that partake of such elegance, and from the munificence vouchsafed to the lilies, in respect of their adorning. For this cause, when He hath decked them out, He doth not so much as call them lilies any more, but "grass of the field." And He is not satisfied even with this name, but again adds another circumstance of vileness, saying, "which to-day is." And He said not, "and to-morrow is not," but what is much baser yet, "is cast into the oven." And He said not, "clothe," but "so clothe."

Seest thou everywhere how He abounds in amplifications and intensities? And this He doth, that He may touch them home: and therefore He hath also added, "shall He not much more clothe you?" For this too hath much emphasis: the force of the word, "you," being no other than to indicate covertly the great value set upon our race, and the concern shown for it; as though He had said, "you, to whom He gave a soul, for whom He fashioned a body, for whose sake He made all the things that are seen, for whose sake He sent prophets, and gave the law, and wrought those innumerable good works; for whose sake He gave up His only begotten Son."

And not till He hath made His proof clear, doth He proceed also to rebuke them, say ing, "O ye of little faith." For this is the quality of an adviser: He doth not admonish only, but reproves also, that He may awaken men the more to the persuasive power of His words.

Hereby He teaches us not only to take no thought, but not even to be dazzled at the costliness of men's apparel. Why, such comeliness is of grass, such beauty of the green herb: or rather, the grass is even more precious than such apparelling. Why then pride thyself on things, whereof the prize rests with the mere plant, with a great balance in its favor?

And see how from the beginning He signifies the injunction to be easy; by the contraries again, and by the things of which they were afraid, leading them away from these cares. Thus, when He had said, "Consider the lilies of the field," He added, "they toil not:" so that in desire to set us free from toils, did He give these commands. In fact, the labor lies, not in taking no thought, but in taking thought for these things. And as in saying, "they sow not," it was not the sowing that He did away with, but the anxious thought; so in saying, "they toil not, neither do they spin," He put an end not to the work, but to the care.

But if Solomon was surpassed by their beauty, and that not once nor twice, but throughout all his reign:—for neither can one say, that at one time He was clothed with such apparel, but after that He was so no more; rather not so much as on one day did He array Himself so beautifully: for this Christ declared by saying, "in all his reign:" and if it was not that He was surpassed by this flower, but vied with that, but He gave place to all alike (wherefore He also said, "as one of these:" for such as between the truth and the counterfeit, so great is the interval between those robes and these flowers):—if then he acknowledged his inferiority, who was more glorious than all kings that ever were: when wilt thou be able to surpass, or rather to approach even faintly to such perfection of form?

After this He instructs us, not to aim at all at such ornament. See at least the end thereof; after its triumph "it is cast into the oven:" and if of things mean, and worthless, and of no great use, God hath displayed so great care, how shall He give up thee, of all living creatures the most important?

Wherefore then did He make them so beautiful? That He might display His own wisdom and the excellency of His power; that from everything we might learn His glory. For not "the Heavens only declare the glory of God," but the earth too; and this David declared when he said, "Praise the Lord, ye fruitful trees, and all cedars." For some by their fruits, some by their greatness, some by their beauty, send up praise to Him who made them: this too being a sign of great excellency of wisdom, when even upon things that are very vile (and what can be viler than that which to-day is, and to-morrow is not?) He pours out such great beauty. If then to the grass He hath given that which it needs not (for what doth the beauty thereof help to the feeding of the fire?) how shall He not give unto thee that which thou needest? If that which is the vilest of all things, He hath lavishly adorned, and that as doing it not for need, but for munificence, how much more will He honor thee, the most honorable of all things, in matters which are of necessity.

2. Now when, as you see, He had demonstrated the greatness of God's providential care, and they were in what follows to be rebuked also, even in this He was sparing, laying to their charge not want, but poverty, of faith. Thus, "if God," saith He, "so clothe the grass of the field, much more you, O ye of little faith."

And yet surely all these things He Himself works. For "all things were made by Him, and without Him was not so much as one thing made." But yet He nowhere as yet makes mention of Himself: it being sufficient for the time, to indicate His full power, that He said at each of the commandments, "Ye have heard that it hath been said to them of old time, but I say unto you."

Marvel not then, when in subsequent instances also He conceals Himself, or speaks something lowly of Himself: since for the present He had but one object, that His word might prove such as they would readily receive, and might in every way demonstrate that He was not a sort of adversary of God, but of one mind, and in agreement with the Father.

Which accordingly He doth here also; for through so many words as He hath spent He ceases not to set Him before us, admiring His wisdom, His providence, His tender care extending through all things, both great and small. Thus, both when He was speaking of Jerusalem, He called it "the city of the Great King;" and when He mentioned Heaven, He spake of it again as "God's throne;" and when He was discoursing of His economy in the world, to Him again He attributes it all, saying, "He maketh His sun to rise on the evil and on the good, and sendeth rain on the just and on the unjust." And in the prayer too He taught us to say, His "is the kingdom and the power and the glory." And here in discoursing of His providence, and signifying how even in little things He is the most excellent of artists, He saith, that "He clothes the grass of the field." And nowhere doth He call Him His own Father, but theirs; in order that by the very honor He might reprove them, and that when He should call Him His Father, they might no more be displeased.

Now if for bare necessaries one is not to take thought, what pardon can we deserve, who take thought for things expensive? Or rather, what pardon can they deserve, who do even without sleep, that they may take the things of others?

3. "Therefore take no thought, saying, what shall we eat? or, what shall we drink? or, wherewithal shall we be clothed? For after all these things do the nations of the world seek."

Seest thou how again He hath both shamed them the more, and hath also shown by the way, that He had commanded nothing grievous nor burdensome? As therefore when He said, "If ye love them which love you," it is nothing great which ye practise, for the very Gentiles do the same; by the mention of the Gentiles He was stirring them up to something greater: so now also He brings them forward to reprove us, and to signify that it is a necessary debt which He is requiring of us. For if we must show forth something more than the Scribes or Pharisees, what can we deserve, who so far from going beyond these, do even abide in the mean estate of the Gentiles, and emulate their littleness of soul?

He doth not however stop at the rebuke, but having by this reproved and roused them, and shamed them with all strength of expression, by another argument He also comforts them, saying, "For your Heavenly Father knoweth that ye have need of all these things." He said not, "God knoweth," but, "your Father knoweth;" to lead them to a greater hope. For if He be a Father, and such a Father, He will not surely be able to overlook His children in extremity of evils; seeing that not even men, being fathers, bear to do so.

And He adds along with this yet another argument. Of what kind then is it? That "ye have need" of them. What He saith is like this. What! are these things superfluous, that He should disregard them? Yet not even in superfluities did He show Himself wanting in regard, in the instance of the grass: but now are these things even necessary. So that what thou considerest a cause for thy being anxious, this I say is sufficient to draw thee from such anxiety. I mean, if thou sayest, "Therefore I must needs take thought, because they are necessary;" on the contrary, I say, "Nay, for this self-same reason take no thought, because they are necessary." Since were they superfluities, not even then ought we to despair, but to feel confident about the supply of them; but now that they are necessary, we must no longer be in doubt. For what kind of father is he, who can endure to fail in supplying to his children even necessaries? So that for this cause again God will most surely bestow them.

For indeed He is the artificer of our nature, and He knows perfectly the wants thereof. So that neither canst thou say, "He is indeed our Father, and the things we seek are necessary, but He knows not that we stand in need of them." For He that knows our nature itself, and was the framer of it, and formed it such as it is; evidently He knows its need also better than thou, who art placed in want of them: it having been by His decree, that our nature is in such need. He will not therefore oppose Himself to what He hath willed, first subjecting it of necessity to so great want, and on the other hand again depriving it of what it wants, and of absolute necessaries.

Let us not therefore be anxious, for we shall gain nothing by it, but tormenting ourselves. For whereas He gives both when we take thought, and when we do not, and more of the two, when we do not; what dost thou gain by thy anxiety, but to exact of thyself a superfluous penalty? Since one on the point of going to a plentiful feast, will not surely permit himself to take thought for food; nor is he that is walking to a fountain anxious about drink. Therefore seeing we have a supply more copious than either any fountain, or innumerable banquets made ready, the providence of God; let us not be beggars, nor little minded.

4. For together with what hath been said, He puts also yet another reason for feeling confidence about such things, saying,

"Seek ye the kingdom of Heaven, and all these things shall be added unto you."

Thus when He had set the soul free from anxiety, then He made mention also of Heaven. For indeed He came to do away with the old things, and to call us to a greater country. Therefore He doeth all, to deliver us from things unnecessary, and from our affection for the earth. For this cause He mentioned the heathens also, saying that "the Gentiles seek after these things;" they whose whole labor is for the present life, who have no regard for the things to come, nor any thought of Heaven. But to you not these present are the chief things, but other than these. For we were not born for this end, that we should eat and drink and be clothed, but that we might please God, and attain unto the good things to come. Therefore as things here are secondary in our labor, so also in our prayers let them be secondary. Therefore He also said, "Seek ye the kingdom of Heaven, and all these things shall be added unto you."

And He said not, "shall be given," but "shall be added," that thou mightest learn, that the things present are no great part of His gifts, compared with the greatness of the things to come. Accordingly, He doth not bid us so much as ask for them, but while we ask for other things, to have confidence, as though these also were added to those. Seek then the things to come, and thou wilt receive the things present also; seek not the things that are seen, and thou shalt surely attain unto them. Yea, for it is unworthy of thee to approach thy Lord for such things. And thou, who oughtest to spend all thy zeal and thy care for those unspeakable blessings, dost greatly disgrace thyself by consuming it on the desire of transitory things.

"How then?" saith one, "did He not bid us ask for bread?" Nay, He added, "daily," and to this again, "this day," which same thing in fact He doth here also. For He said not, "Take no thought," but, "Take no thought for the morrow," at the same time both affording us liberty, and fastening our soul on those things that are more necessary to us.

For to this end also He bade us ask even those, not as though God needed reminding by us, but that we might learn that by His help we accomplish whatever we do accomplish, and that we might be made more His own by our continual prayer for these things.

Seest thou how by this again He would persuade them, that they shall surely receive the things present? For He that bestows the greater, much more will He give the less. "For not for this end," saith He, "did I tell you not to take thought nor to ask, that ye should suffer distress, and go about naked, but in order that ye might be in abundance of these things also:" and this, you see, was suited above all things to attract them to Him. So that like as in almsgiving, when deterring them from making a display to men, He won upon them chiefly by promising to furnish them with it more liberally;—"for thy Father," saith He, "who seeth in secret, shall reward thee openly;"—even so here also, in drawing them off from seeking these things, this is His persuasive topic, that

He promises to bestow it on them, not seeking it, in greater abundance. Thus, to this end, saith He, do I bid thee not seek, not that thou mayest not receive, but that thou mayest receive plentifully; that thou mayest receive in the fashion that becomes thee, with the profit which thou oughtest to have; that thou mayest not, by taking thought, and distracting thyself in anxiety about these, render thyself unworthy both of these, and of the things spiritual; that thou mayest not undergo unnecessary distress, and again fall away from that which is set before thee.

5. "Take therefore no thought for the morrow: for sufficient unto the day is the evil thereof:" that is to say, the affliction, and the bruising thereof. Is it not enough for thee, to eat thy bread in the sweat of thy face? Why add the further affliction that comes of anxiety, when thou art on the point to be delivered henceforth even from the former toils?

By "evil" here He means, not wickedness, far from it, but affliction, and trouble, and calamities; much as in another place also He saith, "Is there evil in a city, which the Lord hath not done?" nor any thing like these, but the scourges which are borne from above. And again, "I," saith He, "make peace, and create evils:" For neither in this place doth He speak of wickedness, but of famines, and pestilences, things accounted evil by most men: the generality being wont to call these things evil. Thus, for example, the priests and prophets of those five lordships, when having yoked the kine to the ark, they let them go without their calves, gave the name of "evil" to those heaven-sent plagues, and the dismay and anguish which thereby sprang up within them.

This then is His meaning here also, when He saith, "sufficient unto the day is the evil thereof." For nothing so pains the soul, as carefulness and anxiety. Thus did Paul also, when urging to celibacy, give counsel, saying, "I would have you without carefulness."

But when He saith, "the morrow shall take thought for itself," He saith it not, as though the day took thought for these things, but forasmuch as He had to speak to a people somewhat imperfect, willing to make what He saith more expressive, He personifies the time, speaking unto them according to the custom of the generality.

And here indeed He advises, but as He proceeds, He even makes it a law, saying, "provide neither gold nor silver, nor scrip for your journey." Thus, having shown it all forth in His actions, then after that He introduces the verbal enactment of it more determinately, the precept too having then become more easy of acceptance, confirmed as it had been previously by His own actions. Where then did He confirm it by His actions? Hear Him saying, "The Son of Man hath not where to lay His head." Neither is He satisfied with this only, but in His disciples also He exhibits His full proof of these things, by fashioning them too in like manner, yet not suffering them to be in want of anything.

But mark His tender care also, how He surpasses the affection of any father. Thus, "This I command," saith He, "for nothing else, but that I may deliver you from superfluous anxieties. For even if to-day thou hast taken thought for to-morrow, thou wilt also have to take thought again to-morrow. Why then what is over and above? Why force the day to receive more than the distress which is allotted to it, and together with its own troubles add to it also the burden of the following day; and this, when there is no chance of thy lightening the other by the addition so taking place, but thou art merely to exhibit thyself as coveting superfluous troubles?" Thus, that He may reprove them the more, He doth all but give life to the very time, and brings it in as one injured, and exclaiming against them for their causeless despite. Why, thou hast received the day, to care for the things thereof. Wherefore then add unto it the things of the other day also? Hath it not then burden enough in its own anxiety? Why now, I pray, dost thou make it yet heavier? Now when the Lawgiver saith these things, and He that is to pass judgment on us, consider the hopes that He suggests to us, how good they are; He Himself testifying, that this life is wretched and wearisome, so that the anxiety even of the one day is enough to hurt and afflict us.

6. Nevertheless, after so many and so grave words, we take thought for these things, but for the things in Heaven no longer: rather we have reversed His order, on either side fighting against His sayings. For mark; "Seek ye not the things present," saith He, "at all;" but we are seeking these things for ever: "seek the things in Heaven," saith He; but those things we seek not so much as for a short hour, but according to the greatness of the anxiety we display about the things of the world, is the carelessness we entertain in things spiritual; or rather even much greater. But this doth not prosper for ever; neither can this be for ever. What if for ten days we think scorn? if for twenty? if for an hundred? must we not of absolute necessity depart, and fall into the hands of the Judge?

"But the delay hath comfort." And what sort of comfort, to be every day looking for punishment and vengeance? Nay, if thou wouldest have some comfort from this delay, take it by gathering for thyself the fruit of amendment after repentance. Since if the mere delay of vengeance seem to thee a sort of refreshment, far more is it gain not to fall into the vengeance. Let us then make full use of this delay, in order to have a full deliverance from the dangers that press upon us. For none of the things enjoined is either burdensome or grievous, but all are so light and easy, that if we only bring a genuine purpose of heart, we may accomplish all, though we be chargeable with countless offenses. For so Manasses had perpetrated innumerable pollutions, having both stretched out his hands against the saints, and brought abominations into the temple, and filled the city with murders, and wrought many other things beyond excuse; yet nevertheless after so long and so great wickedness, he washed away from himself all these things. How and in what manner? By repentance, and consideration.

For there is not, yea, there is not any sin, that doth not yield and give way to the power of repentance, or rather to the grace of Christ. Since if we would but only change, we have Him to assist us. And if thou art desirous to become good, there is none to hinder us; or rather there is one to hinder us, the devil, yet hath he no power, so long as thou choosest what is best, and so attractest God to thine aid. But if thou art not thyself willing, but startest aside, how shall He protect thee? Since not of necessity or compulsion, but of thine own will, He wills thee to be saved. For if thou thyself, having a servant full of hatred and aversion for thee, and continually going off, and fleeing away from thee, wouldest not choose to keep him, and this though needing his services; much less will God, who doeth all things not for His own profit, but for thy salvation, choose to retain thee by compulsion; as on the other hand, if thou show forth a right intention only, He would not choose ever to give thee up, no, not whatever the devil may do. So that we are ourselves to blame for our own destruction. Because we do not approach, nor beseech, nor entreat Him, as we ought: but even if we do draw nigh, it is not as persons who have need to receive, neither is it with the proper faith, nor as making demand, but we do all in a gaping and listless way.

7. And yet God would have us demand things of Him, and for this accounts Himself greatly bound to thee. For He alone of all debtors, when the demand is made, counts it a favor, and gives what we have not lent Him. And if He should see him pressing earnestly that makes the demand, He pays down even what He hath not received of us; but if sluggishly, He too keeps on making delays; not through unwillingness to give, but because He is pleased to have the demand made upon Him by us. For this cause He told thee also the example of that friend, who came by night, and asked a loaf; and of the judge that feared not God, nor regarded men. And He stayed not at similitudes, but signified it also in His very actions, when He dismissed that Phoenician woman, having filled her with His great gift. For through her He signified, that He gives to them that ask earnestly, even the things that pertain not to them. "For it is not meet," saith He, "to take the children's bread, and to give it unto the

dogs." But for all that He gave, because she demanded of him earnestly. But by the Jews He showed, that to them that are careless, He gives not even their own. They accordingly received nothing, but lost what was their own. And while these, because they asked not, did not receive so much as their very own; she, because she assailed Him with earnestness, had power to obtain even what pertained to others, and the dog received what was the children's. So great a good is importunity. For though thou be a dog, yet being importunate, thou shalt be preferred to the child being negligent: for what things affection accomplishes not, these, all of them, importunity did accomplish. Say not therefore, "God is an enemy to me, and will not hearken." He doth straightway answer thee, continually troubling him, if not because thou art His friend, yet because of thine importunity. And neither the enmity, or the unseasonable time, nor anything else becomes an hindrance. Say not, "I am unworthy, and do not pray;" for such was the Syrophoenician woman too. Say not, "I have sinned much, and am not able to entreat Him whom I have angered;" for God looks not at the desert, but at the disposition. For if the ruler that feared not God, neither was ashamed of men, was overcome by the widow, much more will He that is good be won over by continual entreaty.

So that though thou be no friend, though thou be not demanding thy due, though thou hast devoured thy Father's substance, and have been a long time out of sight, though without honor, though last of all, though thou approach Him angry, though much displeased; be willing only to pray, and to return, and thou shalt receive all, and shall quickly extinguish the wrath and the condemnation.

But, "behold, I pray," saith one, "and there is no result." Why, thou prayest not like those; such I mean as the Syrophoenician woman, the friend that came late at night, and the widow that is continually troubling the judge, and the son that consumed his father's goods. For didst thou so pray, thou wouldest quickly obtain. For though despite have been done unto Him, yet is He a Father; and though He have been provoked to anger, yet is He fond of His children; and one thing only doth He seek, not to take vengeance for our affronts, but to see thee repenting and entreating Him. Would that we were warmed in like measure, as those bowels are moved to the love of us. But this fire seeks a beginning only, and if thou afford it a little spark, thou kindlest a full flame of beneficence. For not because He hath been insulted, is He sore vexed, but because it is thou who art insulting Him, and so becoming frenzied. For if we being evil, when our children molest us, grieve on their account; much more is God, who can not so much as suffer insult, sore vexed on account of thee, who hast committed it. If we, who love by nature, much more

He, who is kindly affectioned beyond nature. "For though," saith He, "a woman should forget the fruits of her womb, yet will I not forget thee."

8. Let us therefore draw nigh unto Him, and say, "Truth, Lord; for even the dogs eat of the crumbs which fall from their masters' table." Let us draw nigh "in season, out of season:" or rather, one can never draw nigh out of season, for it is unseasonable not to be continually approaching. For of Him who desires to give it is always seasonable to ask: yea, as breathing is never out of season, so neither is praying unseasonable, but rather not praying. Since as we need this breath, so do we also the help that comes from Him; and if we be willing, we shall easily draw Him to us. And the prophet, to manifest this, and to point out the constant readiness of His beneficence, said, "We shall find Him prepared as the morning." For as often as we may draw nigh, we shall see Him awaiting our movements. And if we fail to draw from out of His ever-springing goodness, the blame is all ours. This, for example, was His complaint against certain Jews, when He said, "My mercy is as a morning cloud, and as the early dew it goeth away." And His meaning is like this; "I indeed have supplied all my part, but ye, as a hot sun coming over scatters both the cloud and the dew, and makes them vanish, so have ye by your great wickedness restrained the unspeakable Beneficence."

Which also itself again is an instance of providential care: that even when He sees us unworthy to receive good, He withholds His benefits, lest He render us careless. But if we change a little, even but so much as to know that we have sinned, He gushes out beyond the fountains, He is poured forth beyond the ocean; and the more thou receivest, so much the more doth He rejoice; and in this way is stirred up again to give us more. For indeed He accounts it as His own wealth, that we should be saved, and that He should give largely to them that ask. And this, it may seem, Paul was declaring when He said, that He is "rich unto all and over all that call upon Him." Because when we pray not, then He is wroth; when we pray not, then doth He turn away from us. For this cause "He became poor, that He might make us rich;" for this cause He underwent all those sufferings, that He might incite us to ask.

Let us not therefore despair, but having so many motives and good hopes, though we sin every day, let us approach Him, entreating, beseeching, asking the forgiveness of our sins. For thus we shall be more backward to sin for the time to come; thus shall we drive away the devil, and shall call forth the lovingkindness of God, and attain unto the good things to come, by the grace and love towards man of our Lord Jesus Christ, to whom be glory and might forever and ever. Amen.

HOMILY XXIII

MATT. VII. 1

"Judge not, that ye be not judged."

What then? Ought we not to blame them that sin? Because Paul also saith this selfsame thing: or rather, there too it is Christ, speaking by Paul, and saying, "Why dost thou judge thy brother? And thou, why dost thou set at nought thy brother?" and, "Who art thou that judgest another man's servant?" And again, "Therefore judge nothing before the time, until the Lord come."

How then doth He say elsewhere, "Reprove, rebuke, exhort," and, "Them that sin rebuke before all?" And Christ too to Peter, "Go and tell him his fault between thee and him alone," and if he neglect to hear, add to thyself another also; and if not even so doth he yield, declare it to the church likewise?" And how hath He set over us so many to reprove; and not only to reprove, but also to punish? For him that hearkens to none of these, He hath commanded to be "as a heathen man and a publican." And how gave He them the keys also? since if they are not to judge, they will be without authority in any matter, and in vain have they received the power to bind and to loose.

And besides, if this were to obtain, all would be lost alike, whether in churches, or in states, or in houses. For except the master judge the servant, and the mistress the maid, and the father the son, and friends one another, there will be an increase of all wickedness. And why say I, friends? unless we judge our enemies, we shall never be able to put an end to our enmity, but all things will be turned upside down.

What then can the saying be? Let us carefully attend, lest the medicines of salvation, and the laws of peace, be accounted by any man laws of overthrow and confusion. First of all, then, even by what follows, He hath pointed out to them that have understanding the excellency of this law, saying, "Why beholdest thou the mote that is in thy brother's eye, but considerest not the beam that is in thine own eye?"

But if to many of the less attentive, it seem yet rather obscure, I will endeavor to explain it from the beginning. In this place, then, as it seems at least to me, He doth not simply command us not to judge any of men's sins, neither doth He simply forbid the doing of such a thing, but to them that are full of innumerable ills, and are trampling upon other men for trifles. And I think that certain Jews too are here hinted at, for that while they were bitter accusing their neighbors for small faults, and such as came to nothing, they were themselves insensibly committing deadly sins. Herewith towards the end also He was upbraiding them, when He said, "Ye bind heavy burdens, and grievous to be borne, but ye will not move them with your finger," and, "ye pay tithe of mint and anise, and have omitted the weightier matters of the law, judgment, mercy, and faith."

Well then, I think that these are comprehended in His invective; that He is checking them beforehand as to those things, wherein they were hereafter to accuse His disciples. For although His disciples had been guilty of no such sin, yet in them were supposed to be offenses; as, for instance, not keeping the sabbath, eating with unwashen hands, sitting at meat with publicans; of which He saith also in another place, "Ye which strain at the gnat, and swallow the camel." But yet it is also a general law that He is laying down on these matters.

And the Corinthians too Paul did not absolutely command not to judge, but not to judge their own superiors, and upon grounds that are not acknowledged; not absolutely to refrain from correcting them that sin. Neither indeed was He then rebuking all without distinction, but disciples doing so to their teachers were the object of His reproof; and they who, being guilty of innumerable sins, bring an evil report upon the guiltless.

This then is the sort of thing which Christ also in this place intimated; not intimated merely, but guarded it too with a great ter ror, and the punishment from which no prayers can deliver.

2. "For with what judgment ye judge," saith He, "ye shall be judged."

That is, "it is not the other," saith Christ, "that thou condemnest, but thyself, and thou art making the judgment-seat dreadful to thyself, and the account strict." As then in the forgiveness of our sins the beginnings are from us, so also in this judgment, it is by ourselves that the measures of our condemnation are laid down. You see, we ought not to upbraid nor trample upon them, but to admonish; not to revile, but to advise; not to assail with pride, but to correct with tenderness. For not him, but thyself, dost thou give over to extreme vengeance, by not sparing him, when it may be needful to give sentence on his offenses.

Seest thou, how these two commandments are both easy, and fraught with great blessings to the obedient, even as of evils on the other hand, to the regardless? For both he that forgives his neighbor, hath freed himself first of the two from the grounds of complaint, and that without any labor; and he that with tenderness and indulgence inquires into other men's offenses, great is the allowance of pardon, which he hath by his judgment laid up beforehand for himself.

"What then!" say you: "if one commit fornication, may I not say that fornication is a bad thing, nor at all correct him that is playing the wanton?" Nay, correct him, but not as a foe, nor as an adversary exacting a penalty, but as a physician providing medicines. For neither did Christ say, "stay not him that is sinning," but "judge not;" that is, be not bitter in pronouncing sentence.

And besides, it is not of great things (as I have already observed), nor of things prohibited, that this is said, but of those which are not even counted offenses. Wherefore He said also.

"Why beholdest thou the mote that is in thy brother's eye?"

Yea, for many now do this; if they see but a monk wearing an unnecessary garment, they produce against him the law of our Lord, while they themselves are extorting without end, and defrauding men every day. If they see him but partaking rather largely of food, they become bitter accusers, while they themselves are daily drinking to excess and surfeiting: not knowing, that besides their own sins, they do hereby gather up for themselves a greater flame, and deprive themselves of every plea. For on this point, that thine own doings must be strictly inquired into, thou thyself hast first made the law, by thus sentencing those of thy neighbor. Account it not then to be a grievous thing, if thou art also thyself to undergo the same kind of trial.

"Thou hypocrite, first cast out the beam out of thine own eye."

Here His will is to signify the great wrath, which He hath against them that do such things. For so, wheresoever He would indicate that the sin is great, and the punishment and wrath in store for it grievous, He begins with a reproach. As then unto him that was exacting the hundred pence, He said in His deep displeasure, "Thou wicked servant, I forgave thee all that debt;" even so here also, "Thou hypocrite." For not of protecting care comes such a judgment, but of ill will to man; and while a man puts forward a mask of benevolence, he is doing a work of the utmost wickedness, causing reproaches without ground, and accusations, to cleave unto his neighbors, and usurping a teacher's rank, when he is not worthy to be so much as a disciple. On account of this He called him "hypocrite." For thou, who in other men's doings art so bitter, as to see even the little things; how hast thou become so remiss in thine own, as that even the great things are hurried over by thee?

"First cast out the beam out of thine own eye."

Seest thou, that He forbids not judging, but commands to cast out first the beam from thine eye, and then to set right the doings of the rest of the world? For indeed each one knows his own things better than those of others; and sees the greater rather than the less; and loves himself more than his neighbor. Wherefore, if thou doest it out of guardian care, I bid thee care for thyself first, in whose case the sin is both more certain and greater. But if thou neglect thyself, it is quite evident that neither dost thou judge thy brother in care for him, but in hatred, and wishing to expose him. For what if he ought to be judged? it should be by one who commits no such sin, not by thee.

Thus, because He had introduced great and high doctrines of self denial, lest any man should say, it is easy so to practise it in words; He willing to signify His entire confidence, and that He was not chargeable with any of the things that had been mentioned, but had duly fulfilled all, spake this parable. And that, because He too was afterwards to judge, saying, "Woe unto you, Scribes and Pharisees, hypocrites." Yet was not he chargeable with what hath been mentioned; for neither did He pull out a mote, nor had He a beam on His eyes, but being clean from all these, He so corrected the faults of all. "For it is not at all meet," saith He, "to judge others, when one is chargeable with the same things." And why marvel at His establishing this law, when even the very thief knew it upon the cross, saying to the other thief, "Dost not thou fear God, seeing we are in the same condemnation;" expressing the same sentiments with Christ?

But thou, so far from casting out thine own beam, dost not even see it, but another's mote thou not only seest, but also judgest, and essayest to cast it out; as if any one seized with a grievous dropsy, or indeed with any other incurable disease, were to neglect this, and find fault with another who was neglecting a slight swelling. And if it be an evil not to see one's own sins, it is a twofold and threefold evil to be even sitting in judgment on others, while men themselves, as if past feeling, are bearing about beams in their own eyes: since no beam is so heavy as sin.

His injunction therefore in these words is as follows, that he who is chargeable with countless evil deeds, should not be a bitter censor of other men's offenses, and especially when these are trifling. He is not overthrowing reproof nor correction, but forbidding men to neglect their own faults, and exult over those of other men.

For indeed this was a cause of men's going unto great vice, bringing in a twofold wickedness. For he, whose practice it had been to slight his own faults, great as they were, and to search bitterly into those of others, being slight and of no account, was spoiling himself two ways: first, by thinking lightly of his own faults; next, by incurring enmities and feuds with all men, and training himself every day to extreme fierceness, and want of feeling for others.

3. Having then put away all these things, by this His excellent legislation, He added yet another charge, saying,

"Give not that which is holy unto the dogs, neither cast ye your pearls before swine."

"Yet surely further on," it will be said, "He commanded, "What ye have heard in the ear, that preach ye upon the housetops." But this is in no wise contrary to the former. For neither in that place did He simply command to tell all men, but to whom it should be spoken, to them He bade speak with freedom. And by "dogs" here He figuratively described them that are living in incurable ungodliness, and affording no hope of change for the better; and by "swine," them that abide continually in an unchaste life, all of whom He hath pronounced unworthy of hearing such things. Paul also, it may be observed, declared this when He said, "But a natural man receiveth not the things of the Spirit, for they are foolishness unto him." And in many other places too He saith that corruption of life is the cause of men's not receiving the more perfect doctrines. Wherefore He commands not to open the doors to them; for indeed they become more insolent after learning. For as to the well-disposed and intelligent, things appear venerable when revealed, so to the insensible, when they are unknown rather. "Since then from their nature, they are not able to learn them, "let the thing be hidden," saith He, "that at least for ignorance they may reverence them. For neither doth the swine know at all what a pearl is. Therefore since he knows not, neither let him see it, lest he trample under foot what he knows not."

For nothing results, beyond greater mischief to them that are so disposed when they hear; for both the holy things are profaned by them, not knowing what they are; and they are the more lifted up and armed against us. For this is meant by, "lest they trample them under their feet, and turn again and rend you."

Nay, "surely," saith one, "they ought to be so strong as to remain equally impregnable after men's learning them, and not to yield to other people occasions against us." But it is not the things that yield it, but that these men are swine; even as when the pearl is trampled under foot, it is not so trampled, because it is really contemptible, but because it fell among swine.

And full well did He say, "turn again and rend you:" for they feign gentleness, so as to be taught: then after they have learnt, quite changing from one sort to another, they jeer, mock and deride us, as deceived persons. Therefore Paul also said to Timothy, "Of whom be thou ware also; for he hath greatly withstood our words;" and again in another place, "From such turn away," and, "A man that is an heretic, after the first and second admonition, reject."

It is not, you see, that those truths furnish them with armor, but they become fools in this way of their own accord, being filled with more willfulness. On this account it is no small gain for them to abide in ignorance, for so they are not such entire scorners. But if they learn, the mischief is twofold. For neither will they themselves be at all profited thereby, but rather the more damaged, and to thee they will cause endless difficulties.

Let them hearken, who shamelessly associate with all, and make the awful things contemptible. For the mysteries we too therefore celebrate with closed doors, and keep out the uninitiated, not for any weakness of which we have convicted our rites, but because the many are as yet imperfectly prepared for them. For this very reason He Himself also discoursed much unto the Jews in parables, "because they seeing saw not." For this, Paul likewise commanded "to know how we ought to answer every man."

4. "Ask, and it shall be given you; seek, and ye shall find; knock, and it shall be opened unto you."

For inasmuch as He had enjoined things great and marvellous, and had commanded men to be superior to all their passions, and had led them up to Heaven itself, and had enjoined them to strive after the resemblance, not of angels and archangels, but (as far as was possible) of the very Lord of all; and had bidden His disciples not only themselves duly to perform all this, but also to correct others, and to distinguish between the evil and them that are not such, the dogs and them that are not dogs (although there be much that is hidden in men):—that they might not say, "these things are grievous and intolerable," (for indeed in the sequel Peter did utter some such things, saying, "Who can be saved?" and again, "If the case of the man be so, it is not good to marry): in order therefore that they might not now likewise say so; as in the first place even by what had gone before He had proved it all to be easy, setting down many reasons one upon another, of power to persuade men: so after all He adds also the pinnacle of all facility, devising as no ordinary relief to our toils, the assistance derived from persevering prayers. Thus, we are not ourselves, saith He, to strive alone, but also to invoke the help from above: and it will surely come and be present with us, and will aid us in our struggles, and make all easy. Therefore He both commanded us to ask, and pledged Himself to the giving.

However, not simply to ask did He command us, but with much assiduity and earnestness. For this is the meaning of "seek." For so he that seeks, putting all things out of his mind, is taken up with that alone which is sought, and forms no idea of any of the persons present. And this which I am saying they know, as many as have lost either gold, or servants, and are seeking diligently after them.

By "seeking," then, He declared this; by "knocking," that we approach with earnestness and a glowing mind.

Despond not therefore, O man, nor show less of zeal about virtue, than they do of desire for wealth. For things of that kind thou hast often sought and not found, but nevertheless, though thou know this, that thou art not sure to find them, thou puttest in motion every mode of search; but here, although having a promise that thou wilt surely receive, thou dost not show even the smallest part of that earnestness. And if thou dost not receive straightway, do not even thus despair. For to this end He said, "knock," to signify that even if He should not straightway open the door, we are to continue there.

5. And if thou doubt my affirmation, at any rate believe His example.

"For what man is there of you," saith He, "whom if his son ask bread, will he give him a stone?"

Because, as among men, if thou keep on doing so, thou art even accounted troublesome, and disgusting: so with God, when thou doest not so, then thou dost more entirely provoke Him. And if thou continue asking, though thou receive not at once, thou surely wilt receive. For to this end was the door shut, that He may induce thee to knock: to this end He doth not straightway assent, that thou mayest ask. Continue then to do these things, and thou wilt surely receive. For that thou mightest not say, "What then if I should ask and not receive?" He hath blocked up thy approach with that similitude, again framing arguments, and by those human things urging us to be confident on these matters; implying by them that we must not only ask, but ask what we ought.

"For which of you is there, a father, of whom if his son shall ask bread, will he give him a stone?" So that if thou receive not, thy asking a stone is the cause of thy not receiving. For though thou be a son, this suffices not for thy receiving: rather this very thing even hinders thy receiving, that being a son, thou askest what is not profitable.

Do thou also therefore ask nothing worldly, but all things spiritual, and thou wilt surely receive. For so Solomon, because he asked what he ought, behold how quickly he received. Two things now, you see, should be in him that prays, asking earnestly, and asking what he ought: "since ye too," saith He, "though ye be fathers, wait for your sons to ask: and if they should ask of you anything inexpedient, ye refuse the gifts; just as, if it be expedient, ye consent and bestow it." Do thou too, considering these things, not withdraw until thou receive; until thou have found, retire not; relax not thy diligence, until the door be opened. For if thou approach with this mind, and say, "Except I receive, I depart not;" thou wilt surely receive, provided thou ask such things, as are both suitable for Him of whom thou askest to give, and expedient for thee the petitioner. But what are these? To seek the things spiritual, all of them; to forgive them that have trespassed, and so to draw nigh asking forgiveness; "to lift up holy hands without wrath and doubting." If we thus ask, we shall receive. As it is, surely our asking is a mockery, and the act of drunken rather than of sober men.

"What then," saith one, "if I ask even spiritual things, and do not receive?" Thou didst not surely knock with earnestness; or thou madest thyself unworthy to receive; or didst quickly leave off.

"And wherefore," it may be inquired, "did He not say, what things we ought to ask"? Nay verily, He hath mentioned them all in what precedes, and hath signified for what things we ought to draw nigh. Say not then, "I drew nigh, and did not receive." For in no case is it owing to God that we receive not, God who loves us so much as to surpass even fathers, to surpass them as far as goodness doth this evil nature.

"For if ye, being evil, know how to give good gifts unto your children, how much more your heavenly Father."

Now this He said, not to bring an evil name on man's nature, nor to condemn our race as bad; but in contrast to His own goodness He calls paternal tenderness evil, so great is the excess of His love to man.

Seest thou an argument unspeakable, of power to arouse to good hopes even him that hath become utterly desperate?

Now here indeed He signifies His goodness by means of our fathers, but in what precedes by the chief among His gifts, by the "soul," by the body. And nowhere doth He set down the chief of all good things, nor bring forward His own coming:—for He who thus made speed to give up His Son to the slaughter, "how shall He not freely give us all things?"—because it had not yet come to pass. But Paul indeed sets it forth, thus saying, "He that spared not His own Son, how shall He not also with Him freely give us all things." But His discourse with them is still from the things of men.

6. After this, to indicate that we ought neither to feel confidence in prayer, while neglecting our own doings; nor, when taking pains, trust only to our own endeavors; but both to seek after the help from above, and contribute withal our own part; He sets forth the one in connection with the other. For so after much exhortation, He taught also how to pray, and when He had taught how to pray, He proceeded again to His exhortation concerning what we are to do; then from that again to the necessity of praying continually, saying, "Ask," and "seek," and "knock." And thence again, to the necessity of being also diligent ourselves.

"For all things," saith He, "whatsoever ye would that men should do to you, do ye also to them."

Summing up all in brief, and signifying, that virtue is compendious, and easy, and readily known of all men.

And He did not merely say, "All things whatsoever ye would," but, "Therefore all things whatsoever ye would." For this word, "therefore," He did not add without purpose, but with a concealed meaning: "if ye desire," saith He, "to be heard, together with what I have said, do these things also." What then are these? "Whatsoever ye would that men should do to you." Seest thou how He hath hereby also signified that together with prayer we need exact conversation? And He did not say, "whatsoever things thou wouldest to be done unto thee of God, those do unto thy neighbor;" lest thou should say, "But how is it possible? He is God and I am man:" but, "whatsoever thou wouldest to be done unto thee of thy fellow servant, these things do thou also thyself show forth towards thy neighbor." What is less burdensome than this? what fairer?

Then the praise also, before the rewards, is exceeding great.

"For this is the law and the prophets." Whence it is evident, that virtue is according to our nature; that we all, of ourselves, know our duties; and that it is not possible for us ever to find refuge in ignorance.

7. "Enter ye in at the strait gate, for wide is the gate and broad is the way that leadeth to destruction, and many there be which go in thereat: and strait is the gate and narrow is the way which leadeth unto life, and few there be that find it."

And yet after this He said, "My yoke is easy, and my burden is light." And in what He hath lately said also, He intimated the same: how then doth He here say it is strait and confined? In the first place, if thou attend, even here He points to it as very light, and easy, and accessible. "And how," it may be said, "is the narrow and confined way easy?" Because it is a way and a gate; even as also the other, though it be wide, though spacious, is also a way and a gate. And of these there is nothing permanent, but all things are passing away, both the pains and the good things of life.

And not only herein is the part of virtue easy, but also by the end again it becomes yet easier. For not the passing away of our labors and toils, but also their issuing in a good end (for they end in life) is enough to console those in conflict. So that both the temporary nature of our labors, and the perpetuity of our crowns, and the fact that the labors come first, and the crowns after, must prove a very great relief in our toils. Wherefore Paul also called their affliction "light"; not from the nature of the events, but because of the mind of the combatants, and the hope of the future. "For our light affliction," saith he, "worketh an eternal weight of glory, while we look not at the things which are seen, but at the things which are not seen." For if to sailors the waves and the seas, to soldiers their slaughters and wounds, to husbandmen the winters and the frosts, to boxers the sharp blows, be light and tolerable things, all of them, for the hope of those rewards which are temporary and perishing; much more when heaven is set forth, and the unspeakable blessings, and the eternal rewards, will no one feel any of the present hardships. Or if any account it, even thus, to be toilsome, the suspicion comes of nothing but their own remissness.

See, at any rate, how He on another side also makes it easy, commanding not to hold intercourse with the dogs, nor to give one's self over to the swine, and to "beware of the false prophets;" thus on all accounts causing men to feel as if in real conflict. And the very fact too of calling it narrow contributed very greatly towards making it easy; for it wrought on them to be vigilant. As Paul then, when he saith, "We wrestle not against flesh and blood," doth so not to cast down, but to rouse up the spirits of the soldiers: even so He also, to shake the travellers out of their sleep, called the way rough. And not in this way only did He work upon men, to be vigilant, but also by adding, that it contains likewise many to supplant them; and, what is yet more grievous, they do not even attack openly, but hiding themselves; for such is the race of the false prophets. "But look not to this," saith He, "that it is rough and narrow, but where it ends; nor that the opposite is wide and spacious, but where it issues."

And all these things He saith, thoroughly to awaken our alacrity; even as elsewhere also He said, "Violent men take it by force." For whoever is in conflict, when he actually sees the judge of the lists marvelling at the painfulness of his efforts, is the more inspirited.

Let it not then bewilder us, when many things spring up hence, that turn to our vexation. For the way is strait, and the gate narrow, but not the city. Therefore must one neither look for rest here, nor there expect any more aught that is painful.

Now in saying, "Few there be that find it," here again He both declared the careless ness of the generality, and instructed His hearers not to regard the felicities of the many, but the labors of the few. For the more part, saith He, so far from walking this way, do not so much as make it their choice: a thing of most extreme criminality. But we should not regard the many, nor be troubled thereat, but emulate the few; and, by all means equipping ourselves, should so walk therein.

For besides that it is strait, there are also many to overthrow us in the way that leads thither. Wherefore He also added,

8. "Beware of false prophets, for they will come to you in sheep's clothing, but inwardly they are ravening wolves." Behold together with the dogs and swine another kind of ambush and conspiracy, far more grievous than that. For

those are acknowledged and open, but these shaded over. For which cause also, while from those He commanded to hold off, these He charged men to watch with exact care, as though it were not possible to see them at the first approach. Wherefore He also said, "beware"; making us more exact to discern them.

Then, lest when they had heard that it was narrow and strait, and that they must walk on a way opposite to the many, and must keep themselves from swine and dogs, and together with these from another more wicked kind, even this of wolves; lest, I say, they should sink down at this multitude of vexations, having both to go a way contrary to most men, and therewith again to have such anxiety about these things: He reminded them of what took place in the days of their fathers, by using the term, "false prophets," for then also no less did such things happen. Be not now, I pray you, troubled (so He speaks), for nothing new nor strange is to befall you. Since for all truth the devil is always secretly substituting its appropriate deceit.

And by the figure of "false prophets," here, I think He shadows out not the heretics, but them that are of a corrupt life, yet wear a mask of virtue; whom the generality are wont to call by the name of impostors. Wherefore He also said further,

"By their fruits ye shall know them."

For amongst heretics one may often find actual goodness, but amongst those whom I was mentioning, by no means.

"What then," it may be said, "if in these things too they counterfeit?" "Nay, they will be easily detected; for such is the nature of this way, in which I commanded men to walk, painful and irksome; but the hypocrite would not choose to take pains, but to make a show only; wherefore also he is easily convicted." Thus, inasmuch as He had said, "there be few that find it," He clears them out again from among those, who find it not, yet feign so to do, by commanding us not to look to them that wear the masks only, but to them who in reality pursue it.

"But wherefore," one may say, "did He not make them manifest, but set us on the search for them?" That we might watch, and be ever prepared for conflict, guarding against our disguised as well as against our open enemies: which kind indeed Paul also was intimating, when he said, that "by their good words they deceive the hearts of the simple." Let us not be troubled therefore, when we see many such even now. Nay, for this too Christ foretold from the beginning.

And see His gentleness: how He said not, "Punish them," but, "Be not hurt by them," "Do not fall amongst them unguarded." Then that thou mightest not say, "it is impossible to distinguish that sort of men," again He states an argument from a human example, thus saying,

"Do men gather grapes of thorns, or figs of thistles? even so every good tree bringeth forth good fruit, but the corrupt tree bringeth forth evil fruit. A good tree cannot bring forth evil fruit, neither can a corrupt tree bring forth good fruit."

Now what He saith is like this: they have nothing gentle nor sweet; it is the sheep only so far as the skin; wherefore also it is easy to discern them. And lest thou shouldest have any the least doubt, He compares it to certain natural necessities, in matters which admit of no result but one. In which sense Paul also said, "The carnal mind is death; for it is not subject to the law of God, neither indeed can be."

And if He states the same thing twice, it is not tautology. But, lest any one should say, "Though the evil tree bear evil fruit, it bears also good, and makes the distinction difficult, the crop being twofold:" "This is not so," saith He, "for it bears evil fruit only, and never can bear good: as indeed in the contrary case also."

"What then? Is there no such thing as a good man becoming wicked? And the contrary again takes place, and life abounds with many such examples."

But Christ saith not this, that for the wicked there is no way to change, or that the good cannot fall away, but that so long as he is living in wickedness, he will not be able to bear good fruit. For he may indeed change to virtue, being evil; but while continuing in wickedness, he will not bear good fruit.

What then? did not David, being good, bear evil fruit? Not continuing good, but being changed; since, undoubtedly, had he remained always what he was, he would not have brought forth such fruit. For not surely while abiding in the habit of virtue, did he commit what he committed.

Now by these words He was also stopping the mouths of those who speak evil at random, and putting a bridle on the lips of all calumniators. I mean, whereas many suspect the good by reason of the bad, He by this saying hath deprived them of all excuse. "For thou canst not say, I am deceived and beguiled;' since I have given thee exactly this way of distinguishing them by their works, having added the injunction to go to their actions, and not to confound all at random."

9. Then forasmuch as He had not commanded to punish, but only to beware of them, He, at once both to comfort those whom they vex, and to alarm and change them, set up as a bulwark against them the punishment they should receive at His hands, saying,

"Every tree that bringeth not forth good fruit is hewn down, and cast into the fire."

Then, to make the saying less grievous, He added,

"Wherefore by their fruits ye shall know them."

That He might not seem to introduce the threatening as His leading topic, but to be stirring up their mind in the way of admonition and counsel.

Here He seems to me to be hinting at the Jews also, who were exhibiting such fruits. Wherefore also He reminded them of the sayings of John, in the very same terms delineating their punishment. For he too said the very same, making mention to them of an "axe," and of a "tree cut down," and of "unquenchable fire."

And though it appear indeed to be some single judgment, the being burnt up, yet if one examine carefully, these are two punishments. For he that is burnt is also cast of course out of God's kingdom; and this latter punishment is more grievous than the other. Now I know indeed that many tremble only at hell, but I affirm the loss of that glory to be a far greater punishment than hell. And if it be not possible to exhibit it such in words, this is nothing marvellous. For neither do we know the blessedness of those good things, that we should on the other hand clearly perceive the wretchedness ensuing on being deprived of them; since Paul, as knowing these things clearly, is aware, that to fall from Christ's glory is more grievous than all. And this we shall know at that time, when we shall fall into the actual trial of it.

But may this never be our case, O thou only-begotten Son of God, neither may we ever have any experience of this irremediable punishment. For how great an evil it is to fall from those good things, cannot indeed be accurately told: nevertheless, as I may be able, I will labor and strive by an example to make it clear to you, though it be but in some small degree.

Let us then imagine a wondrous child, having besides His virtue the dominion of the whole world, and in all respects so virtuous, as to be capable of bringing all men to the yearning of a father's affection. What theft do you think the father of this child would not gladly suffer, not to be cast out of His society? And what evil, small or great, would he not welcome, on condition of seeing and enjoying Him? Now let us reason just so with respect to that glory also. For no child, be he never so virtuous, is so desirable and lovely to a father, as the having our portion in those good things, and "to depart and be with Christ."

No doubt hell, and that punishment, is a thing not to be borne. Yet though one suppose ten thousand hells, he will utter nothing like what it will be to fail of that blessed glory, to be hated of Christ, to hear "I know you not," to be accused for not feeding Him when we saw Him an hungered. Yea, better surely to endure a thousand thunderbolts, than to see that face of mildness turning away from us, and that eye of peace not enduring to look upon us. For if He, while I was an enemy, and hating Him, and turning from Him, did in such wise follow after me, as not to spare even Himself, but to give Himself up unto death: when after all this I do not vouchsafe to Him so much as a loaf in His hunger, with what kind of eyes shall I ever again behold Him?

But mark even here His gentleness; in that He doth not at all speak of His benefits, nor say, "Thou hast despised Him that hath done thee so much good:" neither doth He say, "Me, who brought thee from that which is not into being, who breathed into thee a soul, and set thee over all things on earth, who for thy sake made earth, and heaven, and sea, and air, and all things that are, who had been dishonored by thee, yea accounted of less honor than the devil, and did not even so withdraw Himself, but had innumerable thoughts for thee after it all; who chose to become a slave, who was beaten with rods and spit upon, who was slain, who died the most shameful death, who also on high makes intercession for thee, who freely gives thee His Spirit, who vouchsafes to thee a kingdom, who makes thee such promises, whose will it is to be unto thee Head, and Bridegroom, and Garment, and House, and Root, and Meat, and Drink, and Shepherd, and King, and who hath taken thee to be brother, and heir, and joint-heir with Himself; who hath brought thee out of darkness into the dominion of light." These things, I say, and more than these He might speak of, but He mentions none of these; but what? only the sin itself.

Even here He shows His love, and indicates the yearning which He hath toward thee: not saying, "Depart into the fire prepared for you," but "prepared for the devil." And before He tells them what wrongs they had done, and neither so doth He endure to mention all, but a few. And before these He calls the other sort, those who have done well, to signify from this too that He is blaming them justly.

What amount of punishment, then, is so grievous as these words? For if any one seeing but a man who was his benefactor an hungered, would not neglect him; or if he should neglect him, being upbraided with it, would choose rather to sink into the earth than to hear of it in the presence of two or three friends; what will be our feelings, on hearing these words in the presence of the whole world; such as He would not say even then, were He not earnestly accounting for His own doings? For that not to upbraid did He bring these things forward, but in self-defense, and for the sake of showing, that not without ground nor at random was He saying, "depart from me;" this is evident from His unspeakable benefits. For if He had been minded to upbraid, He would have brought forwards all these, but now He mentions only what treatment He had received.

10. Let us therefore, beloved, fear the hearing these words. Life is not a plaything: or rather our present life is a plaything, but the things to come are not such; or perchance our life is not a plaything only, but even worse than this. For it ends not in laughter, but rather brings exceeding damage on them who are not minded to order their own ways strictly. For what, I pray thee, is the difference between children who are playing at building houses, and us when we are building our fine houses? what again between them making out their dinners, and us in our delicate fare? None, but just that we do it at the risk of being punished. And if we do not yet quite perceive the poverty of what is going on, no wonder, for we are not yet become men; but when we are become so, we shall know that all these things are childish.

For so those other things too, as we grow to manhood, we laugh to scorn; but when we are children we account them to be worth anxiety; and while we are gathering together potsherds and mire we think no less of ourselves than they who are erecting their great circuits of walls. Nevertheless they straightway perish and fall down, and not even when standing can they be of any use to us, as indeed neither can those fine houses. For the citizen of Heaven they cannot receive, neither can he bear to abide in them, who hath his country above; but as we throw down these with our feet, so he too those by his high spirit. And as we laugh at the children, weeping at that overthrow, even so these also, when we are bewailing it all, do not laugh only, but weep also: because both their bowels are compassionate, and great is the mischief thence arising.

Let us therefore become men. How long are we to crawl on the earth, priding ourselves on stones and stocks? How long are we to play? And would we played only! But now we even betray our own salvation; and as children when they neglect their learning, and practise themselves in these things at their leisure, suffer very severe blows; even so we too, spending all our diligence herein, and having then our spiritual lessons required of us in our works, and not being able to produce them, shall have to pay the utmost penalty. And there is none to deliver us; though he be father, brother, what you will. But while these things shall all pass away, the torment ensuing upon them remains immortal and unceasing; which sort of thing indeed takes place with respect to the children as well, their father destroying their childish toys altogether for their idleness, and causing them to weep incessantly.

11. And to convince thee that these things are such, let us bring before us wealth, that which more than anything seems to be worthy of our pains, and let us set against it a virtue of the soul (which soever thou wilt), and then shalt

thou see most clearly the vileness thereof. Let us, I say, suppose there are two men (and I do not now speak of injuriousness, but as yet of honest wealth); and of these two, let the one get together money, and sail on the sea, and till the land, and find many other ways of merchandise (although I know not quite, whether, so doing, he can make honest gains); nevertheless let it be so, and let it be granted that his gains are gotten with honesty; that he buys fields, and slaves, and all such things, and suppose no injustice connected therewith. But let the other one, possessing as much, sell fields, sell houses, and vessels of gold and silver, and give to the poor; let him supply the necessitous, heal the sick, free such as are in straits, some let him deliver from bonds, others let him release that are in mines, these let him bring back from the noose, those, who are captives, let him rescue from their punishment. Of whose side then would you be? And we have not as yet spoken of the future, but as yet of what is here. Of whose part then would ye be? his that is gathering gold, or his that is doing away with calamities? with him that is purchasing fields, or him who is making himself a harbor of refuge for the human race? him that is clothed with much gold, or him that is crowned with innumerable blessings? Is not the one like some angel come down from Heaven for the amendment of the rest of mankind; but the other not so much as like a man, but like some little child that is gathering all together vainly and at random?

But if to get money honestly be thus absurd, and of extreme madness; when not even the honesty is there, how can such a man choose but be more wretched than any? I say, if the absurdity be so great; when hell is added thereto, and the loss of the kingdom, how great wailings are due to him, both living and dead?

12. Or wilt thou that we take in hand some other part also of virtue? Let us then introduce again another man, who is in power, commanding all, invested with great dignity, having a gorgeous herald, and girdle, and lictors, and a large company of attendants. Doth not this seem great, and meet to be called happy? Well then, against this man again let us set another, him that is patient of injuries, and meek, and lowly, and long suffering; and let this last be despitefully used, be beaten, and let him bear it quietly, and bless them that are doing such things.

Now which is the one to be admired, I pray thee? He that is puffed up, and inflamed, or he that is self-subdued? Is not the one again like the powers above, that are so free from passion, but the other like a blown bladder, or a man who hath the dropsy, and great inflammation? The one like a spiritual physician, the other, a ridiculous child that is puffing out his cheeks?

For why dost thou pride thyself, O man? Because thou art borne on high in a chariot? Because a yoke of mules is drawing thee? And what is this? Why, this one may see befalling mere logs of wood and stones. Is it that thou art clothed with beautiful garments? But look at him that is clad with virtue for garments, and thou wilt see thyself to be like withering hay, but him like a tree that bears marvellous fruit, and affords much delight to the beholders. For thou art bearing about food for worms and moths, who, if they should set upon thee, will quickly strip thee bare of this adorning (for truly garments and gold and silver, are the one, the spinning of worms; the other earth and dust, and again become earth and nothing more): but he that is clothed with virtue hath such raiment, as not only worms cannot hurt, but not even death itself. And very naturally; for these virtues of the soul have not their origin from the earth, but are a fruit of the Spirit; wherefore neither are they subject to the mouths of worms. Nay, for these garments are woven in Heaven, where is neither moth, nor worm, nor any other such thing.

Which then is better, tell me? To be rich, or to be poor? To be in power, or in dishonor? In luxury, or in hunger? It is quite clear; to be in honor, and enjoyment, and wealth. Therefore, if thou wouldest have the things and not the names, leave the earth and what is here, and find thee a place to anchor in Heaven: for what is here is a shadow, but all things there are immovable, stedfast, and beyond any assault.

Let us therefore choose them with all diligent care, that we may be delivered from the turmoil of the things here, and having sailed into that calm harbor, may be found with our lading abundant, and with that unspeakable wealth of almsgiving; unto which God grant we may all attain, by the grace and love towards man of our Lord Jesus Christ, to whom be the glory and the might, world without end. Amen.

HOMILY XXIV

MATT. VII. 21

"Not every one that saith unto me, Lord, Lord, shall enter into the kingdom of Heaven, but he that doeth the will of my Father which is in Heaven."

Wherefore said He not, "but he that doeth my will?" Because for the time it was a great gain for them to receive even this first; yea it was very great, considering their weakness. And moreover He intimated the one also by the other. And withal this may be mentioned, that in fact there is no other will of the Son besides that of the Father.

And here He seems to me to be censuring the Jews chiefly, laying as they did the whole stress upon the doctrines, and taking no care of practice. For which Paul also blames them, saying, "Behold thou art called a Jew, and restest in the law, and makest thy boast of God, and knowest His will:" "Who then are these men?" you ask. Many of them that believed received gifts such as he that was casting out devils, and was not with Him; such as Judas; for even he too, wicked as he was, had a gift. And in the Old Testament also this may be found, in that grace hath oftentimes wrought upon unworthy persons, that it might do good to others. That is, since all men were not meet for all things, but some were of a pure life, not having so great faith, and others just the contrary; by these sayings, while He urges the one to show forth much faith, the others too He was summoning by this His unspeakable gift to become better men. Wherefore also with great abundance did He bestow that grace. For "we wrought," it is said, "many mighty works." But "then will I profess unto them, I knew you not." For "now indeed they suppose they are my friends; but then shall they know, that not as to friends did I give to them."

And why marvel if He hath bestowed gifts on men that have believed on Him, though without life suitable to their faith, when even on those who have fallen from both these, He is unquestionably found working? For so Balaam was an alien both from faith and from a truly good life; nevertheless grace wrought on him for the service of other men. And Pharaoh too was of the same sort: yet for all that even to him He signified the things to come. And Nebuchadnezzar was very full of iniquity; yet to him again He revealed what was to follow after many generations. And again to the son of this last, though surpassing his father in iniquity, He signified the things to come, ordering a marvellous and great dispensation. Accordingly because then also the beginnings of the gospel were taking place, and it was requisite that the manifestation of its power should be abundant, many even of the unworthy used to receive gifts. Howbeit, from those miracles no gain accrued to them; rather they are the more punished. Wherefore unto them did He utter even that fearful saying, "I never knew you:" there being many for whom His hatred begins already even here; whom He turns away from, even before the judgment.

Let us fear therefore, beloved; and let us take great heed to our life, neither let us account ourselves worse off, in that we do not work miracles now. For that will never be any advantage to us, as neither any disadvantage in our not working them, if we take heed to all virtue. Because for the miracles we ourselves are debtors, but for our life and our doings we have God our debtor.

3. Having now, you see, finished all, having discoursed accurately of all virtue, and pointed out the pretenders to it, of divers kinds, both such as for display fast and make prayers, and such as come in the sheep's hide; and them too that spoil it, whom He also called swine and dogs: He proceeds to signify how great is the profit of virtue even here, and how great the mischief of wickedness, by saying,

"Whosoever therefore heareth these sayings of mine, and doeth them, shall be likened unto a wise man."

As thus: What they shall suffer who do not (although they work miracles), ye have heard; but ye should know also what such as obey all these sayings shall enjoy; not in the world to come only, but even here. "For whosoever," saith He, "heareth these sayings of mine, and doeth them, shall be likened to a wise man."

Seest thou how He varies His discourse; at one time saying, "Not every one that saith unto me, Lord, Lord," and revealing Himself; at another time, "He that doeth the will of my Father;" and again, bringing in Himself as judge, "For many will say to me in that day, Lord, Lord, have we not prophesied in thy name, and I will say, I know you not." And here again He indicates Himself to have the power over all, this being why He said, "Whosoever heareth these sayings of mine."

Thus whereas all His discourse had been touching the future; of a kingdom, and an unspeakable reward and consolation, and the like; His will is, out of things here also to give them their fruits, and to signify how great is the strength of virtue even in the present life. What then is this her strength? To live in safety, to be easily subdued by no terror, to stand superior to all that despitefully use us. To this what can be equal? For this, not even he that wears the diadem can provide for himself, but that man who follows after virtue. For he alone is possessed of it in full abundance: in the ebb and flow of the things present he enjoys a great calm. The truly marvellous thing being this, that not in fair weather, but when the storm is vehement, and the turmoil great, and the temptations continual, he cannot be shaken ever so little.

"For the rain descended," saith He, "the floods came, the winds blew, and beat upon that house; and it fell not: for it was founded upon the rock."

By "rain" here, and "floods," and "winds," He is expressing metaphorically the calamities and afflictions that befall men; such as false accusations, plots, bereavements, deaths, loss of friends, vexations from strangers, all the ills in our life that any one could mention. "But to none of these," saith He, "doth such a soul give way; and the cause is, it is founded on the rock." He calls the stedfastness of His doctrine a rock; because in truth His commands are stronger than any rock, setting one above all the waves of human affairs. For he who keeps these things strictly, will not have the advantage of men only when they are vexing him, but even of the very devils plotting against him. And that it is not vain boasting so to speak, Job is our witness, who received all the assaults of the devil, and stood unmoveable; and the apostles too are our witnesses, for that when the waves of the whole world were beating against them, when both nations and princes, both their own people and strangers, both the evil spirits, and the devil, and every engine was set in motion, they stood firmer than a rock, and dispersed it all.

And now, what can be happier than this kind of life? For this, not wealth, not strength of body, not glory, not power, nor ought else will be able to secure, but only the possession of virtue. For there is not, nay there is not another life we may find free from all evils, but this alone. And ye are witnesses, who know the plots in king's courts, the turmoils and the troubles in the houses of the rich. But there was not among the apostles any such thing.

What then? Did no such thing befall them? Did they suffer no evil at any man's hand? Nay, the marvel is this above all things, that they were indeed the object of many plots, and many storms burst upon them, but their soul was not overset by them, nor thrown into despair, but with naked bodies they wrestled, prevailed, and triumphed.

Thou then likewise, if thou be willing to perform these things exactly, shall laugh all ills to scorn. Yea, for if thou be but strengthened with such philosophy as is in these admonitions, nothing shall be able to hurt thee. Since in what is he to harm thee, who is minded to lay plots? Will he take away thy money? Well, but before their threatening thou wast commanded to despise it, and to abstain from it so exceedingly, as not so much as even to ask any such thing of thy Lord. But doth he cast thee into prison? Why, before thy prison, thou wast enjoined so to live, as to be crucified even to all the world. But doth he speak evil? Nay, from this pain also Christ hath delivered thee, by promising thee without toil a great reward for the endurance of evil, and making thee so clear from the anger and vexation hence arising, as even to command thee to pray for them. But doth he banish thee and involve thee in innumerable ills? Well, he is making the crown more glorious for thee. But doth he destroy and murder thee? Even hereby he profits thee very greatly, procuring for thee the rewards of the martyrs, and conducting thee more quickly into the untroubled haven, and affording thee matter for a more abundant recompence, and contriving for thee to make a gain of the universal penalty. Which thing indeed is most marvellous of all, that the plotters, so far from injuring at all, do rather make the objects of their despite more approved. To this what can be comparable? I mean, to the choice of such a mode of life as this, and no other, is.

Thus whereas He had called the way strait and narrow; to soothe our labors on this side also, He signifies the security thereof to be great, and great the pleasure; even as of the opposite course great is the unsoundness, and the detriment. For as virtue even from things here was signified by Him to have her rewards, so vice also her penalties. For what I am ever saying, that I will say now also: that in both ways He is everywhere bringing about the salvation of His hearers on the one hand by zeal for virtue, on the other by hatred of vice. Thus, because there would be some to admire what He said, while they yield no proof of it by their works, He by anticipation awakens their fears, saying, Though the things spoken be good, hearing is not sufficient for security, but there is need also of obedience in actions, and the whole lies chiefly in this. And here He ends His discourse, leaving the fear at its height in them.

For as with regard to virtue, not only from the things to come did He urge them (speaking of a kingdom, and of Heaven, and an unspeakable reward, and comfort, and the unnumbered good things): but also from the things present, indicating the firm and immoveable quality of the Rock; so also with respect to wickedness, not from the expected things only doth He excite their fears (as from the tree that is cut down, and the unquenchable fire, and the not entering into the kingdom, and from His saying, "I know you not"): but also from the things present, the downfall, I mean, in what is said of the house.

4. Wherefore also He made His argument more expressive, by trying its force in a parable; for it was not the same thing to say, "The virtuous man shall be impregnable, but the wicked easily subdued," as to suppose a rock, and a house, and rivers, and rain, and wind, and the like.

"And every one," saith He, "that heareth these sayings of mine, and doeth them not, shall be likened to a foolish man, which built his house upon the sand."

And well did He call this man "foolish": for what can be more senseless than one building a house on the sand, and while he submits to the labor, depriving himself of the fruit and refreshment, and instead thereof undergoing punishment? For that they too, who follow after wickedness, do labor, is surely manifest to every one: since both the extortioner, and the adulterer, and the false accuser, toil and weary themselves much to bring their wickedness to effect; but so far from reaping any profit from these their labors, they rather undergo great loss. For Paul too intimated this when he said, "He that soweth to his flesh, shall of his flesh reap corruption." To this man are they like also, who build on the sand; as those that are given up to fornication, to wantonness, to drunkenness, to anger, to all the other things.

Such an one was Ahab, but not such Elijah (since when we have put virtue and vice along side of one another, we shall know more accurately the difference): for the one had built upon the rock, the other on the sand; wherefore though he were a king, he feared and trembled at the prophet, at him that had only his sheepskin. Such were the Jews but not the apostles; and so though they were few and in bonds, they exhibited the steadfastness of the rock; but those, many as they were, and in armor, the weakness of the sand. For so they said, "What shall we do to these men?" Seest thou those in perplexity, not who are in the hands of others, and bound, but who are active in holding down and binding? And what can be more strange than this? Hast thou hold of the other, and art yet in utter perplexity? Yes, and very naturally. For inasmuch as they had built all on the sand, therefore also were they weaker than all. For this cause also they said again, "What do ye, seeking to bring this man's blood upon us?" What saith he? Dost thou scourge, and art thou in fear? entreatest thou despitefully, and art in dismay? Dost thou judge, and yet tremble? So feeble is wickedness.

But the Apostles not so, but how? "We cannot but speak the things which we have seen and heard." Seest thou a noble spirit? seest thou a rock laughing waves to scorn? seest thou a house unshaken? And what is yet more marvellous; so far from turning cowards themselves at the plots formed against them, they even took more courage, and cast the others into greater anxiety. For so he that smites adamant, is himself the one smitten; and he that kicks against the pricks, is himself the one pricked, the one on whom the severe wounds fall: and he who is forming plots against the virtuous, is himself the one in jeopardy. For wickedness becomes so much the weaker, the more it sets itself in array against virtue. And as he who wraps up fire in a garment, extinguishes not the flame, but consumes the garment; so he that is doing despite to virtuous men, and oppressing them, and binding them, makes them more glorious, but destroys himself. For the more ills thou sufferest, living righteously, the stronger art thou become; since the more we honor self-restraint, the less we need anything; and the less we need anything, the stronger we grow, and the more above all. Such a one was John; wherefore him no man pained, but he caused pain to Herod; so he that had nothing prevailed against him that ruled; and he that wore a diadem, and purple, and endless pomp, trembles, and is in fear of him that is stripped of all, and not even when beheaded could he without fear see his head. For that even after his death he had the terror of him in full strength, hear what He saith, "This is John, whom I slew." Now the expression, "I slew," is that of one not exulting, but soothing his own terror, and persuading his troubled soul to call to mind, that he himself slew him. So great is the force of virtue, that even after death it is more powerful than the living. For this same cause again, when he was living, they that possessed much wealth came unto him, and said, "What shall we do?" Is so much yours, and are ye minded to learn the way of your prosperity from him that hath nothing? the rich from the poor? the soldiers from him that hath not even a house?

Such an one was Elias too: wherefore also with the same freedom did he discourse to the people. For as the former said, "Ye generation of vipers;" so this latter, "How long will ye halt upon both your hips?" And the one said, "Hast thou killed, and inherited?" the other, "It is not lawful for thee to have thy brother Philip's wife."

Seest thou the rock? Seest thou the sand; how easily it sinks down, how it yields to calamities? how it is overthrown, though it have the support of royalty, of number, of nobility? For them that pursue it, it makes more senseless than all.

And it doth not merely fall, but with great calamity: for "great indeed," He saith, "was the fall of it." The risk not being of trifles, but of the soul, of the loss of Heaven, and those immortal blessings. Or rather even before that loss, no life so wretched as he must live that follows after this; dwelling with continual despondencies, alarms, cares, anxieties; which a certain wise man also was intimating when he said, "The wicked fleeth, when no man is pursuing." For such men tremble at their shadows, suspect their friends, their enemies, their servants, such as know them, such as know them not; and before their punishment, suffer extreme punishment here. And to declare all this, Christ said, "And great was the fall of it;" shutting up these good commandments with that suitable ending, and persuading even by the things present the most unbelieving to flee from vice.

For although the argument from what is to come be vaster, yet is this of more power to restrain the grosser sort, and to withdraw them from wickedness. Wherefore also he ended with it, that the profit thereof might make its abode in them.

Conscious therefore of all these things, both the present, and the future, let us flee from vice, let us emulate virtue, that we may not labor fruitlessly and at random, but may both enjoy the security here, and partake of the glory there: unto which God grant we may all attain, by the grace and love towards man of our Lord Jesus Christ, to whom be the glory and the might forever and ever. Amen.

HOMILY XXV

MATT. VII. 28

"And it came to pass, when Jesus had ended these sayings, the people were astonished at His doctrine."

Yet was it rather natural for them to grieve at the unpleasantness of His sayings, and to shudder at the loftiness of His injunctions; but now so great was the power of the Teacher, that many of them were even caught thereby, and thrown into very great admiration, and persuaded by reason of the sweetness of His sayings, not even when He ceased to speak, to depart from Him at all afterwards. For neither did the hearers depart, He having come down from the mountain, but even then the whole auditory followed Him; so great a love for His sayings had He instilled into them.

But they were astonished most of all at His authority. For not with reference to another, like the prophet and Moses, did He say what He said; but everywhere indicating Himself to be the person that had the power of deciding. For so, when setting forth His laws, He still kept adding, "But I say unto you." And in reminding them of that day, He declared Himself to be the judge, both by the punishments, and by the honors.

And yet it was likely that this too would disturb them. For if, when they saw Him by His works showing forth His authority, the scribes were for stoning and persecuting Him; while there were words only to prove this, how was it other than likely for them to be offended? and especially when at first setting out these things were said, and before He had given proof of His own power? But however, they felt nothing of this; for when the heart and mind is candid, it is easily persuaded by the words of the truth. And this is just why one sort, even when the miracles were proclaiming His power, were offended; while the other on hearing mere words were persuaded and followed Him. This, I would add, the evangelist too is intimating, when he saith, "great multitudes followed Him," not any of the rulers, nor of the scribes, but as many as were free from vice, and had their judgment uncorrupted. And throughout the whole gospel thou seest that such clave unto Him. For both while He spake, they used to listen in silence, not making any intrusion, nor breaking in upon the connexion of His sayings, nor tempting Him, and desiring to find a handle like the Pharisees; and after His exhortation they followed Him again, marvelling.

But do thou mark, I pray thee, the Lord's consideration, how He varies the mode of profiting His hearers, after miracles entering on words, and again from the instruction by His words passing to miracles. Thus, both before they went up into the mountain, He healed many, preparing the way for His sayings; and after finishing that long discourse to the people, He comes again to miracles, confirming what had been said by what was done. And so, because He was teaching as "one having authority," lest His so teaching should be thought boasting and arrogant, He doth the very same in His works also, as having authority to heal; that they might no more be perplexed at seeing Him teach in this way, when He was working His miracles also in the same.

2. "For when He was come down from the mountain, there came a leper, saying, Lord, if Thou wilt, Thou canst make me clean." Great was the understanding and the faith of him who so drew near. For he did not interrupt the teaching, nor break through the auditory, but awaited the proper time, and approaches Him "when He is come down." And not at random, but with much earnestness, and at His knees, he beseeches Him, as another evangelist saith, and with the genuine faith and right opinion about him. For neither did he say, "If Thou request it of God," nor, "If Thou pray," but, "If Thou wilt, Thou canst make me clean." Nor did he say, "Lord, cleanse me," but leaves all to Him, and makes His recovery depend on Him, and testifies that all the authority is His.

"What then," saith one, "if the leper's opinion was mistaken?" It were meet to do away with it, and to reprove, and set it right. Did He then so do? By no means; but quite on the contrary, He establishes and confirms what had been said. For this cause, you see, neither did He say, "Be thou cleansed," but, "I will, be thou clean;" that the doctrine might no longer be a thing of the other's surmising, but of His own approval.

But the apostles not so: rather in what way? The whole people being in amazement, they said, "Why give heed to us, as though by our own power or authority we had made him to walk?" But the Lord, though He spake oftentimes many things modestly, and beneath His own glory, what saith He here, to establish the doctrine of them that were amazed at Him for His authority? "I will, be thou clean." Although in the many and great signs which He wrought, He nowhere appears to have uttered this word. Here however, to confirm the surmise both of all the people and of the leper touching His authority, He purposely added, "I will."

And it was not that He said this, but did it not; but the work also followed immediately. Whereas, if he had not spoken well, but the saying had been a blasphemy, the work ought to have been interrupted. But now nature herself gave way at His command, and that speedily, as was meet, even more speedily than the evangelist hath said. For the word, "immediately," falls far short of the quickness that there was in the work.

But He did not merely say, "I will, be thou clean," but He also "put forth His hand, and touched him;" a thing especially worthy of inquiry. For wherefore, when cleansing him by will and word, did He add also the touch of His hand? It seems to me, for no other end, but that He might signify by this also, that He is not subject to the law, but is set over it; and that to the clean, henceforth, nothing is unclean. For this cause, we see, Elisha did not so much as see Naaman, but though he perceived that he was offended at his not coming out and touching him, observing the strictness of the law, he abides at home, and sends him to Jordan to wash. Whereas the Lord, to signify that He heals not as a servant, but as absolute master, doth also touch. For His hand became not unclean from the leprosy, but the leprous body was rendered clean by His holy hand.

Because, as we know, He came not to heal bodies only, but also to lead the soul unto self-command. As therefore He from that time forward no more forbad to eat with unwashen hands, introducing that excellent law, which relates to the indifference of meats; just so in this case also, to instruct us for the future, that the soul must be our care;—that leaving the outward purifications, we must wipe that clean, and dread the leprosy thereof alone, which is sin (for to be a leper is no hindrance to virtue):—He Himself first touches the leper, and no man finds fault. For the tribunal was not corrupt, neither were the spectators under the power of envy. Therefore, so far from blaming, they were on the contrary astonished at the miracle, and yielded thereto: and both for what He said, and for what He did, they adored his uncontrollable power.

3. Having therefore healed his body, He bids him,

"Tell no man, but show himself to the priest, and offer the gift that Moses commanded, for a testimony unto them."

Now some say, that for this intent He bade him tell no man, that they might practise no craft about the discerning of his cure; a very foolish suspicion on their part. For He did not so cleanse as to leave the cleansing questionable, but He bids him "tell no man," teaching us to avoid boasting and vainglory. And yet He well knew that the other would not obey, but would proclaim his benefactor: nevertheless He doth His own part.

"How then elsewhere doth He bid them tell of it?" one may ask. Not as jostling with or opposing Himself, but as teaching men to be grateful. For neither in that place did He give command to proclaim Himself, but to "give glory to God;" by this leper training us to be clear of pride and vainglory, by the other to be thankful and grateful; and instructing on every occasion to offer to the Lord the praise of all things that befall us. That is, because men for the most part remember God in sickness, but grow slacker after recovery; He bids them continually both in sickness and in health to give heed to the Lord, in these words, "give glory to God."

But wherefore did He command him also to show himself to the priest, and to offer a gift? To fulfill the law here again. For neither did He in every instance set it aside, nor in every instance keep it, but sometimes He did the one, sometimes the other; by the one making way for the high rule of life that was to come, by the other checking for a while the insolent speech of the Jews, and condescending to their infirmity. And why marvel, if just at the beginning He Himself did this, when even the very apostles, after they were commanded to depart unto the Gentiles, after the doors were opened for their teaching throughout the world, and the law shut up, and the commandments made new, and all the ancient things had ceased, are found sometimes observing the law, sometimes neglecting it?

But what, it may be said, doth this saying, "Show thyself to the priest," contribute to the keeping of the law? No little. Because it was an ancient law, that the leper when cleansed should not entrust to himself the judgment of his cleansing, but should show himself to the priest, and present the demonstration thereof to his eyes, and by that sentence be numbered amongst the clean. For if the priest said not "The leper is cleansed," he remained still with the unclean without the camp. Wherefore he saith, "Show thyself to the priest, and offer the gift that Moses commanded." He said not, "which I command," but for a time remits him to the law, by every means stopping their mouths. Thus, lest they should say, He had seized upon the priests' honor; though He performed the work Himself, yet the approving it He entrusted to them, and made them sit as judges of His own miracles. "Why, I am so far," He saith, "from striving either with Moses or with the priests, that I guide the objects of my favor to submit themselves unto them."

But what is, "for a testimony unto them"? For reproof, for demonstration, for accusation, if they be unthankful. For since they said, as a deceiver and impostor we persecute Him, as an adversary of God, and a transgressor of the law; "Thou shalt bear me witness," saith He, "at that time, that I am not a transgressor of the law. Nay, for having healed thee, I remit thee to the law, and to the approval of the priests;" which was the act of one honoring the law, and admiring Moses, and not setting himself in opposition to the ancient doctrines.

And if they were not in fact to be the better, hereby most of all one may perceive His respect for the law, that although He foreknew they would reap no benefit, He fulfilled all His part. For this very thing He did indeed foreknow, and foretold it: not saying, "for their correction," neither, "for their instruction," but, "for a testimony unto them," that is, for accusation, and for reproof, and for a witness that all hath been done on my part; and though I foreknew they would continue incorrigible, not even so did I omit what ought to be done; only they continued keeping up to the end their own wickedness.

This, we may observe, He saith elsewhere also; "This gospel shall be preached in all the world for a testimony to all the nations, and then shall the end come;" to the nations, to them that obey not, to them that believe not. Thus, lest any one should say, "And wherefore preach to all, if all are not to believe?"—it is that I may be found to have done all my own part, and that no man may hereafter be able to find fault, as though he had not heard. For the very preaching shall bear witness against them, and they will not be able hereafter to say, "We heard not;" for the word of godliness "hath gone out unto the ends of the world."

4. Therefore bearing these things in mind, let us also fulfill all our duties to our neighbor, and to God let us give thanks continually. For it is too monstrous, enjoying as we do His bounty in deed every day, not so much as in word to acknowledge the favor; and this, though the acknowledgment again yield all its profit to us. Since He needs not, be sure, anything of ours: but we stand in need of all things from Him. Thus thanksgiving itself adds nothing to Him, but causes us to be nearer to Him. For if men's bounties, when we call them to memory, do the more warm us with their proper love-charm; much more when we are continually bringing to mind the noble acts of our Lord towards us, shall we be more diligent in regard of His commandments.

For this cause Paul also said, "Be ye thankful." For the best preservative of any benefit is the remembrance of the benefit, and a continual thanksgiving.

For this cause even the awful mysteries, so full of that great salvation, which are celebrated at every communion, are called a sacrifice of thanksgiving, because they are the commemoration of many benefits, and they signify the very sum of God's care for us, and by all means they work upon us to be thankful. For if His being born of a virgin was a great miracle, and the evangelist said in amaze, "now all this was done;" His being also slain, what place shall we find for that? tell me. I mean, if to be born is called "all this;" to be crucified, and to pour forth His blood, and to give Himself to us for a spiritual feast and banquet,—what can that be called? Let us therefore give Him thanks continually, and let this precede both our words and our works.

But let us be thankful not for our own blessings alone, but also for those of others; for in this way we shall be able both to destroy our envy, and to rivet our charity, and make it more genuine. Since it will not even be possible for thee to go on envying them, in behalf of whom thou givest thanks to the Lord.

Wherefore, as you know, the priest also enjoins to give thanks for the world, for the former things, for the things that are now, for what hath been done to us before, for what shall befall us hereafter, when that sacrifice is set forth.

For this is the thing both to free us from earth, and to remove us into heaven, and to make us angels instead of men. Because they too form a choir, and give thanks to God for His good things bestowed on us, saying, "Glory to God in the highest, and on earth peace, good will towards men." "And what is this to us, that are not upon earth, nor are men?" "Nay, it is very much to us, for we have been taught so to love our fellow serv ants, as even to account their blessings ours."

Wherefore Paul also, everywhere in his epistles, gives thanks for God's gracious acts to the world.

Let us too therefore continually give thanks, for our own blessings, and for those of others, alike for the small and for the great. For though the gift be small, it is made great by being God's gift, or rather, there is nothing small that cometh from Him, not only because it is bestowed by Him, but also in its very nature.

And to pass over all the rest, which exceed the sand in multitude; what is equal to the dispensation that hath taken place for our sake? In that what was more precious to Him than all, even His only-begotten Son, Him He gave for us His enemies; and not only gave, but after giving, did even set Him before us as food; Himself doing all things that were for our good, both in giving Him, and in making us thankful for all this. For because man is for the most part unthankful, He doth Himself everywhere take in hand and bring about what is for our good. And what He did with respect to the Jews, by places, and times, and feasts, reminding them of His benefits, that He did in this case also, by the manner of the sacrifice bringing us to a perpetual remembrance of His bounty in these things.

No one hath so labored that we should be approved, and great, and in all things right-minded, as the God who made us. Wherefore both against our will He befriends us often, and without our knowledge oftener than not. And if thou marvel at what I have said, I point to this as having occurred not to any ordinary person, but to the blessed Paul. For even that blessed man, when in much danger and affliction, often besought God that the temptations might depart from him: nevertheless God regarded not his request, but his profit, and to signify this He said, "My grace is sufficient for thee, for my strength is made perfect in weakness." So that before He hath told him the reason, He benefits him against his will, and without his knowing it.

5. Now what great thing doth He ask, in requiring us to be thankful in return for such tender care? Let us then obey, and everywhere keep up this. Since neither were the Jews by anything ruined so much, as by being unthankful; those many stripes, one after another, were brought upon them by nothing else than this; or rather even before those stripes this had ruined and corrupted their soul. "For the hope of the unthankful," saith one, "is like the winter's hoar frost;" it benumbs and deadens the soul, as that doth our bodies.

And this springs from pride, and from thinking one's self worthy of something. But the contrite will acknowledge grounds of thanksgiving to God, not for good things only, but also for what seem to be adverse; and how much soever he may suffer, will count none of his sufferings undeserved. Let us then also, the more we advance in virtue, so much the more make ourselves contrite; for indeed this, more than anything else is virtue. Because, as the sharper our sight is, the more thoroughly do we learn how distant we are from the sky; so the more we advance in virtue, so much the more are we instructed in the difference between God and us. And this is no small part of true wisdom, to be able to perceive our own desert. For he best knows himself, who accounts himself to be nothing. Thus we see that both David and Abraham, when they were come up to the highest pitch of virtue, then best fulfilled this; and would call themselves, the one, "earth and ashes," the other, "a worm;" and all the saints too, like these, acknowledge their own wretchedness. So that he surely who is lifted up in boasting, is the very person to be most ignorant of himself. Wherefore also in our common practice we are wont to say of the proud, "he knows not himself," "he is ignorant of himself." And he that knows not himself, whom will he know? For as he that knows himself will know all things, so he who knows not this, neither will he know the rest.

Such an one was he that saith, "I will exalt my throne above the Heavens." and did not account himself to be worthy so much as of the title of the apostles, after so many and so great deeds of goodness.

Him therefore let us emulate and follow. And we shall follow him, if we rid ourselves of earth, and of things on earth. For nothing makes a man to be so ignorant of himself, as the being rivetted to worldly concerns: nor does anything again so much cause men to be rivetted to worldly concerns, as ignorance of one's self: for these things depend upon each other. I mean, that as he that is fond of outward glory, and highly esteems the things present, if he strive for ever, is not permitted to understand himself; so he that overlooks these things will easily know himself; and having come to the knowledge of himself, he will proceed in order to all the other parts of virtue.

In order therefore that we may learn this good knowledge, let us, disengaged from all the perishable things that kindle in us so great flame, and made aware of their vileness, show forth all lowliness of mind, and self-restraint: that we may attain unto blessings, both present and future: by the grace and love towards man of our Lord Jesus Christ, with whom be glory, might, and honor, to the Father, together with the Holy and Good Spirit, now and ever, and world without end. Amen.

HOMILY XXVI

MATT. VIII. 5

"And when He was entered into Capernaum, there came unto Him a centurion, beseeching Him, and saying, Lord, my servant lieth at home sick of the palsy, grievously tormented."

The leper came unto Him "when He was come down from the mountain," but this centurion, "when He was entered into Capernaum." Wherefore then did neither the one nor the other go up into the mountain? Not out of remissness, for indeed the faith of them both was fervent, but in order not to interrupt His teaching.

But having come unto Him, he saith, "My servant lieth at home sick of the palsy, grievously tormented." Now some say, that by way of excuse he mentioned also the cause, why he had not brought him. "For neither was it possible," saith he, "paralyzed as he was, and tormented, and at his last gasp, to lift and convey him." For that he was at the point of expiring, Luke saith; "He was even ready to die." But I say, this is a sign of his having great faith, even much greater than theirs, who let one down through the roof. For because he knew for certain, that even a mere command was enough for the raising up of the patient, he thought it superfluous to bring him.

What then doth Jesus? What He had in no case done before, here He doeth. For whereas on every occasion He was used to follow the wish of His supplicants, here He rather springs toward it, and offers not only to heal him, but also to come to the house. And this He doth, that we might learn the virtue of the centurion. For if He had not made this offer, but had said, "Go thy way, let thy servant be healed;" we should have known none of these things.

This at least He did, in an opposite way, in the case also of the Phoenician woman. For here, when not summoned to the house, of His own accord He saith, He will come, that thou mightest learn the centurion's faith and great humility; but in the case of the Phoenician woman, He both refuses the grant, and drives her, persevering therein, to great perplexity.

For being a wise physician and full of resources, He knows how to bring about contraries the one by the other. And as here by His freely-offered coming, so there by His peremptory putting off and denial, He unfolds the woman's faith. So likewise He doth in Abraham's case, saying, "I will by no means hide from Abraham my servant;" to make thee know that man's kindly affection, and his care for Sodom. And in the instance of Lot, they that were sent refuse to enter into his house, to make thee know the greatness of that righteous man's hospitality.

What then saith the centurion? "I am not worthy that thou shouldest come under my roof." Let us hearken, as many as are to receive Christ: for it is possible to receive Him even now. Let us hearken, and emulate, and receive Him with as great zeal; for indeed, when thou receivest a poor man who is hungry and naked, thou hast received and cherished Him.

2. "But say in a word only, and my servant shall be healed."

See this man also, how, like the leper, he hath the right opinion touching Him. For neither did this one say, "entreat," nor did he say, "pray, and beseech," but "command only." And then from fear lest out of modesty He refuse, he saith,

"For I also am a man under authority, having under me soldiers; and I say to this man, go, and he goeth; and to another, come, and he cometh; and to my servant, do this, and he doeth it."

"And what of that," saith one, "if the centurion did suspect it to be so? For the question is, whether Christ affirmed and ratified as much." Thou speakest well, and very sensibly. Let us then look to this very thing; and we shall find what happened in the case of the leper, the same happening here likewise. For even as the leper said, "If thou wilt" (and not from the leper only are we positive about His authority, but also from the voice of Christ; in that, so far from putting an end to the suspicion, He did even confirm it more, by adding what were else superfluous to say, in the phrase, "I will, be thou cleansed," in order to establish that man's doctrine): so here too, it is right to see whether any such thing occurred. In fact, we shall find this same thing again taking place. For when the centurion had spoken such words, and had testified His so great prerogative; so far from blaming, He did even approve it, and did somewhat more than approve it. For neither hath the evangelist said, that He praised the saying only, but declaring a certain earnestness in His praise, that He even "marvelled;" and neither did He simply marvel, but in the presence also of the whole people, and set Him as an example to the rest, that they should emulate Him.

Seest thou how each of them that bore witness of His authority is "marvelled at? And the multitudes were astonished at His doctrine, because He taught as one having authority;" and so far from blaming them, He both took them with Him when He came down, and by His words of cleansing to the leper, confirmed their judgment. Again, that leper said, "If thou wilt, thou canst make me clean;" and so far from rebuking, He on the contrary cleansed him by such treatment as He had said. Again, this centurion saith, "Speak the word only, and my servant shall be healed:" and "marvelling" at him, He said, "I have not found so great faith, no, not in Israel."

Now, to convince thee of this by the opposite also; Martha having said nothing of this sort, but on the contrary, "Whatsoever thou wilt ask of God, He will give Thee;" so far from being praised, although an acquaintance, and dear to Him, and one of them that had shown great zeal toward Him, she was rather rebuked and corrected by Him, as not having spoken well; in that He said to her, "Said I not unto thee, that if thou wouldest believe, thou shouldest see the glory of God?" blaming her, as though she did not even yet believe. And again, because she had said, "Whatsoever Thou wilt ask of God, He will give Thee;" to lead her away from such a surmise, and to teach her that He needs not to receive from another, but is Himself the fountain of all good things, He saith, "I am the resurrection and the life;" that is to say, "I wait not to receive active power, but work all of myself."

Wherefore at the centurion He both marvels, and prefers him to all the people, and honors him with the gift of the kingdom, and provokes the rest to the same zeal. And to show thee that for this end He so spake, viz. for the instructing of the rest to believe in like manner, listen to the exactness of the evangelist, how he hath intimated it. For,

"Jesus," saith he, "turned Him about, and said to them that followed Him, I have not found so great faith, no, not in Israel."

It follows, that to have high imaginations concerning Him, this especially is of faith, and tends to procure the kingdom and His other blessings. For neither did His praise reach to words only, but He both restored the sick man whole, in recompence of his faith, and weaves for him a glorious crown, and promises great gifts, saying on this wise,

"Many shall come from the east and west, and shall sit down in the bosoms of Abraham, and Isaac, and Jacob; but the children of the kingdom shall be cast out."

Thus, since He had shown many miracles, He proceeds to talk with them more unreservedly.

Then, that no one might suppose His words to come of flattery, but that all might be aware that such was the mind of the centurion, He saith,

"Go thy way; as thou hast believed, so be it done unto thee."

And straightway the work followed, bearing witness to his character. nothing; for the question is, whether each of them has set before us the zealousness of the man, and his having had the right opinion concerning Christ. But it is likely, that after sending his friends, he himself also came and said these things. And if Luke did not speak of the one, no more did Matthew of the other; and this is not the part of men disagreeing amongst themselves, but rather of those that are filling up the things omitted by one another. But see by another thing also how Luke hath proclaimed his faith, saying that his servant "was ready to die." Nevertheless, not even this cast him into despondency, neither did it cause him to give up: but even so he trusted that he should prevail. And if Matthew affirm Christ to have said, "I have not found so great faith, no, not in Israel," and hereby to show clearly that he was not an Israelite; while Luke saith, "He built our synagogue;" neither is this a contradiction. For it was possible for one, even though not a Jew, both to build the synagogue, and to love the nation.

4. But do not thou, I pray thee, merely inquire what was said by him, but add thereto his rank also, and then thou wilt see the man's excellency. Because in truth great is the pride of them that are in places of command, and not even in afflictions do they take lower ground. He, for example, who is set down in John, is for dragging Him unto his house, and saith, "Come down, for my child is ready to die." But not so this man; rather he is far superior both to him, and to those who let down the bed through the roof. For he seeks not for His bodily presence, neither did He bring the sick man near the physician; a thing which implied no mean imaginations concerning Him, but rather a suspicion of His divine dignity. And he saith, "speak the word only." And at the beginning he saith not even, "speak the word," but only describe his affliction: for neither did he, of great humility, expect that Christ would straightway consent, and inquire for his house. Therefore, when he heard Him say, "I will come and heal him," then, not before he saith, "speak the word." Nor yet did the suffering confound him, but still under calamity he reasons coolly, not looking so much to the health of the servant, as to the avoiding all appearance of doing anything irreverent.

And yet it was not he that pressed it, but Christ that offered it: nevertheless even so he feared, lest perchance he should be thought to be going beyond his own deservings, and to be drawing upon himself a thing above his strength. Seest thou his wisdom? Mark the folly of the Jews, in saying, "He was worthy for whom He should do the favor." For when they should have taken refuge in the love of Jesus towards man, they rather allege this man's worthiness; and know not so much as on what ground to allege it. But not so he, but he affirmed himself even in the utmost degree unworthy, not only of the benefit, but even of receiving the Lord in his house. Wherefore even when he said, "My servant lieth sick," he did not add, "speak," for fear lest he should be unworthy to obtain the gift; but he merely made known his affliction. And when he saw Christ zealous in His turn, not even so did he spring forward, but still continues to keep to the end his own proper measure.

And if any one should say, "wherefore did not Christ honor him in return?" we would say this, that He did make return to him in honor, and that exceedingly: first by bringing out his mind, which thing chiefly appeared by His not coming to his house; and in the second place, by introducing him into His kingdom, and preferring him to the whole Jewish nation. For because he made himself out unworthy even to receive Christ into his house, he became worthy both of a kingdom, and of attaining unto those good things which Abraham enjoyed.

"But wherefore," one may say, "was not the leper commended, who showed forth things greater than these?" For he did not so much as say, "speak the word," but what was far more, "be willing only," which is what the prophet saith concerning the Father, "He hath done whatsoever He pleased." But he also was commended. For when He said, "Offer the gift that Moses commanded, for a testimony unto them," He means nothing else but, "thou shalt be an accuser of them, in that thou didst believe." And besides, it was not the same for one that was a Jew to believe, and for one from without that nation. For that the centurion was not a Jew is evident, both from his being a centurion and from its being said, "I have not found so great faith, no, not in Israel." And it was a very great thing for a man who was out of the list of the Jewish people to admit so great a thought. For he did no less than imagine to himself, as it seems to me, the armies in Heaven; or that the diseases and death, and everything else, were so subject to Him, as his soldiers to himself.

Wherefore he said likewise, "For I also am a man set under authority;" that is, Thou art God, and I man; I under authority, but Thou not under authority. If I therefore, being a man, and under authority, can do so much; far more He, both as God, and as not under authority. Thus with the strongest expression he desires to convince Him, that he saith this, as one giving not a similar example, but one far exceeding. For if I (said he), being equal in honor to them whom I command, and under authority, yet by reason of the trifling superiority of my rank am able to do such great things; and no man contradicts me, but what I command, that is done, though the injunctions be various ("for I say to this man, go, and he goeth; and to another, come, and he cometh":) much more wilt Thou Thyself be able.

And some actually read the place in this way, "For if I, being a man," and having inserted a stop, they add, "having soldiers under authority under me."

But mark thou, I pray thee, how he signified that Christ is able both to overcome even death as a slave, and to command it as its master. For in saying, "come, and he cometh," and "go, and he goeth;" he expresses this: "If Thou shouldest command his end not to come upon him, it will not come."

Seest thou how believing he was? For that which was afterwards to be manifest to all, here is one who already hath made it evident; that He hath power both of death and of life, and "leadeth down to the gates of hell, and bringeth up again." Nor was he speaking of soldiers only, but also of slaves; which related to a more entire obedience.

5. But nevertheless, though having such great faith, he still accounted himself to be unworthy. Christ however, signifying that he was worthy to have Him enter into his house, did much greater things, marvelling at him, and proclaiming him, and giving more than he had asked. For he came indeed seeking for his servant health of body, but went away, having received a kingdom. Seest thou how the saying had been already fulfilled, "Seek ye the kingdom of heaven, and all these things shall be added unto you." For, because he evinced great faith, and lowliness of mind, He both gave him heaven, and added unto him health.

And not by this alone did He honor him, but also by signifying upon whose casting out he is brought in. For now from this time forth He proceeds to make known to all, that salvation is by faith, not by works of the law. And this is why not to Jews only, but to Gentiles also the gift so given shall be proffered, and to the latter rather than to the former. For "think not," saith He, "by any means, that so it hath come to pass in regard of this man alone; nay, so it shall be in regard of the whole world. And this He said, prophesying of the Gentiles, and suggesting to them good hopes. For in fact there were some following Him from Galilee of the Gentiles. And this He said, on the one hand, not letting the Gentiles despair, on the other, putting down the proud spirits of the Jews.

But that His saying might not affront the hearers, nor afford them any handle; He neither brings forward prominently what He hath to say of the Gentiles, but upon occasion taken from the centurion; nor doth He use nakedly the term, Gentiles: not saying, "many of the Gentiles," but, "many from east and west:" which was the language of one pointing out the Gentiles, but did not so much affront the hearers, because His meaning was under a shadow.

Neither in this way only doth He soften the apparent novelty of His doctrine, but also by speaking of "Abraham's bosom" instead of "the kingdom." For neither was that term familiar to them: moreover, the introduction of Abraham would be a sharper sting to them. Wherefore John also spake nothing at first concerning hell, but, what was most apt to grieve them, He saith, "Think not to say, we are children of Abraham."

He is providing for another point also; not to seem in any sense opposed to the ancient polity. For he that admires the patriarchs, and speaks of their bosom as an inheritance of blessings, doth much more than sufficiently remove also this suspicion.

Let no man therefore suppose that the threat is one only, for both the punishment of the one and the joy of the other is double: of the one, not only that they fell away, but that they fell away from their own; of the other, not only that they attained, but that they attained what they had no expectation of: and there is a third together with these, that the one received what pertained to the other. And he calls them "children of the kingdom," for whom the kingdom had been prepared: which also more than all was apt to gall them; in that having pointed to them as being in their bosom by His offer and promise, after all He puts them out.

6. Then, because what He had said was mere affirmation, He confirms it by the miracle; as indeed He shows the miracles in their turn, by the subsequent accomplishment of the prediction. He accordingly, who disbelieves the health which the servant then received, let him from the prophecy, which hath this day come to pass, believe that other also. For so that prophecy again, even before the event, was made manifest to all by the sign which then took place. To this end, you see, having first uttered that prediction, then and not before He raised up the sick of the palsy; that He might make the future credible by the present, and the less by the greater. Since for virtuous men to enjoy His good things, and for the contrary sort to undergo His penalties, were nothing improbable, but a reasonable event, and according to the tenor of laws: but to brace up the feeble, and to raise the dead, was something beyond nature.

But nevertheless, unto this great and marvellous work the centurion too contributed no little; which thing, we see, Christ also declared, saying, "Go thy way, and as thou hast believed, so be it done unto thee." Seest thou how the health of the servant proclaimed aloud both Christ's power, and the faith of the centurion, and also became a pledge of the future? Or rather it was all a proclamation of Christ's power. For not only did He quite heal the servant's body, but the soul also of the centurion He did Himself bring over unto the faith by His miracles.

And do thou look not to this only, that the one believed, and the other was healed, but marvel how quickly also. For this too the evangelist declared, saying, "And his servant was healed in the self-same hour:" even as of the leper also he said, "he was straightway cleansed." For not by healing, but by doing so both in a wonderful manner and in a moment of time, did He display His power. Neither in this way only doth He profit us, but also by his constant practice, in the manifestation of His miracles, of opening incidentally His discourses about His kingdom, and of drawing all men towards it. For, those even whom He was threatening to cast out, He threatened not in order to cast them out, but in order that through such fear, He might draw them into it by His words. And if not even hereby were they profited, theirs is the whole blame, as also of all who are in the like distemper.

For not at all among Jews only may one see this taking place, but also among them that have believed. For Judas too was a child of the kingdom, and it was said to him with the disciples, "Ye shall sit on twelve thrones;" yet he became a child of hell; whereas the Ethiopian, barbarian as he was, and of them "from the east and west," shall enjoy the crowns with Abraham, and Isaac, and Jacob. This takes place among us also now. "For many," saith He, "that are first shall be last, and the last first." And this He saith, that neither the one may grow languid, as unable to return; nor the others be confident, as standing fast. This John also declared before from the beginning, when he said, "God is able of these stones to raise up children unto Abraham." Thus, since it was so to come to pass, it is proclaimed long before; that no one may be confounded at the strangeness of the event. But he indeed speaks of it as a possible thing (for he was first); Christ on the other hand as what will surely be, affording the proof of it from His works.

7. Let us not then be confident, who stand, but let us say to ourselves, "Let him that thinketh he standeth take heed lest he fall;" neither let us who are fallen despair, but let us say to ourselves, "He that falleth, doth he not arise?" For many even who have mounted to the very summit of Heaven, and have shown forth all austerity, and had made their abode in the deserts, nor saw any woman so much as in a dream; having become a little remiss, have been tripped up, and have come unto the very gulf of wickedness. While others again from thence have gone up to Heaven, and from the stage and orchestra have passed over unto the discipline of angels, and have displayed so great virtue, as to drive away devils, and to work many other such miracles. And of

these examples both the Scriptures are full, and our life is also full. Even whoremongers and effeminate persons stop the mouths of the Manichaeans, who say that wickedness is immoveable, enrolling themselves on the devil's side, and weakening the hands of them that would wish to be in earnest, and overturning all our life.

For they who inculcate these things, not only injure men as to the future, but here also turn all things upside down, for their own part at least. Because when will any regard virtue, from among those that are living in wickedness, so long as he accounts his return that way, and his change for the better, a thing impossible? For if now, when both laws exist, and penalties are threatened, and there is common opinion to recall the ordinary sort, and hell is looked for, and a kingdom promised, and wrong things reproached, and the good praised; hardly do any choose the labors that are to be undergone for virtue's sake: shouldest thou take away all these things, what is there to hinder ruin and corruption universal?

Knowing therefore the devil's craft, and that as well the lawgivers of the Gentiles as the oracles of God, and the reasonings of nature, and the common opinion of all men, yea barbarians, and Scythians, and Thracians, and generally all, are directly opposed both to these, and to such as strive to enact the doctrines of fate: let us be sober, beloved, and bidding farewell to all those, let us travel along the narrow way, being both confident and in fear: in fear because of the precipices on either side, confident because of Jesus our guide. Let us travel on, sober and wakeful. For though but for a little while one slumber, he is swept away quickly.

8. For we are not more perfect than David, who by a little carelessness was hurled into the very gulf of sin. Yet he arose again quickly. Look not then to his having sinned only, but also to his having washed away his sin. For to this end He wrote that history, not that thou shouldest behold him fallen, but admire him risen; to teach thee, when thou art fallen, how thou shouldest arise. Thus, as physicians choose out the most grievous diseases, and write them in their books, and teach their method of cure in similar cases; if so be men having practised on the greater, may easily master the less; even so God likewise hath brought forward the greatest of sins, that they also who offend in small things may find the cure of these easy, by means of the other: since if those admitted of healing, much more the less.

Let us look then to the manner both of the sickness, and of the speedy recovery of that blessed man. What then was the manner of his sickness? He committed adultery and murder. For I shrink not from proclaiming these things with a loud voice. Since if the Holy Ghost thought it no shame to record all this history, much less ought we to draw any shade over it. Wherefore I not only proclaim it, but I add another circumstance also. For in fact, whosoever hide these things, they most of all men throw his virtue into the shade. And as they that say nothing of the battle with Goliath deprive him of no small crowns, so also they that hurry by this history. Doth not my saying seem a paradox? Nay, wait a little, and then ye shall know that with reason have we said this. For to this end do I magnify the sin, and make my statement stranger, that I may the more abundantly provide the medicines.

What is it then which I add? The man's virtue; which makes the fault also greater. For all things are not judged alike in all men. "For mighty" men (it is said) "shall be mightily tormented:" and "He that knew his Lord's will, and doeth it not, shall be beaten with many stripes." So that more knowledge is a ground of more punishment. For this same reason the priest, if he commit the same sin as those under government, shall not have the same to endure, but things far more grievous.

Perhaps, seeing the charge against him amplified, ye tremble and fear, and marvel at me, as though I were going down a precipice. But I am so confident on that righteous man's behalf, that I will proceed even farther; for the more I aggravate the charge, so much the more shall I be able to show forth the praise of David.

"And what more than this," you will say, "can be uttered?" Abundantly more. For as in the case of Cain, what was done was not a murder only, but worse than even many murders; for it was not a stranger, but a brother, whom he slew; and a brother who had not done but suffered wrong; not after many murderers, but having first originated the horrid crime: so here too that which was perpetrated was not murder only. For it was no ordinary man that did it, but a prophet: and he slays not him that had done wrong, but him that had suffered wrong; for indeed he had been mortally wronged, by the forcing away his wife: nevertheless after that he added this also.

9. Perceive ye, how I have not spared that righteous one? how without any the least reserve I have mentioned his offenses? But yet, so confident am I concerning his defense, that after so great load as this of his sin, I would there were present both the Manichaeans who most deride all this, and they that are diseased in Marcion's way, that I might fully stop their mouths. For they indeed say "he committed murder and adultery;" but I say not this only, but have also proved the murder to be twofold, first from him who suffered the wrong, then from the quality of the person who offended. For it is not the same thing, for one to whom the Spirit was vouchsafed, and on whom so great benefits had been conferred, and who had been admitted to such freedom of

speech, and at such a time of life, to venture on crimes of that sort; as without all these, to commit this self-same thing. Nevertheless even in this respect is that illustrious man most of all worthy of admiration, that when he had fallen into the very pit of wickedness, he did not sink nor despair, nor cast himself down in supineness, on receiving of the devil so fatal a wound; but quickly, or rather straightway, and with great force, he gave a more fatal blow than he had received.

And the same thing occurred, as if in war and in battle some barbarian had struck his spear into the heart of a chieftain, or shot an arrow into his liver, and had added to the former wound a second more fatal than it, and he that had received these grievous blows, when fallen, and wallowing in much blood all about him, were first to rise up quickly, then to hurl a spear at him that wounded him, and exhibit him dead on the ground in a moment. Even so in this case also, the greater thou declarest the wound, so much the more admirable dost thou imply the soul of him that was wounded to be, that he had power after this grievous wound both to rise up again, and to stand in the very forefront of the battle array, and bear down him that had wounded him.

And how great a thing this is, they best know, whosoever are fallen into grievous sins. For it is not so much a proof of a generous and vigorous soul to walk upright, and to run all the way (for such a soul hath the good hope going along with it, to cheer and to rouse it, to nerve and render it more zealous); as after those innumerable crowns, and so many trophies, and victories, having undergone the utmost loss, to be able to resume the same course. And that what I say may be made plain, I will endeavor to bring before you another example, not at all inferior to the former.

For imagine, I pray thee, some pilot, when he had compassed seas without number, and sailed over the whole ocean; after those many storms, and rocks and waves, to sink, having with him a great freight, in the very mouth of the harbor, and hardly with his naked body to escape this grievous shipwreck; how would he naturally feel towards the sea, and navigation, and such labors? Will such a one then ever choose, unless he be of a very noble soul, to see a beach, or a vessel, or a harbor? I trow not; but he will lie hiding his face, seeing night all through the day, and shrinking from all things; and he will choose rather to live by begging, than to put his hand to the same labors.

But not such was this blessed man; but though he had undergone such a shipwreck, after those innumerable troubles and toils, he stayed not with his face covered, but launched his vessel, and having spread his sails, and taken the rudder in hand, he applies himself to the same labors, and hath made his wealth more abundant again. Now if to stand be so admirable, and not to lie down for ever after one has fallen; to rise up again, and to do such deeds, what crowns would not this deserve?

And yet surely there were many things to drive him to despair; as first, the greatness of his sins; secondly, that not at the beginning of life, when our hopes also are more abundant, but near the end, these things befell him. For neither doth the merchant, who hath just gone out of the harbor and been wrecked, grieve equally with him, who after very many traffickings strikes on a rock. Thirdly, that when he had already obtained great wealth, he incurred this. Yea, for by that time he had stored up no small merchandise: for instance, the deeds of his early youth, when he was a shepherd; those about Goliath, when he set up the glorious trophy; those pertaining to his self-command respecting Saul. Since he showed forth even the evangelical long-suffering, in that he got his enemy ten thousand times into his hands, and continually spared him; and chose rather to be an outcast from his country and from liberty, and from life itself, than to slay him that was unjustly plotting against him. Likewise after his coming to the kingdom, there were noble deeds of his to no small amount.

And besides what I have said, his credit also among the many, and his fall from glory so bright, would cause no ordinary perplexity. For the purple did by no means so much adorn him, as the stain of his sin disgraced him. And ye know of course what a great thing it is for evil deeds to be exposed, and how great a soul is required in such an one, not to despond after the censure of the multitude, and when he hath so many witnesses of his own offenses.

Nevertheless all these darts that noble person drew out of his soul, and so shone forth after this, so wiped out the stain, became so pure, that his offspring even after his death had their sins mitigated by him: and that which was said of Abraham, we find God saying the same of this man also; or rather, much more of the latter. For with respect to the patriarch it is said, "I remembered my covenant with Abraham;" but here He saith not "the covenant," but how? "I will defend this city for my servant David's sake." And besides, on account of His favor towards him, He suffered not Solomon to fall from the kingdom, great as the sin was which he had committed. And so great was the glory of the man, that Peter, so many years after, in exhorting the Jews, spake on this wise: "Let me freely speak unto you of the patriarch David, that he is both dead and buried." And Christ too, discoursing with the Jews, signifies him after his sin to have had the Spirit vouchsafed to such a degree, that he was counted worthy to prophesy again even concerning His Godhead; and thereby stopping their mouths, He said, "How then doth David in spirit call Him Lord, saying, The Lord said unto my Lord, Sit thou on my right hand ?" And much as with

Moses, so it fell out also with David. For as Miriam, even against Moses' will, was punished by God for insolence to her brother, because He greatly loved the holy man; even so this man, injuriously treated by his son, God did swiftly avenge, and that against his will.

These things then are sufficient, yea rather before all others these are sufficient to indicate the man's excellency. For when God pronounces His judgment, we ought to inquire no further. But if ye would become particularly acquainted with His self command, ye may by perusing his history after his sin, perceive his confidence towards God, his benevolence, his growth in virtue, his strictness unto his last breath.

10. Having then these examples, let us be sober, and let us strive not to despond, and if at any time we fall, not to lie prostrate. For not to cast you into slothfulness, did I speak of the sins of David, but to work in you more fear. For if that righteous man through a little remissness received such wounds, what shall we have to suffer, who are every day negligent? Do not therefore look at his fall, and be remiss, but consider what great things he did even after this, what great mournings, how much repentance he showed forth, adding his nights to his days, pouring forth fountains of tears, washing his couch with his tears, withal clothing himself in sackcloth.

Now if he needed so great a conversion, when will it be possible for us to be saved, feeling insensible after so many sins? For he that hath many good deeds, would easily even by this throw a shade over his sins; but he that is unarmed, wherever he may receive a dart, receives a mortal wound.

In order therefore that this may not be so, let us arm ourselves with good works; and if any offense have befallen us, let us wash it away: that we may be counted worthy, after having lived the present life to the glory of God, to enjoy the life to come; unto which may we all attain, by the grace and love towards man of our Lord Jesus Christ, to whom be glory and might forever and ever. Amen.

HOMILY XXVII

MATT. VIII. 14

"And when Jesus was come into Peter's house, He saw his wife's mother laid and sick of a fever: and He touched her hand, and the fever left her, and she arose and ministered unto Him."

But Mark adds also, "immediately," meaning to declare the time as well; but this evangelist hath set down only the miracle, without signifying besides the time. And whereas the others say, that she that lay ill did also entreat Him, this too he hath passed over in silence. But this comes not of any dissonance, but the one of brevity, the other of exact narrative. But for what intent did He go into Peter's house? As it seems to me, to take food. This at least is declared when it is said,

"She arose and ministered unto Him."

For He used to visit His disciples (as Matthew likewise, when He had called him), so honoring them and making them more zealous.

But do thou mark, I pray thee, herein also Peter's reverence towards Him. For though he had his wife's mother at home lying ill, and very sick of a fever, he drew Him not into his house, but waited first for the teaching to be finished, then for all the others to be healed; and then when He had come in, besought Him. Thus from the beginning was he instructed to prefer the things of all others to his own.

Therefore neither doth he himself bring Him in, but He entered of His own accord (after the centurion had said, "I am not worthy that Thou shouldest come under my roof"): to show how much favor He bestowed on His disciple. And yet consider of what sort were the houses of these fishermen; but for all that, He disdained not to enter into their mean huts, teaching thee by all means to trample under foot human pride.

And sometimes He heals by words only, sometimes He even stretches forth His hand, sometimes He doeth both these things, to bring into sight His way of healing. For it was not His will always to work miracles in the more surpassing manner: it being needful for Him to be concealed awhile, and especially as concerned His disciples; since they out of their great delight would have proclaimed everything. And this was evident from the fact, that even after coming to the mount, it was needful to charge them that they should tell no man.

Having therefore touched her body, He not only quenched the fever, but also gave her back perfect health. Thus, the disease being an ordinary one, He displayed His power by the manner of healing; a thing which no physician's art could have wrought. For ye know that even after the departing of fevers, the patients yet need much time to return to their former health. But then all took place at once.

And not in this case only, but also in that of the sea. For neither there did He quiet the winds only and the storm, but He also stayed at once the swelling of the waves; and this also was a strange thing. For even if the tempest should cease, the waves continue to swell for a long time.

But with Christ it was not so, but all at once was ended: and so it befell this woman also. Wherefore also the evangelist, to declare this, said, "She arose and ministered unto Him;" which was a sign both of Christ's power, and of the disposition of the woman, which she showed towards Christ.

And another thing together with these we may hence observe, that Christ grants the healing of some to the faith even of others. Since in this case too, others besought Him, as also in the instance of the centurion's servant. And this grant He makes, when there is no unbelief in him that is to be healed, but either through disease he cannot come unto Him, or through ignorance imagines nothing great of Him, or because of His immature age.

2. "When the even was come, they brought unto Him many that were possessed with devils: and He cast out the spirits from them with a word, and healed all that were sick: that it might be fulfilled which was spoken by the Prophet Esaias, that He took our infirmities, and bare our sicknesses."

Seest thou the multitude, by this time growing in faith? For not even when the time pressed could they endure to depart, nor did they account it unseasonable to bring their sick to Him at eventide.

But mark, I pray thee, how great a multitude of persons healed the evangelists pass quickly over, not mentioning one by one, and giving us an account of them, but in one word traversing an unspeakable sea of miracles. Then lest the greatness of the wonder should drive us again to unbelief, that even so great a people and their various diseases should be delivered and healed by Him in one moment of time, He brings in the prophet also to bear witness to what is going on: indicating the abundance of the proof we have, in every case, out of the Scriptures; such, that from the miracles themselves we have no more; and He saith, that Esaias also spake of these things; "He took our infirmities, and bare our sicknesses." He said not, "He did them away," but "He took and bare them;" which seems to me to be spoken rather of sins, by the prophet, in harmony with John, where he saith, "Behold the Lamb of God, that beareth the sin of the world."

How then doth the evangelist here apply it to diseases? Either as rehearsing the passage in the historical sense, or to show that most of our diseases arise from sins of the soul. For if the sum of all, death itself, hath its root and foundation from sin, much more the majority of our diseases also: since our very capability of suffering did itself originate there.

3. "Now when Jesus saw great multitudes about Him, He gave commandment to depart unto the other side."

Seest thou again His freedom from ostentation? in that as the others say, "He charged the devils not to say it was He," so this writer saith, He repels the multitudes from Him. Now in so doing, He was at once both training us to be moderate, and at the same time allaying the envy of the Jews, and teaching us to do nothing for display. For He was not, we know, a healer to bodies only, but a curer also of the soul, and a teacher of self-restraint; by both disclosing Himself, both by putting away their diseases, and by doing nought for display. Because they indeed were cleaving unto Him, loving Him, and marvelling at Him, and desiring to look upon Him. For who would depart from one who was doing such miracles? Who would not long, were it only to see the face, and the mouth that was uttering such words?

For not by any means in working wonders only was He wonderful, but even when merely showing Himself, He was full of great grace; and to declare this the prophet said, "Fair in beauty beyond the children of men." And if Esaias saith, "He hath no form nor comeliness," he affirms it either in comparison of the glory of His Godhead, which surpasses all utterance and description; or as declaring what took place at His passion, and the dishonor which He underwent at the season of the cross, and the mean estate which throughout His life He exemplified in all respects.

Further: He did not first give "commandment to depart unto the other side," nor until He had healed them. For surely they could not have borne it. As therefore on the mountain they not only continued with Him while exhorting them, but also when it was silence followed Him; so here too, not in His miracles only did they wait on Him, but also when He had ceased again, from His very countenance receiving no small benefit. For if Moses had his face made glorious, and Stephen like that of an angel; consider thou our common Lord, what manner of person it was likely He would appear at such a time.

Many now perchance have fallen into a passionate desire of seeing that form; but if we are willing we shall behold one far better than that. For if we can pass through our present life with Christian boldness, we shall receive Him in the clouds, meeting Him in an immortal and incorruptible body.

But observe how He doth not simply drive them away, lest He should hurt them. For He did not say, "withdraw," but "gave commandment to depart to the other side," giving them to expect that He would surely come thither.

4. And the multitudes for their part evinced this great love, and were following with much affection; but some one person, a slave of wealth, and possessed with much arrogance, approaches Him, and saith,

"Master, I will follow Thee whithersoever Thou goest."

Seest thou how great his arrogance? For as not deigning to be numbered with the multitude, and indicating that he is above the common sort, so he comes near. Because such is the Jewish character; full of unseasonable confidence. So too another afterwards, when all men were keeping silence, of his own accord springs up, and saith, "Which is the first commandment?"

Yet nevertheless the Lord rebuked not his unseasonable confidence, teaching us to bear even with such as these. Therefore He doth not openly convict them who are devising mischief, but replies to their secret thought, leaving it to themselves only to know that they are convicted, and doubly doing them good, first by showing that He knows what is in their conscience, next by granting unto them concealment after this manifestation, and allowing them to recover themselves again, if they will: which thing He doth in the case of this man also.

For he, seeing the many signs, and many drawn after Him, thought to make a gain out of such miracles; wherefore also he was forward to follow Him. And whence is this manifest? From the answer which Christ makes, meeting not the question, as it stands verbally, but the temper shown in its meaning. For, "What?" saith He, "dost thou look to gather wealth by following me? Seest thou not then that I have not even a lodging, not even so much as the birds have?"

For "the foxes," saith He, "have holes, and the birds of the air have nests, but the Son of Man hath not where to lay His head."

Now these were not the words of one turning Himself away, but of one who while putting to the proof his evil disposition, yet permitted him (if he were willing with such a prospect) to follow Him. And to convince thee of his wickedness, when he had heard these things, and had been proved, he did not say, "I am ready to follow Thee."

5. And in many other places also Christ is clearly doing this; He doth not openly convict, but by His answer He manifests the purpose of them that are coming unto Him. Thus to him again that said, "Good Master," and had thought by such flattery to gain His favor, according to his purpose He made answer, saying, "Why callest thou me good? There is none good but one, that is, God."

And when they said unto Him, "Behold, Thy mother and Thy brethren seek Thee;" forasmuch as these were under the influence of some human infirmity, not desiring to hear something profitable, but to make a display of their relationship to Him, and therein to be vainglorious; hear what He saith: "Who is my mother, and who are my brethren?"

And again to His brethren themselves, saying unto Him, "Show thyself to the world," and wishing thence to feed their vainglory, He said, "Your time" (so He speaks) "is always ready, but my time is not yet come."

And in the opposite cases too He doth so; as in that of Nathanael, saying, "Behold an Israelite indeed, in whom is no guile." And again, "Go and show John again those things which ye do hear and see." For neither in this did He reply to the words, but to the intention of him that sent them. And with the people again in like manner, He addresses His discourse unto their conscience, saying, "What went ye out into the wilderness to see?" That is because they were probably feeling about John, as though he had been a sort of easy and wavering person; to correct this their suspicion, He saith, "What went ye out into the wilderness to see? A reed shaken with the wind?" or, "a man clothed with soft raiment?" by both these figures declaring, that he was neither of himself a waverer, nor would be softened by any luxury. Thus then in the present case also He makes His answer to their meaning.

And see how in this also He shows forth great moderation: in that He said not, "I have it indeed, but despise it," but "I have it not." Seest thou what exact care goes along with His condescension? Even as when He eats and drinks, when He seems to be acting in an opposite way to John, this too He doeth for the sake of the Jews' salvation, or rather for that of the whole world, at once both stopping the mouths of the heretics, and desiring to win also more abundantly those of that day to Himself.

6. But a certain other one, we read, said unto Him,

"Lord, suffer me first to go and bury my father."

Didst thou mark the difference? how one impudently saith, "I will follow Thee whithersoever Thou goest;" but this other, although asking a thing of sacred duty, saith, "Suffer me." Yet He suffered him not, but saith, "Let the dead bury their dead, but do thou follow me." For in every case He had regard to the intention. And wherefore did He not suffer him? one may ask. Because, on the one hand, there were those that would fulfill that duty, and the dead was not going to remain unburied; on the other, it was not fit for this man to be taken away from the weightier matters. But by saying, "their own dead," He implies that this is not one of His dead. And that because he that was dead, was, at least as I suppose, of the unbelievers.

Now if thou admire the young man, that for a matter so necessary he besought Jesus, and did not go away of his own accord; much rather do thou admire him for staying also when forbidden.

Was it not then, one may say, extreme ingratitude, not to be present at the burial of his father? If indeed he did so out of negligence, it was ingratitude, but if in order not to interrupt a more needful work, his departing would most surely have been of extreme inconsideration. For Jesus forbad him, not as commanding to think lightly of the honor due to our parents, but signifying that nothing ought to be to us more urgent than the things of Heaven, and that we ought with all diligence to cleave to these, and not to put them off for ever so little, though our engagements be exceeding indispensable and pressing.

For what can be more needful than to bury a father? what more easy? since it would not even consume any long time.

But if one ought not to spend even as much time as is required for a father's burial, nor is it safe to be parted even so long from our spiritual concerns; consider what we deserve, who all our time stand off from the things that pertain to Christ, and prefer things very ordinary to such as are needful, and are remiss, when there is nothing to press on us?

And herein too we should admire the instructiveness of His teaching, that He nailed him fast to His word, and with this freed him from those endless evils, such as lamentations, and mournings, and the things that follow thereafter. For after the burial he must of necessity proceed to inquire about the will, then about the distribution of the inheritance, and all the other things that follow thereupon; and thus waves after waves coming in succession upon him, would bear him away very far from the harbor of truth. For this cause He draws him, and fastens him to Himself.

But if thou still marvellest, and art perplexed, that he was not permitted to be present at his father's burial; consider that many suffer not the sick, if it be a father that is dead, or a mother, or a child, or any other of their kinsmen, to know it, nor to follow him to the tomb; and we do not for this charge them with cruelty nor inhumanity: and very reasonably. For, on the contrary, it were cruelty to bring out to the funeral solemnity men in such a state.

But if to mourn and be afflicted in mind for them that are of our kindred is evil, much more our being withdrawn from spiritual discourses. For this same cause He said elsewhere also, "No man having put his hand to the plough, and looking back, is fit for the kingdom of Heaven." And surely it is far better to proclaim the kingdom, and draw back others from death, than to bury the dead body, that is nothing advantaged thereby; and especially, when there are some to fulfill all these duties.

7. Nothing else then do we learn hereby, but that we must not wantonly lose any, no not the smallest time, though there be ten thousand things to press on us; but to set what is spiritual before all, even the most indispensable matters, and to know both what is life, and what is death. Since many even of them that seem to live are nothing better than dead men, living as they do in wickedness; or rather these are worse than the dead; "For he that is dead," it is said, "is freed from sin," but this man is a slave to sin. For tell me not of this, that he is not eaten of worms, nor lies in a coffin, nor hath closed his eyes, nor is bound in graveclothes. Nay, for these things he undergoes more grievously than the dead, no worms devouring him, but the passions of his soul tearing him to pieces more fiercely than wild beasts.

And if his eyes be open, this too again is far worse than having closed them. For those of the dead see no evil thing, but this man is gathering unto himself diseases without number, while his eyes are open. And whereas the other lies in a coffin, unmoved by anything, this one is buried in the tomb of his innumerable distempers.

But thou seest not his body in a state of decay. And what of that? Since before his body, his soul is corrupted and destroyed, and undergoes greater rottenness. For the other stinketh a few days, but this for the whole of his life exhales evil odors, having a mouth more foul than sewers.

And so the one differs from the other, by just so much as this, that the dead indeed undergoes that decay only which comes of nature, but this man together with that, brings in also that rottenness which is from intemperance, devising each day unnumbered causes of corruption.

But is he borne on horseback? And what of that? Why, so is the other on a couch. And what is very hard, while the other is seen by no one in his dissolution and decay, but hath his coffin for a veil, this man is going about everywhere with his evil savor, bearing about a dead soul in his body as in a tomb.

And if one could but once see a man's soul who is living in luxury and vice, thou wouldest perceive that it is far better to lie bound in a grave than to be rivetted by the chains of our sins; and to have a stone laid over thee, than that heavy cover of insensibility. Wherefore above all things it behooves the friends of these dead men, seeing that they are past feeling, to come near to Jesus in their behalf, as Mary then did in the case of Lazarus. Though he "stinketh," though he be "dead four days," do not despair, but approach, and remove the stone first. Yea, for then thou shalt see him lying as in a tomb, and bound in his grave clothes.

And if ye will, let it be some one of them that are great and distinguished, whom we bring before you. Nay, fear not, for I will state the example without a name: or rather, though I should mention the name, not even so need there be any fear: for who ever fears a dead man? seeing that whatever one may do, he continues dead, and the dead cannot injure the living either little or much.

Let us then behold their head bound up. For indeed, when they are for ever drunken, even as the dead by their many wrappers and grave-clothes, so are all their organs of sense closed and bound up. And if thou wilt look at their hands too, thou shalt see these again bound to their belly, like those of the dead, and fastened about not with grave-clothes, but what is far more grievous, with the bands of covetousness: obtaining as they do no leave from her to be stretched out for alms-giving, or for any other of such like good deeds; rather she renders them more useless than those of the dead. Wouldest thou also see their feet bound together? See them again fastened about with cares, and for this cause never able to run unto the house of God.

Hast thou seen the dead? behold also the embalmer. Who then is the embalmer of these? The devil, who carefully fastens them about, and suffers not the man any longer to appear a man, but a dry stock. For where there is no eye, nor hands, nor feet, nor any other such thing, how can such an one appear a man? Even so may we see their soul also swaddled up, and rather an image than a soul.

Forasmuch then as they are in a sort of senseless state, being turned to dead men, let us in their behalf draw nigh unto Jesus, let us entreat Him to raise them up, let us take away the stone, let us loosen the grave clothes. For if thou take away the stone, that is, their insensibility to their own miseries, thou wilt quickly be able to bring them also out of the tomb; and having brought them out, thou wilt more easily rid them of their bonds. Then shall Christ know thee, when thou art risen, when unbound; then will He call thee even unto His own supper. As many therefore of you as are friends of Christ, as many as are disciples, as many as love him that is gone, draw near unto Jesus, and pray. For even though his ill savor abound and be ever so intense, nevertheless not even so should we, his friends, forsake him, but so much the rather draw near; even as the sisters of Lazarus then did; neither should we leave interceding, beseeching, entreating, until we have received him alive.

For if we thus order our own affairs, and those of our neighbors, we shall also attain speedily unto the life to come; unto which may we all attain, by the grace and love to man of our Lord Jesus Christ, to whom be glory forever and ever. Amen.

HOMILY XXVIII

MATT. VIII. 23, 24

"And when He was entered into a ship, His disciples followed Him. And, behold, there arose a great tempest in the sea, insomuch that the ship was covered with the waves, but He was asleep."

Now Luke, to free himself from having the order of time required of him, saith thus, "And it came to pass on a certain day that He went into a ship with His disciples;" and Mark in like manner. But this evangelist not so, but he maintains the order in this place also. For they did not all of them write all things in this way. And these things I have mentioned before, lest any one from the omission should suppose there was a discordance.

The multitudes then He sent on, but the disciples He took with Himself: for the others mention this too. And He took them with Him, not for nought, nor at hazard, but in order to make them spectators of the miracle that was to take place. For like a most excellent trainer, He was anointing them with a view to both objects; as well to be undismayed in dangers, as to be modest in honors. Thus, that they might not be high minded, because having sent away the rest, He retained them, He suffers them to be tossed with the tempest; at once correcting this, and disciplining them to bear trials nobly.

For great indeed were the former miracles too, but this contained also in it a kind of discipline, and that no inconsiderable one, and was a sign akin to that of old. For this cause He takes the disciples only with Himself. For as, when there was a display of miracles, He suffers the people also to be present; so when trial and terrors were rising up against Him, then He takes with Him none but the champions of the whole world, whom He was to discipline.

And while Matthew merely mentioned that "He was asleep," Luke saith that it was "on a pillow;" signifying both His freedom from pride, and to teach us hereby a high degree of austerity.

The tempest therefore being thoroughly excited, and the sea raging, "They awake Him, saying, Lord, save us: we perish." But He rebuked them before He rebuked the sea. Because as I said, for discipline these things were permitted, and they were a type of the temptations that were to overtake them. Yea, for after these things again, He often suffered them to fall into more grievous tempests of fortune, and bare long with them. Wherefore Paul also said, "I would not, brethren, have you ignorant, that we were pressed out of measure beyond strength, insomuch that we despaired even of life;" and after this again, "Who delivered us from so great deaths." Signifying therefore hereby, that they ought to be confident, though the waves rise high, and that He orders all things for good, He first of all reproves them. For indeed their very alarm was a profitable occurrence, that the miracle might appear greater, and their remembrance of the event be rendered lasting. Since when anything strange is about to happen, there are prepared beforehand many things to cause remembrance, lest after the miracle hath passed by, men should sink into forgetfulness.

Thus Moses also first is in fear of the serpent, and not merely in fear, but even with much distress: and then he sees that strange thing come to pass. So these too, having first looked to perish, were then saved, that having confessed the danger, they might learn the greatness of the miracle.

Therefore also He sleeps: for had He been awake when it happened, either they would not have feared, or they would not have besought Him, or they would not so much as have thought of His being able to do any such thing.

Therefore He sleeps, to give occasion for their timidity, and to make their perception of what was happening more distinct. For a man looks not with the same eyes on what happens in the persons of others, as in his own. Therefore since they had seen all benefitted, while themselves had enjoyed no benefit, and were supine (for neither were they lame, nor had they any other such infirmity); and it was meet they should enjoy His benefits by their own perception: He permits the storm, that by their deliverance they might attain to a clearer perception of the benefit.

Therefore neither doth He this in the presence of the multitudes, that they might not be condemned for little faith, but He has them apart, and corrects them, and before the tempest of the waters He puts an end to the tempests of their soul, rebuking them, and saying,

"Why are ye fearful, O ye of little faith:" instructing them also, that men's fear is wrought not by the approach of the temptations, but by the weakness of their mind.

But should any one say, that it was not fearfulness, or little faith, to come near and awaken Him; I would say this, that that very thing was an especial sign of their wanting the right opinion concerning Him. That is, His power to rebuke when awakened they knew, but that He could do so even sleeping, they knew not as yet.

And why at all marvel that it was so now, when even after many other miracles their impressions were still rather imperfect? wherefore also they are often rebuked; as when He saith, "Are ye also yet without understanding?" Marvel not then, if when the disciples were in such imperfect dispositions, the multitudes had no exalted imagination of Him. For

"They marvelled, saying, What manner of man is this, that even the sea and the winds obey Him?"

But Christ chode not with them for calling Him a man, but waited to teach them by His signs, that their supposition was mistaken. But from what did they think Him a man? First from His appearance, then from His sleeping, and His making use of a ship. So on this account they were cast into perplexity, saying, "What manner of man is this?" since while the sleep and the outward appearance showed man, the sea and the calm declared Him God.

For because Moses had once done some such thing, in this regard also doth He signify His own superiority, and that the one works miracles as a slave, the other as Lord. Thus, He put forth no rod, as Moses did, neither did He stretch forth His hands to Heaven, nor did He need any prayer, but, as was meet for a master commanding His handmaid, or a creator His creature, so did He quiet and curb it by word and command only; and all the surge was straightway at an end, and not one trace of the disturbance remained. For this the evangelist declared saying, "And there was a great calm." And that which had been spoken of the Father as a great thing, this He showed forth again by His works. And what had been said concerning Him? "He spake," it saith, "and the stormy wind ceased." So here likewise, He spake, and "there was a great calm." And for this most of all did the multitudes marvel at him; who would not have marvelled, had He done it in such manner as did Moses.

2. Now when He is departed from the sea, there follows another miracle yet more awful. For men possessed with devils, like wicked runaways at sight of their master, said,

"What have we to do with Thee, Jesus, Thou Son of God? Art Thou come hither to torment us before the time?"

For, because the multitudes called Him man, the devils came proclaiming His Godhead, and they that heard not the sea swelling and subsiding, heard from the devils the same cry, as it by its calm was loudly uttering.

Then, lest the thing might seem to come of flattery, according to their actual experience they cry out and say, "Art Thou come hither to torment us before the time?" With this view, then, their enmity is avowed beforehand, that their entreaty may not incur suspicion. For indeed they were invisibly receiving stripes, and the sea was not in such a storm as they; galled, and inflamed, and suffering things intolerable from His mere presence. Accordingly, no man daring to bring them to Him, Christ of Himself goes unto them.

And Matthew indeed relates that they said, "Art Thou come hither before the time to torment us?" but the other evangelists have added, that they also entreated and adjured Him not to cast them into the deep. For they supposed that their punishment was now close upon them, and feared, as even now about to fall into vengeance.

And though Luke and those who follow him say that it was one person, but this evangelist two, this doth not exhibit any discrepancy at all. I grant if they had said, there was only one, and no other, they would appear to disagree with Matthew; but if that spake of the one, this of the two, the statement comes not of disagreement, but of a different manner of narration. That is, I for my part think, Luke singled out the fiercest one of them for his narrative, wherefore also in more tragical wise doth he report their miserable case; as, for instance, that bursting his bonds and chains he used to wander about the wilderness. And Mark saith, that he also cut himself with the stones.

And their words too are such as well betray their implacable and shameless nature. For, saith he, "Art thou come hither to torment us before the time?" You see, that they had sinned, they could not deny, but they demand not to suffer their punishment before the time. For, since He had caught them in the act of perpetrating those horrors so incurable and lawless, and deforming and punishing His creature in every way; and they supposed that He, for the excess of their crimes, would not await the time of their punishment: therefore they besought and entreated Him: and they that endured not even bands of iron come bound, and they that run about the mountains, are gone forth into the plain; and those who hinder all others from passing, at sight of Him blocking up the way, stand still.

3. But what can be the reason that they love also to dwell in the tombs? They would fain suggest to the multitude a pernicious opinion, as though the souls of the dead become demons, which God forbid we should ever admit into our conception. "But what then wilt thou say," one may ask, "when many of the sorcerers take children and slay them, in order to have the soul afterwards to assist them?" Why, whence is this evident? for of their slaying them, indeed, many tell us, but as to the souls of the slain being with them, whence knowest thou it, I pray thee? "The possessed themselves," it is replied, "cry out, I am the soul of such a one." But this too is a kind of stage-play, and devilish deceit. For it is not the spirit of the dead that cries out, but the evil spirit that feigns these things in order to deceive the hearers. For if it were possible for a soul to enter into the substance of an evil spirit, much more into its own body.

And besides, it stands not to reason that the injured soul should co-operate with the wrong-doer, or that a man should be able to change an incorporeal power into another substance. For if in bodies this were impossible, and one could not make a man's body become that of an ass; much more were this impossible in the invisible soul; neither could one transform it into the substance of an evil spirit. So that these are the sayings of besotted old wives, and spectres to frighten children.

Nor indeed is it possible for a soul, torn away from the body, to wander here any more. For "the souls of the righteous are in the hand of God;" and if of the righteous, then those children's souls also; for neither are they wicked: and the souls too of sinners are straightway led away hence. And it is evident from Lazarus and the rich man; and elsewhere too Christ saith, "This day they require thy soul of thee." And it may not be that a soul, when it is gone forth from the body, should wander here; nor is the reason hard to see. For if we, going about on the earth which is familiar and well known to us, being encompassed with a body, when we are journeying in a strange road, know not which way to go unless we have some one to lead us; how should the soul, being rent away from the body, and having gone out from all her accustomed region, know where to walk without one to show her the way?

And from many other things too one might perceive, that it is not possible for a disembodied soul to remain here. For both Stephen saith, "Receive my spirit;" and Paul, "To depart and to be with Christ is far better;" and of the patriarch too the Scripture saith, that "he was gathered unto his fathers, being cherished in a good old age." And as to the proof, that neither can the souls of sinners continue here; hear the rich man making much entreaty for this, and not obtaining it; since had it been at all possible, he would have come, and have told what had come to pass there. Whence it is evident that after their departure hence our souls are led away into some place, having no more power of themselves to come back again, but awaiting that dreadful day.

4. Now, should any one say, "And wherefore did Christ fulfill the devils' request, suffering them to depart into the herd of swine?" this would be our reply, that He did so, not as yielding to them, but as providing for many objects thereby. One, to teach them that are delivered from those wicked tyrants, how great the malice of their insidious enemies: another, that all might learn, how not even against swine are they bold, except He allow them; a third, that they would have treated those men more grievously than the swine, unless even in their calamity they had enjoyed much of God's providential care. For that they hate us more than the brutes is surely evident to every man. So then they that spared not the swine, but in one moment of time cast them all down the precipice, much more would they have done so to the men whom they possessed, leading them towards the desert, and carrying them away, unless even in their very tyranny the guardian care of God had abounded, to curb and check the excess of their violence. Whence it is manifest that there is no one, who doth not enjoy the benefit of God's providence. And if not all alike, nor after one manner, this is itself a very great instance of providence; in that according to each man's profit, the work also of providence is displayed.

And besides what hath been mentioned, there is another thing also, which we learn from this; that His providence is not only over all in common, but also over each in particular; which He also declared with respect to His disciples, saying, "But the very hairs of your head are numbered." And from these demoniacs too, one may clearly perceive this; who would have "been choked" long before, if they had not enjoyed the benefit of much tender care from above.

For these reasons then He suffered them to depart into the herd of swine, and that they also who dwelt in those places should learn His power. For where His name was great, He did not greatly display Himself: but where no one knew Him, but they were still in an insensible condition, He made His miracles to shine out, so as to bring them over to the knowledge of His Godhead. For it is evident from the event that the inhabitants of that city were a sort of senseless people; for when they ought to have adored and marvelled at His power, they sent Him away, and "besought Him that He would depart out of their coasts."

But for what intent did the devils destroy the swine? Everywhere they have labored to drive men to dismay, and everywhere they rejoice in destruction. This, for instance, the devil did with respect to Job, although in that case too God suffered it, but neither in that case as complying with the devil, but willing to show His own servant the more glorious, cutting off from the evil spirit all pretext for his shamelessness, and turning on his own head what was done against the righteous man. Because now also the contrary of what they wished came to pass. For the power of Christ was gloriously proclaimed, and the wickedness of the demons, from which He delivered those possessed by them, was more plainly indicated; and how they want power to touch even swine, without permission from the God of all.

And if any would take these things in a hidden sense, there is nothing to hinder. For the history indeed is this, but we are to know assuredly, that the swinish sort of men are especially liable to the operations of the demons. And as long as they are men that suffer such things, they are often able yet to prevail; but if they are become altogether swine, they are not only possessed, but are also cast down the precipice. And besides, lest any should suppose what was done to be mere acting, instead of distinctly believing that the devils were gone out; by the death of the swine this is rendered manifest.

And mark also His meekness together with His power. For when the inhabitants of that country, after having received such benefits, were driving Him away, He resisted not, but retired, and left those who had shown themselves unworthy of His teaching, having given them for teachers them that had been freed from the demons, and the swine-herds, that they might of them learn all that had happened; whilst Himself retiring leaves the fear vigorous in them. For the greatness withal of the loss was spreading the fame of what had been done, and the event penetrated their mind. And from many quarters were wafted sounds, proclaiming the strangeness of the miracle; from the cured, and from the drowned, from the owners of the swine, from the men that were feeding them.

5. These things any one may see happening now also, even many in the tombs possessed of evil spirits, whom nothing restrains from their madness; not iron, nor chain, nor multitude of men, nor advice, nor admonition, nor terror, nor threat, nor any other such thing.

For so when any man is dissolute, eager after all embraces, he differs not at all from the demoniac, but goes about naked like him, clad indeed in garments, but deprived of the true covering, and stripped of his proper glory; cutting himself not with stones, but with sins more hurtful than many stones. Who then shall be able to bind such a one? Who, to stay his unseemliness and frenzy, his way of never coming to himself, but forever haunting the tombs? For such are the resorts of the harlots, full of much evil savor, of much rottenness.

And what of the covetous man? Is he not like this? For who will be able ever to bind him? Are there not fears and daily threats, and admonitions, and counsels? Nay, all these bonds he bursts asunder; and if any one come to set him free, he adjures him that he may not be freed, accounting it the greatest torture not to be in torture: than which what can be more wretched? For as to that evil spirit, even though he despised men, yet he yielded to the command of Christ, and quickly sprang out of the man's body; but this man yields not even to His commandment. See at least how he daily hears Him saying, "Ye cannot serve God and mammon," and threatening hell, and the incurable torments, and obeys not: not that He is stronger than Christ, but because against our will Christ corrects us not. Therefore such men live as in desert places, though they be in the midst of cities. For who, that hath reason, would choose to be with such men? I for my part would sooner consent to dwell with ten thousand demoniacs, than with one diseased in this way.

And that I am not mistaken in saying this, is manifest from their respective feelings. For these last account him an enemy that hath done them no wrong, and desire even to take him for a slave when he is free, and encompass him with ten thousand evils; but the demoniacs do no such thing, but toss their disease to and for within themselves. And while these overturn many houses, and cause the name of God to be blasphemed, and are a pest to the city and to the whole earth; they that are troubled by evil spirits, deserve rather our pity and our tears. And the one for the more part act in insensibility, but the others are frantic while they reason, keeping their orgies in the midst of cities, and maddened with some new kind of madness. For what do all the demoniacs so bad, as what Judas dared to do, when he showed forth that extremity of wickedness? And all too that imitate him, like fierce wild beasts escaped from their cage, trouble their cities, no man restraining them. For these also have bonds upon them on every side; such as the fears of the judges, the threatening of the laws, the condemnation of the multitude, and other things more than these; yet bursting asunder even these, they turn all things upside down. And should any one remove these altogether from them, then would he know assuredly the demon that is in them to be far fiercer, and more frantic than he who is just now gone forth.

But since this may not be, let us for the time suppose it for argument's sake: and let us take off from him all his chains, and then shall we clearly know his manifest madness. But be not afraid of the monster, when we uncover it; for it is the representation in word, not the thing in truth. Let there be then some man, darting fire from his eyes, black, having from either shoulder serpents hanging down instead of hands; and let him have also a mouth, with sharp swords set in it instead of teeth, and for a tongue a gushing fountain of poison and some baneful drug; and a belly more consuming than any furnace, devouring all that is cast unto it, and a sort of winged feet more vehement than any flame; and let his face be made up of a dog and of a wolf; and let him utter nothing human, but something discordant, and unpleasing, and terrible; and let him have also in his hands a firebrand. Perhaps what we have said seems to you to be terrible, but we have not even yet fashioned him worthily; for together with these things we must add others besides. I mean, that he is also to slay them that meet with him, to devour them, to fasten upon their flesh.

Yet is the covetous man much more fierce even than this, assailing all like hell, swallowing all up, going about a common enemy to the race of men. Why, he would have no man exist, that he may possess all things. And he stops not even at this, but when in his longing he shall have destroyed all men, he longs also to mar the substance of the earth, and to see it all become gold; nay, not the earth only, but hills also, and woods, and fountains, and in a word all things that appear.

And to convince you that not even yet have we set forth his madness, let there be no man to accuse and frighten him, but take away the terror of the laws in supposition awhile, and thou wilt see him snatching up a sword, laying violent hands on all, and sparing none; neither friend, nor kinsman, nor brother, nor even his very parent. Nay rather, in this case there is not even need of supposing, but let us ask him, if he is not for ever framing to himself such imaginations, and if he does not in thought range among all men to destroy them; both friends and kinsmen, and even his very parents. Nay rather there is no need even to ask, because in truth all men know that they who are under the power of this disease are wearied even of their father's old age; and that which is sweet, and universally desirable, the having children, they esteem grievous and unwelcome: many at least with this view have even paid money to be childless, and have maimed their nature, not only by slaying their children after birth, but by not suffering them even to be born at all.

6. Marvel not, therefore, if we have thus sketched the covetous man (for in truth he is far worse than what we have said); but let us consider how we shall deliver him from the demon. How then shall we deliver him? If he may be clearly made aware, that his love of money stands very much in his way in respect of this very object, the gaining of money; for they that wish to gain in little things undergo great losses; whence accordingly a proverb hath been put forth to this same effect. Many, for instance, on many occasions, wishing to lend at large usury, and through the expectation of gain not having inquired about them who receive their money, have together with the interest lost also all their capital. Others again falling into dangers, and not willing to give up a little have together with the substance lost their life too.

Again, when it has been in men's power to purchase either gainful offices, or some other such thing, by some trifling meanness they have lost all. For because they know not how to sow, but have ever practised reaping, they of course continually fail of their harvest. For no man can be always reaping, as neither can he be always gaining. Therefore since they are not willing to spend, neither do they know how to gain. And should they have to take a wife, the same thing again befalls them; for either they are deceived into taking a poor wife for a rich one, or when they have brought home one that is rich, but full of faults without number, here too they have incurred more loss than gain. For it is not superfluity but virtue, that causes wealth. For what profit is there of her wealth, when she is expensive and dissolute, and scatters all abroad more vehemently than any wind? What if she be unchaste, and bring in numberless lovers? what if she be drunken? Will she not quickly make her husband the poorest of men? But they do not only marry, but also buy at great risk, from their great covetousness, laboring to find not good slaves, but cheap ones.

Consider then all these things (for the words concerning hell and the kingdom ye are not yet able to hear), and bearing in mind the losses which ye have often undergone from your love of money, in loans, and in purchases, and in marriages, and in offices of power, and in all the rest; withdraw yourselves from doating on money.

For so shall ye be able to live the present life in security, and after a little advance to hear also the words that treat on self-government, and see through and look upon the very Sun of Righteousness, and to attain unto the good things promised by Him; unto which God grant we may all attain, by the grace and love towards man of our Lord Jesus Christ, to whom be glory and might forever and ever. Amen.

HOMILY XXIX

MATT. IX. 1, 2

"And He entered into a ship, and passed over, and came into His own city. And, behold, they brought to Him a man sick of the palsy, lying on a bed: and Jesus seeing their faith said unto the sick of the palsy; Son, be of good cheer; thy sins be forgiven thee."

By His own city here he means Capernaum. For that which gave Him birth was Bethlehem; that which brought Him up, Nazareth; that which had Him continually inhabiting it, Capernaum.

This paralytic, however, was different from that one who is set forth in John. For he lay at the pool, but this at Capernaum; and that man had his infirmity thirty and eight years, but concerning this, no such thing is mentioned; and the other was in a state destitute of protectors, but this had some to take care of him, who also took him up, and carried him. And to this He saith, "Son, thy sins be forgiven thee," but to that He saith, "Wilt thou be made whole?" And the other He healed on a sabbath day, but this not on a sabbath, for else the Jews would have laid this also to His charge; and in the case of this man they were silent, but in that of the other they were instant in persecuting him.

And this I have said, not without purpose, lest any one should think there is a discrepancy from suspecting it to be one and the same paralytic.

But do thou, I pray thee, mark the humility and meekness of our Lord. For He had also before this put away the multitudes from Him, and moreover when sent away by them at Gadara, He withstood not, but retired, not however to any great distance.

And again He entered into the ship and passed over, when He might have gone over afoot. For it was His will not to be always doing miracles, that He might not injure the doctrine of His humanity.

Now Matthew indeed saith, that "they brought him," but the others, that they also broke up the roof, and let him down. And they put the sick man before Christ, saying nothing, but committing the whole to Him. For though in the beginning He Himself went about, and did not require so much faith of them that came unto Him; yet in this case they both approached Him, and had faith required on their part. For, "Seeing," it is said, "their faith;" that is, the faith of them that had let the man down. For He doth not on all occasions require faith on the part of the sick only: as for instance, when they are insane, or in any other way, through their disease, are out of their own control. Or rather, in this case the sick man too had part in the faith; for he would not have suffered himself to be let down, unless he had believed.

Forasmuch then as they had evinced so great faith, He also evinces His own power, with all authority absolving his sins, and signifying in all ways that He is equal in honor with Him that begat Him. And mark; He implied it from the beginning, by His teaching, when He taught them as one having authority; by the leper, when He said, "I will, be thou clean," by the centurion, when upon his saying, "Speak the word only, and my servant shall be healed, He marvelled at him," and celebrated him above all men; by the sea, when He curbed it with a mere word; by the devils, when they acknowledged Him as their judge, and He cast them out with great authority.

Here again in another and a greater way He constrains His very enemies to confess His equality in honor, and by their own mouth He makes it manifest. For He, to signify His indifference to honor (for there stood a great company of spectators shutting up the entrance, wherefore also they let him down from above), did not straightway hasten to heal the visible body, but He takes His occasion from them; and He healed first that which is invisible, the soul, by forgiving his sins; which indeed saved the other, but brought no great glory to Himself. They themselves rather, troubled by their malice, and wishing to assail Him, caused even against their will what was done to be conspicuous. He, in fact, in His abundance of counsel, made use of their envy for the manifestation of the miracle.

Upon their murmuring, then, and saying, "This man blasphemeth; who can forgive sins but God only?" let us see what He saith. Did He indeed take away the suspicion? And yet if He were not equal, He should have said, "Why fix upon me a notion which is not convenient? I am far from this power." But now hath He said none of these things, but quite the contrary He hath both affirmed and ratified, as well by His own voice, as by the performance of the miracle. Thus, it appearing that His saying certain things of Himself gave disgust to his hearers, He affirms what He had to say concerning Himself by the others; and what is truly marvellous, not by His friends only, but also by His enemies; for this is the excellency of His wisdom. By His friends on the one hand, when He said, "I will, be thou clean," and when He said, "I have not found so great faith, no, not in Israel;" but by His enemies, now. For because they had said, "No man can forgive sins but God only," He subjoined,

"But that ye may know that the Son of Man hath power to forgive sins upon the earth (then saith He to the sick of the palsy), Arise, and take up thy bed, and go unto thine house."

And not here only, but also in another case again, when they were saying, "For a good work we stone thee not, but for blasphemy, and because that thou, being a man, makest thyself God," neither in that instance did He put down this opinion, but again confirmed it, saying, "If I do not the works of my Father, believe me not; but if I do, though ye believe not me, believe the works."

2. In this case indeed He discloses also another sign, and that no small one, of His own Godhead, and of His equality in honor with the Father. For whereas they said, "To unbind sins pertains to God only," He not only unbinds sins, but also before this He makes another kind of display in a thing which pertained to God only; the publishing the secrets in the heart. For neither had they uttered what they were thinking.

For "behold, certain of the scribes," it saith, "said within themselves, This man blasphemeth. And Jesus knowing their thoughts, said, Wherefore think ye evil in your hearts?"

But that it belongs to God only to know men's secrets, hear what saith the prophet, "Thou most entirely alone knowest the hearts;" and again, "God trieth the hearts and reins; " and Jeremiah too saith, "The heart is deep above all things, and it is man, and who shall know him?" and, "Man shall look on the face, but God on the heart." And by many things one may see, that to know what is in the mind belongs to God alone.

Implying therefore that He is God, equal to Him that begat Him; what things they were reasoning in themselves (for through fear of the multitude, they durst not utter their mind), this their opinion He unveils and makes manifest, evincing herein also His great gentleness.

"For wherefore," saith He, "think ye evil in your hearts?"

And yet if there were cause for displeasure, it was the sick man who should have been displeased, as being altogether deceived, and should have said "One thing I came to have healed, and amendest Thou another? Why, whence is it manifest that my sins are forgiven?"

But now he for his part utters no such word, but gives himself up to the power of the healer; but these being curious and envious, plot against the good deeds of others. Wherefore He rebukes them indeed, but with all gentleness. "Why, if ye disbelieve," saith He, "what went before, and account my saying a boast; behold I add to it also another, the uncovering of your secrets; and after that again another." What then is this? The giving tone to the body of the paralyzed.

And whereas, when He spake unto the sick of the palsy, He spake without clearly manifesting His own authority: for He said not, "I forgive thee thy sins," but, "thy sins be forgiven thee:" upon their constraining, He discloses His authority more clearly, saying, "But that ye may know that the Son of Man hath power on earth to forgive sins."

Seest thou, how far He was from unwillingness to be thought equal to the Father? For He said not at all, "The Son of Man hath need of another;" or, "He hath given Him authority," but, "He hath authority." Neither doth He say it for love of honor, but "to convince you," so He speaks, "that I do not blaspheme in making myself equal with God."

Thus everywhere His will is to offer proofs clear and indisputable; as when He saith, "Go thy way, show thyself to the priest;" and when He points to Peter's wife's mother ministering, and permits the swine to cast themselves down headlong. And in the same manner here also; first, for a certain token of the forgiveness of his sins, He provides the giving tone to his body: and of that again, his carrying his bed; to hinder the fact from being thought a mere fancy. And He doeth not this, before He had asked them a question. "For whether is easier," saith He, "to say, Thy sins be forgiven thee? or to say, Take up thy bed, and go unto thine house?" Now what He saith is like this, "Which seems to you easier, to bind up a disorganized body, or to undo the sins of a soul? It is quite manifest; to bind up a body. For by how much a soul is better than a body, by so much is the doing away sins a greater work than this; but because the one is unseen, the other in sight, I throw in that, which although an inferior thing, is yet more open to sense; that the greater also and the unseen may thereby receive its proof;" thus by His works anticipating even now the revelation of what had been said by John, that "He taketh away the sins of the world."

Well then, having raised him up, He sends him to his house; here again signifying His unboastfulness, and that the event was not a mere imagination; for He makes the same persons witnesses of his infirmity, and also of his health. For I indeed had desired, saith He, through thy calamity to heal those also, that seem to be in health, but are diseased in mind; but since they will not, depart thou home, to heal them that are there.

Seest thou how He indicates Him to be Creator both of souls and bodies? He heals therefore the palsy in each of the two substances, and makes the invisible evident by that which is in sight. But nevertheless they still creep upon the earth.

"For when the multitudes saw it, they marvelled, and glorified God, which" (it is said) "had given such power unto men:" for the flesh was an offense unto them. But He did not rebuke them, but proceeds by His works to arouse them, and exalt their thoughts. Since for the time it was no small thing for

Him to be thought greater than all men, as having come from God. For had they well established these things in their own minds, going on orderly they would have known, that He was even the Son of God. But they did not retain these things clearly, wherefore neither were they able to approach Him. For they said again, "This man is not of God;" "how is this man of God?" And they were continually harping on these things, putting them forward as cloaks for their own passions.

3. Which thing many now also do; and thinking to avenge God, fulfill their own passions, when they ought to go about all with moderation. For even the God of all, having power to launch His thunderbolt against them that blaspheme Him, makes the sun to rise, and sends forth the showers, and affords them all other things in abundance; whom we ought to imitate, and so to entreat, advise, admonish, with meekness, not angry, not making ourselves wild beasts.

For no harm at all ensues unto God by their blasphemy, that thou shouldest be angered, but he who blasphemed hath himself also received the wound. Wherefore groan, bewail, for the calamity indeed deserves tears. And the wounded man, again,—noth ing can so heal him as gentleness: gentleness, I say, which is mightier than any force.

See, for example, how He Himself, the insulted one, discourses with us, both in the Old Testament, and in the New; in the one saying, "O my people, what have I done unto thee?" in the other, "Saul, Saul, why persecutest thou me." And Paul too bids, "In meekness instruct those that oppose themselves." And Christ again, when His disciples had come to Him, requiring fire to come down from heaven, strongly rebuked them, saying, "Ye know not what manner of spirit ye are of."

And here again He said not, "O accursed, and sorcerers as ye are; O ye envious, and enemies of men's salvation;" but, "Wherefore think ye evil in your hearts?"

We must, you see, use gentleness to eradicate the disease. Since he who is become better through the fear of man, will quickly return to wickedness again. For this cause He commanded also the tares to be left, giving an appointed day of repentance. Yea, and many of them in fact repented, and became good, who before were bad; as for instance, Paul, the Publican, the Thief; for these being really tares turned into kindly wheat. Because, although in the seeds this cannot be, yet in the human will it is both manageable and easy; for our will is bound by no limits of nature, but hath freedom of choice for its privilege.

Accordingly, when thou seest an enemy of the truth, wait on him, take care of him, lead him back into virtue, by showing forth an excellent life, by applying "speech that cannot be condemned," by bestowing attention and tender care, by trying every means of amendment, in imitation of the best physicians. For neither do they cure in one manner only, but when they see the wound not yield to the first remedy, they add another, and after that again another; and now they use the knife, and now bind up. And do thou accordingly, having become a physician of souls, put in practice every mode of cure according to Christ's laws; that thou mayest receive the reward both of saving thyself and of profiting others, doing all to the glory of God, and so being glorified also thyself. "For them that glorify me," saith He, "I will glorify; and they that despise me, shall be lightly esteemed."

Let us, I say, do all things unto His glory; that we may attain unto that blessed portion, unto which God grant we may all attain, by the grace and love towards man of our Lord Jesus Christ, to whom be glory and might forever and ever. Amen.

HOMILY XXX

MATT. IX. 9

"And as Jesus passed forth from thence, He saw a man sitting at the receipt of custom, named Matthew; and He saith unto him, Follow me."

For when He had performed the miracle, He did not remain, lest, being in sight, He should kindle their jealousy the more; but He indulges them by retiring, and soothing their passion. This then let us also do, not encountering them that are plotting against us; let us rather soothe their wound, giving way and relaxing their vehemence.

But wherefore did He not call him together with Peter and John and the rest? As in their case He had come at that time, when He knew the men would obey Him; so Matthew also He then called when He was assured he would yield himself. And therefore Paul again He took, as a fisher his prey, after the resurrection. Because He who is acquainted with the hearts, and knows the secrets of each man's mind, knew also when each of these would obey. Therefore not at the beginning did He call him, when he was yet in rather a hardened state, but after His countless miracles, and the great fame concerning Him, when He knew him to have actually become more prepared for obedience.

And we have cause also to admire the self-denial of the evangelist, how he disguises not his own former life, but adds even his name, when the others had concealed him under another appellation.

But why did he say he was "sitting at the receipt of custom?" To indicate the power of Him that called him, that it was not when he had left off or forsaken this wicked trade, but from the midst of the evils He drew him up; much as He converted the blessed Paul also when frantic and raging, and darting fire; which thing he himself makes a proof of the power of Him that called him, saying to the Galatians, "Ye have heard of my conversation in time past in the Jews' religion, how that beyond measure I persecuted the church of God." And the fishermen too He called when they were in the midst of their business. But that was a craft not indeed in bad report, but of men rather rudely bred, not mingling with others, and endowed with great simplicity; whereas the pursuit now in question was one full of all insolence and boldness, and a mode of gain whereof no fair account could be given, a shameless traffic, a robbery under cloak of law: yet nevertheless He who uttered the call was ashamed of none of these things.

And why talk I of His not being ashamed of a publican? since even with regard to a harlot woman, so far from being ashamed to call her, He actually permitted her to kiss His feet, and to moisten them with her tears. Yea, for to this end He came, not to cure bodies only, but to heal likewise the wickedness of the soul. Which He did also in the case of the paralytic; and having shown clearly that He is able to forgive sins, then, not before, He comes to him whom we are now speaking of; that they might no more be troubled at seeing a publican chosen into the choir of the disciples. For He that hath power to undo all our offenses, why marvel if He even make this man an apostle?

But as thou hast seen the power of Him that called, so consider also the obedience of him that was called: how he neither resisted, nor disputing said, "What is this? Is it not indeed a deceitful calling, wherewith He calls me, being such as I am?" nay; for this humility again had been out of season: but he obeyed straightway, and did not even request to go home, and to communicate with his relations concerning this matter; as neither indeed did the fishermen; but as they left their net and their ship and their father, so did he his receipt of custom and his gain, and followed, exhibiting a mind prepared for all things; and breaking himself at once away from all worldly things, by his complete obedience he bare witness that He who called him had chosen a good time.

And wherefore can it be, one may say, that he hath not told us of the others also, how and in what manner they were called; but only of Peter and James, and John and Philip, and nowhere of the others?

Because these more than others were in so strange and mean ways of life. For there is nothing either worse than the publican's business, or more ordinary than fishing. And that Philip also was among the very ignoble, is manifest from his country. Therefore these especially they proclaim to us, with their ways of life, to show that we ought to believe them in the glorious parts of their histories also. For they who choose not to pass by any of the things which are accounted reproachful, but are exact in publishing these more than the rest, whether they relate to the Teacher or to the disciples; how can they be suspected in the parts which claim reverence? more especially since many signs and miracles are passed over by them, while the events of the cross, accounted to be reproaches, they utter with exact care and loudly; and the disciples' pursuits too, and their faults, and those of their Master's ancestry who were notorious for sins, they discover with a clear voice. Whence it is manifest that they made much account of truth, and wrote nothing for favor, nor for display.

2. Having therefore called him, He also honored him with a very great honor by partaking straightway of his table; for in this way He would both give him good hope for the future, and lead him on to a greater confidence. For not in a long time, but at once, He healed his vice. And not with him only doth He sit down to meat, but with many others also; although this very thing was accounted a charge against Him, that He chased not away the sinners. But neither do they conceal this point, what sort of blame is endeavored to be fixed on His proceedings.

Now the publicans come together as to one of the same trade; for he, exulting in the entrance of Christ, had called them all together. The fact is, Christ used to try every kind of treatment; and not when discoursing only, nor when healing, nor when reproving His enemies, but even at His morning meal, He would often correct such as were in a bad way; hereby teaching us, that every season and every work may by possibility afford us profit. And yet surely what was then set before them came of injustice and covetousness; but Christ refused not to partake of it, because the ensuing gain was to be great: yea rather He becomes partaker of the same roof and table with them that have committed such offenses. For such is the quality of a physician; unless he endure the corruption of the sick, he frees them not from their infirmity.

And yet undoubtedly He incurred hence an evil report: first by eating with him, then in Matthew's house, and thirdly, in company with many publicans. See at least how they reproach Him with this. "Behold a man gluttonous, and a wine-bibber, a friend of publicans and sinners."

Let them hear, as many as are striving to deck themselves with great honor for fasting, and let them consider that our Lord was called "a man gluttonous and a winebibber," and He was not ashamed, but overlooked all these things, that he might accomplish what He had set before him; which indeed was accordingly done. For the publican was actually converted, and thus became a better man.

And to teach thee that this great thing was wrought by his partaking of the table with Him, hear what Zacchaeus saith, another publican. I mean, when he heard Christ saying, "To-day, I must abide in thy house," the delight gave him wings, and he saith, "The half of my goods I give to the poor, and if I have taken anything from any man by false accusation, I restore him fourfold." And to him Jesus saith, "This day is salvation come to this house." So possible is it by all ways to give instruction.

But how is it, one may say, that Paul commands, "If any man that is called a brother be a fornicator or covetous, with such an one no, not to eat?" In the first place, it is not as yet manifest, whether to teachers also he gives this charge, and not rather to brethren only. Next, these were not yet of the number of the perfect, nor of those who had become brethren. And besides, Paul commands, even with respect to them that had become brethren, then to shrink from them, when they continue as they were, but these had now ceased, and were converted.

3. But none of these things shamed the Pharisees, but they accuse Him to His disciples, saying,

"Why eateth your Master with publicans and sinners?"

And when the disciples seem to be doing wrong, they intercede with Him, saying, "Behold thy disciples do that which is not lawful to do on the sabbath-day;" but here to them they discredit Him. All which was the part of men dealing craftily, and wishing to separate from the Master the choir of the disciples. What then saith Infinite Wisdom?

"They that be whole need not a physician," saith He, "but they that are sick."

See how He turned their reasoning to the opposite conclusion. That is, while they made it a charge against Him that He was in company with these men: He on the contrary saith, that His not being with them would be unworthy of Him, and of His love of man; and that to amend such persons is not only blameless, but excellent, and necessary, and deserving of all sorts of praise.

After this, that He might not seem to put them that were bidden to shame, by saying, "they that are sick;" see how He makes up for it again, by reproving the others, and saying,

"Go ye and learn what that meaneth, I will have mercy, and not sacrifice."

Now this He said, to upbraid them with their ignorance of the Scriptures. Wherefore also He orders His discourse more sharply, not Himself in anger, far from it; but so as that the publicans might not be in utter perplexity.

And yet of course He might say, "Did ye not mark, how I remitted the sins of the sick of the palsy, how I braced up his body?" But He saith no such thing, but argues with them first from men's common reasonings, and then from the Scriptures. For having said, "They that be whole need not a physician, but they that are sick;" and having covertly indicated that He Himself was the Physician; after that He said, "Go ye and learn what that meaneth, I will have mercy, and not sacrifice." Thus doth Paul also: when he had first established his reasoning by illustrations from common things, and had said, "Who feedeth a flock, and eateth not of the milk thereof?" then he brings in the Scriptures also, saying, "It is written in the law of Moses, Thou shalt not muzzle the ox that treadeth out the corn;" and again, "Even so hath the Lord ordained, that they which preach the gospel should live of the gospel."

But to His disciples not so, but He puts them in mind of His signs, saying on this wise, "Do ye not yet remember the five loaves of the five thousand, and how many baskets ye took up?" Not so however with these, but He reminds them of our common infirmity, and signifies them at any rate to be of the number of the infirm; who did not so much as know the Scriptures, but making light of the rest of virtue, laid all the stress on their sacrifices; which thing He is also earnestly intimating unto them, when He sets down in brief what had been affirmed by all the prophets, saying, "Learn ye what that meaneth, I will have mercy, and not sacrifice."

The fact is, He is signifying hereby that not He was transgressing the law, but they; as if He had said, "Wherefore accuse me? Because I bring sinners to amendment? Why then ye must accuse the Father also for this." Much as He said also elsewhere, establishing this point: "My Father worketh hitherto, and I work:" so here again, "Go ye and learn what that meaneth, I will have mercy, and not sacrifice." "For as this is His will, saith Christ, so also mine." Seest thou how the one is superfluous, the other necessary? For neither did He say, "I will have mercy, and sacrifice," but, "I will have mercy, and not sacrifice." That is, the one thing He allowed, the other He cast out; and proved that what they blamed, so far from being forbidden, was even ordained by the law, and more so than sacrifice; and He brings in the Old Testament, speaking words and ordaining laws in harmony with Himself.

Having then reproved them, both by common illustrations and by the Scriptures, He adds again,

"I am not come to call righteous men, but sinners to repentance."

And this He saith unto them in irony; as when He said, "Behold, Adam is become as one of us;" and again, "If I were hungry, I would not tell thee." For that no man on earth was righteous, Paul declared, saying, "For all have sinned, and come short of the glory of God." And by this too the others were comforted, I mean, the guests. "Why, I am so far," saith He, "from loathing sinners, that even for their sakes only am I come." Then, lest He should make them more careless, He staid not at the word "sinners," but added, "unto repentance." "For I am not come that they should continue sinners, but that they should alter, and amend."

4. He then having stopped their mouths every way, as well from the Scriptures as from the natural consequence of things; and they having nothing to say, proved as they were obnoxious to the charges which they had brought against Him, and adversaries of the law and the Old Testament; they leave Him, and again transfer their accusation to the disciples.

And Luke indeed affirms that the Pharisees said it, but this evangelist, that it was the disciples of John; but it is likely that both said it. That is, they being, as might be expected, in utter perplexity, take the other sort with them; as they did afterwards with the Herodians likewise. Since in truth John's disciples were always disposed to be jealous of Him, and reasoned against Him: being then only humbled, when first John abode in the prison. They came at least then, "and told Jesus;" but afterwards they returned to their former envy.

Now what say they? "Why do we and the Pharisees fast oft, but thy disciples fast not?"

This is the disease, which Christ long before was eradicating, in the words, "When thou fastest, anoint thy head, and wash thy face;" foreknowing the evils that spring therefrom. But yet He doth not rebuke even these, nor say, "O ye vainglorious and over-busy;" but He discourses to them with all gentleness, saying, "The children of the bride-chamber cannot fast, as long as the bridegroom is with them." Thus, when others were to be spoken for, the publicans I mean, to soothe their wounded soul, He was more severe in His reproof of their revilers; but when they were deriding Himself and His disciples, He makes His reply with all gentleness.

Now their meaning is like this; "Granted," say they, "Thou doest this as a physician; why do Thy disciples also leave fasting, and cleave to such tables?" Then, to make the accusation heavier, they put themselves first, and then the Pharisees; wishing by the comparison to aggravate the charge. For indeed "both we," it is said, "and the Pharisees, fast oft." And in truth they did fast, the one having learnt it from John, the other from the law; even as also the Pharisee said, "I fast twice in the week."

What then saith Jesus? "Can the children of the bridechamber fast, while the bridegroom is with them." Before, He called Himself a physician, but here a bridegroom; by these names revealing His unspeakable mysteries. Yet of course He might have told them, more sharply, "These things depend not on you, that you should make such laws. For of what use is fasting, when the mind is full of wickedness; when ye blame others, when ye condemn them, bearing about beams in your eyes, and do all for display? Nay, before all this ye ought to have cast out vainglory, to be proficients in all the other duties, in charity, meekness, brotherly love." However, nothing of this kind doth He say, but with all gentleness, "The children of the bridechamber cannot fast, so long as the bridegroom is with them;" recalling to their mind John's words, when he said, "He that hath the bride, is the bridegroom, but the friend of the bridegroom, which standeth and heareth Him, rejoiceth greatly because of the bridegroom's voice."

Now His meaning is like this: The present time is of joy and gladness, therefore do not bring in the things which are melancholy. For fasting is a melancholy thing, not in its own nature, but to them that are yet in rather a feeble state; for to those at least that are willing to practise self-command, the observance is exceedingly pleasant and desirable. For as when the body is in health, the spirits are high, so when the soul is well conditioned, the pleasure is greater. But according to their previous impression He saith this. So also Isaiah, discoursing of it, calls it "an affliction of the soul;" and Moses too in like manner.

Not however by this only doth He stop their mouths, but by another topic also, saying,

"Days will come, when the bridegroom shall be taken from them, and then shall they fast."

For hereby He signifies, that what they did was not of gluttony, but pertained to some marvellous dispensation. And at the same time He lays beforehand the foundation of what He was to say touching His passion, in His controversies with others instructing His disciples, and training them now to be versed in the things which are deemed sorrowful. Because for themselves already to have this said to them, would have been grievous and galling, since we know that afterwards, being uttered, it troubled them; but spoken to others, it would become rather less intolerable to them.

It being also natural for them to pride themselves on John's calamity, He from this topic represses likewise such their elation: the doctrine however of His resurrection He adds not yet, it not being yet time. For so much indeed was natural, that one supposed to be a man should die, but that other was beyond nature.

5. Then what He had done before, this He doth here again. I mean, that as He, when they were attempting to prove Him blameable for eating with sinners, proved to them on the contrary, that His proceeding was not only no blame, but an absolute praise to Him: so here too, when they wanted to show of Him, that He knows not how to manage His disciples, He signifies that such language was the part of men not knowing how to manage their inferences, but finding fault at random.

"For no man," saith He, "putteth a piece of new cloth unto an old garment."

He is again establishing His argument by illustrations from common life. And what He saith is like this, "The disciples have not yet become strong, but still need much condescension. They have not yet been renewed by the Spirit, and on persons in that state one ought not to lay any burden of injunctions."

And these things He said, setting laws and rules for His own disciples, that when they should have to receive as disciples those of all sorts that should come from the whole world, they might deal with them very gently.

"Neither do men put new wine into old bottles."

Seest thou His illustrations, how like the Old Testament? the garment? the wine skins? For Jeremiah too calls the people "a girdle," and makes mention again of "bottles" and of "wine." Thus, the discourse being about gluttony and a table, He takes His illustrations from the same.

But Luke the same words, a second and a third time and often; not however in a wearisome kind of way, but sport ively, and do thou now turn from her, now flatter and court her.

Seest thou not the painters, how much they rub out, how much they insert, when they are making a beautiful portrait? Well then, do not thou prove inferior to these. For if these, in drawing the likeness of a body, used such great diligence, how much more were it meet for us, in fashioning a soul, to use every contrivance. For if thou shouldest fashion well the form of this soul, thou wilt not see the countenance of the body looking unseemly, nor lips stained, nor a mouth like a bear's mouth dyed with blood, nor eyebrows blackened as with the smut of some kitchen vessel, nor cheeks whitened with dust like the walls of the tombs. For all these things are smut, and cinders, and dust, and signals of extreme deformity.

But stay: I have been led on unobserving, I know not how, into these expressions; and while admonishing another to teach with gentleness, I have been myself hurried away into wrath. Let us return therefore again unto the more gentle way of admonition, and let us bear with all the faults of our wives, that we may succeed in doing what we would. Seest thou not how we bear with the cries of children, when we would wean them from the breast, how we endure all for this object only, that we may persuade them to despise their former food? Thus let us do in this case also, let us bear with all the rest, that we may accomplish this. For when this hath been amended, thou wilt see the other too proceeding in due order, and thou wilt come again unto the ornaments of gold, and in the same way wilt reason concerning them likewise, and thus by little and little bringing thy wife unto the right rule, thou wilt be a beautiful painter, a faithful servant, an excellent husbandman.

Together with these things remind her also of the women of old, of Sarah, of Rebecca, both of the fair and of them that were not so, and point out how all equally practised modesty. For even Leah, the wife of the patriarch, not being fair, was not constrained to devise any such thing, but although she were uncomely, and not very much beloved by her husband, she neither devised any such thing, nor marred her countenance, but continued to preserve the lineaments thereof undisfigured, and this though brought up by Gentiles.

But thou that art a believing woman, thou that hast Christ for thine head, art thou bringing in upon us a satanic art? And dost thou not call to mind the water that dashed over thy countenance, the sacrifice that adorns thy lips, the blood that hath reddened thy tongue? For if thou wouldest consider all these things, though thou wert fond of dress to the ten thousandth degree, thou wilt not venture nor endure to put upon thee that dust and those cinders. Learn that thou hast been joined unto Christ, and refrain from this unseemliness. For neither is He delighted with these colorings, but He seeks after another beauty, of which He is in an exceeding degree a lover, I mean, that in the soul. This the prophet likewise hath charged thee to cherish, and hath said, "So shall the King have pleasure in thy beauty."

Let us not therefore be curious in making ourselves unseemly. For neither is any one of God's works imperfect, nor doth it need to be set right by thee. For not even if to an image of the emperor, after it was set up, any one were to seek to add his own work, would the attempt be safe, but he will incur extreme danger. Well then, man works and thou addest not; but doth God work, and dost thou amend it? And dost thou not consider the fire of hell? Dost thou not consider the destitution of thy soul? For on this account it is neglected, because all thy care is wasted on the flesh.

But why do I speak of the soul? For to the very flesh everything falls out contrary to what ye have sought. Consider it. Dost thou wish to appear beautiful? This shows thee uncomely. Dost thou wish to please thy husband? This rather grieves him; and causes not him only, but strangers also, to become thine accusers. Wouldest thou appear young? This will quickly bring thee to old age. Wouldest thou wish to array thyself honorably? This makes thee to be ashamed. For such an one is ashamed not only before those of her own rank, but even those of her maids who are in her secret, and those of her servants who know; and, above all, before herself.

But why need I say these things? For that which is more grievous than all I have now omitted, namely, that thou dost offend God; thou underminest modesty, kindlest the flame of jealousy, emulatest the harlot women at their brothel.

All these things then consider, ye women, and laugh to scorn the pomp of Satan and the craft of the devil; and letting go this adorning, or rather disfiguring, cultivate that beauty in your own souls which is lovely even to angels and desired of God, and delightful to your husbands; that ye may attain both unto present glory, and unto that which is to come. To which God grant that we may all attain, by the grace and love towards man of our Lord Jesus Christ, to whom be glory and might forever and ever. Amen.

HOMILY XXXI

MATT. IX. 18

"While He spake these things unto them, behold, there came in a ruler, and worshipped Him, saying, My daughter is even now dead; but come and lay Thy hand upon her, and she shall live."

The deed overtook the words; so that the mouths of the Pharisees were the more stopped. For both he that came was a ruler of the synagogue, and his affliction terrible. For the young damsel was both his only child, and twelve years old, the very flower of her age; on which account especially He raised her up again, and that immediately.

And if Luke say that men came, saying, "Trouble not the Master, for she is dead;" we will say this, that the expression, "she is even now dead," was that of one conjecturing from the time of his journeying, or exaggerating his affliction. For it is an usual thing with persons in need to heighten their own evils by their report, and to say something more than is really true, the more to attract those whom they are beseeching.

But see his dullness: how he requires of Christ two things, both His actual presence, and the laying on of His hand: and this by the way is a sign that he had left her still breathing. This Naaman also, that Syrian, required of the prophet. "For I thought," saith he, "he will surely come out, and will lay on his hand." For in truth they who are more or less dull of temper, require sight and sensible things.

And whereas Mark saith, He took the three disciples, and so doth Luke; our evangelist merely saith, "the disciples." Wherefore then did He not take with Him Matthew, though he had but just come unto Him? To bring him to a more earnest longing, and because he was yet rather in an imperfect state. For to this intent doth He honor those, that these may grow such as those are. But for him it sufficed for the present, to see what befell the woman with the issue of blood, and to be honored by His table, and by His partaking of his salt.

And when He had risen up many followed Him, as for a great miracle, both on account of the person who had come, and because the more part being of a grosser disposition were seeking not so much the care of the soul, as the healing of the body; and they flowed together, some urged by their own afflictions, some hastening to behold how other men's were cured: however, there were as yet but few in the habit of coming principally for the sake of His words and doctrine. Nevertheless, He did not suffer them to enter into the house, but His disciples only; and not even all of these, everywhere instructing us to repel the applause of the multitude.

2. "And, behold," it is said, "a woman that had an issue of blood twelve years, came behind Him, and touched the hem of His garment. For she said within herself, If I may but touch His garment, I shall be whole."

Wherefore did she not approach Him boldly? She was ashamed on account of her affliction, accounting herself to be unclean. For if the menstruous woman was judged not to be clean, much more would she have the same thought, who was afflicted with such a disease; since in fact that complaint was under the law accounted a great uncleanness. Therefore she lies hidden, and conceals herself. For neither had she as yet the proper and correct opinion concerning Him: else she would not have thought to be concealed. And this is the first woman that came unto Him in public, having heard of course that He heals women also, and that He is on His way to the little daughter that was dead.

And she durst not invite Him to her house, although she was wealthy; nay, neither did she approach publicly, but secretly with faith she touched His garments. For she did not doubt, nor say in herself, "Shall I indeed be delivered from the disease? shall I indeed fail of deliverance?" But confident of her health, she so approached Him. "For she said," we read, "in herself, If I may only touch His garment, I shall be whole." Yea, for she saw out of what manner of house He was come, that of the publicans, and who they were that followed Him, sinners and publicans; and all these things made her to be of good hope.

What then doth Christ? He suffers her not to be hid, but brings her into the midst, and makes her manifest for many purposes.

It is true indeed that some of the senseless ones say, "He does this for love of glory. For why," say they, "did He not suffer her to be hid?" What sayest thou, unholy, yea, all unholy one? He that enjoins silence, He that passes by miracles innumerable, is He in love with glory?

For what intent then doth He bring her forward? In the first place He puts an end to the woman's fear, lest being pricked by her conscience, as having stolen the gift, she should abide in agony. In the second place, He sets her right, in respect of her thinking to be hid. Thirdly, He exhibits her faith to all, so as to provoke the rest also to emulation; and His staying of the fountains of her blood was no greater sign than He affords in signifying His knowledge of all things. Moreover the ruler of the synagogue, who was on the point of thorough unbelief, and so of utter ruin, He corrects by the woman. Since both they that came said, "Trouble not the Master, for the damsel is dead;" and those in the house laughed Him to scorn, when He said, "She sleepeth;" and it was likely that the father too should have experienced some such feeling. Therefore to correct this weakness beforehand, He brings forward the simple woman. For as to that ruler being quite of the grosser sort, hear what He saith unto him: "Fear not, do thou believe only, and she shall be made whole."

Thus He waited also on purpose for death to come on, and that then He should arrive; in order that the proof of the resurrection might be distinct. With this view He both walks more leisurely, and discourses more with the woman; that He might give time for the damsel to die, and for those to come, who told of it, and said, "Trouble not the Master." This again surely the evangelist obscurely signifies, when he saith, "While He yet spake, there came from the house certain which said, Thy daughter is dead, trouble not the Master." For His will was that her death should be believed, that her resurrection might not be suspected. And this He doth in every instance. So also in the case of Lazarus, He waited a first and a second and a third day.

On account then of all these things He brings her forward, and saith, "Daughter, be of good cheer," even as He had said also to the paralyzed person, "Son, be of good cheer." Because in truth the woman was exceedingly alarmed; therefore He saith, "be of good cheer," and He calls her "daughter;" for her faith had made her a daughter. After that comes also her praise: "Thy faith hath made thee whole."

But Luke tells us also other things more than these concerning the woman. Thus, when she had approached Him, saith he, and had received her health, Christ did not immediately call her, but first He saith, "Which is he that touched me?" Then when Peter and they that were with Him said, Master, the multitude throng Thee, and press Thee, and sayest Thou, who touched me?" (which was a very sure sign both that He was encompassed with real flesh, and that He trampled on all vainglory, for they did not follow Him at all afar off, but thronged Him on every side); He for His part continued to say, "Somebody hath touched me, for I perceive that virtue is gone out of me;" answering after a grosser manner according to the impression of His hearers. But these things He said, that He might also induce her of herself to make confession. For on this account neither did He immediately convict her, in order that having signified that He knows all things clearly, He might induce her of her own accord to publish all, and work upon her to proclaim herself what had been done, and that He might not incur suspicion by saying it.

Seest thou the woman superior to the ruler of the synagogue? She detained Him not, she took no hold of Him, but touched Him only with the end of her fingers, and though she came later, she first went away healed. And he indeed was bringing the Physician altogether to his house, but for her a mere touch suffered. For though she was bound by her affliction, yet her faith had given her wings. And mark how He comforts her, saying, "Thy faith hath saved thee." Now surely, had He drawn her forward for display, He would not have added this; but He saith this, partly teaching the ruler of the synagogue to believe, partly proclaiming the woman's praise, and affording her by these words delight and advantage equal to her bodily health.

For that He did this as minded to glorify her, and to amend others, and not to show Himself glorious, is manifest from hence; that He indeed would have been equally an object of admiration even without this (for the miracles were pouring around Him faster than the snow-flakes, and He both had done and was to do far greater things than these): but the woman, had this not happened, would have gone away hid, deprived of those great praises. For this cause He brought her forward, and proclaimed her praise, and cast out her fear, (for "she came," it is said, "trembling"); and He caused her to be of good courage, and together with health of body, He gave her also other provisions for her journey, in that He said, "Go in peace."

3. "And when He came into the ruler's house, and saw the minstrels and the people making a noise, He saith unto them, Give place, for the maid is not dead, but sleepeth. And they laughed Him to scorn."

Noble tokens, surely, these, of the rulers of synagogues; in the moment of her death pipes and cymbals raising a dirge! What then doth Christ? All the rest He cast out, but the parents He brought in; to leave no room for saying that He healed her in any other way. And before her resurrection too, He raises her in His word; saying, "The maid is not dead, but sleepeth." And in many instances besides He doeth this. As then on the sea He expels tumult from the mind of the by-standers, at the same time both signifying that it is easy for Him to raise the dead (which same thing He did with respect to Lazarus also, saying, "Our friend Lazarus sleepeth ;" and also teaching us not to fear death; for that it is not death, but is henceforth become a sleep. Thus, since He Himself was to die, He doth in the persons of others prepare His disciples beforehand to be of good courage, and to bear the end meekly. Since in truth, when He had come, death was from that time forward a sleep.

But yet they laughed Him to scorn: He however was not indignant at being disbelieved by those for whom He was a little afterwards to work miracles; neither did He rebuke their laughter, in order that both it and the pipes, and the cymbals, and all the other things, might be a sure proof of her death. For since for the most part, after the miracles are done, men disbelieve, He takes them beforehand by their own answers; which was done in the case both of Lazarus and of Moses. For to Moses first He saith, "What is that in thine hand?" in order that when he saw it become a serpent, He should not forget that it was a rod before, but being reminded of his own saying, might be amazed at what was done. And with regard to Lazarus He saith, "Where have ye laid him?" that they who had said, "Come and see," and "he stinketh, for he hath been dead four days," might no longer be able to disbelieve His having raised a dead man.

Seeing then the cymbals and the multitude, He put them all out, and in the presence of the parents works the miracle; not introducing another soul, but recalling the same that had gone out, and awakening her as it were out of a sleep.

And He holds her by the hand, assuring the beholders; so as by that sight to make a way for the belief of her resurrection. For whereas the father said, "Lay thy hand upon her;" He on His part doth somewhat more, for He lays no hand on her, but rather takes hold of her, and raises her, implying that to Him all things are ready. And He not only raises her up, but also commands to give her meat, that the event might not seem to be an illusion. And He doth not give it Himself, but commands them; as also with regard to Lazarus He said, "Loose him, and let him go," and afterwards makes him partaker of His table.

For so is He wont always to establish both points, making out with all completeness the demonstration alike of the death and of the resurrection.

But do thou mark, I pray thee, not her resurrection only, but also His commanding "to tell no man;" and by all learn thou this especially, His freedom from haughtiness and vainglory. And withal learn this other thing also, that He cast them that were beating themselves out of the house, and declared them unworthy of such a sight; and do not thou go out with the minstrels, but remain with Peter, and John, and James.

For if He cast them out then, much more now. For then it was not yet manifest that death was become a sleep, but now this is clearer than the very sun itself. But is it that He hath not raised thy daughter now? But surely He will raise her, and with more abundant glory. For that damsel, when she had risen, died again; but thy child, if she rise again, abides thenceforth in immortal being.

4. Let no man therefore beat himself any more, nor wail, neither disparage Christ's achievement. For indeed He overcame death. Why then dost thou wail for nought? The thing is become a sleep. Why lament and weep? Why, even if Greeks did this, they should be laughed to scorn; but when the believer behaves himself unseemly in these things, what plea hath he? What excuse will there be for them that are guilty of such folly, and this, after so long a time, and so clear proof of the resurrection?

But thou, as though laboring to add to the charge against thee, dost also bring us in heathen women singing dirges, to kindle thy feelings, and to stir up the furnace thoroughly: and thou hearkenest not to Paul, saying, "What concord hath Christ with Belial? or what part hath he that believeth with an infidel?"

And while the children of heathens, who know nothing of resurrection, do yet find words of consolation, saying, "Bear it manfully, for it is not possible to undo what hath taken place, nor to amend it by lamentations;" art not thou, who hearest sayings wiser and better than these, ashamed to behave thyself more unseemly than they? For we say not at all, "Bear it manfully, because it is not possible to undo what hath taken place," but, "bear it manfully, because he will surely rise again;" the child sleeps and is not dead; he is at rest and hath not perished. For resurrection will be his final lot, and eternal life, and immortality, and an angel's portion. Hearest thou not the Psalm that saith, "Return unto thy rest, O my soul, for the Lord hath dealt bountifully with thee?" God calleth it "bountiful dealing," and dost thou make lamentation?

And what more couldest thou have done, if thou wert a foe and an enemy of the dead? Why, if there must be mourning, it is the devil that ought to mourn. He may beat himself, he may wail, at our journeying to greater blessings. This lamentation becomes his wickedness, not thee, who art going to be crowned and to rest. Yea, for death is a fair haven. Consider, at any rate, with how many evils our present life is filled; reflect how often thou thyself hast cursed our present life. For indeed things go on to worse, and from the very beginning thou wert involved in no small condemnation. For, saith He, "In sorrow thou shalt bring forth children;" and, "In the sweat of thy face shalt thou eat thy bread;" and, "In the world ye shall have tribulation."

But of our state there, no such word at all is spoken, but all the contrary; that "grief and sorrow and sighing have fled away." And that "men shall come from the east and from the west, and shall recline in the bosoms of Abraham and Isaac and Jacob." And that the region there is a spiritual bride-chamber, and bright lamps, and a translation to Heaven.

5. Why then disgrace the departed? Why dispose the rest to fear and tremble at death? Why cause many to accuse God, as though He had done very dreadful things? Or rather, why after this invite poor persons, and entreat priests to pray? "In order," saith he, "that the dead may depart into rest; that he may find the Judge propitious." For these things then art thou mourning and wailing? Thou art therefore fighting and warring with thyself: exciting a storm against thyself on account of his having entered into harbor.

"But what can I do?" saith he: "such a thing is nature." The blame is not nature's, neither doth it belong to the necessary consequence of the thing; but it is we that are turning all things upside down, are overcome with softness, are giving up our proper nobility, and are making the unbelievers worse. For how shall we reason with another concerning immortality? how shall we persuade the heathen, when we fear death, and shudder at it more than he? Many, for instance, among the Greeks although they knew nothing of course about immortality, have crowned themselves at the decrease of their children, and appeared in white garments, that they might reap the present glory; but thou not even for the future glory's sake ceasest thy woman's behavior and wailing.

But hast thou no heirs, nor any to succeed to thy goods? And which wouldest thou rather, that he should be heir of thy possessions, or of Heaven? And which didst thou desire, that he should succeed to the things that perish, which he must have let go soon after, or to things that remain, and are immoveable? Thou hadst him not for heir, but God had him instead of thee; he became not joint-heir with his own brethren, but he became "joint-heir with Christ."

"But to whom," saith he, "are we to leave our garments, to whom our houses, to whom our slaves and our lands?" To him again, and more securely than if he lived; for there is nothing to hinder. For if barbarians burn the goods of the departed together with them, much more were it a righteous thing for thee to send away with the dead what things he hath: not to be turned to ashes, like those, but to invest him with more glory; and that if he departed a sinner, it may do away his sins; but if righteous, that it may become an increase of reward and recompense.

But dost thou long to see him? Then live the same life with him, and thou wilt soon obtain that sacred vision.

And herewith consider this also, that though thou shouldest not hearken to us, thou wilt certainly yield to time. But no reward then for thee; for the consolation comes of the number of the days. Whereas if thou art willing now to command thyself, thou wilt gain two very great points: first, thou wilt deliver thyself from the intervening ills, next, thou wilt be crowned with the brighter crown from God. For indeed neither almsgiving nor anything else is nearly so great as bearing affliction meekly.

Bear in mind, that even the Son of God died: and He indeed for thee, but thou for thyself. And when He said, "If it be possible, let the cup pass from me," and suffered pain, and was in agony, nevertheless He shunned not the end, but underwent it, and that with its whole course of exceeding woe. That is, He did by no means simply endure death, but the most shameful death; and before His death, stripes; and before His stripes, upbraidings, and jeers, and revilings; instructing thee to bear all manfully. And though He died, and put off His body, He resumed it again in greater glory, herein also holding out to thee good hopes. If these things be not a fable, lament not. If thou account these things to be sure, weep not; but if thou dost weep, how wilt thou be able to persuade the Greek that thou believest?

6. But even so doth the event still appear intolerable to thee? Well then, for this very cause it is not meet to lament for him, for he is delivered from many such calamities. Grudge not therefore against him, neither envy him: for to ask death for yourself because of his premature end, and to lament for him that he did not live to endure many such things, is rather the part of one grudging and envying.

And think not of this, that he will no more return home: but that thyself also art a little while after to go to him. Regard not this, that he returns here no more, but that neither do these things that are seen remain such as they are, but these too are being transformed. Yea, for heaven, and earth, and sea, and all, are being put together afresh, and then shalt thou recover thy child in greater glory.

And if indeed he departed a sinner, his wickedness is stayed; for certainly, had God known that he was being converted, He would not have snatched him away before his repentance: but if he ended his life righteous, he now possesses all good in safety. Whence it is manifest that thy tears are not of kindly affection, but of unreasoning passion. For if thou lovedst the departed, thou shouldest rejoice and be glad that he is delivered from the present waves.

For what is there more, I pray thee? What is there fresh and new? Do we not see the same things daily revolving? Day and night, night and day, winter and summer, summer and winter, and nothing more. And these indeed are ever the same; but our evils are fresh, and newer. Wouldest thou then have him every day drawing up more of these things, and abiding here, and sickening, and mourning, and in fear and trembling, and enduring some of the ills of life, dreading others lest he some time endure them? Since assuredly thou canst not say this, that one sailing over this great sea might possibly be free from despondency and cares, and from all other such things.

And withal take this also into account, that thou didst not bring him forth immortal; and that if he had not died now, he must have endured it soon after. But is it that thou hadst not thy fill of him? But thou wilt of a certainty enjoy him there. But longest thou to see him here also? And what is there to hinder thee? For thou art permitted even here, if thou be watchful; for the hope of the things to come is clearer than sight.

But thou, if he were in some king's court wouldest not ever seek to see him, so long as thou heardest of his good report: and seeing him departed to the things that are far better, art thou faint-hearted about a little time; and that, when thou hast in his place one to dwell with thee?

But hast thou no husband? yet hast thou a consolation, even the Father of the orphans, and Judge of the widows. Hear even Paul pronouncing this widowhood blessed, and saying, "Now she that is a widow indeed and desolate, trusteth in the Lord." Because such an one will appear more approved, evincing as she doth greater patience. Mourn not therefore for that which is thy crown, that for which thou demandest a reward.

Since thou hast also restored His deposit, if thou hast exhibited the very thing entrusted to thee. Be not in care any more, having laid up the possession in an inviolable treasure-house.

But if thou wouldest really learn, both what is our present being, and what our life to come; and that the one is a spider's web and a shadow, but the things there, all of them, immoveable and immortal; thou wouldest not after that want other arguments. For whereas now thy child is delivered from all change; if he were here, perhaps he might continue good, perhaps not so. Seest thou not how many openly cast off their own children? how many are constrained to keep them at home, although worse than the open outcasts?

Let us make account of all these things and practise self-command; for so shall we at once show regard to the deceased, and enjoy much praise from men, and receive from God the great rewards of patience, and attain unto the good things eternal; unto which may we all attain, by the grace and love towards man of our Lord Jesus Christ, to whom be glory and might forever and ever. Amen.

HOMILY XXXII

MATT. IX. 27–30

"And when Jesus departed thence, two blind men followed Him, crying, and saying, Thou Son of David, have mercy on us. And when He was come into the house, the blind men came to Him: and Jesus saith unto them, Believe ye that I am able to do this? They say unto Him, Yea, Lord. Then touched He their eyes, saying, According to your faith be it unto you. And their eyes were opened."

Wherefore can it be that He puts them off, and they crying out? Here again teaching us utterly to repel the glory that cometh from the multitude. For because the house was near, He leads them thither to heal them in private. And this is evident from the fact, that He charged them moreover to tell no man.

But this is no light charge against the Jews; when these men, though their eyes were struck out, receive the faith by hearing alone, but they beholding the miracles, and having their sight to witness what was happening, do all just contrary. And see their earnestness also, both by their cry, and by their prayer itself. For they did not merely approach Him, but with loud cries, and alleging nought else but "mercy."

And they called Him "Son of David," because the name was thought to be honorable. In many passages, for instance, did the prophets likewise so call the kings, whom they wished to honor, and to declare great.

And having brought them into the house, He puts to them a further question. For in many cases He made a point of healing on entreaty, lest any should suppose Him to be rushing upon these miracles through vainglory: and not on this account alone, but to indicate also that they deserve healing, and that no one should say, "If it was of mere mercy that He saved, all men ought to be saved." For even His love to man hath a kind of proportion; depending on the faith of them that are healed. But not for these causes only doth He require faith of them, but forasmuch as they called Him "Son of David," He to lead them up to what is higher, and to teach them to entertain the imaginations they ought of Himself, saith, "Believe ye that I am able to do this?" He did not say, "Believe ye that I am able to entreat my Father, that I am able to pray" but, "that I am able to do this?"

What then is their word? "Yea, Lord." They call Him no more Son of David, but soar higher, and acknowledge His dominion.

And then at last He for His part lays His hand upon them, saying, "According to your faith be it unto you." And this He doth to confirm their faith, and to show that they are participators in the good work, and to witness that their words were not words of flattery. For neither did He say, "Let your eyes be opened," but, "According to your faith be it unto you;" which He saith to many of them that came unto Him; before the healing of their bodies, hastening to proclaim the faith in their soul; so as both to make them more approved, and to render others more serious.

Thus with respect to the sick of the palsy also; for there too before giving nerve to the body, He raises up the fallen soul, saying, "Son, be of good cheer, thy sins be forgiven thee." And the young damsel too, when He had raised her up, He detained, and by the food taught her her Benefactor; and in the case of the centurion also He did in like manner, leaving the whole to his faith; and as to His disciples again, when delivering them from the storm on the sea, He delivered them first from their want of faith. Just so likewise in this case: He knew indeed, even before their cry, the secrets of their mind; but that He might lead on others also to the same earnestness, He makes them known to the rest as well, by the result of their cure proclaiming their hidden faith.

Then after their cure He commands them to tell no man; neither doth He merely command them, but with much strictness.

"For Jesus," it is said, "straitly charged them, saying, See that no man know it. But they, when they were departed, spread abroad His fame in all that country."

They however did not endure this, but became preachers, and evangelists; and when bidden to hide what had been done, they endured it not.

And if in another place we find Him saying, "Go thy way, and declare the glory of God," that is not contrary to this, but even highly in agreement herewith. For He instructs us to say nothing ourselves, concerning ourselves, but even to forbid them that would eulogise us: but if the glory be referred to God, then not only not to forbid, but to command men to do this.

2. "And as they went out," it is said, "behold, they brought unto Him a dumb man possessed with a devil."

For the affliction was not natural, but the device of the evil spirit; wherefore also he needs others to bring him. For he could neither make entreaty himself, being speechless, nor supplicate others, when the evil spirit had bound his tongue, and together with his tongue had fettered his soul.

For this cause neither doth He require faith of him, but straightway heals the disease.

"For when the devil was cast out," it saith, "the dumb spake: and the multitudes marvelled, saying, It was never so seen in Israel."

Now this especially vexed the Pharisees, that they preferred Him to all, not only that then were, but that had ever been. And they preferred Him, not for His healing, but for His doing it easily and quickly, and to diseases innumerable and incurable.

And thus the multitude; but the Pharisees quite contrariwise; not only disparaging the works, but saying things contradictory to themselves, and not ashamed. Such a thing is wickedness. For what say they?

"He casteth out devils through the prince of the devils."

What can be more foolish than this? For in the first place, as He also saith further on, it is impossible that a devil should cast out a devil, for that being is wont to repair what belongs to himself, not to pull it down. But He did not cast out devils only, but also cleansed lepers, and raised the dead, and curbed the sea, and remitted sins, and preached the kingdom, and brought men unto the Father; things which a demon would never either choose, or at any time be able to effect. For the devils bring men to idols, and withdraw them from God, and persuade them to disbelieve the life to come. The devil doth not bestow kindness when he is insulted; forasmuch as even when not insulted, he harms those that court and honor him.

But He doeth the contrary. For after these their insults and revilings,

3. "He went about," it is said, "all the cities and villages, teaching in their synagogues, and preaching the gospel of the kingdom, and healing every sickness and every disease."

And so far from punishing them for their insensibility, He did not even simply rebuke them; at once both evincing His meekness, and so refuting the calumny; and at the same time minded also by the signs which followed to exhibit His proof more completely: and then to adduce also the refutation by words. He went about therefore both in cities, and in countries, and in their synagogues; instructing us to requite our calumniators, not with fresh calumnies, but with greater benefits. Since, if not for man's sake, but God's, thou doest good to thy fellow-servants; whatsoever they may do, leave not thou off doing them good, that thy reward may be greater; since he surely, who upon their calumny leaves off his doing good, signifies that for their praise' sake, not for God's sake, he applies himself to that kind of virtue.

For this cause Christ, to teach us that of mere goodness He had entered on this, so far from waiting for the sick to come to Him, of Himself hastened unto them, bearing them two of the greatest blessings; one, the gospel of the kingdom; another, the perfect cure of all their diseases. And not a city did He overlook, not a village did He hasten by, but visited every place.

4. And not even at this doth He stop, but He exhibits also another instance of His forethought. That is,

"When He saw," it is said, "the multitudes, He was moved with compassion on them, because they were troubled, and scattered abroad, as sheep having no shepherd. Then saith He unto His disciples, The harvest truly is plenteous, but the laborers are few, pray ye therefore the Lord of the harvest, that He will send forth laborers into His harvest."

See again His freedom from vainglory. That He may not draw all men unto Himself, He sends out His disciples.

And not with this view only, but that He might also teach them, after practising in Palestine, as in a sort of training-school, to strip themselves for their conflicts with the world. For this purpose then He makes the exercises even more serious than the actual conflicts, so far as pertained to their own virtue; that they might more easily engage in the struggles that were to ensue; as it were a sort of tender nestlings whom He was at length leading out to fly. And for the present He makes them physicians of bodies, dispensing to them afterwards the cure of the soul, which is the principal thing.

And mark how He points out the facility and necessity of the thing. For what saith He? "The harvest truly is plenteous, but the laborers are few." That is, "not to the sowing," saith He, "but to the reaping do I send you." Which in John He expressed by, "Other men labored, and ye are entered into their labors."

And these things he said, at once repressing their pride, and preparing them to be of good courage, and signifying that the greater part of the labor came first.

And contemplate Him here too beginning from love to man, not with any requital. "For He had compassion, because they were troubled and scattered abroad as sheep having no shepherd." This is His charge against the rulers of the Jews, that being shepherds they acted the part of wolves. For so far from amending the multitude, they even marred their progress. For instance, when they were marvelling and saying, "It was never so seen in Israel:" these were affirming the contrary, "He casteth out devils through the prince of the devils."

But of what laborers doth He speak here? Of the twelve disciples. What then? whereas He had said, "But the laborers are few," did He add to their number? By no means, but He sent them out alone. Wherefore then did He say, "Pray ye the Lord of the harvest, that He would send forth laborers into His harvest;" and made no addition to their number? Because though they were but twelve, He made them many from that time forward, not by adding to their number, but by giving them power.

Then to signify how great the gift is, He saith, "Pray ye the Lord of the harvest;" and indirectly declares it to be His own prerogative. For after having said, "Pray ye the Lord of the harvest;" when they had not made any entreaty nor prayer, He Himself at once ordains them, reminding them also of the sayings of John, of the threshing floor, and of the Person winnowing, and of the chaff, and of the wheat. Whence it is evident that Himself is the husbandman, Himself the Lord of the harvest, Himself the master and owner of the prophets. For if He sent them to reap, clearly it was not to reap what belongs to another, but what Himself had sown by the prophets.

But not in this way only was He indirectly encouraging them, in calling their ministry a harvest; but also by making them able for the ministry.

"And when He had called unto Him," it saith, "His twelve disciples, He gave them power against unclean spirits, to cast them out, and to heal all manner of sickness, and all manner of disease."

Still the Spirit was not yet given. For "there was not yet," it saith, "a Spirit, because that Jesus was not yet glorified." How then did they cast out the spirits? By His command, by His authority.

And mark, I pray thee, also, how well timed was the mission. For not at the beginning did He send them; but when they had enjoyed sufficiently the advantage of following Him, and had seen a dead person raised, and the sea rebuked, and devils expelled, and a paralytic new-strung, and sins remitted, and a leper cleansed, and had received a sufficient proof of His power, both by deeds and words, then He sends them forth: and not to dangerous acts, for as yet there was no danger in Palestine, but they had only to stand against evil speakings. However, even of this He forewarns them, I mean of their perils; preparing them even before the time, and making them feel as in conflict by His continual predictions of that sort.

5. Then, since He had mentioned to us two pairs of apostles, that of Peter, and that of John, and after those had pointed out the calling of Matthew, but had said nothing to us either of the calling or of the name of the other apostles; here of necessity He sets down the list of them, and their number, and makes known their names, saying thus:

"Now the names of the twelve apostles are these; first, Simon, who is called Peter."

Because there was also another Simon, the Canaanite; and there was Judas Iscariot, and Judas the brother of James; and James the son of Alphaeus, and James the son of Zebedee.

Now Mark doth also put them according to their dignity; for after the two leaders, He then numbers Andrew; but our evangelist not so, but without distinction; or rather He sets before himself even Thomas who came far short of him.

But let us look at the list of them from the beginning.

"First, Simon, who is called Peter, and Andrew his brother."

Even this is no small praise. For the one he named from his virtue, the other from his high kindred, which was in conformity to his disposition.

Then, "James the son of Zebedee, and John his brother."

Seest thou how He arranges them not according to their dignity. For to me John seems to be greater, not only than the others, but even than his brother.

After this, when he had said, "Philip, and Bartholomew," he added, "Thomas, and Matthew the Publican."

But Luke not so, but in the opposite order, and he puts him before Thomas.

Next, "James the son of Alphaeus." For there was, as I have already said, the son of Zebedee also. Then after having mentioned "Lebbaeus, whose surname was Thaddaeus," and "Simon" Zelotes, whom he calls also "the Canaanite," he comes to the traitor. And not as a sort of enemy or foe, but as one writing a history, so hath he described him. He saith not, "the unholy, the all unholy one," but hath named him from his city, "Judas Iscariot." Because there was also another Judas, "Lebbaeus, whose surname was Thaddaeus," who, Luke saith, was the brother of James, saying, "Judas the brother of James." Therefore to distinguish him from this man, it saith, "Judas Iscariot, who also betrayed Him." And he is not ashamed to say, "who also betrayed Him." So far were they from ever disguising aught even of those things that seem to be matters of reproach.

And first of all, and leader of the choir, is the "unlearned, the ignorant man."

But let us see whither, and to whom, He sends them.

"These twelve," it is said, "Jesus sent forth."

What manner of men were these? The fishermen, the publicans: for indeed four were fishermen and two publicans, Matthew and James, and one was even a traitor. And what saith He to them? He presently charges them, saying,

"Go not into the way of the Gentiles, and into any city of the Samaritans enter ye not; but go rather to the lost sheep of the house of Israel."

"For think not at all," saith He, "because they insult me, and call me demoniac, that I hate them and turn away from them. Nay, as I sought earnestly to amend them in the first place, so keeping you away from all the rest, to them do I send you as teachers and physicians. And I not only forbid you to preach to others before these, but I do not suffer you so much as to touch upon the road that leads thither, nor to enter into such a city." Because the Samaritans too are in a state of enmity with the Jews. And yet it was an easier thing to deal with them, for they were much more favorably disposed to the faith; but the case of these was more difficult. But for all this, He sends them on the harder task, indicating his guardian care of them, and stopping the mouths of the Jews, and preparing the way for the teaching of the apostles, that people might not hereafter blame them for "entering in to men uncircumcised," and think they had a just cause for shunning and abhorring them. And he calls them "lost," not "stray," "sheep," in every way contriving how to excuse them, and winning their mind to himself.

6. "And as ye go," saith He, "preach, saying, The kingdom of Heaven is at hand."

Seest thou the greatness of their ministry? Seest thou the dignity of apostles? Of nothing that is the object of sense are they commanded to speak, nor such as Moses spake of, and the prophets before them, but of some new and strange things. For while the former preached no such things, but earth, and the good things in the earth, these preached the kingdom of Heaven, and whatever is there.

And not from this circumstance only were these the greater, but also from their obedience: in that they shrink not, nor are they backward, like those of old; but, warned as they are of perils, and wars, and of those insupportable evils, they receive with great obedience His injunctions, as being heralds of a kingdom.

"And what marvel," saith one, "if having nothing to preach that is dismal or grievous, they readily obeyed?" What sayest thou? nothing grievous enjoined them? Dost thou not hear of the prisons, the executions, the civil wars, the hatred of all men? all which, He said a little while after, they must undergo. True, as to other men, He sent them to be procurers and heralds of innumerable blessings: but for themselves, He said and proclaimed beforehand, that they were to suffer terrible and incurable ills.

After this, to make them trustworthy, He saith,

"Heal the sick, cleanse the lepers, cast out devils: freely ye have received, freely give."

See how He provides for their conduct, and that no less than for their miracles, implying that the miracles without this are nothing. Thus He both quells their pride by saying, "Freely ye have received, freely give;" and takes order for their being clear of covetousness. Moreover, lest it should be thought their own work, and they be lifted up by the signs that were wrought, He saith, "freely ye have received." "Ye bestow no favor on them that receive you, for not for a price did ye receive these things, nor after toil: for the grace is mine. In like manner therefore give ye to them also, for there is no finding a price worthy of them."

7. After this plucking up immediately the root of the evils, He saith,

"Provide neither gold, nor silver, nor brass in your purses, nor scrip for your journey, neither two coats, neither shoes, nor yet a staff."

He said not, "take them not with you," but, "even if you can obtain them from another, flee the evil disease." And you see that hereby He was answering many good pur poses; first setting His disciples above suspicion; secondly, freeing them from all care, so that they might give all their leisure to the word; thirdly, teaching them His own power. Of this accordingly He quite speaks out to them afterwards, "Lacked ye anything, when I sent you naked and unshod?"

He did not at once say, "Provide not," but when He had said, "Cleanse the lepers, cast out devils," then He said, "Provide nothing; freely ye have received, freely give;" by His way of ordering things consulting at once for their interest, their credit, and their ability.

But perhaps some one may say, that the rest may not be unaccountable, but "not to have a scrip for the journey, neither two coats, nor a staff, nor shoes," why did He enjoin this? Being minded to train them up unto all perfection; since even further back, He had suffered them not to take thought so much as for the next day. For even to the whole world He was to send them out as teachers. Therefore of men He makes them even angels (so to speak); releasing them from all worldly care, so that they should be possessed with one care alone, that of their teaching; or rather even from that He releases them, saying, "Take no thought how or what ye shall speak."

And thus, what seems to be very grievous and galling, this He shows to be especially light and easy for them. For nothing makes men so cheerful as being freed from anxiety and care; and especially when it is granted them, being so freed, to lack nothing, God being present, and becoming to them instead of all things.

Next, lest they should say, "whence then are we to obtain our necessary food?" He saith not unto them, "Ye have heard that I have told you before, Behold the fowls of the air;'" (for they were not yet able to realise this commandment in their actions); but He added what came far short of this, saying, "For the workman is worthy of his meat;" declaring that they must be nourished by their disciples, that neither they might be high minded towards those whom they were teaching, as though giving all and receiving nothing at their hands; nor these again break away, as being despised by their teachers.

After this, that they may not say, "Dost thou then command us to live by begging?" and be ashamed of this, He signifies the thing to be a debt, both by calling them "workmen," and by terming what was given, "hire." For "think not," saith He, "because the labor is in words, that the benefit conferred by you is small; nay, for the thing hath much toil; and whatsoever they that are taught may give, it is not a free gift which they bestow, but a recompence which they render: "for the workman is worthy of his meat." But this He said, not as declaring so much to be the worth of the apostles' labors, far from it; God forbid: but as both making it a law for them to seek nothing more, and as convincing the givers, that what they do is not an act of liberality, but a debt.

8. "And into whatsoever city or town ye shall enter, inquire who in it is worthy: and there abide till ye go thence."

That is, "it follows not," saith He, "from my saying, The workman is worthy of his meat,' that I have opened to you all men's doors: but herein also do I require you to use much circumspection. For this will profit you both in respect of your credit, and for your very maintenance. For if he is worthy, he will surely give you food; more especially when ye ask nothing beyond mere necessaries."

And He not only requires them to seek out worthy persons, but also not to change house for house, whereby they would neither vex him that is receiving them, nor themselves get the character of gluttony and self-indulgence. For this He declared by saying, "There abide till ye go thence." And this one may perceive from the other evangelists also.

Seest thou how He made them honorable by this also, and those that received them careful; by signifying that they rather are the gainers, both in honor, and in respect of advantage?

Then pursuing again the same subject, He saith,

"And when ye come into an house, salute it. And if the house be worthy, let your peace come upon it; but if it be not worthy, let your peace return to you."

Seest thou how far He declines not to carry His injunctions? And very fitly. For as champions of godliness, and preachers to the whole world, was He training them. And in that regard disposing them to practise moderation, and making them objects of love, He saith,

"And whosoever shall not receive you, nor hear your words, when ye depart out of that house or city, shake off the dust of your feet. Verily I say unto you, it shall be more tolerable for the land of Sodom and Gomorrah in the day of judgment, than for that city."

That is, "do not," saith He, "because ye are teachers, therefore wait to be saluted by others, but be first in showing that respect." Then, implying that this is not a mere salutation, but a blessing, He saith, "If the house be worthy, it shall come upon it," but if it deal insolently, its first punishment will be, not to have the benefit of your peace; and the second, that it shall suffer the doom of Sodom." "And what," it will be said, "is their punishment to us?" Ye will have the houses of such as are worthy.

But what means, "Shake off the dust of your feet?" It is either to signify their having received nothing of them, or to be a witness to them of the long journey, which they had travelled for their sake.

But mark, I pray thee, how He doth not even yet give the whole to them. For neither doth He as yet bestow upon them foreknowledge, so as to learn who is worthy, and who is not so; but He bids them inquire, and await the trial. How then did He Himself abide with a publican? Because he was become worthy by his conversion.

And mark, I pray thee, how when He had stripped them of all, He gave them all, by suffering them to abide in the houses of those who became disciples, and to enter therein, having nothing. For thus both themselves were freed from anxiety, and they would convince the others, that for their salvation only are they come; first by bringing in nothing with them, then by requiring no more of them than necessaries, lastly, by not entering all their houses without distinction.

Since not by the signs only did He desire them to appear illustrious, but even before the signs, by their own virtue. For nothing so much characterizes strictness of life, as to be free from superfluities, and so far as may be, from wants. This even the false apostles knew. Wherefore Paul also said, "That wherein they glory, they may be found even as we."

But if when we are in a strange country, and are going unto persons unknown to us, we must seek nothing more than our food for the day, much more when abiding at home.

9. These things let us not hear only, but also imitate. For not of the apostles alone are they said, but also of the saints afterwards. Let us therefore become worthy to entertain them. For according to the disposition of the entertainers

this peace both comes and flies away again. For not only on the courageous speaking of them that teach, but also on the worthiness of them that receive, doth this effect follow.

Neither let us account it a small loss, not to enjoy such peace. For this peace the prophet also from of old proclaims, saying, "How beautiful are the feet of them that bring good tidings of peace." Then to explain the value thereof he added, "That bring good tidings of good things."

This peace Christ also declared to be great, when He said, "Peace I leave with you, my peace I give unto you." And we should do all things, so as to enjoy it, both at home and in church. For in the very church too the presiding minister gives peace. And this which we speak of is a type of that. And you should receive it with all alacrity, in heart before the actual communion. For if not to impart it after the communion be disgusting, how much more disgusting to repel from you him that pronounces it!

For thee the presbyter sits, for thee the teacher stands, laboring and toiling. What plea then wilt thou have, for not affording him so much welcome as to listen to Him? For indeed the church is the common home of all, and when ye have first occupied it, we enter in, strictly observing the type which they exhibited. For this cause we also pronounce "peace" in common to all, directly as we enter, according to that law.

Let no one therefore be careless, no one inattentive, when the priests have entered in and are teaching; for there is really no small punishment appointed for this. Yea, and I for one would rather enter into any of your houses ten thousand times, and find myself baffled, than not be heard when I speak here. This latter is to me harder to bear than the other, by how much this house is of greater dignity; our great possessions being verily laid up here, here all the hopes we have. For what is here, that is not great and awful? Thus both this table is far more precious and delightful than the other, and this candlestick than the candlestick there. And this they know, as many as have put away diseases by anointing themselves with oil in faith and in due season. And this coffer too is far better and more indispensable than that other chest; for it hath not clothes but alms shut up in it; even though they be few that own them. Here too is a couch better than that other; for the repose of the divine Scriptures is more delightful than any couch.

And had we attained to excellence in respect of concord, then had we no other home beside this. And that there is nothing over-burdensome in this saying, the "three thousand," bear witness, and the "five thousand," who had but one home, one table, one soul; for "the multitude of them that believed," we read, "were of one heart and of one soul." But since we fall far short of their virtue, and dwell scattered in our several homes, let us at least, when we meet here, be earnest in so doing. Because though in all other things we be destitute and poor, yet in these we are rich. Wherefore here at least receive us with love when we come in unto you. And when I say, "Peace be unto you," and ye say, "And with thy spirit," say it not with the voice only, but also with the mind; not in mouth, but in understanding also. But if, while here thou sayest, "Peace also to thy spirit," out of doors thou art mine enemy, spitting at and calumniating me, and secretly aspersing me with innumerable reproaches; what manner of peace is this?

For I indeed, though thou speak evil of me ten thousand times, give thee that peace with a pure heart, with sincerity of purpose, and I can say nothing evil at any time of thee; for I have a father's bowels. And if I rebuke thee at any time, I do it out of concern for thee. But as for thee, by thy secret carping at me, and not receiving me in the Lord's house, I fear lest thou shouldest in return add to my despondency; not for thine insulting me, not for thy casting me out, but for thy rejecting our peace, and drawing down upon thyself that grievous punishment.

For though I shake not off the dust, though I turn not away, what is threatened remains unchanged. For I indeed oftentimes pronounce peace to you, and will not cease from continually speaking it; and if, besides your insults, ye receive me not, even then I shake not off the dust; not that I am disobedient to our Lord, but that I vehemently burn for you. And besides, I have suffered nothing at all for you; I have neither come a long journey, nor with that garb and that voluntary poverty am I come (therefore we first blame ourselves), nor without shoes and a second coat; and perhaps this is why ye also fail of your part. However, this is not a sufficient plea for you; but while our condemnation is greater, to you it imparts no excuse.

10. Then the houses were churches, but now the church is become a house. Then one might say nothing worldly in a house, now one may say nothing spiritual in a church, but even here ye bring in the business from the market place, and while God is discoursing, ye leave off listening in silence to His sayings, and bring in the contrary things, and make discord. And I would it were your own affairs, but now the things which are nothing to you, those ye both speak and hear.

For this I lament, and will not cease lamenting. For I have no power to quit this house, but here we must needs remain until we depart from this present life. "Receive us" therefore, as Paul commanded. For his language in that place related not to a meal, but to the temper and mind. This we also seek of you, even love, that fervent and genuine affection. But if ye endure not even this, at least love yourselves, and lay aside your present remissness. This is sufficient for our consolation, if we see you approving yourselves, and becoming better men. So will I also myself show forth increased love, even "though the more abundantly I love you, the less I be loved."

For indeed there are many things to bind us together. One table is set before all, one Father begat us, we are all the issue of the same throes, the same drink hath been given to all; or rather not only the same drink, but also to drink out of one cup. For our Father desiring to lead us to a kindly affection, hath devised this also, that we should drink out of one cup; a thing which belongs to intense love.

But "there is no comparison between the apostles and us." I confess it too, and would never deny it. For I say not, to themselves, but not even to their shadows are we comparable.

But nevertheless, let your part be done. This will have no tendency to disgrace you but rather to profit you the more. For when even to unworthy persons ye show so much love and obedience, then shall ye receive the greater reward.

For neither are they our own words which we speak, since ye have no teacher at all on earth; but what we have received, that we also give, and in giving we seek for nothing else from you, but to be loved only. And if we be unworthy even of this, yet by our loving you we shall quickly be worthy. Although we are commanded to love not them only that love us, but even our enemies. Who then is so hardhearted, who so savage, that after having received such a law, he should abhor and hate even them that love him, full as he may be of innumerable evils?

We have partaken of a spiritual table, let us be partakers also of spiritual love. For if robbers, on partaking of salt, forget their character; what excuse shall we have, who are continually partaking of the Lord's body, and do not imitate even their gentleness? And yet to many, not one table only, but even to be of one city, hath sufficed for friendship; but we, when we have the same city, and the same house, and table, and way, and door, and root, and life, and head, and the same shepherd, and king, and teacher, and judge, and maker, and father, and to whom all things are common; what indulgence can we deserve, if we be divided one from another?

11. But the miracles, perhaps, are what ye seek after, such as they wrought when they entered in; the lepers cleansed, the devils driven out, and the dead raised? Nay, but this is the great indication of your high birth, and of your love, that ye should believe God without pledges. And in fact this, and one other thing, were the reasons why God made miracles to cease. I mean, that if

when miracles are not performed, they that plume themselves on other advantages,—for instance, either on the word of wisdom, or on show of piety,—grow vainglorious, are puffed up, are separated one from another; did miracles also take place, how could there but be violent rendings? And that what I say is not mere conjecture, the Corinthians bear witness, who from this cause were divided into many parties.

Do not thou therefore seek signs, but the soul's health. Seek not to see one dead man raised; nay, for thou hast learnt that the whole world is arising. Seek not to see a blind man healed, but behold all now restored unto that better and more profitable sight; and do thou too learn to look chastely, and amend thine eye.

For in truth, if we all lived as we ought, workers of miracles would not be admired so much as we by the children of the heathen. For as to the signs, they often carry with them either a notion of mere fancy, or another evil suspicion, although ours be not such. But a pure life cannot admit of any such reproach; yea, all men's mouths are stopped by the acquisition of virtue.

Let virtue then be our study: for abundant are her riches, and great the wonder wrought in her. She bestows the true freedom, and causes the same to be discerned even in slavery, not releasing from slavery, but while men continue slaves, exhibiting them more honorable than freemen; which is much more than giving them freedom: not making the poor man rich, but while he continues poor, exhibiting him wealthier than the rich.

But if thou wouldest work miracles also, be rid of transgressions, and thou hast quite accomplished it. Yea, for sin is a great demon, beloved; and if thou exterminate this, thou hast wrought a greater thing than they who drive out ten thousand demons. Do thou listen to Paul, how he speaks, and prefers virtue to miracles. "But covet earnestly," saith he, "the best gifts: and yet show I unto you a more excellent way." And when he was to declare this "way," he spoke not of raising the dead, not of cleansing of lepers, not of any other such thing; but in place of all these he set charity. Hearken also unto Christ, saying, "Rejoice not that the demons obey you, but that your names are written in Heaven." And again before this, "Many will say to me in that day, Have we not prophesied in Thy name, and cast out devils, and done many mighty works, and then I will profess unto them, I know you not." And when He was about to be crucified, He called His disciples, and said unto them, "By this shall all men know that ye are my disciples," not "if ye cast out devils," but "if ye have love one to another." And again, "Hereby shall all men know that Thou hast sent me;" not "if these men raise the dead," but, "if they be one."

For, as to miracles, they oftentimes, while they profited another, have injured him who had the power, by lifting him up to pride and vainglory, or haply in some other way: but in our works there is no place for any such suspicion, but they profit both such as follow them, and many others.

These then let us perform with much diligence. For if thou change from inhumanity to almsgiving, thou hast stretched forth the hand that was withered. If thou withdraw from theatres and go to the church, thou hast cured the lame foot. If thou draw back thine eyes from an harlot, and from beauty not thine own, thou hast opened them when they were blind. If instead of satanical songs, thou hast learnt spiritual psalms, being dumb, thou hast spoken.

These are the greatest miracles, these the wonderful signs. If we go on working these signs, we shall both ourselves be a great and admirable sort of persons through these, and shall win over all the wicked unto virtue, and shall enjoy the life to come; unto which may we all attain, by the grace and love towards man of our Lord Jesus Christ, to whom be glory and might forever and ever. Amen.

HOMILY XXXIII

MATT. X. 16

"Behold, I send you forth as sheep in the midst of wolves; be ye therefore wise as serpents, and harmless as doves."

Having made them feel confident about their necessary food, and opened unto them all men's houses, and having invested their entrance with an appearance to attract veneration, charging them not to come in as wanderers, and beggars, but as much more venerable than those who received them (for this He signifies by His saying, "the workman is worthy of his hire;" and by His commanding them to inquire, who was worthy, and there to remain, and enjoining them to salute such as receive them; and by His threatening such as receive them not with those incurable evils): having I say, in this way cast out their anxiety, and armed them with the display of miracles, and made them as it were all iron and adamant, by delivering them from all worldly things, and enfranchising them from all temporal care: He speaks in what follows of the evils also that were to befall them; not only those that were to happen soon after, but those too that were to be in long course of time; from the first, even long beforehand, preparing them for the war against the devil. Yea, and many advantages were hence secured; and first, that they learnt the power of His foreknowledge; secondly, that no one should suspect, that through weakness of their Master came these evils upon them; thirdly, that such as undergo these things should not be dismayed by their falling out unexpectedly, and against hope; fourthly, that they might not at the very time of the cross be troubled on hearing these things. For indeed, they were just so affected at that time; when also He upbraided them, saying, "Because I have said these things unto you, sorrow hath filled your hearts; and none of you asketh me, whither goest Thou?" And yet He had said nothing as yet touching Himself, as that He should be bound, and scourged, and put to death, that He might not hereby also confound their minds; but for the present He announces before what should happen to themselves.

Then, that they might learn that this system of war is new, and the manner of the array unwonted; as He sends them bare, and with one coat, and unshod, and without staff, and without girdle or scrip, and bids them be maintained by such as receive them; so neither here did He stay His speech, but to signify His unspeakable power, He saith, "Even thus setting out, exhibit the gentleness of "sheep," and this, though ye are to go unto "wolves;" and not simply unto wolves, but "into the midst of wolves."

And He bids them have not only gentleness as sheep, but also the harmlessness of the dove. "For thus shall I best show forth my might, when sheep get the better of wolves, and being in the midst of wolves, and receiving a thousand bites, so far from being consumed, do even work a change on them a thing far greater and more marvellous than killing them, to alter their spirit, and to reform their mind; and this, being only twelve, while the whole world is filled with the wolves."

Let us then be ashamed, who do the contrary, who set like wolves upon our enemies. For so long as we are sheep, we conquer: though ten thousand wolves prowl around, we overcome and prevail. But if we become wolves, we are worsted, for the help of our Shepherd departs from us: for He feeds not wolves, but sheep: and He forsakes thee, and retires, for neither dost thou allow His might to be shown. Because, as He accounts the whole triumph His own, if thou being ill used, show forth gentleness; so if thou follow it up and give blows, thou obscurest His victory.

2. But do thou consider, I pray thee, who they are that hear these injunctions, so hard and laborious: the timid and ignorant; the unlettered and uninstructed; such as are in every respect obscure, who have never been trained up in the Gentile laws, who do not readily present themselves in the public places; the fishermen, the publicans, men full of innumerable deficiencies. For if these things were enough to confound even the lofty and great, how were they not enough to cast down and dismay them that were in all respects untried, and

had never entertained any noble imagination? But they did not cast them down.

"And very naturally," some one may perhaps say; "because He gave them power to cleanse lepers, to drive out devils." I would answer as follows: Nay, this very thing was enough especially to perplex them, that for all their raising the dead, they were to undergo these intolerable evils, both judgments, and executions, and the wars which all would wage on them, and the common hatred of the world; and that such terrors await them, while themselves are working miracles.

3. What then is their consolation for all these things? The power of Him that sends them. Wherefore also He puts this before all, saying, "Behold, I send you." This suffices for your encouragement, this for confidence, and fearing none of your assailants.

Seest thou authority? seest thou prerogative? seest thou invincible might? Now His meaning is like this: "Be not troubled" (so He speaks), "that sending you among wolves, I command you to be like sheep and like doves. For I might indeed have done the contrary, and have suffered you to undergo nothing terrible, nor as sheep to be exposed to wolves; I might have rendered you more formidable than lions; but it is expedient that so it should be. This makes you also more glorious; this proclaims also my power."

This He said also unto Paul: "My grace is sufficient for thee, for my strength is made perfect in weakness." "It is I, now mark it, who have caused you so to be." For in saying, "I send you forth as sheep," He intimates this. "Do not therefore despond, for I know, I know certainly, that in this way more than any other ye will be invincible to all."

After this, that they may contribute something on their own part also, and that all might not seem to be of His grace, nor they supposed to be crowned at random, and vainly, He saith, "Be ye therefore wise as serpents, and harmless as doves." "But what," it might be said, "will our wisdom avail in so great dangers? nay, how shall we be able to have wisdom at all, when so many waves are drenching us all over? For let a sheep be ever so wise, when it is in the midst of wolves, and so many wolves, what will it be able to do? Let the dove be ever so harmless, what will it profit, when so many hawks are assailing it?" In the brutes indeed, not at all: but in you as much as possible.

But let us see what manner of wisdom He here requires. That of the serpent, He saith. For even as that animal gives up everything, and if its very body must be cut off, doth not very earnestly defend it, so that it may save its head; in like manner do thou also, saith He, give up every thing but the faith; though goods, body, life itself, must be yielded. For that is the head and the root; and if that be preserved, though thou lose all, thou wilt recover all with so much the more splendor.

On this account then He neither commanded to be merely a simple and single-hearted sort of person, nor merely wise; but hath mixed up both these, so that they may become virtue; taking in the wisdom of the serpent that we may not be wounded in our vitals; and the harmlessness of the dove, that we may not retaliate on our wrongdoers, nor avenge ourselves on them that lay snares; since wisdom again is useless, except this be added. Now what, I ask, could be more strict than these injunctions? Why, was it not enough to suffer wrong? Nay, saith He, but I do not permit thee so much as to be indignant. For this is "the dove." As though one should cast a reed into fire, and command it not to be burnt by the fire, but to quench it.

However, let us not be troubled; nay, for these things have come to pass, and have had an accomplishment, and have been shown in very deed, and men became wise as serpents, and harmless as doves; not being of another nature, but of the same with us.

Let not then any one account His injunctions impracticable. For He beyond all others knows the nature of things; He knows that fierceness is not quenched by fierceness, but by gentleness. And if in men's actual deeds too thou wouldest see this result, read the book of the Acts of the Apostles, and thou wilt see how often, when the people of the Jews had risen up against them and were sharpening their teeth, these men, imitating the dove, and answering with suitable meekness, did away with their wrath, quenched their madness, broke their impetuosity. As when they said, "Did not we straitly command you, that ye should not speak in this name?" although able to work any number of miracles, they neither said nor did anything harsh, but answered for themselves with all meekness, saying, "Whether it be right to hearken unto you more than unto God, judge ye."

Hast thou seen the harmlessness of the dove? Behold the wisdom of the serpent. "For we cannot but speak the things, which we know and have heard." Seest thou how we must be perfect on all points, so as neither to be abased by dangers, nor provoked by anger?

4. Therefore He said also,

"Beware of men, for they shall deliver you up to councils, and they shall scourge you in their synagogues: and ye shall be brought before governors and kings for my sake, for a testimony to them and the Gentiles."

Thus again is He preparing them to be vigilant, in every case assigning to them the sufferance of wrong, and permitting the infliction of it to others; to teach thee that the victory is in suffering evil, and that His glorious trophies are thereby set up. For He said not at all, "Fight ye also, and resist them that would vex you," but only, "Ye shall suffer the utmost ills."

O how great is the power of Him that speaks! How great the self-command of them that hear! For indeed we have great cause to marvel, how they did not straightway dart away from Him on hearing these things, apt as they were to be startled at every sound, and such as had never gone further than that lake, around which they used to fish; and how they did not reflect, and say to themselves, "And whither after all this are we to flee? The courts of justice against us, the kings against us, the governors, the synagogues of the Jews, the nations of the Gentiles, the rulers, and the ruled." (For hereby He not only forewarned them of Palestine, and the ills therein, but discovered also the wars throughout the world, saying, "Ye shall be brought before kings and governors;" signifying that to the Gentiles also He was afterwards to send them as heralds.) "Thou hast made the world our enemy, Thou hast armed against us all them that dwell on the earth, peoples, tyrants, kings."

And what follows again is much more fearful, since men are to become on our account murderers of brothers, of children, of fathers.

"For the brother," saith He, "shall deliver up the brother to death, and the father the child; and children shall rise up against their parents, and cause them to be put to death."

"How, then," one might say, "will the rest of men believe, when they see on our account, children slain by their fathers, and brethren by brethren, and all things filled with abominations?" What? will not men, as though we were destructive demons, will they not, as though we were devoted, and pests of the world, drive us out from every quarter, seeing the earth filled with blood of kinsmen, and with so many murderers? Surely fair is the peace (is it not?) which we are to bring into men's houses and give them, while we are filling those houses with so many slaughters. Why, had we been some great number of us, instead of twelve; had we been, instead of "unlearned and ignorant," wise, and skilled in rhetoric, and mighty in speech; nay more, had we been even kings, and in possession of armies and abundance of wealth; how could we have persuaded any, while kindling up civil wars, yea, and other wars far worse than they? Why, though we were to despise our own safety, which of all other men will give heed to us?"

But none of these things did they either think or say, neither did they require any account of His injunctions, but simply yielded and obeyed. And this came not from their own virtue only, but also of the wisdom of their Teacher. For see how to each of the fearful things He annexed an encouragement; as in the case of such as received them not, He said, "It shall be more tolerable for the land of Sodom and Gomorrha in the day of judgment, than for that city;" so here again, when He had said, "Ye shall be brought before governors and kings," He added, "for my sake, for a testimony to them, and the Gentiles." And this is no small consolation, that they are suffering these things both for Christ, and for the Gentiles' conviction. Thus God, though no one regard, is found to be everywhere doing His own works. Now these things were a comfort to them, not that they desired the punishment of other men, but that they might have ground of confidence, as sure to have Him everywhere present with them, who had both foretold and foreknown these things; and because not as wicked men, and as pests, were they to suffer all this.

And together with these, He adds another, and that no small consolation for them, saying,

"But when they deliver you up, take no thought how or what ye shall speak, for it shall be given you in that hour what ye shall speak. For it is not ye that speak, but the Spirit of your Father that speaketh in you."

For lest they should say, "How shall we be able to persuade men, when such things are taking place?" He bids them be confident as to their defense also. And elsewhere indeed He saith, "I will give you a mouth and wisdom;" but here, "It is the Spirit of your Father that speaketh in you," advancing them unto the dignity of the prophets. Therefore, when He had spoken of the power that was given, then He added also the terrors, the murders, and the slaughters.

"For the brother shall deliver up the brother," saith He, "to death, and the father the child, and the children shall rise up against their parents, and cause them to be put to death."

And not even at this did He stop, but added also what was greatly more fearful, and enough to shiver a rock to pieces: "And ye shall be hated of all men." And here again the consolation is at the doors, for, "For my name's sake," saith He, "ye shall suffer these things." And with this again another, "But he that endureth to the end, the same shall be saved."

And these things in another point of view likewise were sufficient to rouse up their spirits; since at any rate the power of their gospel was to blaze up so high, as that nature should be despised, and kindred rejected, and the Word preferred to all, chasing all mightily away. For if no tyranny of nature is strong enough to withstand your sayings, but it is dissolved and trodden under foot, what else shall be able to get the better of you? Not, however, that your life will be in security, because these things shall be; but rather ye will have for your common enemies and foes them that dwell in the whole world.

5. Where now is Plato? Where Pythagoras? Where the long chain of the Stoics? For the first, after having enjoyed great honor, was so practically refut-

ed, as even to be sold out of the country, and to succeed in none of his objects, no, not go much as in respect of one tyrant: yea, he betrayed his disciples, and ended his life miserably. And the Cynics, mere pollutions as they were, have all passed by like a dream and a shadow. And yet assuredly no such thing ever befell them, but rather they were accounted glorious for their heathen philosophy, and the Athenians made a public monument of the epistles of Plato, sent them by Dion; and they passed all their time at ease, and abounded in wealth not a little. Thus, for instance, Aristippus was used to purchase costly harlots; and another made a will, leaving no common inheritance; and another, when his disciples had laid themselves down like a bridge, walked on them; and he of Sinope, they say, even behaved himself unseemly in the market place.

Yea, these are their honorable things. But there is no such thing here, but a strict temperance, and a perfect decency, and a war against the whole world in behalf of truth and godliness, and to be slain every day, and not until hereafter their glorious trophies.

But there are some also, one may say, skilled in war amongst them; as Themistocles, Pericles. But these things too are children's toys, compared with the acts of the fishermen. For what canst thou say? That he persuaded the Athenians to embark in their ships, when Xerxes was marching upon Greece? Why in this case, when it is not Xerxes marching, but the devil with the whole world, and his evil spirits innumerable assailing these twelve men, not at one crisis only, but throughout their whole life, they prevailed and vanquished; and what was truly marvellous, not by slaying their adversaries, but by converting and reforming them.

For this especially you should observe throughout, that they slew not, nor destroyed such as were plotting against them, but having found them as bad as devils, they made them rivals of angels, enfranchising human nature from this evil tyranny, while as to those execrable demons that were confounding all things, they drave them out of the midst of markets, and houses, or rather even from the very wilderness. And to this the choirs of the monks bear witness, whom they have planted everywhere, clearing out not the habitable only, but even the uninhabitable land. And what is yet more marvellous, they did not this in fair conflict, but in the enduring of evil they accomplished it all. Since men actually had them in the midst, twelve unlearned persons, binding, scourging, dragging them about, and were not able to stop their mouths; but as it is impossible to bind the sunbeam, so also their tongue. And the reason was, "it was not they" themselves "that spake," but the power of the Spirit. Thus for instance did Paul overcome Agrippa, and Nero, who surpassed all men in wickedness. "For the Lord," saith he, "stood with me, and strengthened me, and delivered me out of the mouth of the lion."

But do thou also admire them, how when it was said to them, "Take no thought," they yet believed, and accepted it, and none of the terrors amazed them. And if thou say, He gave them encouragement enough, by saying, "It shall be the Spirit of your Father that shall speak;" even for this am I most amazed at them, that they doubted not, nor sought deliverance from their perils; and this, when not for two or three years were they to suffer these things, but all their life long. For the saying, "He that endureth to the end, the same shall be saved," is an intimation of this.

For His will is, that not His part only should be contributed, but that the good deeds should be also done of them. Mark, for instance, how from the first, part is His, part His disciples.' Thus, to do miracles is His, but to provide nothing is theirs. Again, to open all men's houses, was of the grace from above; but to require no more than was needful, of their own self-denial. "For the workman is worthy of his hire." Their bestowing peace was of the gift of God, their inquiring for the worthy, and not entering in without distinction unto all, of their own self command. Again, to punish such as received them not was His, but to retire with gentleness from them, without reviling or insulting them, was of the apostles' meekness. To give the Spirit, and cause them not to take thought, was of Him that sent them, but to become like sheep and doves, and to bear all things nobly, was of their calmness and prudence. To be hated and not to despond, and to endure, was their own; to save them that endured, was of Him who sent them.

Wherefore also He said, "He that endureth to the end, the same shall be saved." That is, because the more part are wont at the beginning indeed to be vehement, but afterwards to faint, therefore saith He, "I require the end." For what is the use of seeds, flourishing indeed at first, but a little after fading away? Therefore it is continued patience that He requires of them. I mean, lest any say, He wrought the whole Himself, and it was no wonder that they should prove such, suffering as they did nothing intolerable; therefore He saith unto them, "There is need also of patience on your part. For though I should rescue you from the first dangers, I am reserving you for others more grievous, and after these again others will succeed; and ye shall not cease to have snares laid for you, so long as ye have breath." For this He intimated in saying, "But he that endureth to the end, the same shall be saved."

For this cause then, though He said, "Take no thought what ye shall speak;" yet elsewhere He saith, "Be ready to give an answer to every man that asketh you a reason of the hope that is in you." That is, as long as the contest is among friends, He commands us also to take thought; but when there is a terrible tribunal, and frantic assemblies, and terrors on all sides, He bestows the influence from Himself, that they may take courage and speak out, and not be discouraged, nor betray the righteous cause.

For in truth it was a very great thing, for a man occupied about lakes, and skins, and receipt of custom, when tyrants were on their thrones, and satraps, and guards standing by them, and the swords drawn, and all standing on their side; to enter in alone, bound, hanging down his head, and yet be able to open his mouth. For indeed they allowed them neither speech nor defense with respect to their doctrines, but set about torturing them to death, as common pests of the world. For "They," it is said, "that have turned the world upside down, are come hither also;" and again, "They preach things contrary to the decrees of Caesar, saying that Jesus Christ is king." And everywhere the courts of justice were preoccupied by such suspicions, and much influence from above was needed, for their showing both the truth of the doctrine they preached, and that they are not violating the common laws; so that they should neither, while earnest to speak of the doctrine, fall under suspicion of overturning the laws; nor again, while earnest to show that they were not overturning the common government, corrupt the perfection of their doctrines: all which thou wilt see accomplished with all due consideration, both in Peter and in Paul, and in all the rest. Yea, and as rebels and innovators, and revolutionists, they were accused all over the world; yet nevertheless they both repelled this impression, and invested themselves with the contrary, all men celebrating them as saviors, and guardians, and benefactors. And all this they achieved by their much patience. Wherefore also Paul said, "I die daily;" and he continued to "stand in jeopardy" unto the end.

6. What then must we deserve, having such high patterns, and in peace giving way to effeminacy, and remissness? With none to make war (it is too evident) we are slain; we faint when no man pursues, in peace we are required to be saved, and even for this we are not sufficient. And they indeed, when the world was on fire, and the pile was being kindled over the whole earth, entering, snatched from within, out of the midst of the flame, such as were burning; but thou art not able so much as to preserve thyself.

What confidence then will there be for us? What favor? There are no stripes, no prisons, no rulers, no synagogues, nor aught else of that kind to set upon us; yea, quite on the contrary we rule and prevail. For both kings are godly, and there are many honors for Christians, and precedences, and distinctions, and immunities, and not even so do we prevail. And whereas they being daily led to execution, both teachers and disciples, and bearing innumerable stripes, and continual brandings, were in greater luxury than such as abide in Paradise; we who have endured no such thing, not even in a dream, are softer than any wax. "But they," it will be said, "wrought miracles." Did this then keep them from the scourge? did it free them from persecution? Nay, for this is the strange thing, that they suffered such things often even at the hands of them whom they benefited, and not even so were they confounded, receiving only evil for good. But thou if thou bestow on any one any little benefit, and then be requited with anything unpleasant, art confounded, art troubled, and repentest of that which thou hast done.

If now it should happen, as I pray it may not happen nor at any time fall out, that there be a war against churches, and a persecution, imagine how great will be the ridicule, how sore the reproaches. And very naturally; for when no one exercises himself in the wrestling school, how shall he be distinguished in the contests? What champion, not being used to the trainer, will be able, when summoned by the Olympic contests, to show forth anything great and noble against his antagonist? Ought we not every day to wrestle and fight and run? See ye not them that are called Pentathli, when they have no antagonists, how they fill a sack with much sand, and hanging it up try their full strength thereupon? And they that are still younger, practise the fight against their enemies upon the persons of their companions.

These do thou also emulate, and practise the wrestlings of self denial. For indeed there are many that provoke to anger, and incite to lust, and kindle a great flame. Stand therefore against thy passions, bear nobly the mental pangs, that thou mayest endure also those of the body.

7. For so the blessed Job, if he had not exercised himself well before his conflicts, would not have shone so brightly in the same. Unless he had practised freedom from all despondency, he would have uttered some rash word, when his children died. But as it was he stood against all the assaults, against ruin of fortune, and destruction of so great affluence: against loss of children, against his wife's commiseration, against plagues in body, against reproaches of friends, against revilings of servants.

And if thou wouldest see his ways of exercise also, hear him saying, how he used to despise wealth: "If I did but rejoice," saith he, "because my wealth was great: if I set gold up for a heap, if I put my trust in a precious stone." Therefore neither was he confounded at their being taken away, since he desired them not when present.

Hear how he also managed what related to his children, not giving way to undue softness, as we do, but requiring of them all circumspection. For he who offered sacrifice even for their secret sins, imagine how strict a judge he was of such as were manifest.

And if thou wouldest also hear of his strivings after continence, hearken to him when he saith, "I made a covenant with mine eyes, that I should not think upon a maid." For this cause his wife did not break his spirit, for he loved her even before this, not however immoderately, but as is due to a wife.

Wherefore I am led even to marvel, whence it came into the devil's thought to stir up the contest, knowing as he did of his previous training. Whence then did it occur to him? The monster is wicked, and never despairs: and this turns out to us a very great condemnation that he indeed never gives up the hope of our destruction, but we despair of our own salvation.

But for bodily mutilation and indignity, mark how he practised himself. Why, inasmuch as he himself had never undergone any such thing, but had continued to live in wealth and luxury, and in all other splendor, he used to divine other men's calamities, one by one. And this he declared, when he said, "For the thing which I greatly feared is come upon me; and that which I was afraid of is come unto me." And again, "But I wept for every helpless man, and groaned when I saw a man in distress."

So because of this, nothing of what happened confounded him, none of those great and intolerable ills. For I bid thee not look at the ruin of his substance, nor at the loss of his children, nor at that incurable plague, nor at his wife's device against him; but at those things which are far more grievous than these.

"And what," saith one, "did Job suffer more grievous than these? for from his history there is nothing more than these for us to learn." Because we are asleep, we do not learn, since he surely that is anxious, and searches well for the pearl, will know of many more particulars than these. For the more grievous, and apt to infuse greater perplexity, were different.

And first, his knowing nothing certain about the kingdom of heaven, and the resurrection; which indeed he also spoke of, lamenting. "For I shall not live alway, that I should suffer long." Next, his being conscious to himself of many good works. Thirdly, his being conscious of no evil thing. Fourthly, his supposing that at God's hands he was undergoing it; or if at the devil's, this again was enough to offend him. Fifthly, his hearing his friends accusing him of wickedness, "For thou hast not been scourged," say they, "according to what thy sins deserve." Sixthly, his seeing such as lived in wickedness prospering, and exulting over him. Seventhly, not having any other to whom he might look as even having ever suffered such things.

8. And if thou wouldest learn how great these things are, consider our present state. For if now, when we are looking for a kingdom, and hoping for a resurrection, and for the unutterable blessings, and are conscious to ourselves of countless evil deeds, and when we have so many examples, and are partakers of so high a philosophy; should any persons lose a little gold, and this often, after having taken it by violence, they deem life not to be lived in, having no wife to lay sore on them, nor bereaved of children, nor reproached by friends, nor insulted by servants, but rather having many to comfort them, some by words, some by deeds; of how noble crowns must not he be worthy, who seeing what he had gotten together by honest labor, snatched away from him for nought and at random, and after all that, undergoing temptations without number, like sleet, yet throughout all abides unmoved, and offers to the Lord his due thanksgiving for it all?

Why, though no one had spoken any of the other taunts, yet his wife's words alone were sufficient utterly to shake a very rock. Look, for example, at her craft. No mention of money, none of camels, and flocks, and herds, (for she was conscious of her husband's self command with regard to these), but of what was harder to bear than all these, I mean, their children; and she deepens the tragedy, and adds to it her own influence.

Now if when men were in wealth, and suffering no distress, in many things and oft have women prevailed on them: imagine how courageous was that soul, which repulsed her, assaulting him with such powerful weapons, and which trod under foot the two most tyrannical passions, desire and pity. And yet many having conquered desire, have yielded to pity. That noble Joseph, for instance, held in subjection the most tyrannical of pleasures, and repulsed that strange woman, plying him as she did with innumerable devices; but his tears he contained not, but when he saw his brethren that had wronged him, he was all on fire with that passion, and quickly cast off the mask, and discovered the part he had been playing. But when first of all she is his wife, and when her words are piteous, and the moment favorable for her, as well as his wounds and his stripes, and those countless waves of calamities; how can one otherwise than rightly pronounce the soul impassive to so great a storm to be firmer than any adamant?

Allow me freely to say, that the very apostles, if not inferior to this blessed man, are at least not greater than he was. For they indeed were comforted by the suffering for Christ; and this medicine was so sufficient daily to relieve them, that the Lord puts it everywhere, saying, "for me, for my sake," and, "If they call me, the master of the house, Beelzebub." But he was destitute of this encouragement, and of that from miracles, and of that from grace; for neither had he so great power of the Spirit.

And what is yet greater, nourished in much delicacy, not from amongst fishermen, and publicans, and such as lived frugally, but after enjoyment of so much honor, he suffered all that he did suffer. And what seemed hardest to bear in the case of the apostles, this same he also underwent, being hated of friends, of servants, of enemies, of them who had received kindness of him: and the sacred anchor, the harbor without waves, namely, that which was said to the apostles, "for my sake," of this he had no sight.

I admire again the three children, for that they dared the furnace, that they stood up against a tyrant. But hear what they say, "We serve not thy Gods, nor worship the image which thou hast set up." A thing which was the greatest encouragement to them, to know of a certainty that for God they are suffering all whatsoever they suffer. But this man knew not that it was all conflicts, and a wrestling; for had he known it, he would not have felt what was happening. At any rate, when he heard, "Thinkest thou that I have uttered to thee mine oracles for nought, or that thou mightest be proved righteous?" consider how straightway, at a bare word, he breathed again, how he made himself of no account, how he accounted himself not so much as to have suffered what he had suffered, thus saying, "Why do I plead any more, being admonished and reproved of the Lord, hearing such things, I being nothing?" And again, "I have heard of Thee before, as far as hearing of the ear; but now mine eye hath seen Thee; wherefore I have made myself vile, and have melted away; and I accounted myself earth and ashes."

This fortitude then, this moderation, of him that was before law and grace, let us also emulate, who are after law and grace; that we may also be able to share with him the eternal tabernacles; unto which may we all attain, by the grace and love towards man of our Lord Jesus Christ, to whom be the glory and the victory forever and ever. Amen.

HOMILY XXXIV

MATT. X. 23

"But when they persecute you in this city, flee ye into the other; for verily I say unto you, ye shall not have gone over the cities of Israel, till the Son of Man be come."

Having spoken of those fearful and horrible things, enough to melt very adamant, which after His cross, and resurrection, and assumption, were to befall them, He directs again His discourse to what was of more tranquil character, allowing those whom He is training to recover breath, and affording them full security. For He did not at all command them, when persecuted, to close with the enemy, but to fly. That is, it being so far but a beginning, and a prelude, He gave His discourse a very condescending turn. For not now of the ensuing persecutions is He speaking, but of those before the cross and the passion. And this He showed by saying, "Ye shall not have gone over the cities of Israel, till the Son of Man be come." That is, lest they should say, "What then, if when persecuted we flee, and there again they overtake us, and drive us out?"—to destroy this fear, He saith, "Ye shall not have gone round Palestine first, but I will straightway come upon you."

And see how here again He doeth not away with the terrors, but stands by them in their perils. For He said not, "I will snatch you out, and will put an end to the persecutions;" but what? "Ye shall not have gone over the cities of Israel, till the Son of Man be come." Yea, for it sufficed for their consolation, simply to see Him.

But do thou observe, I pray thee, how He doth not on every occasion leave all to grace, but requires something also to be contributed on their part. "For if ye fear," saith He, "flee," for this He signified by saying, "flee ye," and "fear not." And He did not command them to flee at first, but when persecuted to withdraw; neither is it a great distance that He allows them, but so much as to go about the cities of Israel.

Then again, He trains them for another branch of self-command; first, casting out all care for their food: secondly, all fear of their perils; and now, that of calumny. Since from that first anxiety He freed them, by saying, "The workman is worthy of his hire," and by signifying that many would receive them; and from their distress about their dangers, by saying, "Take no thought how or what ye shall speak," and, "He that endureth unto the end, the same shall be saved."

But since withal it was likely that they should also bring upon themselves an evil report, which to many seems harder to bear than all; see whence He comforts them even in this case, deriving the encouragement from Himself, and from all that had been said touching Himself; to which nothing else was equal. For as He said in that other place, "Ye shall be hated of all men," and added, "for my name's sake," so also here.

And in another way He mitigates it, joining a fresh topic to that former. What kind of one then is it?

"The disciple," saith He, "is not above his Master, nor the servant above his Lord. It is enough for the disciple that he be as his Master, and the servant as his Lord. If they have called the Master of the house Beelzebub, how much more shall they call them of His household? Fear them not therefore."

See how He discovers Himself to be the Lord and God and Creator of all things. What then? Is there not any disciple above his Master, or servant above his Lord? So long as he is a disciple, and a servant, he is not, by the nature of that honor. For tell me not here of the rare instances, but take the principle from the majority. And He saith not, "How much more His servants," but "them of His household," to show how very near He felt them to be to Him. And elsewhere too He said, "Henceforth I call you not servants; ye are my friends." And He said not, If they have insulted the Master of the house, and calumniated Him; but states also the very form of the insult, that they "called Him Beelzebub."

Then He gives also another consolation, not inferior to this: for this indeed is the greatest; but because for them who were not yet living strictly, there was need also of another, such as might have special power to refresh them, He states it likewise. And the saying seems indeed in form to be an universal proposition, nevertheless not of all matters, but of those in hand only, is it spoken. For what saith He?

"There is nothing covered, that shall not be revealed; nor hid, that shall not be known." Now what He saith is like this. It is indeed sufficient for your encouragement, that I also shared with you in the same reproach; I who am your Master and Lord. But if it still grieve you to hear these words, consider this other thing too, that even from this suspicion ye will soon be released. For why do ye grieve? At their calling you sorcerers and deceivers? But wait a little, and all men will address you as saviors, and benefactors of the world. Yea, for time discovers all things that are concealed, it will both refute their false accusation, and make manifest your virtue. For when the event shows you saviors, and benefactors, and examples of all virtue, men will not give heed to their words, but to the real state of the case; and they will appear false accusers, and liars, and slanderers, but ye brighter than the sun, length of time revealing and proclaiming you, and uttering a voice clearer than a trumpet, and making all men witnesses of your virtue. Let not therefore what is now said humble you, but let the hope of the good things to come raise you up. For it cannot be, that what relates to you should be hid.

2. Then, having rid them of all distress, and fears, and anxiety, and set them above men's reproaches, then, and not till then, He seasonably discourses to them also of boldness in their preaching.

For, "What I tell you," saith He, "in darkness, that speak ye in light; and what ye have heard in the ear, that preach ye upon the housetops."

Yet it was not at all darkness, when He was saying these things; neither was He dis coursing unto them in the ear; but He used a strong figure, thus speaking. That is, because He was conversing with them alone, and in a small corner of Palestine, therefore He said, "in darkness," and "in the ear;" contrasting the boldness of speech, which He was hereafter to confer on them, with the tone of the conversation which was then going on. "For not to one, or two, or three cities, but to the whole world ye shall preach," saith He, "traversing land and sea, the inhabited country, and the desert; to princes alike and tribes, to philosophers and orators, saying all with open face, and with all boldness of speech." Therefore, He said, "On the house tops," and, "In the light," without any shrinking, and with all freedom.

And wherefore said He not only, "Preach on the housetops," and "Speak in the light," but added also, "What I tell you in darkness," and "What ye hear in the ear"? It was to raise up their spirits. As therefore when He said, "He that believeth on me, the works that I do shall he do also, and greater works than these shall he do;" even so here too, to signify that He will do it all by them, and more than by Himself, He inserted this. For "the beginning indeed," saith He, "I have given, and the prelude; but the greater part it is my will to effect through you." Now this is the language of one not commanding only, but also declaring beforehand what was to be, and encouraging them with His sayings, and implying that they should prevail over all, and quietly also removing again their distress at the evil report. For as this doctrine, after lying hid for a while, shall overspread all things, so also the evil suspicion of the Jews shall quickly perish.

Then, because He had lifted them up on high, He again gives warning of the perils also, adding wings to their mind, and exalting them high above all. For what saith He? "Fear not them which kill the body, but are not able to kill the soul." Seest thou how He set them far above all things, persuading them to despise not anxiety only and calumny, dangers and plots, but even that which is esteemed of all things most terrible, death? And not death alone, but by violence too? And He said not, "ye shall be slain," but with the dignity that became Him, He set this before them, saying, "Fear not them which kill the body, but are not able to kill the soul; but rather fear Him which is able to destroy both soul and body in hell;" bringing round the argument, as He ever doth, to its opposite. For what? is your fear, saith He, of death? and are ye therefore slow to preach? Nay for this very cause I bid you preach, that ye fear death: for this shall deliver you from that which is really death. What though they shall slay you? yet over the better part they shall not prevail, though they strive ten thousand ways. Therefore He said not, "Who do not kill the soul," but, who "are not able to kill." For wish it as they may, they shall not prevail. Wherefore, if thou fear punishment, fear that, the more grievous by far.

Seest thou how again He doth not promise them deliverance from death, but permits them to die, granting them more than if He had not allowed them to suffer it? Because deliverance from death is not near so great as persuading men to despise death. You see now, He doth not push them into dangers, but sets them above dangers, and in a short sentence fixes in their mind the doctrines that relate to the immortality of the soul, and having in two or three words implanted a saving doctrine, He comforts them also by other considerations.

Thus, lest they should think, when killed and butchered, that as men forsaken they suffered this, He introduces again the argument of God's providence, saying on this wise: "Are not two sparrows sold for a farthing? And one of them shall not fall into a snare without your Father. But the very hairs of your head are all numbered." "For what is viler than they?" saith He; "nevertheless, not even these shall be taken without God's knowledge." For He means not this, "by His operation they fall," for this were unworthy of God; but, "nothing that is done is hid from Him." If then He is not ignorant of anything that befalls us, and loves us more truly than a father, and so loves us, as to have numbered our very hairs; we ought not to be afraid. And this He said, not that God numbers our hairs, but that He might indicate His perfect knowledge, and His great providence over them. If therefore He both knows all the things that are done, and is able to save you, and willing; whatever ye may have to suffer, think not that as persons forsaken ye suffer. For neither is it His will to deliver you from the terrors, but to persuade you to despise them, since this is, more than anything, deliverance from the terrors.

3. "Fear ye not therefore; ye are of more value than many sparrows." Seest thou that the fear had already prevailed over them? Yea, for He knew the secrets of the heart; therefore He added, "Fear them not therefore;" for even should they prevail, it will be over the inferior part, I mean, the body; which though they should not kill, nature will surely take with her and depart. So that not even this depends on them, but men have it from nature. And if thou fear this, much more shouldest thou fear what is greater, and dread "Him who is able to destroy both soul and body in hell." And He saith not openly now, that it is Himself, "Who is able to destroy both soul and body," but where He before declared Himself to be judge, He made it manifest.

But now the contrary takes place: Him, namely, who is able to destroy the soul, that is, to punish it, we fear not, but those who slay the body, we shudder at. Yet surely while He together with the soul punishes the body also, they cannot even chasten the body, much less the soul: and though they chasten it ever so severely, yet in that way they rather make it more glorious.

Seest thou how He signifies the conflicts to be easy? Because in truth, death did exceedingly agitate their souls, inspiring terror for a time, for that it had not as yet been made easy to overcome, neither had they that were to despise it partaken of the grace of the Spirit.

Having, you see, cast out the fear and distress that was agitating their soul; by what follows He also encourages them again, casting out fear by fear; and not by fear only, but also by the hope of great prizes; and He threatens with much authority, in both ways urging them to speak boldly for the truth; and saith further,

"Whosoever therefore shall confess me before men, him will I also confess before my Father which is in Heaven. But whosoever shall deny me before men, him will I also deny before my Father which is in Heaven."

Thus not from the good things only, but also from the opposites, doth He urge them; and He concludes with the dismal part.

And mark His exact care; He said not "me," but "in me," implying that not by a power of his own, but by the help of grace from above, the confessor makes his confession. But of him that denies, He said not, "in me," but "me;" for he having become destitute of the gift, his denial ensues.

"Why then is he blamed," one may say, "if being forsaken, he denies?" Because the being forsaken is the fault of the forsaken person himself.

But why is He not satisfied with the faith in the mind, but requires also the confession with the mouth? To train us up to boldness in speech, and a more abundant love and determination, and to raise us on high. Wherefore also He addresses Himself to all. Nor doth He at all apply this to the disciples only in person, for not them, but their disciples too, He is now rendering noble hearted. Because he that hath learnt this lesson will not only teach with boldness, but will likewise suffer all things easily, and with ready mind. This at any rate brought over many to the apostles, even their belief in this word. Because both in the punishment the infliction is heavier, and in the good things the recompense greater. I mean, whereas he that doeth right hath the advantage in time, and the delay of the penalty is counted for gain by the sinner: He hath introduced an equivalent, or rather a much greater advantage, the increase of the recompenses. "Hast thou the advantage," saith He, "by having first confessed me here? I also will have the advantage of thee, by giving thee greater things, and unspeakably greater; for I will confess thee there." Seest thou that both the good things and the evil things are there to be dispensed? Why then hasten and hurry thyself? and why seek thy rewards here, thou who art "saved by hope?"

Wherefore, whether thou hast done anything good, and not received its recompense here, be not troubled (for with increase, in the time to come, the reward thereof awaits thee): or whether thou hast done any evil, and not paid the penalty, be not easy; for there will vengeance receive thee, if thou turn not and amend.

But if thou believe it not, from the things here form thy conjecture about things to come also. Why, if in the season of the conflicts they that confess are so glorious, imagine what they will be in the season of the crowns. If the enemies here applaud, how shall that tenderest of all fathers fail to admire and proclaim thee? Yea, then shall we have both our gifts for the good, and our punishments for the evil. So that such as deny shall suffer harm, both here and there; here living with an evil conscience, though they were never to die, they shall be surely dead; and there, undergoing the last penalty: but the other sort will profit both here and there, both here making a gain of their death, and in this way becoming more glorious than the living, and there enjoying those unspeakable blessings.

God then is in no wise prompt to punish only, but also to confer benefits; and for this last more than for the first. But why hath He put the reward once only, the punishment twice? He knows that this would be more apt to correct us. For this cause when He had said, "Fear Him which is able to destroy both soul and body in hell," He saith again, "Him will I also deny." So doth Paul also, continually making mention of hell.

Thus we see that He, having by all ways trained on His scholar (both by opening Heaven to him, and by setting before him that fearful judgment-seat, and by pointing to the amphitheatre of angels, and how in the midst of them the crowns shall be proclaimed, which thing would thenceforth prepare the way for the word of godliness to be very easily received); in what follows, lest they grow timid and the word be hindered, He bids them be prepared even for slaughter itself; to make them aware that such as continue in their error, will have to suffer (among other things) for plotting against them.

4. Let us therefore despise death, although the time be not come that requires it of us; for indeed it will translate us to a far better life. "But the body decays." Why, on this account most especially we ought to rejoice, because death decays, and mortality perishes, not the substance of the body. For neither, shouldest thou see a statue being cast, wouldest thou call the process destruction, but an improved formation. Just so do thou reason also concerning the body, and do not bewail. Then it were right to bewail, had it remained in its chastisement.

"But," saith one, "this ought to take place without the decay of our bodies; they should continue entire." And what would this have advantaged either the living or the departed? How long are ye lovers of the body? How long are ye rivetted to the earth and gaping after shadows? Why, what good would this have done? or rather, what harm would it not have done? For did our bodies not decay, in the first place the greatest of all evils, pride, would have continued with many. For if even while this is going on, and worms gushing out, many have earnestly sought to be gods; what would not have been the result did the body continue?

In the second place, it would not be believed to be of earth; for if, its end witnessing this, some yet doubt; what would they not have suspected if they did not see this? Thirdly, the bodies would have been excessively loved; and most men would have become more carnal and gross; and if even now some cleave to men's tombs and coffins, after that themselves have perished, what would they not have done, if they had even their image preserved? Fourthly, they would not have earnestly desired the things to come. Fifthly, they that say the world is eternal, would have been more confirmed, and would have denied God as Creator. Sixthly, they would not have known the excellence of the soul, and how great a thing is the presence of a soul in a body. Seventhly, many of them that lose their relations would have left their cities, and have dwelt in the tombs, and have become frantic, conversing continually with their own dead. For if even now men form to themselves images, since they cannot keep the body (for neither is it possible, but whether they will or no it glides and hurries from them), and are rivetted to the planks of wood; what monstrous thing would they not then have devised? To my thinking, the generality would have even built temples for such bodies, and they that are skilled in such sorceries would have persuaded evil spirits to speak through them; since at least even now, they that venture on the arts of necromancy attempt many things more out of the way than these. And how many idolatries would not have arisen from hence? when men even after the dust and ashes, are yet eager in those practices.

God therefore, to take away all our extravagances, and to teach us to stand off from all earthly things, destroys the bodies before our eyes. For even he that is enamored of bodies, and is greatly affected at the sight of a beautiful damsel, if he will not learn by discourse the deformity of that substance, shall know it by the very sight. Yea, many of the like age with her whom he loves, and oftentimes also fairer, being dead, after the first or second day, have emitted an ill savor, and foul matter, and decay with worms. Imagine then what sort of beauty thou lovest, and what sort of elegance has power so to disturb thee. But if bodies did not decay, this would not be well known: but as evil spirits run unto men's graves, so also many of our lovers, continually sitting by the tombs, would have received evil spirits in their soul, and would quickly have perished in this grievous madness.

But as it is, together with all other things this also comforts the soul, that the form is not seen: it brings men to forgetfulness of their affliction. Indeed, if this were not so, there would be no tombs at all, but thou wouldest see our cities having corpses instead of statues, each man desiring to look upon his own dead. And much confusion would arise hence, and none of the ordinary sort would attend to his soul, nor would give room to the doctrine of immortality to enter in: and many other things too, more shocking than these, would have resulted, which even to speak of were unseemly. Wherefore it decays presently, that thou mightest see unveiled the beauty of the soul. For if she be the procurer of all that beauty and life, much more excellent must she herself be. And if she preserve that which is so deformed and unsightly, much more herself.

5. For it is not the body wherein the beauty lies, but the expression, and the bloom which is shed over its substance by the soul. Now then, I bid thee love that which makes the body also to appear such as it is. And why speak I of death? Nay even in life itself, I would have thee mark how all is hers that is beautiful. For whether she be pleased, she showers roses over the cheeks; or whether she be pained, she takes that beauty, and involves it all in a dark robe. And if she be continually in mirth, the body improves in condition; if in grief, she renders the same thinner and weaker than a spider's web; if in wrath, she hath made it again abominable and foul; if she show the eye calm, great is the beauty that she bestows; if she express envy, very pale and livid is the hue she sheds over us; if love, abundant the gracefulness she at once confers. Thus in fact many women, not being beautiful in feature, have derived much grace from the soul; others again of brilliant bloom, by having an ungracious soul, have marred their beauty. Consider how a face that is pale grows red, and by the variation of color produces great delight, when there is need of shame and blushing. As, on the other hand, if it be shameless, it makes the countenance more unpleasing than any monster.

For nothing is fairer, nothing sweeter than a beauteous soul. For while as to bodies, the longing is with pain, in the case of souls the pleasure is pure and calm. Why then let go the king, and be wild about the herald? Why leave the philosopher, and gape after his interpreter? Hast thou seen a beautiful eye? acquaint thyself with that which is within; and if that be not beautiful, despise this likewise. For surely, didst thou see an ill-favored woman wearing a beautiful mask, she would make no impression on thee: just as on the other hand, neither wouldest thou suffer one fair and beautiful to be disguised by the mask, but wouldest take it away, as choosing to see her beauty unveiled.

This then I bid thee do in regard of the soul also, and acquaint thyself with it first; for this is clad with the body instead of a mask; wherefore also that abides such as it is; but the other, though it be mishapen, may quickly become beautiful. Though it have an eye that is unsightly, and harsh, and fierce, it may become beautiful, mild, calm, sweet-tempered, gentle.

This beauty therefore let us seek, this countenance let us adorn; that God also may "have pleasure in our beauty," and impart to us of His everlasting blessings, by the grace and love towards man of our Lord Jesus Christ, to whom be glory and might forever and ever. Amen.

HOMILY XXXV

MATT. X. 34

"Think not that I am come to send peace on earth; I am not come to send peace, but a sword."

Again, He sets forth the things that are more painful, and that with great aggravation: and the objection they were sure to meet Him with, He prevents them by stating. I mean, lest hearing this, they should say, "For, this then art Thou come, to destroy both us, and them that obey us, and to fill the earth with war?" He first saith Himself, "I am not come to send peace on earth."

How then did He enjoin them to pronounce peace on entering into each house? And again, how did the angels say, "Glory to God in the highest, and on earth peace"? And how came all the prophets too to publish it for good tidings? Because this more than anything is peace, when the diseased is cut off, when the mutinous is removed. For thus it is possible for Heaven to be united to earth. Since the physician too in this way preserves the rest of the body, when he amputates the incurable part; and the general, when he has brought to a separation them that were agreed in mischief. Thus it came to pass also in the case of that famous tower; for their evil peace was ended by their good discord, and peace made thereby. Thus Paul also divided them that were conspiring against him. And in Naboth's case that agreement was at the same time more grievous than any war. For concord is not in every case a good thing, since even robbers agree together.

The war is not then the effect of His purpose, but of their temper. For His will indeed was that all should agree in the word of godliness; but because they fell to dissension, war arises. Yet He spake not so; but what saith He? "I am not come to send peace;" comforting them. As if He said, For think not that ye are to blame for these things; it is I who order them so, because men are so disposed. Be not ye therefore confounded, as though the events happened against expectation. To this end am I come, to send war among men; for this is my will. Be not ye therefore troubled, when the earth is at war, as though it were subject to some hostile device. For when the worse part is rent away, then after that Heaven is knit unto the better.

And these things He saith, as strengthening them against the evil suspicion of the multitude.

And He said not "war," but what was more grievous than it, "a sword." And if there be somewhat painful in these expressions, and of an alarming emphasis, marvel not. For, it being His will to train their ears by the severity of His words, lest in their difficult circumstances they should start aside, He fashioned His discourse accordingly; lest any one should say it was by flattery He persuaded them, and by concealing the hardships; therefore even to those things which merited to be otherwise expressed, He gave by His words the more galling and painful turn. For it is better to see persons' gentleness in things, than in words.

2. Wherefore neither with this was He satisfied, but unfolds also the very nature of the war, signifying it to be far more grievous even than a civil war; and He saith, "I am come to set a man at variance against his father, and the daughter against her mother, and the daughter-in-law against her mother-in-law."

For not friends only, saith He, nor fellow citizens, but even kinsmen shall stand against one another, and nature shall be divided against herself. "For I am come," saith He, "to set a man at variance against his father, and the daughter against her mother, and a daughter-in-law against her mother-in-law." That is, not merely among those of the same household is the war, but among those that are dearest, and extremely near to each other. And this more than anything signifies His power, that hearing these things, they both accepted Him, and set about persuading all others.

Yet was it not He that did this: of course not: but the wickedness of the other sort: nevertheless He saith it is His own doing. For such is the custom of the Scripture. Yea, and elsewhere also He saith, "God hath given them eyes that they should not see:" and here He speaks in this way, in order that having, as I said before, exercised themselves in these words, they might not be confounded on suffering reproaches and insults.

But if any think these things intolerable, let them be reminded of an ancient history. For in times of old also this came to pass, which thing especially shows the old covenant to be akin to the new, and Him who is here speaking, the same with the giver of those commands. I mean that in the case of the Jews also, when each had slain his neighbor, then He laid aside His anger against them; both when they made the calf, and when they were joined to Baal Peor. Where then are they that say, "That God is evil, and this good?" For behold He hath filled the world with blood, shed by kinsmen. Nevertheless even this we affirm to be a work of great love towards man.

Therefore, you see, implying that it was He who approved those other acts also, He makes mention also of a prophecy, which if not spoken for this end, yet involves the same meaning. And what is this?

"A man's foes shall be they of his own household."

For indeed among the Jews also something of the kind took place. That is, there were prophets, and false prophets, and the people was divided, and families were in dissension; and some believed the one, and some the other. Wherefore the prophet admonishes, saying, "Trust ye not in friends, have not hope in guides; yea, even of her that lieth in thy bosom beware, in respect of communicating aught to her:" and, "A man's enemies are the men that are in his own house."

And this He said, preparing him that should receive the word to be above all. For to die is not evil, but to die an evil death. On this account He said moreover, "I am come to cast fire upon the earth." And this He said, to declare the vehemence and warmth of the love which He required. For, because He loved us very much, so He will likewise be loved of us. And these sayings would strengthen the persons present also, and lift them higher. "For if those others," saith He, "are to despise kinsmen, and children, and parents, imagine what manner of men ye their teachers ought to be. Since neither will the hardships stop with you, but will also pass on to the rest. For since I am come bringing great blessings, I demand also great obedience, and purpose of heart."

3. "He that loveth father or mother more than me, is not worthy of me; and he that loveth son or daughter more than me, is not worthy of me; and he that taketh not his cross and followeth after me, is not worthy of me."

Seest thou a teacher's dignity? Seest thou, how He signifies himself a true Son of Him that begat Him, commanding us to let go all things beneath, and to take in preference the love of Him?

"And why speak I," saith He, "of friends and kinsmen? Even if it be thine own life which thou preferrest to my love, thy place is far from my disciples." What then? Are not these things contrary to the Old Testament? Far from it, rather they are very much in harmony therewith. For there too He commands not only to hate the worshippers of idols, but even to stone them; and in

Deuteronomy again, admiring these, He saith, "Who said unto his father, and to his mother, I have not seen thee; neither did he acknowledge his brethren, and his own sons he disowned: he kept Thy oracles." And if Paul gives many directions touching parents, commanding us to obey them in all things, marvel not; for in those things only doth he mean us to obey, as many as do not hinder godliness. For indeed it is a sacred duty to render them all other honors: but when they demand more than is due, one ought not to obey. For this reason Luke saith, "If any man come to me, and hate not his father, and mother, and wife, and children, and brethren, and sisters, yea, and his own life also, he cannot be my disciple;" not commanding simply to hate them, since this were even quite contrary to the law; but "when one desires to be loved more than I am, hate him in this respect. For this ruins both the beloved himself, and the lover." And these things He said, both to render the children more determined, and to make the fathers more gentle, that would hinder them. For when they saw He had such strength and power as to sever their children from them, they, as attempting things impossible, would even desist. Wherefore also He leaves the fathers, and addresses His discourse to the children, instructing the former not to make the attempt, as attempting things impracticable.

Then lest they should be indignant, or count it hard, see which way He makes His argument tend: in that having said, "Who hateth not father and mother," He adds, "and his own life." For why dost thou speak to me of parents, saith He, and brothers, and sisters, and wife? Nothing is nearer than the life to any man: yet if thou hate not this also, thou must bear in all things the opposite of his lot who loveth me.

And not even simply to hate it was His command, but so as to expose it to war, and to battles, and to slaughters, and blood. "For he that beareth not his cross, and cometh after me, cannot be my disciple." Thus He said not merely that we must stand against death, but also against a violent death; and not violent only, but ignominious too.

And He discourses nothing as yet of His own passion, that when they had been for a time instructed in these things, they might more easily receive His word concerning it. Is there not, therefore, cause for amazement, how on their hearing these things, their soul did not wing its way from the body, the hardships being everywhere at hand, and the good things in expectation? How then did it not flee away? Great was both the power of the speaker, and the love of the hearers. Wherefore though hearing things far more intolera ble and galling than those great men, Moses and Jeremiah, they continued to obey, and to say nothing against it.

"He that findeth his life," saith He, "shall lose it: and he that loseth his life for my sake, shall find it." Seest thou how great the damage to such as love it unduly? how great the gain to them that hate it? I mean, because the injunctions were disagreeable, when He was bidding them set themselves against parents, and children, and nature, and kindred, and the world, and their very soul, He sets forth the profit also, being very great. Thus, "These things," saith He, "so far from harming, will very greatly profit; and their opposites will injure;" urging them, as He ever doth, by the very things which they desire. For why art thou willing to despise thy life? Because thou lovest it? Then for that very reason despise it, and so thou wilt advantage it in the highest degree, and do the part of one that loves it.

And mark an instance of unspeakable consideration. For not in respect of our parents only doth He practise this reasoning, nor of our children, but with regard to our life, which is nearer than all; that the other point may thenceforth become unquestionable, and they may learn that they will in this way profit those of their kindred likewise, as much as may be; since so it is in the case even of our life, which is more essential to us than all.

4. Now these things were enough to recommend men to receive them, their appointed healers. Yea, who would choose but receive with all readiness them that were so noble, such true heroes, and as lions running about the earth, and despising all that pertained to themselves, so that others might be saved? Yet nevertheless He proffers also another reward, indicating that He is caring here for the entertainers more than for the guests.

And the first honor He confers is by saying,

"He that receiveth you, receiveth me, and he that receiveth me, receiveth Him that sent me."

With this, what may compare? that one should receive the Father and the Son! But He holds out herewith another reward also.

" He," saith He, "that receiveth a prophet in the name of a prophet, shall receive a prophet's reward; and he that receiveth a righteous man in the name of a righteous man, shall receive a righteous man's reward."

And as before He threatens punishment to such as do not receive them, here He defines also a certain refreshment for the good. And to teach thee His greater care for them, He said not simply, "He that receiveth a prophet," or "He that receiveth a righteous man," but subjoined, "in the name of a prophet," and, "in the name of a righteous man;" that is, if not for any worldly preferment, nor for any other temporal thing, he receive him, but because he is either a prophet or a righteous man, he shall receive a prophet's reward, and a righteous man's reward; such as it were meet for him to have, that hath received a prophet, or a righteous man; or, such as that other is himself to receive. Which kind of thing Paul also said: "That your abundance may be a supply for their want, that their abundance also may be a supply for your want."

Then, lest any one should allege poverty, He saith,

"Or whosoever shall give to drink unto one of these little ones a cup of cold water only in the name of a disciple, verily I say unto you, he shall in no wise lose his reward."

"Though a cup of cold water be thy gift, on which there is nothing laid out, even of this shall a reward be stored up for thee. For I do all things for the sake of you the receivers."

Seest thou what mighty persuasions He used, and how He opened to them the houses of the whole world? Yea, He signified that men are their debtors: first, by saying, "The workman is worthy of his hire;" secondly, by sending them forth having nothing; thirdly, by giving them up to wars and fightings in behalf of them that receive them; fourthly, by committing to them miracles also; fifthly, in that He did by their lips introduce peace, the cause of all blessings, into the houses of such as receive them; sixthly, by threatening things more grievous than Sodom to such as receive them not: seventhly, by signifying that as many as welcome them are receiving both Himself and the Father; eighthly, by promising both a prophet's and a righteous man's reward: ninthly, by undertaking that the recompenses shall be great, even for a cup of cold water. Now each one of these things, even by itself, were enough to attract them. For who, tell me, when a leader of armies wounded in innumerable places, and dyed in blood, came in sight, returning after many trophies from war and conflict, would not receive him, throwing open every door in his house?

5. But who now is like this? one may say. Therefore He added, "In the name of a disciple, and of a prophet, and of a righteous man;" to instruct thee that not for the worthiness of the visitor, but for the purpose of him that gives welcome, is His reward appointed. For though here He speak of prophets, and righteous men, and disciples, yet elsewhere He bids men receive the veriest outcasts, and punishes such as fail to do so. For, "Inasmuch as ye did it not to one of the least of these, ye did it not to me;" and the converse again He affirms with respect to the same persons.

Since though he may be doing no such great work, he is a man, inhabiting the same world with thee, beholding the same sun having the same soul, the same Lord, a partaker with thee of the same mysteries, called to the same heaven with thee; having a strong claim, his poverty, and his want of necessary food. But now they that waken thee with flutes and pipes in the winter season, and disturb thee without purpose or fruit, depart from thee receiving many gifts. And they that carry about swallows, and smut themselves over, and abuse every one, receive a reward for this their conjuration. But if there come to thee a poor man wanting bread, there is no end of revilings, and reproaches, and charges of idleness, and upbraidings, and insults, and jeers; and thou considerest not with thyself, that thou too art idle, and yet God giveth thee His gifts. For tell me not this, that thou too art doing somewhat, but point me out this rather, if it be anything really needful that thou doest, and art busy about. But if thou tellest one of money-getting, and of traffic, and of the care and increase of thy goods, I also would say unto thee, Not these, but alms, and prayers, and the protection of the injured, and all such things, are truly works, with respect to which we live in thorough idleness. Yet God never told us, "Because thou art idle, I light not up the sun for thee; because thou doest nothing of real consequence, I quench the moon, I paralyze the womb of the earth, I restrain the lakes, the fountains, the rivers, I blot out the atmosphere: I withhold the annual rains:" but He gives us all abundantly. And to some that are not merely idle, but even doing evil, He freely gives the benefit of these things.

When therefore thou seest a poor man, and sayest, "It stops my breath that this fellow, young as he is and healthy, having nothing, would fain be fed in idleness; he is surely some slave and runaway, and hath deserted his proper master:" I bid thee speak these same words to thyself; or rather, permit him freely to speak them unto thee, and he will say with more justice, "It stops my breath that thou, being healthy, art idle, and practisest none of the things which God hath commanded, but having run away from the commandments of thy Lord, goest about dwelling in wickedness, as in a strange land, in drunkenness, in surfeiting, in theft, in extortion, in subverting other men's houses." And thou indeed imputest idleness, but I evil works; in thy plotting, in thy swearing, in thy lying, in thy spoiling, in thy doing innumerable such things.

And this I say, not as making a law in favor of idleness, far from it; but rather very earnestly wishing all to be employed; for sloth is the teacher of all wickedness: but I beseech you not to be unmerciful, nor cruel. Since Paul also, having made infinite complaints, and said, "If any will not work, neither let him eat," stopped not at this, but added, "But ye, be not weary in well doing." "Nay, but these things are contradictory. For if thou hast commanded for them not to eat, how exhortest thou us to give?" I do so, saith He, for I have also commanded to avoid them, and "to have no company with them;" and again I said, "Count them not as enemies, but admonish them;" not making contradictory laws, but such as are quite in unison with each other. Because, if thou art prompt to mercy, both he, the poor man, will soon be rid of his idleness, and thou of thy cruelty.

"But he hath many lies and inventions," you reply. Well, hence again is he pitiable, for that he hath fallen into such distress, as to be hardened even in such doings. But we, so far from pitying, add even those cruel words, "Hast thou not received once and again?" so we talk. What then? because he was once fed, hath he no need to be fed again? Why dost thou not make these laws for thine own belly also, and say to it likewise, Thou wert filled yesterday, and the day before, seek it not now? But while thou fillest that beyond measure, even to bursting, from him thou turnest away, when he asks but what is moderate; whereas thou oughtest therefore to pity him, because he is constrained to come to thee every day. Yea, if nought else incline thee to him, thou shouldest pity him because of this; for by the constraint of his poverty he is forced on these things, and doeth them. And thou dost not pity him, because, being so spoken to, he feels no shame: the reason being, that his want is too strong for him.

Nay, thou instead of pitying, dost even make a show of him; and whereas God hath commanded to give secretly, thou standest exposing publicly him that hath accosted thee, and upbraiding him, for what ought to move thy pity. Why, if thou art not minded to give, to what end add reproach, and bruise that weary and wretched soul? He came as into a harbor, seeking help at thine hands; why stir up waves, and make the storm more grievous? Why dost thou condemn him of meanness? What? had he thought to hear such things, would he have come to thee? Or if he actually came foreseeing this, good cause therefore both to pity him, and to shudder at thine own cruelty, that not even so, when thou seest an inexorable necessity laid upon him, dost thou become more gentle, nor judgest him to have a sufficient excuse for his importunity in the dread of hunger, but accusest him of impudence: and yet hast thou often thyself practised greater impudence, yea in respect of grievous matters. For while here the very impudence brings with it ground of pardon, we, often doing things punishable, brazen it out: and when we ought to bear all that in mind, and be humble, we even trample on those miserable men, and when they ask medicines, we add to their wounds. I say, if thou wilt not give, yet why dost thou strike? If thou wilt not be bounteous, yet why be insolent?

"But he submits not to be put off in any other way." Well then, as that wise man commanded, so do. "Answer him peaceable words with meekness." For not of his own accord, surely, is he so very importunate. For there is not, there cannot be, any man desiring to be put to shame for its own sake. How much soever any may contend, I cannot yield ever to be convinced that a man who was living in plenty would choose to beg.

6. Let no man then beguile us with arguments. But although Paul saith, "If any will not work, neither let him eat," to them he saith it; but to us he saith not this, but, on the contrary, "Be not weary in well doing." Even thus do we at home; when any two are striving with each other, we take each apart, and give them the opposite advice. This did God also, and Moses. For while to God he said, "If thou wilt forgive them their sin, forgive it; else blot me out also;" them on the contrary he commanded to slay one another, and all that pertained to them. Yet these things are contrary; nevertheless, both looked to one end.

Again, God said to Moses in the hearing of the Jews, "Let me alone, that I may consume the people," (for though they were not present when God was saying this, yet they were to hear it afterwards): but privately He gives him directions of the opposite tenor. And this, Moses upon constraint revealed afterwards, thus saying, "What? did I conceive them, that thou sayest to me, Carry them, as a nurse would carry the sucking child in her bosom?"

These things are done also in houses, and often a father while he blames the tutor in private for having used his child reproachfully, saying, "Be not rough, nor hard," to the youth speaks in the contrary way, "Though thou be reproached unjustly, bear it;" out of those opposites making up some one wholesome result. Thus also Paul said to such as are in health and beg, "If any man will not work, neither let him eat," that he may urge them into employment: but to such as can show mercy, "Ye, for your part, be not weary in well doing:" that he may lead them to give alms.

So also, when he was admonishing those of the Gentiles, in his Epistle to the Romans, not to be highminded against the Jews, he brought forward also the wild olive, and he seems to be saying one thing to these, another to those.

Let us not therefore fall away into cruelty, but let us listen to Paul, saying, "Be not weary in well doing;" let us listen to the Lord, who saith, "Give to every man that asketh of thee," and, "Be ye merciful as your Father." And though He hath spoken of many things, He hath nowhere used this expression, but with regard to our deeds of mercy only. For nothing so equals us with God, as doing good.

"But nothing is more shameless," saith one, "than a poor man." Why, I pray thee? Because he runs up, and cries out after thee? Wilt thou then let me point out, how we are more importunate than they, and very shameless? Remember, I say, now at the season of the fast, how often, when thy table was spread at eventide, and thou hadst called thy ministering servant; on his moving rather leisurely, thou hast overset everything, kicking, insulting, reviling, merely about a little delay; although fully assured, that if not immediately, yet a little after thou shalt enjoy thy victuals. Upon which thou dost not call thyself impudent, changed as thou art into a wild beast for nothing; but the poor man, alarmed and trembling about his greater interests (for not about delay, but about famine, is all his fear), him dost thou call audacious, and shameless, and impudent, and all the most opprobrious names? Nay, how is this anything but extreme impudence.

But these things we do not consider: therefore we account such men troublesome: since if we at all searched into our own doings, and compared them with theirs, we should not have thought them intolerable.

Be not then a severe judge. Why, if thou wert clear of all sins, not even then would the law of God permit thee to be strict in searching out other men's sins. And if the Pharisee perished on this account, what defense are we to find? If He suffer not such as have done well to be bitter in searching out other men's doings, much less them that have offended.

7. Let us not then be savage, nor cruel, not without natural feeling, not implacable, not worse than wild beasts. For I know many to have gone even so far in brutishness, as for a little trouble to slight famishing persons, and to say these words: "I have no servant now with me; we are far from home; there is no money-changer that I know." Oh cruelty! Didst thou promise the greater, and dost thou not fulfill the less? To save thy walking a little way, doth he perish with hunger? Oh insolence! Oh pride! Why, if it were ten furlongs to be walked, oughtest thou to be backward? Doth it not even come into thy mind that so thy reward is made greater? For whereas, when thou givest, thou receivest reward for the gift only: when thou thyself also goest, for this again is appointed thee a recompense.

Yea, the patriarch himself we admire for this, that in his own person he ran to the herd, and snatched up the calf, and that, when he had three hundred and eighteen servants born in his house. But now some are filled with so much pride, as to do these things by servants, and not to be ashamed. "But dost thou require me to do these things myself?" one may say. "How then shall I not seem to be vainglorious?" Nay, but as it is, thou art led by another kind of vainglory to do this, being ashamed to be seen talking with a poor man.

But I am in no respect strict about this; only give, whether by thyself or by another thou art minded to do so; and do not accuse, do not smite, do not revile. For medicines, not wounds, doth he need who comes unto thee; mercy, not a sword. For tell me, if any one who had been smitten with a stone, and had received a wound in his head, were to let go all others, and run unto thy knees, drenched in his blood; wouldest thou indeed smite him with another stone, and add unto him another wound? I, for my part, think not; but even as it was, thou wouldest endeavor to cure it. Why then doest thou the contrary with respect to the poor? Knowest thou not how much power a word hath, both to raise up, and to cast down? "For a word," it is said, "is better than a gift."

Dost thou not consider that thou art thrusting the sword into thyself, and art receiving a more grievous wound, when he, being reviled, silently withdraws, with groans and many tears? Since indeed of God he is sent unto thee. Consider then, in insulting him, upon whom thou art causing the insult to pass; when God indeed sends him unto thee, and commands thee to give, but thou, so far from giving, dost even insult him on his coming.

And if thou art not aware how exceedingly amiss this is, look at it as among men, and then thou wilt fully know the greatness of the sin. As thus: if a servant of thine had been commanded by thee to go to another servant, who had money of thine, to receive it, and were to come back not only with empty hands, but also with despiteful usage; what wouldest thou not do to him that had wrought the insult? What penalty wouldest thou not exact, as though, after this, it were thyself that had been ill used?

This reckoning do thou make in regard of God also; for truly it is He that sends the poor to us, and of His we give, if indeed we do give. But if, besides not giving, we also send them away insulted, consider how many bolts, how many thunders, that which we are doing deserves.

Duly considering then all these things, let us both bridle our tongue, and put away inhumanity, and let us stretch forth the hand to give alms, and not with money only, but with words also, let us relieve such as are in need; that we may both escape the punishment for reviling, and may inherit the kingdom which is for blessing and almsgiving, by the grace and love towards man of our Lord Jesus Christ, to whom be glory and might forever and ever. Amen.

HOMILY XXXVI

MATT. XI. 1

"And it came to pass, when Jesus had made an end of commanding His twelve disciples, He departed thence to teach and to preach in their cities."

That is, after He had sent them, He proceeded to withdraw Himself, to give them room and opportunity to do what He had enjoined. For while He was present and healing, no one would be willing to approach them.

"Now when John had heard in the prison the works of Jesus, he sent two of his disciples, and asked Him, saying, Art thou He that should come, or do we look for another?"

But Luke saith, they also told John of the miracles, and then he sent them. However, this contains no matter of difficulty, but of consideration only; for this, among other things, indicates their jealousy towards Him.

But what follows is completely among the controverted points. Of what nature then is this? Their saying, "Art Thou He that should come, or do we look for another?" That is, he that knew Him before His miracles, he that had learned it of the Spirit, he that heard it of the Father, he who had proclaimed Him before all men; doth he now send to learn of Him, whether it be Himself or no? And if yet thou didst not know that it is surely He, how thinkest thou thyself credible, affirming as thou dost concerning things, whereof thou art ignorant? For he that is to bear witness to others, must be first worthy of credit himself. Didst thou not say, "I am not meet to loose the latchet of His shoe?" Didst thou not say, "I knew Him not, but He that sent me to baptize with water, the same said unto me, Upon whom thou shalt see the Spirit descending and resting upon Him, the same is He which baptizeth with the Holy Ghost?" Didst thou not see the Spirit in form of a dove? didst thou not hear the voice? Didst thou not utterly forbid Him, saying, "I have need to be baptized of Thee?" Didst thou not say even to thy disciples, "He must increase, I must decrease?" Didst thou not teach all the people, that "He should baptize them with the Holy Ghost and with fire?" and that He "is the Lamb of God that taketh away the sin of the world?" Didst thou not before His signs and miracles proclaim all these things? How then now, when He hath been made manifest to all, and the fame of Him hath gone out everywhere, and dead men have been raised, and devils driven away, and a display made of so great miracles, dost thou after this send to learn of Him?

What then is the fact? Were all these sayings a kind of fraud: a stage play and fables? Nay, who that hath any understanding would say so? I say not, John, who leaped in the womb, who before his own birth proclaimed Him, the citizen of the wilderness, the exhibitor of the conversation of angels; but even though he were one of the common sort, and of them that are utterly outcast, he would not have hesitated, after so many testimonies, both on his own part and on the part of others.

Whence it is evident, that neither did he send as being himself in doubt, nor did he ask in ignorance. Since no one surely could say this, that though he knew it fully, yet on account of his prison he was become rather timid: for neither was he looking to be delivered therefrom, nor if he did look for it, would he have betrayed his duty to God, armed as he was against various kinds of death. For unless he had been prepared for this, he would not have evinced so great courage towards a whole people, practised in shedding blood of prophets; nor would he have rebuked that savage tyrant with so much boldness in the midst of the city and the forum, severely chiding him, as though he were a little child, in hearing of all men. And even if he were grown more timid, how was he not ashamed before his own disciples, in whose presence he had so often borne witness unto Him, but asked his question by them, which he should have done by others? And yet surely he knew full well, that they too were jealous of Christ, and desired to find some handle against Him. And how could he but be abashed before the Jewish people, in whose presence he had proclaimed such high things? Or what advantage accrued to him thereby, towards deliverance from his bonds? For not for Christ's sake had he been cast into prison, nor for having proclaimed His power, but for his own rebuke touching the unlawful marriage. And what child so silly, what person so frantic, but that so he would have put on himself their character?

2. What then is it which he is bringing about? For that it belongs not to John to have doubt hereupon, no nor to any ordinary person, nor even to one extremely foolish and frenzied; so much is evident from what we have said. And now we have only to add the solution.

For what intent then did he send to ask? John's disciples were starting aside from Jesus, and this surely any one may see, and they had always a jealous feeling towards Him. And it is plain, from what they said to their master: "He that was with thee," it is said, "beyond Jordan, to whom thou barest witness, behold, the same baptizeth, and all men come unto Him." And again, "There arose a question between John's disciples and the Jews about purifying." And again they came unto Him, and said, "Why do we and the Pharisees fast oft, but Thy disciples fast not?" For as yet they knew not who Christ was, but imagining Jesus to be a mere man, but John greater than after the manner of man, were vexed at seeing the former held in estimation, but the latter, as he had said, now ceasing. And this hindered them from coming unto Him, their jealousy quite blocking up the access. Now so long as John was with them, he was exhorting them continually and instructing them, and not even so did he persuade them; but when he was now on the point of dying, he uses the more diligence: fearing as he did lest he might leave a foundation for bad doctrine, and they continue broken off from Christ. For as he was diligent even at first to bring to Christ all that pertained to himself; so on his failing to persuade them, now towards his end he does but exert the more zeal.

Now if he had said, "Go ye away unto Him, He is better than I," he would not have persuaded them, minded as they were not easily to be separated from him, but rather he would have been thought to say it out of modesty, and they would have been the more rivetted to him; or if he had held his peace, then again nothing was gained. What then doth he? He waits to hear from them that Christ is working miracles, and not even so doth he admonish them, nor doth he send all, but some two (whom he perhaps knew to be more teachable than the rest); that the inquiry might be made without suspicion, in order that from His acts they might learn the difference between Jesus and himself. And he saith, Go ye, and say, "Art thou He that should come, or do we look for another?"

But Christ knowing the purpose of John, did not say, I am He; for this would again have offended the hearers, although this was what it naturally followed for Him to say, but He leaves them to learn it from His acts. For it saith, "when these were come to Him, then "He cured many." And yet what congruity was there, that being asked, "Art thou He," He should say nothing to that, but should presently cure them that were sick; unless it had been His mind to establish this which I have mentioned? Because they of course would account the testimony of His deeds surer, and more above suspicion than that of His words.

Knowing therefore, as being God, the mind with which John had sent them, He straightway cured blind, lame, and many others; not to teach him (for how should He him that was convinced), but these that were doubting: and having healed them, He saith,

"Go and show John again those things which ye do hear and see; the blind receive their sight, and the lame walk, and the lepers are cleansed, and the deaf hear, and the dead are raised up, and the poor have the gospel preached unto them." And he added, "And blessed is he, whosoever shall not be offended in me;" implying that He knows even their unuttered thoughts. For if He had said, "I am He," both this would have offended them, as I have already said; and they would have thought, even if they had not spoken, much as the Jews said to Him, "Thou bearest record of Thyself." Wherefore He saith not this Himself, but leaves them to learn all from the miracles, freeing what He taught from suspicion, and making it plainer. Wherefore also He covertly added His reproof of them. That is, because they were "offended in Him," He by setting forth their case and leaving it to their own conscience alone, and by calling no witness of this His accusation, but only themselves that knew it all, did thus also draw them the more unto Himself, in saying, Blessed is he, whosoever shall not be offended in me." For indeed His secret meaning was of them when He said this.

3. But in order to our making the truth more evident to you by the comparison of the several statements, producing not only our own sayings, but also what is stated by others; we must needs add some account of them.

What then do some affirm? That this which we have stated was not the cause, but that John was in ignorance, yet not in ignorance of all; but that He was the Christ, he knew, but whether He was also to die for mankind, he knew not, therefore he said, "Art Thou He that should come?" that is, He that is to descend into hell. But this is not tenable; for neither of this was John ignorant. This at least he proclaimed even before all the others, and bare record of this first, "Behold," saith he, "the Lamb of God, which taketh away the sin of the world." Now he called Him a lamb, as proclaiming the cross, and again in saying, "That taketh away the sin of the world," he declared this same thing. For not otherwise than by the cross did He effect this; as Paul likewise said: "And the handwriting which was contrary to us, even it He took out of the way, nailing it to His cross." And his saying too, "He shall baptize you with the Spirit," is that of one who was foretelling the events after the resurrection.

Well: that He was to rise again, he knew, say they, and that He was to give the Holy Ghost; but that He should likewise be crucified, he knew not. How then was He to rise again, who had not suffered, nor been crucified? And how was this man greater than a prophet, who knew not even what the prophets knew? For that he was greater than a prophet, even Christ Himself bare record, but that the prophets knew of the passion is surely plain to every one. For so Isaiah saith, "He is brought as a lamb to the slaughter, and as a sheep before her shearer is dumb." And before this testimony also he saith, "There shall be a root of Jesse, and He that shall rise again to rule the Gentiles, in Him shall the Gentiles trust." Then speaking of His passion, and of the ensuing glory, he added, "And His rest shall be honor." And this prophet foretold not only that He should be crucified, but also with whom. "For," saith he, "He was numbered with the transgressors." And not this only, but that He should not even plead for Himself; "For this man," he saith, "openeth not His mouth:" and that He should be unjustly condemned; "For in His humiliation," saith he, "His judgment was taken away." And before this again, David both saith this, and describes the judgment hall. "Why," saith he, "do the heathen rage, and the people imagine a vain thing? The kings of the earth stand up, and the rulers are gathered together against the Lord, and against His anointed." And elsewhere he mentions also the image of the cross, saying on this wise, "They pierced my hand and my feet," and those things which the soldiers were emboldened to do, he adds with all exactness, "For they parted my garments," saith he, "among them, and for my vesture they did cast lots." And elsewhere again he saith, that they also offered Him vinegar; "For they gave me," saith He, "gall for my meat, and for my thirst they made me drink vinegar."

So then the prophets, so many years before, speak of the hall of judgment, and of the condemnation, and of them that were crucified with Him, and of the division of the garments, and of the lot cast upon them, and of many more things besides (for indeed it is unnecessary to allege all now, lest we make our discourse long): and was this man, greater than them all, ignorant of all these things? Nay, how should this be reasonable?

And why did he not say, "Art thou He that should come to hell," but simply, "He that should come?" Although this were far more absurd than the others, I mean their saying, "he therefore said these things, that he might preach there also after his departure." To whom it were seasonable to say, "Brethren, be not children in understanding, howbeit in malice be ye children." For the present life indeed is the season for right conversation, but after death is judgment and punishment. "For in hell," it is said, "who will confess unto thee?"

How then were "the gates of brass burst, and the bars of iron broken in sunder"? By His body; for then first was a body shown, immortal, and destroying the tyranny of death. And besides, this indicates the destruction of the might of death, not the loosing of the sins of those who had died before His coming. And if this were not so, but He have delivered all that were before Him from hell, how saith He, "It shall be more tolerable for the land of Sodom and Gomorrah?" For this saying supposes that those are also to be punished; more mildly indeed, yet still that they are to be punished. And yet they did also suffer here the most extreme punishment, nevertheless not even this will deliver them. And if it is so with them, much more with such as have suffered nothing.

"What then?" one may say, "were they wronged, who lived before His coming?" By no means, for men might then be saved, even though they had not confessed Christ. For this was not required of them, but not to worship idols, and to know the true God. "For the Lord thy God," it is said, "is one Lord." Therefore the Maccabees were admired, because for the observance of the law they suffered what they did suffer; and the three children, and many others too amongst the Jews, having shown forth a very virtuous life, and having maintained the standard of this their knowledge, had nothing more required of them. For then it was sufficient for salvation, as I have said already, to know God only; but now it is so no more, but there is need also of the knowledge of

Christ. Therefore He said, "If I had not come and spoken unto them, they had not had sin, but now they have no cloak for their sin."

So likewise with regard to the rule of practice. Then murder was the destruction of him that committed it, but now even to be angry. And then to commit adultery, and to lie with another man's wife, brought punishment, but now even to look with unchaste eyes. For as the knowledge, so also the rule of life is now made stricter. So that there was no need of a forerunner there.

And besides, if unbelievers are after death to be saved on their believing, no man shall ever perish. For all will then repent and adore. And in proof that this is true, hear Paul saying, "Every tongue shall confess, and every knee shall bow, of things in heaven, and things in earth, and things under the earth." And, "The last enemy that shall be destroyed is death." But there is no advantage in that submission, for it comes not of a rightly disposed choice, but of the necessity of things, as one may say, thenceforth taking place.

Let us not then any more bring in such old wives' doctrines, and Jewish fables. Hear at least what Paul saith touching these things. "For as many as have sinned without law, shall also perish without law;" where his discourse is of those who lived in the time before the law; and, "As many as have sinned in the law, shall be judged by the law," speaking of all after Moses. And, "That the wrath of God is revealed from heaven against all ungodliness, and unrighteousness of men," and, "indignation and wrath, tribulation and anguish upon every soul of man that worketh evil, of the Jew first, and also of the Gentile." And yet countless were the evils which the Gentiles have suffered in this world, and this is declared alike by the histories of the heathens, and by the Scriptures that are in our hands. For who could recount the tragic calamities of the Babylonians, or those of the Egyptians? But in proof that they who, not having known Christ before His coming in the flesh, yet refrained from idolatry and worshipped God only, and showed forth an excellent life, shall enjoy all the blessings; hear what is said: "But glory, and honor, and peace to every one that worketh good, to the Jew first, and also to the Gentile." Seest thou that for their good deeds there are many rewards, and chastisements again, and penalties for such as have done the contrary?

4. Where now, tell me, are the utter unbelievers in hell? Why, if those before Christ's coming, who had not so much as heard the name of hell, nor of a resurrection, and were punished here, shall suffer punishment there also; how much more we that have been nurtured in so many lessons of strict virtue?

And how is it reasonable, asks one, that they that have never heard of hell, should fall into hell? For they will say, "If thou hadst threatened hell, we should have feared more, and have been sobered." To be sure; (is it not so?) at our rate of living now, who hear daily the sayings about hell, and give no heed at all.

And besides, there is this also to be said; that he who is not restrained by the judgments in sight, much less will he be restrained by those others. For the less reasonable sort, and those of a grosser disposition, are wont to be sobered rather by things which are at hand, and straightway to happen, than by such as will come to pass a long time after. "But over us," one may say, "a greater fear is suspended, and herein were they wronged." By no means. For first, there are not the same measures set to us as to them, but much greater for us. Now they that have undertaken greater labors, ought to enjoy greater help. And it is no little help, that our fear has been increased. And if we have an advantage over them in knowing things to come, they have an advantage over us in that the severe punishments are presently laid upon them.

But there is something else, which the multitude say with respect to this also. For "where," say they, "is God's justice, when any one for sinning here, is punished both here and there?" Would ye then I should put you in mind of your own sayings, that ye may no longer give us trouble, but furnish the solution from within yourselves. I have heard many of our people, if haply they were told of a murderer cut off in a court of justice, how they had indignation, and talked in this way: "This unholy and accursed wretch, having perpetrated thirty murders, or even many more, hath himself undergone one death only; and where is the justice of it?" So that ye yourselves confess, that one death is not sufficient for punishment; how give ye then an opposite sentence now. Because not others but yourselves are the objects of your judgment: so great a hindrance is self-love to our perceiving what is just. Because of this, when we are judging others, we search out all things with strictness, but when we are sitting in judgment on ourselves, we are blinded. Since if we were to search into these things in our own case too, as we do with regard to other men, we should give an uncorrupt sentence. For we also have sins, deserving not two or three, but ten thousand deaths. And to pass over all the rest, let us recollect ourselves, as many of us as partake unworthily of the mysteries; such men being guilty of the body and blood of Christ. Wherefore, when thou art talking of the murderer, take account of thyself also. For he indeed hath murdered a man, but thou art under the guilt of slaying the Lord; and he, not having partaken of mysteries, but we, while enjoying the benefit of the sacred table.

And what are they that bite and devour their brethren, and pour out such abundance of venom? What is he that robs the poor of their food? For if he who imparts not of his own, is such as I have said, much more he that takes the things of others. How many robbers do the covetous surpass in wickedness!

how many murderers and robbers of tombs, the rapacious! and how many after spoiling men are desirous even of their blood!

"Nay," saith he, "God forbid." Now thou sayest, God forbid. When thou hast an enemy, then say, God forbid, and call to mind what hath been said, and show forth a life full of great strictness; lest the portion of Sodom await us also, lest we suffer the lot of Gomorrha, lest we undergo the ills of the Tyrians and Sidonians; or rather, lest we offend Christ, which were a thing more grievous and more to be feared than all.

For though to many hell seem to be a fearful thing, yet I for my part will not cease continually to say, that this is more grievous and fearful than any hell; and you I entreat to be of the same mind. For so shall we both be delivered from hell, and enjoy the glory that is bestowed of Christ; unto which may we all attain, by the grace and love towards man of our Lord Jesus Christ, to whom be glory and might forever and ever. Amen.

HOMILY XXXVII

MATT. X. 7, 8, 9

"And as they departed, Jesus began to say unto the multitudes concerning John, What went ye out into the wilderness to see? A reed shaken with the wind? But what went ye out for to see? A man clothed in soft raiment; behold, they that wear soft clothing are in kings' houses. But what went ye out for to see? A prophet? yea, I say unto you, and more than a prophet."

For the matter indeed of John's disciples had been ordered well, and they were gone away assured by the miracles which had just been performed; but there was need after that of remedy as regarded the people. For although they could not suspect anything of the kind of their own master, the common people might from the inquiry of John's disciples form many strange suspicions, not knowing the mind with which he sent his disciples. And it was natural for them to reason with themselves, and say, "He that bore such abundant witness, hath he now changed his persuasion, and doth he doubt whether this or another be He that should come? Can it be, that in dissension with Jesus he saith this? that the prison hath made him more timid? that his former words were spoken vainly, and at random?" It being then natural for them to suspect many such things, see how He corrects their weakness, and removes these their suspicions. For "as they departed, He began to say to the multitudes." Why, "as they departed?" That He might not seem to be flattering the man.

And in correcting the people, He doth not publish their suspicion, but adds only the solution of the thoughts that were mentally disturbing them: signifying that He knew the secrets of all men. For He saith not, as unto the Jews, "Wherefore think ye evil?" Because if they had it in their minds, not of wickedness did they so reason, but of ignorance on the points that had been spoken of. Wherefore neither doth He discourse unto them in the way of rebuke, but merely sets right their understanding, and defends John, and signifies that he is not fallen away from his former opinion, neither is he changed, not being at all a man easily swayed and fickle, but steadfast and sure, and far from being such as to betray the things committed unto him.

And in establishing this, He employs not at first his own sentence, but their former testimony, pointing out how they bare record of his firmness, not by their words only, but also by their deeds.

Wherefore He saith, "What went ye out into the wilderness to see?" as though He had said, Wherefore did ye leave your cities, and your houses, and come together all of you into the wilderness? To see a pitiful and flexible kind of person? Nay, this were out of all reason, this is not what is indicated by that earnestness, and the concourse of all men unto the wilderness. So much people and so many cities would not have poured themselves out with so great zeal towards the wilderness and the river Jordan at that time, had ye not expected to see some great and marvellous one, one firmer than any rock. Yea, it was not "a reed" surely, that "ye went out to see shaken by the wind:" for the flexible and such as are lightly brought round, and now say one thing, now another, and stand firm in nothing, are most like that.

And see how He omits all wickedness, and mentions this, which then especially haunted them; and removes the suspicion of lightness.

"But what went ye out for to see? a man clothed in soft raiment? Behold, they that wear soft clothing are in kings' houses."

Now His meaning is like this: He was not of himself a waverer; and this ye yourselves showed by your earnestness. Much less could any one say this, that he was indeed firm, but having made himself a slave to luxury, he afterwards became languid. For among men, some are such as they are of themselves, others become so; for instance, one man is passionate by nature, and another from having fallen into a long illness gets this infirmity. Again, some men are flexible and fickle by nature, while others become so by being slaves to luxury, and by living effeminately. "But John," saith He, "neither was such a character by nature, for neither was it a reed that ye went out to see; nor by giving himself to luxury did he lose the advantage he possessed." For that he did not make himself a slave to luxury, his garb shows, and the wilderness, and the prison. Since, had he been minded to wear soft raiment, he would not have lived in the wilderness, nor in the prison, but in the king's courts: it being in his power, merely by keeping silence, to have enjoyed honor without limit. For since Herod so reverenced him, even when he had rebuked him, and was in chains, much more would he have courted him, had he held his peace. You see, he had indeed given proof of his firmness and fortitude; and how could he justly incur suspicions of that kind?

2. When therefore as well by the place, as by his garments, and by their concourse unto Him, He had delineated his character, He proceeds to bring in the prophet. For having said, "Why went ye out? To see a prophet? Yea I say unto you, and more than a prophet;" He goes on, "For this is he of whom it is written, Behold, I send my messenger before Thy face, which shall prepare Thy way before Thee." Having before set down the testimony of the Jews, He then applies that of the prophets; or rather, He puts in the first place the sentence of the Jews, which must have been a very strong demonstration, the witness being borne by his enemies; secondly, the man's life; thirdly, His own judgment; fourthly, the prophet; by all means stopping their mouths.

Then lest they should say, "But what if at that time indeed he were such an one, but now is changed?" He added also what follows; his garments, his prison, and together with these the prophecy.

Then having said, that he is greater than a prophet, He signifies also in what he is greater. And in what is he greater? In being near Him that was come. For, "I send," saith He, "my messenger before Thy face;" that is, nigh Thee. For as with kings, they who ride near the chariot, these are more illustrious than the rest, just so John also appears in his course near the advent itself. See how He signified John's excellency by this also; and not even here doth He stop, but adds afterwards His own suffrage as well, saying, "Verily I say unto you, among them that are born of women, there hath not arisen a greater than John the Baptist."

Now what He said is like this: "woman hath not borne a greater than this man." And His very sentence is indeed sufficient; but if thou art minded to learn from facts also, consider his table, his manner of life, the height of his soul. For he so lived as though he were in heaven: and having got above the necessities of nature, he travelled as it were a new way, spending all his time in hymns and prayers, and holding intercourse with none among men, but with God alone continually. For he did not so much as see any of his fellow-servants, neither was he seen by any one of them; he fed not on milk, he enjoyed not the comfort of bed, or roof, or market, or any other of the things of men; and yet he was at once mild and earnest. Hear, for example, how considerately he reasons with his own disciples, courageously with the people of the Jews, how openly with the king. For this cause He said also, "There hath not risen among them that are born of women a greater than John the Baptist."

3. But lest the exceeding greatness of His praises should produce a sort of extravagant feeling, the Jews honoring John above Christ; mark how He corrects this also. For as the things which edified His own disciples did harm to the multitudes, they supposing Him an easy kind of person; so again the remedies employed for the multitudes might have proved more mischievous, they deriving from Christ's words a more reverential opinion of John than of Himself.

Wherefore this also, in an unsuspected way, He corrects by saying, "He that is less, in the kingdom of Heaven is greater than he." Less in age, and according to the opinion of the multitude, since they even called Him "a gluttonous man and a winebibber;" and, "Is not this the carpenter's son?" and on every occasion they used to make light of Him.

"What then?" it may be said, "is it by comparison that He is greater than John?" Far from it. For neither when John saith, "He is mightier than I," doth he say it as comparing them; nor Paul, when remembering Moses he writes, "For this man was counted worthy of more glory than Moses," doth he so write by way of comparison; and He Himself too, in saying, "Behold, a greater than Solomon is here," speaks not as making a comparison.

Or if we should even grant that this was said by Him in the way of comparison, this was done in condescension, because of the weakness of the hearers. For the men really had their gaze very much fixed upon John; and then he was rendered the more illustrious both by his imprisonment, and by his plainness of speech to the king; and it was a great point for the present, that even so much should be received among the multitude. And so too, the Old Testament uses in the same way to correct the souls of the erring, by putting together in a way of comparison things that cannot be compared; as when it saith, "Among the gods there is none like unto Thee, O Lord:" and again, "There is no god like our God."

Now some affirm, that Christ said this of the apostles, others again, of angels. Thus, when any have turned aside from the truth, they are wont to wander many ways. For what sort of connexion hath it, to speak either of angels or of apostles? And besides, if He were speaking of the apostles, what hindered his bringing them forward by name? whereas, when He is speaking of Himself, He naturally conceals His person, because of the still prevailing suspicion, and that

He may not seem to say anything great of Himself; yea, and we often find Him doing so.

But what is, "In the kingdom of heaven?" Among spiritual beings, and all them that are in heaven.

And moreover His saying, "There hath not risen among them that are born of women a greater than John," suited one contrasting John with Himself, and thus tacitly excepting Himself. For though He too were born of a woman, yet not as John, for He was not a mere man, neither was He born in like manner as a man, but by a strange and wondrous kind of birth.

4. "And from the days of John the Baptist," saith He, "until now, the kingdom of heaven suffereth violence, and the violent take it by force."

And what sort of connexion may this have with what was said before? Much, assuredly, and in full accordance therewith. Yea, by this topic also He proceeds to urge and press them into the faith of Himself; and at the same time likewise, He is speaking in agreement with what had been before said by John. "For if all things are fulfilled even down to John, I am "He that should come."

"For all the prophets," saith He, "and the law prophesied until John."

For the prophets would not have ceased, unless I were come. Expect therefore nothing further, neither wait for any one else. For that I am He is manifest both from the prophets ceasing, and from those that every day "take by force" the faith that is in me. For so manifest is it and certain, that many even take it by force. Why, who hath so taken it? tell me. All who approach it with earnestness of mind.

Then He states also another infallible sign, saying, "If ye will receive it, he is Elias, which was for to come." For "I will send you," it is said, "Elias the Tishbite, who shall turn the heart of the father to the children." This man then is Elias, if ye attend exactly, saith He. For "I will send," saith He, "my messenger before Thy face."

And well hath He said, "If ye will receive it," to show the absence of force. For I do not constrain, saith He. And this He said, as requiring a candid mind, and showing that John is Elias, and Elias John. For both of them received one ministry, and both of them became forerunners. Wherefore neither did He simply say, "This is Elias," but, "If ye are willing to receive it, this is he," that is, if with a candid mind ye give heed to what is going on. And He did not stop even at this, but to the words, "This is Elias, which was for to come," He added, to show that understanding is needed, He that hath ears to hear, let him hear."

Now He used so many dark sayings, to stir them up to inquiry. And if not even so were they awakened, much more, had all been plain and clear. For this surely no man could say, that they dared not ask Him, and that He was difficult of approach. For they that were asking him questions, and tempting Him about common matters, and whose mouths were stopped a thousand times, yet they did not withdraw from Him; how should they but have inquired of Him, and besought Him touching the indispensable things, had they indeed been desirous to learn? For if concerning the matters of the law they asked, "Which is the first commandment," and all such questions, although there was of course no need of His telling them that; how should they but ask the meaning of what He Himself said, for which also He was bound to give account in His answers? And especially when it was He Himself that was encouraging and drawing them on to do this. For by saying, "The violent take it by force," He stirs them up to earnestness of mind; and by saying, "He that hath ears to hear, let him hear," He doth just the same thing.

5. "But whereunto shall I liken this generation?" saith He, "It is like unto children sitting in the market place, and saying, We have piped unto you, and ye have not danced; we have mourned unto you, and ye have not lamented." This again seems to be unconnected with what came before, but it is the most natural consequence thereof. Yea, He still keeps to the same point, the showing that John is acting in harmony with Himself, although the results were opposite; as indeed with respect to his inquiry also. And He implies that there was nothing that ought to have been done for their salvation, and was omitted; which thing the prophet saith of the vineyard; "What ought I to have done to this vineyard, and have not done it? For whereunto," saith He, "shall I liken this generation? It is like unto children sitting in the market, and saying, We have piped unto you, and ye have not danced, we have mourned unto you, and ye have not lamented. For John came neither eating nor drinking, and they say, He hath a devil. The Son of Man came eating and drinking, and they say, Behold a man gluttonous, and a winebibber, a friend of publicans and sinners."

Now what He saith is like this: We have come each of us an opposite way, I and John; and we have done just as if it were some hunters with a wild beast that was hard to catch, and which might by two ways fall into the toils; as if each of the two were to cut it off his several way, and drive it, taking his stand opposite to the other; so that it must needs fall into one of the two snares. Mark, for instance, the whole race of man, how it is astonished at the wonder of men's fasting, and at this hard and self-denying life. For this reason it had been so ordered, that John should be thus brought up from his earliest youth, so that hereby (among other things) his sayings might obtain credit.

But wherefore, it may be asked, did not He Himself choose that way? In the first place He did also Himself proceed by it, when He fasted the forty days, and went about teaching, and not having where to lay His head. Nevertheless He did also in another mode accomplish this same object, and provide for the advantage thence accruing. For to be testified of by him that came this way was the same thing, or even a much greater thing than to have come this way Himself.

And besides, John indeed exhibited no more than his life and conversation; for "John," it is said, "did no sign," but He Himself had the testimony also from signs and from miracles. Leaving therefore John to be illustrious by his fasting, He Himself came the opposite way, both coming unto publicans' tables, and eating and drinking.

Let us ask the Jews then, "Is fasting a good thing, and to be admired? you should then have obeyed John, and received him, and believed his sayings. For so would those sayings have led you towards Jesus. Is fasting, on the other hand, a thing grievous, and burdensome? then should you have obeyed Jesus, and have believed in Him that came the opposite way. Thus, either way, ye would have found yourselves in the kingdom." But, like an intractable wild beast, they were speaking evil of both. The fault is not then theirs who were not believed, but they are to be blamed who did not believe. For no man would ever choose to speak evil of opposite things, any more than he would on the other hand commend them. I mean thus: he that approves the cheerful and free character, will not approve him that is sad and grave; he that commends the man of a sad countenance will not commend the cheerful man. For it is a thing impossible to give your vote both ways at once. Therefore also He saith, "We have piped unto you, and ye have not danced;" that is, "I have exhibited the freer kind of life, and ye obeyed not:" and, "We have mourned, and ye have not lamented;" that is, "John followed the rugged and grave life, and ye took no heed." And He saith not, "he this, I that," but the purpose of both being one, although their modes of life were opposite, for this cause He speaks of their doings as common. Yea, for even their coming by opposite ways arose out of a most exact accordance, such as continued looking to one and the same end. What sort of excuse then can ye have after all this?

Wherefore He subjoined, "And wisdom is justified of her children;" that is, though ye be not persuaded, yet with me after this ye cannot find fault. As the prophet saith touching the Father, "That Thou mightest be justified in Thy sayings." For God, though He should effect nothing more by His care over us, fulfills all His part, so as to leave to them that will be shameless not so much as a shadow of excuse for uncandid doubt.

And if the similitudes be mean, and of an ill sound, marvel not, for He was discoursing with a view to the weakness of His hearers. Since Ezekiel too mentions many similitudes like them, and unworthy of God's majesty. But this too especially becomes His tender care.

And mark them, how in another respect also they are carried about into contradictory opinions. For whereas they had said of John, "he hath a devil," they stopped not at this, but said the very same again concerning Him, taking as He did the opposite course; thus were they forever carried about into conflicting opinions.

But Luke herewith sets down also another and a heavier charge against them, saying, "For the publicans justified God, having received the baptism of John."

6. Then He proceeds to upbraid the cities now that wisdom hath been justified; now that He hath shown all to be fully performed. That is, having failed to persuade them, He now doth but lament over them; which is more than terrifying. For He had exhibited both His teaching by His words, and His wonder-working power by His signs. But forasmuch as they abode in their own unbelief, He now does but upbraid.

For "then," it is said, "began Jesus to upbraid the cities, wherein most of His mighty works were done, because they repented not; saying, Woe unto thee, Chorazin! woe unto thee, Bethsaida!"

Then, to show thee that they are not such by nature, He states also the name of the city out of which proceeded five apostles. For both Philip, and those two pairs of the chief apostles, were from thence.

"For if," saith He, "the mighty works which were done in you had been done in Tyre and Sidon, they would have repented in sackcloth and ashes. But I say unto you, It shall be more tolerable for Tyre and Sidon, at the day of judgment, than for you. And thou, Capernaum, which art exalted unto heaven, shalt be brought down to hell, for if the mighty works which have been done in thee had been done in Sodom, it would have remained until this day. But I say unto you, It shall be more tolerable for the land of Sodom in the day of judgment, than for thee."

And He adds not Sodom with the others for nought, but to aggravate the charge against them. Yea, for it is a very great proof of wickedness, when not only of them that now are, but even of all those that ever were wicked, none are found so bad as they.

Thus elsewhere also He makes a comparison, condemning them by the Ninevites, and by the Queen of the south; there, however, it was by them that did right, here, even by them that sinned; a thing far more grievous. With this law of condemnation, Ezekiel too was acquainted: wherefore also he said to Jerusalem, "Thou hast justified thy sisters in all thy sins." Thus everywhere is He wont to linger in the Old Testament, as in a favored place. And not even at this doth He stay His speech, but makes their fears yet more intense, by saying, that they should suffer things more grievous than Sodomites and Tyrians, so as by every means to gather them in, both by bewailing, and by alarming them.

7. To these same things let us also listen: since not for the unbelievers only, but for us also, hath He appointed a punishment more grievous than that of the Sodomites, if we will not receive the strangers that come in unto us; I mean, when He commanded to shake off the very dust: and very fitly. For as to the Sodomites, although they committed a great transgression, yet it was before the law and grace; but we, after so much care shown towards us, of what indulgence should we be worthy, showing so much inhospitality, and shutting our doors against them that are in need, and before our doors our ears? or rather not against the poor only, but against the apostles themselves? For therefore we do it to the poor, because we do it to the very apostles. For whereas Paul is read, and thou attendest not; whereas John preaches, and thou hearest not: when wilt thou receive a poor man, who wilt not receive an apostle?

In order then that both our houses may be continually open to the one, and our ears to the others, let us purge away the filth from the ears of our soul. For as filth and mud close up the ears of our flesh, so do the harlot's songs, and worldly news, and debts, and the business of usury and loans, close up the ear of the mind, worse than any filth; nay rather, they do not close it up only, but also make it unclean. And they are putting dung in your ears, who tell you of these things. And that which the barbarian threatened, saying, "Ye shall eat your own dung," and what follows; this do these men also make you undergo, not in word, but in deeds; or rather, somewhat even much worse. For truly those songs are more loathsome even than all this; and what is yet worse, so far from feeling annoyance when ye hear them, ye rather laugh, when ye ought to abominate them and fly.

But if they be not abominable, go down unto the stage, imitate that which thou praisest; or rather, do thou merely take a walk with him that is exciting that laugh. Nay, thou couldest not bear it. Why then bestow on him so great honor? Yea, while the laws that are enacted by the Gentiles would have them to be dishonored, thou receivest them with thy whole city, like ambassadors and generals, and dost convoke all men, to receive dung in their ears. And thy servant, if he say anything filthy in thy hearing, will receive stripes in abundance; and be it a son, a wife, whoever it may, that doth as I have said, thou callest the act an affront; but if worthless fellows, that deserve the scourge, should invite thee to hear the filthy words, not only art thou not indignant, thou dost even rejoice and applaud. And what could be equal to this folly?

But dost thou thyself never utter these base words? Why what is the profit? or rather, this very fact, whence is it manifest? For if thou didst not utter these things, neither wouldest thou at all laugh at hearing them, nor wouldest thou run with such zeal to the voice that makes thee ashamed.

For tell me, art thou pleased at hearing men blaspheme? Dost thou not rather shudder, and stop thine ears? Surely I think thou dost. Why so? Because thou blasphemest not thyself. Just so do thou act with respect to filthy talking also; and if thou wouldest show us clearly, that thou hast no pleasure in filthy speaking, endure not so much as to hear them. For when wilt thou be able to become good, bred up as thou art with such sounds in thine ears? When wilt thou venture to undergo such labors as chastity requires, now that thou art falling gradually away through this laughter, these songs, and filthy words? Yea, it is a great thing for a soul that keeps itself pure from all this, to be able to become grave and chaste; how much more for one that is nourished up in such hearings? Know ye not, that we are of the two more inclined to evil? While then we make it even an art, and a business, when shall we escape that furnace?

8. Heardest thou not what Paul saith, "Rejoice in the Lord?" He said not, "in the devil." When then wilt thou be able to hear Paul? when, to gain a sense of thy wrong actions? drunken as thou art, ever and incessantly, with the spectacle I was speaking of. For thy having come here is nothing wonderful nor great; or rather it is wonderful. For here thou comest any how, and so as just to satisfy a scruple, but there with diligence and speed, and great readiness. And it is evident from what thou bringest home, on returning thence.

For even all the mire that is there poured out for you, by the speeches, by the songs, by the laughter, ye collect and take every man to his home, or rather not to his home only, but every man even into his own mind.

And from things not worthy of abhorrence thou turnest away; while others which are to be abhorred, so far from hating, thou dost even court. Many, for instance, on coming back from tombs, are used to wash themselves, but on returning from theatres they have never groaned, nor poured forth any fountains of tears; yet surely the dead man is no unclean thing, whereas sin induces such a blot, that not even with ten thousand fountains could one purge it away, but with tears only, and with confessions. But no one hath any sense of this blot. Thus because we fear not what we ought, therefore we shrink from what we ought not.

And what again is the applause? what the tumult, and the satanical cries, and the devilish gestures? For first one, being a young man, wears his hair long behind, and changing his nature into that of a woman, is striving both in aspect, and in gesture, and in garments, and generally in all ways, to pass into the likeness of a tender damsel. Then another who is grown old, in the opposite way to this, having his hair shaven, and with his loins girt about, his shame cut off before his hair, stands ready to be smitten with the rod, prepared both to say and do anything. The women again, their heads uncovered, stand without a blush, discoursing with a whole people, so complete is their practice in shamelessness; and thus pour forth all effrontery and impurity into the souls of their hearers. And their one study is, to pluck up all chastity from the foundations, to disgrace our nature, to satiate the desire of the wicked demon. Yea, and there are both foul sayings, and gestures yet fouler; and the dressing of the hair tends that way, and the gait, and apparel, and voice, and flexure of the limbs; and there are turnings of the eyes, and flutes, and pipes, and dramas, and plots; and all things, in short, full of the most extreme impurity. When then wilt thou be sober again, I pray thee, now that the devil is pouring out for thee so much of the strong wine of whoredom, mingling so many cups of unchastity? For indeed both adulteries and stolen marriages are there, and there are women playing the harlot, men prostituting, youths corrupting themselves: all there is iniquity to the full, all sorcery, all shame. Wherefore they that sit by should not laugh at these things, but weep and groan bitterly.

"What then? Are we to shut up the stage?" it will be said, "and are all things to be turned upside down at thy word?" Nay, but as it is, all things are turned upside down. For whence are they, tell me, that plot against our marriages? Is it not from this theatre? Whence are they that dig through into chambers? Is it not from that stage? Comes it not of this, when husbands are insupportable to their wives? of this, when the wives are contemptible to their husbands? of this, that the more part are adulterers? So that the subverter of all things is he that goes to the theatre; it is he that brings in a grievous tyranny. "Nay," thou wilt say, "this is appointed by the good order of the laws." Why, to tear away men's wives, and to insult young boys, and to overthrow houses, is proper to those who have seized on citadels. "And what adulterer," wilt thou say, "hath been made such by these spectacles?" Nay, who hath not been made an adulterer? And if one might but mention them now by name, I could point out how many husbands those harlots have severed from their wives, how many they have taken captive, drawing some even from the marriage bed itself, not suffering others so much as to live at all in marriage.

"What then? I pray thee, are we to overthrow all the laws?" Nay, but it is overthrowing lawlessness, if we do away with these spectacles. For hence are they that make havoc in our cities; hence, for example, are seditions and tumults. For they that are maintained by the dancers, and who sell their own voice to the belly, whose work it is to shout, and to practise everything that is monstrous, these especially are the men that stir up the populace, that make the tumults in our cities. For youth, when it hath joined hands with idleness, and is brought up in so great evils, becomes fiercer than any wild beast. The necromancers too, I pray thee, whence are they? Is it not from hence, that in order to excite the people who are idling without object, and make the dancing men have the benefit of much and loud applause, and fortify the harlot women against the chaste, they proceed so far in sorcery, as not even to shrink from disturbing the bones of the dead? Comes it not hence, when men are forced to spend without limit on that wicked choir of the devil? And lasciviousness, whence is that, and its innumerable mischiefs? Thou seest, it is thou who art subverting our life, by drawing men to these things, while I am recruiting it by putting them down.

"Let us then pull down the stage," say they. Would that it were possible to pull it down; or rather, if ye be willing, as far as regards us, it is pulled down, and digged up. Nevertheless, I enjoin no such thing. Standing as these places are, I bid you make them of no effect; which thing were a greater praise than pulling them down.

9. Imitate at least the barbarians, if no one else; for they verily are altogether clean from seeking such sights. What excuse then can we have after all this, we, the citizens of Heaven, and partners in the choirs of the cherubim, and in fellowship with the angels, making ourselves in this respect worse even than the barbarians, and this, when innumerable other pleasures, better than these, are within our reach?

Why, if thou desirest that thy soul may find delight, go to pleasure grounds, to a river flowing by, and to lakes, take notice of gardens, listen to grasshoppers as they sing, be continually by the coffins of martyrs, where is health of body and benefit of soul, and no hurt, no remorse after the pleasure, as there is here.

Thou hast a wife, thou hast children; what is equal to this pleasure? Thou hast a house, thou hast friends, these are the true delights: besides their purity, great is the advantage they bestow. For what, I pray thee, is sweeter than children? what sweeter than a wife, to him that will be chaste in mind?

To this purpose, we are told, that the barbarians uttered on some occasion a saying full of wise severity. I mean, that having heard of these wicked spectacles, and the unseasonable delight of them; "why the Romans," say they, "have devised these pleasures, as though they had not wives and children;" implying that nothing is sweeter than children and wife, if thou art willing to live honestly.

"What then," one may say, "if I point to some, who are nothing hurt by their pastime in that place?" In the first place, even this is a hurt, to spend one's time without object or fruit, and to become an offense to others. For even if thou shouldest not be hurt, thou makest some other more eager herein. And how canst thou but be thyself hurt, giving occasion to what goes on? Yea, both the fortune-teller, and the prostitute boy, and the harlot woman, and all those choirs of the devil, cast upon thy head the blame of their proceedings. For as surely as, if there were no spectators, there would be none to follow these employments; so, since there are, they too have their share of the fire due to such deeds. So that even if in chastity thou wert quite unhurt (a thing impossible), yet for others' ruin thou wilt render a grievous account; both the spectators,' and that of those who assemble them.

And in chastity too thou wouldest profit more, didst thou refrain from going thither. For if even now thou art chaste, thou wouldest have become chaster by avoiding such sights. Let us not then delight in useless argument, nor devise unprofitable apologies: there being but one apology, to flee from the Babylonian furnace, to keep far from the Egyptian harlot, though one must escape her hands naked.

For so shall we both enjoy much delight, our conscience not accusing us, and we shall live this present life with chastity, and attain unto the good things to come, by the grace and love towards man of our Lord Jesus Christ; to whom be glory and might, now and ever, and world without end. Amen.

HOMILY XXXVIII

MATT. XI. 25, 26

"At that time Jesus answered and said, I make acknowledgment unto Thee, O Father, Lord of Heaven and earth; because Thou hast hid these things from the wise and prudent, and hast revealed them unto babes. Even so, Father, for so it seemed good in Thy sight."

Seest thou, how many ways He leads them on to the faith? First, by His praises of John. For by pointing to him as a great and marvellous one, He proved likewise all his sayings credible, whereby he used to draw them on to the knowledge of Him. Secondly, by saying, "The kingdom of Heaven suffereth violence, and the violent take it by force;" for this is the language of one who is pressing and urging them. Thirdly, by signifying that the number of the prophets was finished; for this too manifested Himself to be the person that was announced beforehand by them. Fourthly, by pointing out that whatsoever things should be done by him, were all accomplished; at which time also He made mention of the parable of the children. Fifthly, by His upbraiding them that had not believed, and by His alarming and threatening them greatly. Sixthly, by His giving thanks for them that believed. For the expression, "I make acknowledgment to Thee," here is, "I thank Thee." "I thank Thee," He saith, "because Thou hast hid these things from the wise and prudent."

What then? doth He rejoice in destruction, and in the others not having received this knowledge? By no means; but this is a most excellent way of His to save men, His not forcing them that utterly reject, and are not willing to receive His sayings; that, since they were not bettered by His call, but fell back, and despised it, His casting them out might cause them to fall into a longing for these things. And so likewise the attentive would grow more earnest.

And while His being revealed to these was fit matter of joy, His concealment from those was no more of joy but of tears. Thus at any rate He acts, where He weeps for the city. Not therefore because of this doth He rejoice, but because what wise men knew not, was known to these. As when Paul saith, "I thank God, that ye were servants of sin, but ye obeyed from the heart the form of doctrine which was delivered unto you." You see, neither doth Paul therefore rejoice, because they were "servants of sin," but because being such, they had been so highly favored.

Now by the "wise," here, He means the Scribes, and the Pharisees. And these things He saith, to make the disciples more earnest, and to show what had been vouchsafed to the fishermen, when all those others had missed of it. And in calling them "wise," He means not the true and commendable wisdom, but this which they seemed to have through natural shrewdness. Wherefore neither did He say, "thou hast revealed it to fools," but "to babes;" to unsophisticated, that is, to simple-minded men; and He implies that so far from their missing these privileges contrary to their desert, it was just what might be expected. And He instructs us throughout, to be free from pride, and to follow after simplicity. For this cause Paul also expressed it with more exceeding earnestness, writing on this wise: "If any man among you seemeth to be wise in this world, let him become a fool, that he may be wise." For thus is God's grace manifested.

But wherefore doth He give thanks to the Father, although of course it was Himself who wrought this? As He prays and intercedes with God, showing His great love towards us, in the same way doth He this too: for this also is of much love. And He signifies, that not from Him only had they fallen away, but also from the Father. Thus, what He said, speaking to His disciples, "Cast not the holy things unto dogs," this He Himself anticipated them in performing.

Moreover He signifies hereby both His own principal will, and that of the Father; His own, I say, by His giving thanks and rejoicing at what had taken place; His Father's, by intimating that neither had He done this upon entreaty, but of Himself upon His own will; "For so," saith He, "it seemed good in Thy sight:" that is, "so it pleased Thee."

And wherefore was it hidden from them? Hear Paul, saying, that "Seeking to establish their own righteousness, they have not submitted themselves to the righteousness of God."

Consider now how it was likely the disciples should be affected, hearing this; that what wise men knew not, these knew, and knew it continuing babes, and knew it by God's revelation. But Luke saith, that "at the very hour," when the seventy came telling Him about the devils, then He "rejoiced" and spake these things, which, besides increasing their diligence, would also dispose them to be modest. That is, since it was natural for them to pride themselves on their driving away devils, on this among other grounds He refrains them; that it was a revelation, whatever had been done, no diligence on their part. Wherefore also the scribes, and the wise men, thinking to be intelligent for themselves, fell away through their own vanity. Well then, if for this cause it was hidden from them, "do you also," saith He, "fear, and continue babes." For this caused you to have the benefit of the revelation, as indeed on the other hand the contrary made them be deprived of it. For by no means, when He saith, "Thou hast hid," doth He mean that it is all God's doing: but as when Paul saith, "He gave them over to a reprobate mind," and, "He hath blinded their minds," it is not meant to bring Him in as the doer of it, but those who gave the occasion: so here also He uses the expression, "Thou hast hid."

For since He had said, "I thank Thee, because Thou hast hid them, and hast revealed them unto babes;" to hinder thy supposing that as being Himself deprived of this power, and unable to effect it, so He offers thanks, He saith,

"All things are delivered unto me of my Father." And to them that are rejoicing, because the devils obey them, "Nay, why marvel," saith He, "that devils yield to you? All things are mine; "All things are delivered unto me."

But when thou hearest, "they are delivered," do not surmise anything human. For He uses this expression, to prevent thine imagining two unoriginate Gods. Since, that He was at the same time both begotten, and Lord of all, He declares in many ways, and in other places also.

2. Then He saith what is even greater than this, lifting up thy mind; "And no man knoweth the Son, but the Father; neither knoweth any man the Father, but the Son." Which seems indeed to the ignorant unconnected with what went before, but hath full accordance therewith. As thus: having said, "All things are delivered unto me of my Father," He adds, "And what marvel," so He speaks, "if I be Lord of all? I who have also another greater privilege, the knowing the Father, and being of the same substance." Yea, for this too He covertly signifies by His being the only one who so knew Him. For this is His meaning, when He saith, "No man knoweth the Father but the Son."

And see at what time He saith this. When they by His works had received the certain proof of His might, not only seeing Him work miracles, but endowed also in His name with so great powers. Then, since He had said, "Thou hast revealed them unto babes," He signifies this also to pertain to Himself; for "neither knoweth any man the Father," saith He, "save the Son, and he to whomsoever the Son is willing to reveal Him; not "to whomsoever He may be enjoined," "to whomsoever He may be commanded." But if He reveals Him, then Himself too. This however He let pass as acknowledged, but the other He hath set down. And everywhere He affirms this; as when He saith, "No man cometh unto the Father, but by me."

And thereby he establishes another point also, His being in harmony and of one mind with Him. "Why," saith He, "I am so far from fighting and warring with Him, that no one can even come to Him but by me." For because this most offended them, His seeming to be a rival God, He by all means doth away with this; and interested Himself about this not less earnestly, but even more so, than about His miracles.

But when He saith, "Neither knoweth any man the Father, save the Son," He means not this, that all men were ignorant of Him, but that with the knowledge wherewith He knows Him, no man is acquainted with Him; which may be said of the Son too. For it was not of some God unknown, and revealed to no man, that He was so speaking, as Marcion saith; but it is the perfection of knowledge that He is here intimating, since neither do we know the Son as He should be known; and this very thing, to add no more, Paul was declaring, when he said, "We know in part, and we prophesy in part."

3. Next, having brought them by His words to an earnest desire, and having signified His unspeakable power, He after that invites them, saying, "Come

unto me, all ye that labor and are heavy laden, and I will give you rest." Not this or that person, but all that are in anxiety, in sorrows, in sins. Come, not that I may call you to account, but that I may do away your sins; come, not that I want your honor, but that I want your salvation. "For I," saith He, "will give you rest." He said not, "I will save you," only; but what was much more, "I will place you in all security."

"Take my yoke upon you, and learn of me, for I am meek and lowly in heart; and ye shall find rest unto your souls. For my yoke is easy, and my burden is light." Thus, "be not afraid," saith He, "hearing of a yoke, for it is easy: fear not, because I said, "a burden," for it is light."

And how said He before, "The gate is narrow and the way strait?" Whilst thou art careless, whilst thou art supine; whereas, if thou duly perform His words, the burden will be light; wherefore also He hath now called it so.

But how are they duly performed? If thou art become lowly, and meek, and gentle. For this virtue is the mother of all strictness of life. Wherefore also, when beginning those divine laws, with this He began. And here again He doeth the very same, and exceeding great is the reward He appoints. "For not to another only dost thou become serviceable; but thyself also above all thou refreshest," saith He. "For ye shall find rest unto your souls."

Even before the things to come, He gives thee here thy recompense, and bestows the prize already, making the saying acceptable, both hereby, and by setting Himself forward as an example. For, "Of what art thou afraid?" saith He, "lest thou shouldest be a loser by thy low estate? Look to me, and to all that is mine; learn of me, and then shalt thou know distinctly how great thy blessing." Seest thou how in all ways He is leading them to humility? By His own doings: "Learn of me, for I am meek." By what themselves are to gain; for, "Ye shall find," saith He," rest unto your souls." By what He bestows on them; for, "I too will refresh you," saith He. By rendering it light; "For my yoke is easy, and my burden is light." So likewise doth Paul, saying, "For the present light affliction, which is but for a moment, worketh a far more exceeding and eternal weight of glory."

And how, some one may say, is the burden light, when He saith, "Except one hate father and mother;" and, "Whosoever taketh not up his cross, and followeth after me, is not worthy of me:" and, "Whosoever forsaketh not all that he hath, cannot be my disciple:" when He commands even to give up our very life? Let Paul teach thee, saying, "Who shall separate us from the love of Christ? Shall tribulation, or distress, or persecution, or famine, or nakedness, or peril, or sword? " And that, "The sufferings of this present time are not worthy to be compared with the glory that shall be revealed in us." Let those teach thee, who return from the council of the Jews after plenty of stripes, and "rejoice that they were counted worthy to suffer shame for the name of Christ." And if thou art still afraid and tremblest at hearing of the yoke and the burden, the fear comes not of the nature of the thing, but of thy remissness; since if thou art prepared, and in earnest, all will be easy to thee and light. Since for this cause Christ also, to signify that we too must needs labor ourselves, did not mention the gracious things only, and then hold His peace, nor the painful things only, but set down both. Thus He both spake of "a yoke," and called it "easy;" both named a burden, and added that it was "light;" that thou shouldest neither flee from them as toilsome, nor despise them as over easy.

But if even after all this, virtue seem to thee an irksome thing, consider that vice is more irksome. And this very thing He was intimating, in that He said not first, "Take my yoke upon you," but before that, "Come, ye that labor and are heavy laden;" implying that sin too hath labor, and a burden that is heavy and hard to bear. For He said not only, "Ye that labor," but also, "that are heavy laden." This the prophet too was speaking of, when in that description of her nature, "As an heavy burden they weighed heavy upon me." And Zacharias too, describing her, saith she is "A talent of lead."

And this moreover experience itself proves. For nothing so weighs upon the soul, and presses it down, as consciousness of sin; nothing so much gives it wings, and raises it on high, as the attainment of righteousness and virtue.

And mark it: what is more grievous, I pray thee, than to have no possessions? to turn the cheek, and when smitten not to smite again? to die by a violent death? Yet nevertheless, if we practise self-command, all these things are light and easy, and pleasurable.

But be not disturbed; rather let us take up each of these, and inquire about it accurately; and if ye will, that first which many count most painful. Which then of the two, tell me, is grievous and burdensome, to be in care for one belly, or to be anxious about ten thousand? To be clothed with one outer garment, and seek for nothing more; or having many in one's house, to bemoan one's self every day and night in fear, in trembling, about the preservation of them, grieved, and ready to choke about the loss of them; lest one should be moth-eaten, lest a servant purloin and go off with them?

4. But whatever I may say, my speech will present no such proof as the actual trial. Wherefore I would there were present here with us some one of those who have attained unto that summit of self-restraint, and then you would know assuredly the delight thereof; and that none of those that are enamored

of voluntary poverty would accept wealth, though ten thousand were to offer it.

But would these, say you, ever consent to become poor, and to cast away the anxieties which they have? And what of that? This is but a proof of their madness and grievous disease, not of anything very pleasurable in the thing. And this even themselves would testify to us, who are daily lamenting over these their anxieties, and accounting their life to be not worth living. But not so those others; rather they laugh, leap for joy, and the wearers of the diadem do not so glory, as they do in their poverty.

Again, to turn the cheek is, to him that gives heed, a less grievous thing than to smite another; for from this the contest hath beginning, in that termination: and whereas by the former thou hast kindled the other's pile too, by the latter thou hast quenched even thine own flames. But that not to be burnt is a pleasanter thing than to be burnt, is surely plain to every man. And if this hold in regard of bodies, much more in a soul.

And whether is lighter, to contend, or to be crowned? to fight, or to have the prize? and to endure waves, or to run into harbor? Therefore also, to die is better than to live. For the one withdraws us from waves and dangers, while the other adds unto them, and makes a man subject to numberless plots and distresses, which have made life not worth living in thine account.

And if thou disbelievest our sayings, hearken to them that have seen the countenances of the martyrs in the time of their conflicts, how when scourged and flayed, they were exceeding joyful and glad, and when exposed upon hot irons, rejoiced, and were glad of heart, more than such as lie upon a bed of roses. Wherefore Paul also said, when he was at the point of departing hence, and closing his life by a violent death, "I joy, and rejoice with you all; for the same cause also do ye joy, and rejoice with me." Seest thou with what exceeding strength of language he invites the whole world to partake in his gladness? So great a good did he know his departure hence to be, so desirable, and lovely, and worthy of prayer, that formidable thing, death.

5. But that virtue's yoke is sweet and light, is manifest many other ways also; but to conclude, if you please, let us look also at the burdens of sin. Let us then bring forward the covetous, the retailers and second-hand dealers in shameless bargains. What now could be a heavier burden than such transactions? how many sorrows, how many anxieties, how many disappointments, how many dangers, how many plots and wars, daily spring up from these gains? how many troubles and disturbances? For as one can never see the sea without waves, so neither such a soul without anxiety, and despondency, and

fear, and disturbance; yea, the second overtakes the first, and again others come up, and when these are not yet ceased, others come to a head.

Or wouldest thou see the souls of the revilers, and of the passionate? Why, what is worse than this torture? what, than the wounds they have within? what, than the furnace that is continually burning, and the flame that is never quenched?

Or of the sensual, and of such as cleave unto this present life? Why, what more grievous than this bondage? They live the life of Cain, dwelling in continual trembling and fear at every death that happens; the kinsmen of the dead mourn not so much, as these do for their own end.

What again fuller of turmoil, and more frantic, than such as are puffed up with pride? "For learn," saith He, "of me, for I am meek and lowly in heart, and ye shall find rest unto your souls." Because long-suffering is the mother of all good things.

Fear thou not therefore, neither start away from the yoke that lightens thee of all these things, but put thyself under it with all forwardness, and then thou shalt know well the pleasure thereof. For it doth not at all bruise thy neck, but is put on thee for good order's sake only, and to persuade thee to walk seemly, and to lead thee unto the royal road, and to deliver thee from the precipices on either side, and to make thee walk with ease in the narrow way.

Since then so great are its benefits, so great its security, so great its gladness, let us with all our soul, with all our diligence, draw this yoke; that we may both here "find rest unto our souls," and attain unto the good things to come, by the grace and love towards man of our Lord Jesus Christ, to whom be glory and might, now and ever, and world without end. Amen.

HOMILY XXXIX

MATT. XII. 1

"At that time Jesus went on the Sabbath day through the corn; and His disciples were a hungered, and began to pluck the ears of corn, and to eat."

But Luke saith, "On a double Sabbath." Now what is a double Sabbath? When the cessation from toil is twofold, both that of the regular Sabbath, and that of another feast coming upon it. For they call every cessation from toil, a sabbath.

But why could He have led them away from it, who foreknew all, unless it had been His will that the Sabbath should be broken? It was His will indeed, but not simply so; wherefore He never breaks it without a cause, but giving reasonable excuses: that He might at once bring the law to an end, and not startle them. But there are occasions on which He even repeals it directly, and not with circumstance: as when He anoints with the clay the eyes of the blind man; as when He saith, "My Father worketh hitherto, and I work." And He doth so, by this to glorify His own Father, by the other to soothe the infirmity of the Jews. At which last He is laboring here, putting forward as a plea the necessity of nature; although in the case of acknowledged sins, that could not of course ever be an excuse. For neither may the murderer make his anger a plea, nor the adulterer allege his lust, no, nor any other excuse; but here, by mentioning their hunger, He freed them from all blame.

But do thou, I pray thee, admire the disciples, how entirely they control themselves, and make no account of the things of the body, but esteem the table of the flesh a secondary thing, and though they have to struggle with continual hunger, do not even so withdraw themselves. For except hunger had sorely constrained them, they would not have done so much as this.

What then do the Pharisees? "When they saw it," it is said, "they said unto Him, Behold, Thy disciples do that which is not lawful to do upon the Sabbath day."

Now here indeed with no great vehemence (yet surely that would have been consistent in them),—nevertheless they are not vehemently provoked, but simply find fault. But when He stretched out the withered hand and healed it, then they were so infuriated, as even to consult together about slaying and destroying Him. For where nothing great and noble is done, they are calm; but where they see any made whole, they are savage, and fret themselves, and none so intolerable as they are: such enemies are they of the salvation of men.

How then doth Jesus defend His disciples? "Have ye not read," saith He, "what David did in the temple, when he was an hungered, himself and all they that were with him? how he entered into the house of God, and did eat the show-bread, which was not lawful for him to eat, neither for them which were with him, but only for the priests?"

Thus, whereas in pleading for His disciples, He brings forward David; for Himself, it is the Father.

And observe His reproving manner: "Have ye not read what David did?" For great indeed was that prophet's glory, so that Peter also afterwards pleading with the Jews, spake on this wise, "Let me freely speak unto you of the patriarch David, that he is both dead and buried."

But wherefore doth He not call him by the name of his rank, either on this occasion or afterwards? Perhaps because He derived His race from him.

Now had they been a candid sort of persons, He would have turned His discourse to the disciples' suffering from hunger; but abominable as they were and inhuman, He rather rehearses unto them a history.

But Mark saith, "In the days of Abiathar the High Priest:" not stating what was con trary to the history, but implying that he had two names; and adds that "he gave unto him," indicating that herein also David had much to say for himself, since even the very priest suffered him; and not only suffered, but even ministered unto him. For tell me not that David was a prophet, for not even so was it lawful, but the privilege was the priests': wherefore also He added, "but for the priests only." For though he were ten thousand times a prophet, yet was he not a priest; and though he were himself a prophet, yet not so they that were with him; since to them too we know that he gave.

"What then," it might be said, "were they all one with David?" Why talk to me of dignity, where there seems to be a transgression of the law, even though it be the constraint of nature? Yea, and in this way too He hath the more entirely acquitted them of the charges, in that he who is greater is found to have done the same.

"And what is this to the question," one may say; "for it was not surely the Sabbath, that he transgressed?" Thou tellest me of that which is greater, and which especially shows the wisdom of Christ, that letting go the Sabbath, He brings another example greater than the Sabbath. For it is by no means the same, to break in upon a day, and to touch that holy table, which it was not lawful for any man to touch. Since the Sabbath indeed hath been violated, and that often; nay rather it is continually being violated, both by circumcision, and by many other works; and at Jericho too one may see the same to have happened; but this happened then only. So that He more than obtains the victory. How then did no man blame David, although there was yet another ground of charge heavier than this, that of the priests' murder, which had its origin from this? But He states it not, as applying himself to the present subject only.

2. Afterwards again He refutes it in another way also. For as at first He brought in David, by the dignity of the person quelling their pride; so when He had stopped their mouths, and had put down their boasting, then He adds also the more appropriate refutation. And of what sort is this? "Know ye not, that in the temple the priests profane the Sabbath, and are blameless?" For in that other instance indeed, saith He, the emergency made the relaxation, but here is the relaxation even without emergency. He did not however at once thus refute them but first by way of permission, afterwards as insisting upon

his argument. Because it was meet to draw the stronger inference last, although the former argument also had of course its proper weight.

For tell me not, that it is not freeing one's self from blame, to bring forward another who is committing the same sin. For when the doer incurs no blame, the act on which he hath ventured becomes a rule for others to plead.

Nevertheless He was not satisfied with this, but subjoins also what is more decisive, saying that the deed is no sin at all; and this more than anything was the sign of a glorious victory, to point to the law repealing itself, and in two ways doing so, first by the place, then by the Sabbath; or rather even in three ways, in that both the work is twofold that is done, and with it goes also another thing, its being done by the priests; and what is yet more, that it is not even brought as a charge. "For they," saith He, "are blameless."

Seest thou how many points He hath stated? the place; for He saith, "In the temple;" the persons, for they are "the priests;" the time, for He saith, "the Sabbath;" the act itself, for "they profane;" (He not having said, "they break," but what is more grievous, "they profane;") that they not only escape punishment, but are even free from blame, "for they," saith He, "are blameless."

Do not ye therefore account this, He saith, like the former instance. For that indeed was done both but once, and not by a priest, and was of necessity; wherefore also they were deserving of excuse; but this last is both done every Sabbath, and by priests, and in the temple, and according to the law. And therefore again not by favor, but in a legal way, they are acquitted of the charges. For not at all as blaming them did I so speak, saith He, nor yet as freeing them from blame in the way of indulgence, but according to the principle of justice.

And He seems indeed to be defending them, but it is His disciples whom He is clearing of the alleged faults. For when He saith, "those are blameless," He means, "much more are these."

"But they are not priests." Nay, they are greater than priests. For the Lord of the temple Himself is here: the truth, not the type. Wherefore He said also, "But I say unto you, That in this place is one greater than the temple."

Nevertheless, great as the sayings were which they heard, they made no reply, for the salvation of men was not their object.

Then, because to the hearers it would seem harsh, He quickly draws a veil over it, giving His discourse, as before, a lenient turn, yet even so expressing Himself with a rebuke. "But if ye had known what this meaneth, I will have mercy and not sacrifice, ye would not have condemned the guiltless."

Seest thou how again He inclines His speech to lenity, yet again shows them to be out of the reach of lenity? "For ye would not have condemned," saith He, "the guiltless." Before indeed He inferred the same from what is said of the priests, in the words, "they are guiltless;" but here He states it on His own authority; or rather, this too is out of the law, for He was quoting a prophetic saying.

3. After this He mentions another reason likewise; "For the Son of man," saith He, "is Lord of the Sabbath day;" speaking it of Himself. But Mark relates Him to have said this of our common nature also; for He said, "The Sabbath was made for man, not man for the Sabbath."

Wherefore then was he punished that was gathering the sticks? Because if the laws were to be despised even at the beginning, of course they would scarcely be observed afterwards.

For indeed the Sabbath did at the first confer many and great benefits; for instance, it made them gentle towards those of their household, and humane; it taught them God's providence and the creation, as Ezekiel saith; it trained them by degrees to abstain from wickedness, and disposed them to regard the things of the Spirit.

For because they could not have borne it, if when He was giving the law for the Sabbath, He had said, "Do your good works on the Sabbath, but do not the works which are evil," therefore He restrained them from all alike for, "Ye must do nothing at all," saith He: and not even so were they kept in order. But He Himself, in the very act of giving the law of the Sabbath, did even therein darkly signify that He will have them refrain from the evil works only, by the saying, "Ye must do no work, except what shall be done for your life." And in the temple too all went on, and with more diligence and double toil. Thus even by the very shadow He was secretly opening unto them the truth.

Did Christ then, it will be said, repeal a thing so highly profitable? Far from it; nay, He greatly enhanced it. For it was time for them to be trained in all things by the higher rules, and it was unnecessary that his hands should be bound, who was freed from wickedness, winged for all good works; or that men should hereby learn that God made all things; or that they should so be made gentle, who are called to imitate God's own love to mankind (for He saith, "Be ye merciful, as your Heavenly Father"); or that they should make one day a festival, who are commanded to keep a feast all their life long; ("For let us keep the feast," it is said, "not with old leaven, neither with leaven of malice and wickedness; but with unleavened bread of sincerity and truth"); as neither need they stand by an ark and a golden altar, who have the very Lord of all for their inmate, and in all things hold communion with Him; by prayer, and by oblation, and by scriptures, and by almsgiving, and by having Him within them. Lo now, why is any Sabbath required, by him who is always keeping the feast, whose conversation is in Heaven?

4. Let us keep the feast then continually, and do no evil thing; for this is a feast: and let our spiritual things be made intense, while our earthly things give place: and let us rest a spiritual rest, refraining our hands from covetousness; withdrawing our body from our superfluous and unprofitable toils, from such as the people of the Hebrews did of old endure in Egypt. For there is no difference betwixt us who are gathering gold, and those that were bound in the mire, working at those bricks, and gathering stubble, and being beaten. Yea, for now too the devil bids us make bricks, as Pharaoh did then. For what else is gold, than mire? and what else is silver, than stubble? Like stubble, at least, it kindles the flame of desire; like mire, so doth gold defile him that possesses it.

Wherefore He sent us, not Moses from the wilderness, but His Son from Heaven. If then, after He is come, thou abide in Egypt, thou wilt suffer with the Egyptians: but if leaving that land thou go up with the spiritual Israel, thou shalt see all the miracles.

Yet not even this suffices for salvation. For we must not only be delivered out of Egypt, but we must also enter into the promise. Since the Jews too, as Paul saith, both went through the Red Sea, and ate manna, and drank spiritual drink, but nevertheless they all perished.

Lest then the same befall us also, let us not be slow, neither draw back; but when thou hearest wicked spies even now bringing up an evil report against the strait and narrow way, and uttering the same kind of talk as those spies of old, let not the multitude, but Joshua, be our pattern, and Caleb the son of Jephunneh; and do not thou give up, until thou have attained the promise, and entered into the Heavens.

Neither account the journey to be difficult. "For if when we were enemies, we were reconciled to God, much more, being reconciled, shall we be saved." "But this way," it will be said, "is strait and narrow." Well, but the former, through which thou hast come, is not strait and narrow only, but even impassable, and full of savage wild beasts. And as there was no passing through the Red Sea, unless that miracle had been wrought, so neither could we, abiding in our former life, have gone up into Heaven, but only by baptism intervening. Now if the impossible hath become possible, much more will the difficult be easy.

"But that," it will be said, "was of grace only." Why, for this reason especially thou hast just cause to take courage. For if, where it was grace alone, He wrought with you; will He not much more be your aid, where ye also show forth laborious works? If He saved thee, doing nothing, will He not much more help thee, working?

Above indeed I was saying, that from the impossibilities thou oughtest to take courage about the difficulties also; but now I add this, that if we are vigilant, these will not be so much as difficult. For mark it: death is trodden under foot, the devil hath fallen, the law of sin is extinguished, the grace of the Spirit is given, life is contracted into a small space, the heavy burdens are abridged.

And to convince thee hereof by the actual results, see how many have overshot the injunctions of Christ; and art thou afraid of that which is just their measure? What plea then wilt thou have, when others are leaping beyond the bounds, and thou thyself too slothful for what is enacted?

Thus, thee we admonish to give alms of such things as thou hast, but another hath even stripped himself of all his possessions: thee we require to live chastely with thy wife, but another hath not so much as entered into marriage: and thee we entreat not to be envious, but another we find giving up even his own life for charity: thee again we entreat to be lenient in judgments, and not severe to them that sin, but another, even when smitten, hath turned the other cheek also.

What then shall we say, I pray thee? What excuse shall we make, not doing even these things, when others go so far beyond us? And they would not have gone beyond us, had not the thing been very easy. For which pines away, he who envies other men's blessings, or he who takes pleasure with them, and rejoices? Which eyes all things with suspicion and continual trembling, the chaste man, or the adulterer? Which is cheered by good hopes, he that spoils by violence, or he that shows mercy, and imparts of his own to the needy?

Let us then bear in mind these things, and not be torpid in our career for virtue's sake; but having stripped ourselves with all readiness for these glorious wrestlings, let us labor for a little while, that we may win the perpetual and imperishable crowns; unto which may we all attain, by the grace and love towards man of our Lord Jesus Christ, to whom be glory and might forever and ever. Amen.

THE CHURCH FATHERS

COMPLETE SET: 3 SERIES, 63 VOLUMES

A E T E R N A P R E S S

THE CHURCH FATHERS COMPLETE COLLECTION: COMPOSED OF 3 SERIES, 63 VOLUMES, 65 AUTHORS, 500 TEXTS COMPOSED OF 1,000 BOOKS, 18,000 CHAPTERS, 16 MILLION WORDS.

CATHOLIC EDITION. CONTAINS CHURCH FATHERS AUTHOR TEXTS ONLY, WITHOUT PROTESTANT INTRODUCTIONS, ELUCIDATIONS, PREFACES OR FOOTNOTES.

NPNF1-01. SAINT AUGUSTINE: THE CONFESSIONS OF SAINT AUGUSTIN: CE
NPNF1: 25 VOLUMES. VOLUME: 1. 978-1-78516-260-2. PAPERBACK 6X9

NPNF1-02. SAINT AUGUSTINE: LETTERS OF SAINT AUGUSTIN: CE
NPNF1: 25 VOLUMES. VOLUME: 2. 978-1-78516-261-9. PAPERBACK 6X9

NPNF1-03. SAINT AUGUSTINE: THE CITY OF GOD: PART 1: CE
NPNF1: 25 VOLUMES. VOLUME: 3. 978-1-78516-262-6. PAPERBACK 6X9

NPNF1-04. SAINT AUGUSTINE: THE CITY OF GOD: PART 2: CE
NPNF1: 25 VOLUMES. VOLUME: 4. 978-1-78516-263-3. PAPERBACK 6X9

NPNF1-05. SAINT AUGUSTINE: ON CHRISTIAN DOCTRINE, MORAL TREATISES OF SAINT AUGUSTIN: CE
NPNF1: 25 VOLUMES. VOLUME: 5. 978-1-78516-264-0. PAPERBACK 6X9

NPNF1-06. SAINT AUGUSTINE: DOCTRINAL TREATISES OF SAINT AUGUSTIN: CE
NPNF1: 25 VOLUMES. VOLUME: 6. 978-1-78516-265-7. PAPERBACK 6X9

NPNF1-07. SAINT AUGUSTINE: THE ANTI-MANICHAEAN WRITINGS: CE
NPNF1: 25 VOLUMES. VOLUME: 7. 978-1-78516-266-4. PAPERBACK 6X9

NPNF1-08. SAINT AUGUSTINE: THE ANTI-DONATIST WRITINGS: CE
NPNF1: 25 VOLUMES. VOLUME: 8. 978-1-78516-267-1. PAPERBACK 6X9

NPNF1-09. SAINT AUGUSTINE: ANTI-PELAGIAN WORKS: PART 1: CE
NPNF1: 25 VOLUMES. VOLUME: 9. 978-1-78516-268-8. PAPERBACK 6X9

NPNF1-10. SAINT AUGUSTINE: ANTI-PELAGIAN WORKS: PART 2: CE
NPNF1: 25 VOLUMES. VOLUME: 10. 978-1-78516-269-5. PAPERBACK 6X9

NPNF1-11. SAINT AUGUSTINE: OUR LORD'S SERMON ON THE MOUNT, THE HARMONY OF THE GOSPELS: CE
NPNF1: 25 VOLUMES. VOLUME: 11. 978-1-78516-270-1. PAPERBACK 6X9

NPNF1-12. SAINT AUGUSTINE: SERMONS ON SELECTED LESSONS OF THE NEW TESTAMENT: CE
NPNF1: 25 VOLUMES. VOLUME: 12. 978-1-78516-271-8. PAPERBACK 6X9

NPNF1-13. SAINT AUGUSTINE: LECTURES OR TRACTATES ON THE GOSPEL ACCORDING TO SAINT JOHN: CE
NPNF1: 25 VOLUMES. VOLUME: 13. 978-1-78516-272-5. PAPERBACK 6X9

NPNF1-14. SAINT AUGUSTINE -TEN HOMILIES ON THE FIRST EPISTLE OF JOHN TO THE PARTHIANS, TWO BOOKS OF SOLILOQUIES, EXPOSITIONS ON THE BOOK OF PSALMS: PART 1: CE
NPNF1: 25 VOLUMES. VOLUME: 14. 978-1-78516-273-2. PAPERBACK 6X9

NPNF1-15. SAINT AUGUSTINE: EXPOSITIONS ON THE BOOK OF PSALMS: PART 2: CE
NPNF1: 25 VOLUMES. VOLUME: 15. 978-1-78516-274-9. PAPERBACK 6X9

NPNF1-16. SAINT CHRYSOSTOM: ON THE PRIESTHOOD, ASCETIC TREATISES, SELECT HOMILIES AND LETTERS, HOMILIES ON THE STATUTES: CE
NPNF1: 25 VOLUMES. VOLUME: 16. 978-1-78516-275-6. PAPERBACK 6X9

NPNF1-17. SAINT CHRYSOSTOM: HOMILIES ON THE GOSPEL OF SAINT MATTHEW: PART 1: CE
NPNF1: 25 VOLUMES. VOLUME: 17. 978-1-78516-276-3. PAPERBACK 6X9

NPNF1-18. SAINT CHRYSOSTOM: HOMILIES ON THE GOSPEL OF SAINT MATTHEW: PART 2: CE
NPNF1: 25 VOLUMES. VOLUME: 18. 978-1-78516-277-0. PAPERBACK 6X9

NPNF1-19. SAINT CHRYSOSTOM: HOMILIES ON THE ACTS OF THE APOSTLES: CE
NPNF1: 25 VOLUMES. VOLUME: 19. 978-1-78516-278-7. PAPERBACK 6X9

NPNF1-20. SAINT CHRYSOSTOM: HOMILIES ON THE EPISTLE OF SAINT PAUL THE APOSTLE TO THE ROMANS: CE
NPNF1: 25 VOLUMES. VOLUME: 20. 978-1-78516-279-4. PAPERBACK 6X9

NPNF1-21. SAINT CHRYSOSTOM: HOMILIES ON THE EPISTLES OF PAUL TO THE CORINTHIANS, HOMILIES ON THE SECOND EPISTLE OF SAINT PAUL THE APOSTLE TO THE CORINTHIANS: CE
NPNF1: 25 VOLUMES. VOLUME: 21. 978-1-78516-280-0. PAPERBACK 6X9

NPNF1-22. SAINT CHRYSOSTOM: HOMILIES ON GALATIANS, EPHESIANS, PHILIPPIANS, COLOSSIANS AND THESSALONIANS: CE
NPNF1: 25 VOLUMES. VOLUME: 22. 978-1-78516-281-7. PAPERBACK 6X9

NPNF1-23. SAINT CHRYSOSTOM: HOMILIES ON THE EPISTLES OF SAINT PAUL THE APOSTLE TO TIMOTHY, TITUS, AND PHILEMON: CE
NPNF1: 25 VOLUMES. VOLUME: 23. 978-1-78516-282-4. PAPERBACK 6X9

NPNF1-24. SAINT CHRYSOSTOM: HOMILIES ON THE GOSPEL OF SAINT JOHN: CE
NPNF1: 25 VOLUMES. VOLUME: 24. 978-1-78516-283-1. PAPERBACK 6X9

NPNF1-25. SAINT CHRYSOSTOM: HOMILIES ON THE EPISTLE TO THE HEBREWS: CE
NPNF1: 25 VOLUMES. VOLUME: 25. 978-1-78516-284-8. PAPERBACK 6X9

NPNF2-01. THE CHURCH HISTORY OF EUSEBIUS, THE LIFE OF THE BLESSED EMPEROR CONSTANTINE, THE ORATION OF THE EMPEROR CONSTANTINE, THE ORATION OF EUSEBIUS PAMPHILUS: CE
NPNF2: 21 VOLUMES. VOLUME: 1. 978-1-78516-285-5. PAPERBACK 6X9

NPNF2-02. THE ECCLESIASTICAL HISTORY OF SOCRATES, THE ECCLESIASTICAL HISTORY OF SOZOMEN: CE
NPNF2: 21 VOLUMES. VOLUME: 2. 978-1-78516-286-2. PAPERBACK 6X9

NPNF2-03. THE ECCLESIASTICAL HISTORY, DIALOGUES, AND LETTERS OF THEODORET, DIALOGUES, THE ERANISTES OR POLYMORPHUS OF THE BLESSED THEODORETUS: CE
NPNF2: 21 VOLUMES. VOLUME: 3. 978-1-78516-287-9. PAPERBACK 6X9

NPNF2-04. LETTERS OF THE BLESSED THEODORET, JEROME AND GENNADIUS LIVES OF ILLUSTRIOUS MEN, LIFE AND WORKS OF RUFINUS WITH JEROME'S APOLOGY AGAINST RUFINUS: CE
NPNF2: 21 VOLUMES. VOLUME: 4. 978-1-78516-288-6. PAPERBACK 6X9

NPNF2-05. SAINT ATHANASIUS OF ALEXANDRIA: SELECT WORKS AND LETTERS: PART 1: CE
NPNF2: 21 VOLUMES. VOLUME: 5. 978-1-78516-289-3. PAPERBACK 6X9

NPNF2-06. SAINT ATHANASIUS OF ALEXANDRIA: SELECT WORKS AND LETTERS: PART 2: CE
NPNF2: 21 VOLUMES. VOLUME: 6. 978-1-78516-290-9. PAPERBACK 6X9

NPNF2-07. SAINT GREGORY OF NYSSA: DOGMATIC TREATISES: CE
NPNF2: 21 VOLUMES. VOLUME: 7. 978-1-78516-291-6. PAPERBACK 6X9

NPNF2-08. SAINT GREGORY OF NYSSA: ASCETIC AND MORAL TREATISES, PHILOSOPHICAL WORKS, APOLOGETIC WORKS, ORATORICAL WORKS, LETTERS: CE
NPNF2: 21 VOLUMES. VOLUME: 8. 978-1-78516-292-3. PAPERBACK 6X9

NPNF2-09. SAINT JEROME: LETTERS: CE
NPNF2: 21 VOLUMES. VOLUME: 9. 978-1-78516-293-0. PAPERBACK 6X9

NPNF2-10. SAINT JEROME: TREATISES: CE
NPNF2: 21 VOLUMES. VOLUME: 10. 978-1-78516-294-7. PAPERBACK 6X9

NPNF2-11. THE CATECHETICAL LECTURES OF SAINT CYRIL, SELECT ORATIONS OF SAINT GREGORY NAZIANZEN, SELECT LETTERS OF SAINT GREGORY NAZIANZEN: CE
NPNF2: 21 VOLUMES. VOLUME: 11. 978-1-78516-295-4. PAPERBACK 6X9

NPNF2-12. SAINT BASIL: DE SPIRITU SANCTO, THE HEXAEMERON, THE LETTERS: CE
NPNF2: 21 VOLUMES. VOLUME: 12. 978-1-78516-296-1. PAPERBACK 6X9

NPNF2-13. SAINT HILARY OF POITIERS: TREATISE DE SYNODIS, DE TRINITATE, THE HOMILIES ON PSALMS I, LIII, CXXX, EXPOSITION OF THE ORTHODOX FAITH BY JOHN OF DAMASCUS: CE
NPNF2: 21 VOLUMES. VOLUME: 13. 978-1-78516-297-8. PAPERBACK 6X9

NPNF2-14. SAINT AMBROSE: DOGMATIC TREATISES, ETHICAL WORKS, AND SERMONS, SELECTIONS FROM THE LETTERS OF SAINT AMBROSE: CE
NPNF2: 21 VOLUMES. VOLUME: 14. 978-1-78516-298-5. PAPERBACK 6X9

NPNF2-15. THE WORKS OF SULPITIUS SEVERUS: CE
NPNF2: 21 VOLUMES. VOLUME: 15. 978-1-78516-299-2. PAPERBACK 6X9

NPNF2-16. THE WORKS OF JOHN CASSIAN: CE
NPNF2: 21 VOLUMES. VOLUME: 16. 978-1-78516-300-5. PAPERBACK 6X9

NPNF2-17. THE LETTERS AND SERMONS OF SAINT LEO THE GREAT: CE
NPNF2: 21 VOLUMES. VOLUME: 17. 978-1-78516-301-2. PAPERBACK 6X9

NPNF2-18. SAINT GREGORY THE GREAT: THE BOOK OF PASTORAL RULE, REGISTER OF THE EPISTLES, SELECTED EPISTLES: CE
NPNF2: 21 VOLUMES. VOLUME: 18. 978-1-78516-302-9. PAPERBACK 6X9

NPNF2-19. EPHRAIM SYRUS, APHRAHAT: CE
NPNF2: 21 VOLUMES. VOLUME: 19. 978-1-78516-303-6. PAPERBACK 6X9

NPNF2-20. THE SEVEN ECUMENICAL COUNCILS: PART 1: CE
NPNF2: 21 VOLUMES. VOLUME: 20. 978-1-78516-304-3. PAPERBACK 6X9

NPNF2-21. THE SEVEN ECUMENICAL COUNCILS: PART 2: CE
NPNF2: 21 VOLUMES. VOLUME: 21. 978-1-78516-305-0. PAPERBACK 6X9

Made in the USA
San Bernardino, CA
16 March 2017